DEEPER INTO THE DARKNESS

DEEPER
INTO THE
DARKNESS

ROD MACDONALD

Whittles Publishing

Published by
Whittles Publishing Ltd.,
Dunbeath,
Caithness, KW6 6EG,
Scotland, UK

www.whittlespublishing.com

ISBN 978-184995-360-3

Printed by Cambrian Printers

Also by Rod Macdonald:

Dive and history guides:

Dive Scapa Flow
Dive Scotland's Greatest Wrecks
Dive England's Greatest Wrecks
Great British Shipwrecks – a Personal Adventure
Force Z Shipwrecks of the South China Sea – HMS Prince of Wales and HMS Repulse
Dive Truk Lagoon –the Japanese World War II Pacific Shipwrecks
Dive Palau – the Shipwrecks
Shipwrecks of Truk Lagoon

The Technical Diving Trilogy: diving adventures, from novice diver
to mixed-gas closed-circuit rebreather technical diver

1. Into the Abyss – Diving to Adventure in the Liquid World
2. The Darkness Below
3. Deeper Into the Darkness

www.rod-macdonald.co.uk
http://www.whittlespublishing.com/Rod_Macdonald
http://www.amazon.co.uk/Rod-Macdonald

CONTENTS

Book Three *Latest Developments* 279

Acknowledgements

As ever, I am grateful to my long time (and long-suffering) dive buddies, Paul Haynes, Gary Petrie and Greg Booth, for taking part in my adventures in the UK and around the world in such far-flung places as Truk and Palau.

For providing some wonderful underwater shots, I am grateful to Bob Anderson of the Scapa Flow-based dive boat MV *Halton*, and Ewan Rowell, Barry McGill and Richard Barnden.

I am also grateful to those in the many dive centres and dive boats who have gone out of their way to accommodate my unusual requests when out of the blue I pitch up on their doorsteps with an idea for another book, determined to dive only metal, and avoid at all costs fish, fauna and wet rock:

> In Scapa Flow, I inflict myself on Bob Anderson and the MV *Halton*, and Ben Wade and Emily Turton of the MV *Huskyan*.
>
> In Truk Lagoon, Truk Stop Dive Center & Hotel on Weno are particularly accommodating of my needy requests, kindly assigning a private boat to my team where needed.
>
> In Palau, I use Sam's Tours based in Koror, where they have a great setup and location. Without exception, Sam's is staffed by lovely people who also go out of their way to accommodate my requests to dive the World War II shipwrecks, which are mainly overlooked by visiting divers in favour of the stunning reef and wall diving, truly some of the best in the world.
>
> In Guadalcanal, I used Tulagi Dive based at the Point Cruz Yacht Club in Honiara, where Neil Yates and Troy effortlessly and expertly sorted me out.

For archive photographs, I am grateful to the Imperial War Museum (IWM), Orkney Library and the U.S. National Archives.

Finally I'd like to say thank you to my editor, Caroline Petherick, for all her hard work bringing this book together. Over the years I've struggled with some editors of my books due to the technical nature of diving, ships and the nautical terminology involved. But Caroline has worked with me on my last three books – and seems to be all things to all people. As well as being a gifted wordsmith, she dives, has a pilot's licence, and has a good grasp of the sea and all things nautical. It has been a pleasure dealing with her again.

Cover shoot

When looking to come up with an eye-catching cover image for the book I managed to prevail upon Bob Anderson, skipper of the Scapa Flow dive boat MV *Halton*. Rather than a blurry, dark underwater image, a sharp, moody image of a diver at the surface with a dive boat behind would, I thought, work. Bob, who did much of the underwater photography for *Dive Scapa Flow*, graciously agreed and we set up a few days for a shoot in November 2017. It was, in reality, partly an excuse for me to jump on to the *Halton* and get some diving in Scapa. In between dives we would muck about on the surface and see if we could get the shot I was after.

I arrived aboard the Halton, which was tied up in Stromness harbour, in darkness on a cold, windy November night. After getting a couple of days' fine diving done on the German World War I shipwrecks, as the weather broke and the seas picked up Bob took the Halton into a small bay in the lee of the island of Cava. There, bobbing about on the surface, we got calm enough water to spend an hour trying all sorts of different shots and angles, which involved positioning the Halton to get it in the background, until we got the final photo you see on the cover. I'm very much obliged, Bob!

Left: The author. (Author's collection)

Right: Bob Anderson in the foreground and the author to the rear having a laugh during the cover shoot on a stormy day at Scapa Flow in the lee of Cava. © Bob Anderson.

You can see the cover reveal and a bit of background to the book on my YouTube channel here:

INTRODUCTION

My first book, *Dive Scapa Flow*, was published by Mainstream, Edinburgh, in 1990. It set the scene for diving at Scapa Flow by covering the scuttling of the 74 interned German High Seas Fleet warships there on 21 June 1919 and the subsequent momentous salvage work over the coming decades that saw the majority of those ships lifted to the surface. Three complete German World War I High Seas Fleet battleships and four cruisers were left on the bottom of the Flow. The book also covered the many other Scapa Flow wrecks, such as the blockships, World War II wrecks and more recent sinkings.

The book came out at a time when there was an absolute dearth of information about what the ships left on the bottom were like and how to dive them. It was an immediate success.

Mainstream had taken a leap in the dark with me as an unpublished author and my idea for a book, and had published it in paperback initially. As the first paperback print run quickly sold out, it was reprinted in 1992 – and sold out again. In 1993, happy with the figures, Mainstream put out a hardback version that underwent a number of revisions and editions before in 2017, my current publishers, Whittles Publishing, put out a fully rewritten centenary edition to coincide with the series of 100th anniversary events taking place in and around Orkney, such as the Battle of Jutland, the losses of HMS *Hampshire* and HMS *Vanguard*, the arrival of the German High Seas Fleet at Scapa Flow for internment, and of course the subsequent scuttle of the fleet on 21 June 1919. The book was given a full 21st-century makeover with new photography, new wreck illustrations and stunning cutting-edge scans that showed the wrecks in incredible detail, as they have never been seen before.

After the success of the first edition of *Dive Scapa Flow*, I researched and wrote about 14 of the most popular wrecks around Scotland in *Dive Scotland's Greatest Wrecks*, published in 1993. It sold well enough, and a second edition was published in 2000. After a break from writing, following the birth of my two daughters, I put out a companion guide, *Dive England's Greatest Wrecks*, in 2003.

Having now written about the greatest shipwrecks around the UK, as I brainstormed for a way of writing professionally about a subject other than shipwrecks, I came up with the idea of writing a book that charted the highs and lows of my diving career, which had begun back in the early 1980s as a novice diver and progressed through the development of our sport up until the advent of technical diving. The resultant book, *Into the Abyss – Diving to Adventure in the Liquid World*, was published in 2003 and was a collection of true life stories of my diving adventures, such as diving into the heart of the Corryvreckan Whirlpool off Jura, in western Scotland – a dive that seemed to resonate and attract a lot of attention. Diving like this was just what my group of divers did. We didn't think it was anything special – but some of the stories seemed to have had readers breaking out in cold sweats if the reviews, which were unanimously positive, were to be believed. The review I liked best featured in *Diver* magazine in 2004 and ran:

> As much as people try to portray diving as adventurous, very often these days it isn't. You board a charter boat with 20 other people and get taken to a dive site that's been visited a million times before, and picked clean by everyone before you. And that's while you're being led by a divemaster who still uses acne cream.
>
> In short, diving these days is a little tame. We need a lesson or two from those who started when George Michael was still in Wham and Frankie Goes to Hollywood were telling everyone to relax.
>
> Enter wreck guru Rod Macdonald, and his book *Into the Abyss*. For divers who started diving when BSAC clubs were full of men with more facial hair than Dave Lee Travis, when RIBs were actually Zodiacs and, if you hired a hardboat, it came with a lovely smell of fish from the morning's catch; this book is a trip down memory lane.
>
> For those of you who didn't know a time before mandatory life-rafts, back-lifts, wing systems and nitrox, this will be a revelation. Six months' pre-training before getting in the water, panic stricken first boat dives, awe-inspiring virgin wreck dives – this book has the lot. Macdonald really was on a voyage of discovery, and he shares it in intricate detail, as if he was sitting beside you, telling the story in person.
>
> All the essence of diving at the cusp of the technical revolution is here. Forget biographies by 20-something pop stars or TV actors with mediocre lives; this is the life of a man who was out there pioneering and discovering. ... This book is utterly marvellous and deeply interesting.
>
> *Diver* Magazine, December 2004.

My life as a Scots lawyer seemed to consume me after those two last books were published in 2003, and I wrote no more until I retired from law aged 50 in 2010. Suddenly I now had a lot of free time and it just felt natural to return to writing. My first post-retirement book was called *The Darkness Below* and was published in 2011. This book picked up the story from the end of *Into the Abyss*, charting more of our adventures as diving moved forward from open-circuit trimix diving to closed-circuit mixed-gas rebreather diving. It again got great reviews – my favourite being from *Divers Inc* in 2012:

> Even the name of Rod Macdonald's latest book has the air of a thriller novel; and if you're a dive junkie like me, then that's exactly what it is.

Although I'm not a techy, I love wreck diving within my limits and like many other devotees, I've made pilgrimages to dive wrecks in Scapa Flow, the Sound of Mull, the North Atlantic and a few more exotic locations around the globe. And that's the real thriller of 'The Darkness Below'. Rod not only reveals the facts of lesser known and enduringly fascinating wrecks in locations I'm familiar with, he goes even further; exposing the history of other maritime classics I would never have known about. That's why this book is so different.

Like many other commentators, Rod could have chosen the easy path and concentrated on the more commonly known wrecks. But he'd just have been delivering re-hashed information presented from his perspective. Because Rod refuses to do that, it's what makes 'The Darkness Below' a refreshingly great read.

The book itself is excellently arranged. The many illustrations combined with Rod's in-depth descriptions and the wealth of both historical and anecdotal information doesn't leave the reader wanting.

Often I'll read a book on wrecks only to find myself disappointingly asking very obvious questions due to the lack of basic information. You won't find that in 'The Darkness Below'. It challenges and pulverises the senses with information. It truly is an excellent and informative read and a book you'll find yourself returning to repeatedly for another fix.

If I could sum it all up, I'd say for me 'The Darkness Below' is like a fusion of the most exciting presentations I've watched on National Geographic or Discovery; and reminiscent of the pioneering explorations of Cousteau. And as the opening chapter acknowledges: the late great Monsieur Cousteau may have been your idol, Rod, but you're equally trail-blazing an awe-inspiring path yourself.

After this book was published, I returned to type (!) and in quick succession put out *Great British Shipwrecks – A Personal Adventure* in 2012, followed by *Force Z Shipwrecks of the South China Sea – HMS Prince of Wales and HMS Repulse* in 2013. In 2015 *Dive Truk Lagoon – the Japanese World War II Pacific Shipwrecks* was published, followed by *Dive Palau – the Shipwrecks* in 2016, and then in 2017, *Shipwrecks of Truk Lagoon*, which my daughter Nicola designed and produced.

In the intervening years since *The Darkness Below* was published in 2011, I had spent a lot of time exploring the Pacific War shipwrecks of Truk Lagoon and Palau for my two manuals about diving the wrecks there. Of necessity, my descriptions of the wrecks there had to be regimented, clinical and almost dispassionate. But, as ever with my diving, there had been many adventures along the way as I explored and researched the wrecks – and I had seen so many things that simply couldn't go in the wreck manuals. In *The Darkness Below* I wrote a chapter about the SS *Creemuir* and the subsequent friendship I had developed with Noel Blacklock, the former Royal Navy radio officer on the ship when it was torpedoed off north-east Scotland in 1940. A couple of years after the book was published there was another exciting development to that story which I felt really needed to go into print. Read Chapter 14 to learn what it was – I won't spoil it here for you!

So gradually, as my head was bursting with all these stories, I decided to write a follow-on to *Into the Abyss* and *The Darkness Below* – a third volume in the story of my diving career, which by complete chance, mirrors and charts the development of our sport of technical diving from its origins in the dangerous deep air days of the late 1980s, through concepts such as extended range diving, the use of decompression gases such as nitrox, the use of deep diving trimix gases using helium, through open-circuit trimix diving and on to the present day, when we use amazingly complicated closed-circuit rebreathers that greatly extend the time you can spend on the bottom and the depth you can go to with ease, whilst minimising as far as possible the length of time it takes to ascend safely and decompress.

Of necessity, reading about diving, and particularly technical diving, means grappling with a number of specialist concepts and pieces of kit that can seem confusing and daunting to the non-diver to begin with. Rather than providing a dull glossary, each time something specialist comes up for the first time I've tried to explain it in simple terms so that as you progress through the book, these concepts and pieces of kit will become more familiar. Don't worry if you don't understand something at a first reading; you will by the end of the book!

So here is my humble effort – an originally unintended trilogy is now formed. I hope you enjoy it.

Fair winds and following seas

Rod Macdonald
2018

Author's note: For the last 10 years or so I have been using an underwater video camera to record the ship wrecks I dive. I now have my own YouTube channel on which I post short videos of the wrecks. Throughout this book, where there is a video of the particular wreck being described available on my channel I have inserted a QR Code to allow you to go straight to the channel and dive with me on the wreck.

If you don't use a QR reader then simply go to YouTube and type in my name and the wreck you wish to dive with me – e.g. "Rod Macdonald Aikoku Maru" (using double quote marks helps google find the correct site). You will then be whisked magically to the bottom of Truk Lagoon. If you wish to be notified of future videos as they are posted please subscribe to the channel.

BOOK ONE

WORLD WAR I NAVAL WRECKS AROUND THE UK

Author's note

At the time of writing this book we were in the midst of a number of important 100th anniversaries of the momentous events of World War I. The great land battles were being remembered at a number of ceremonies as the dates occurred. The great clash of steel titans at sea, the Battle of Jutland, was poignantly remembered, as were the individual sinkings of some famous ships such as HMS *Hampshire* and HMS *Vanguard*. But for many ships and their crews, sent to the bottom by mine, torpedo or collision, there was no such act of remembrance. Now, therefore, as these great 100th anniversaries passed, it seemed an appropriate time to write about some of the famous World War I naval shipwrecks that lie around our British coastline, in my own act of remembrance to those who perished.

1

HMS *PATHFINDER*

5 September 1914 – the first warship sunk by a torpedo fired by a submarine

The British scout cruiser HMS *Pathfinder* had the misfortune of being the first ship sunk by a locomotive torpedo fired from a submarine in warfare. To be clear, she was not the first ship *sunk* by a submarine in combat – which, as history records, was the 1,240-ton American Civil War three-masted screw sloop USS *Housatonic*. She was blockading the Confederate-held port of Charleston when, on the night of 17 February 1864, she was attacked by the Confederate submarine *H. L. Hunley*. The small 40ft-long *Hunley* carried a crew of eight: seven to turn the hand-cranked propeller and an officer to navigate and steer. The *Hunley* made a stealth approach just under the surface towards the Union ship, and although she was spotted on her final approach, was able to ram a spar torpedo attached to her bow into the starboard beam of the Union ship. The *Hunley* then withdrew, and the torpedo

The 2,940-ton scout cruiser HMS Pathfinder – the first warship to be sunk by a torpedo fired by a submarine.

exploded and sent the *Housatonic* to the bottom. Then the *Hunley* herself sank with the loss of all hands, for unknown reasons, shortly after the attack.

HMS *Pathfinder* was launched on 16 July 1904 at Cammell Laird's yard in Birkenhead, on the River Mersey at Liverpool. (Cammell Laird is one of the most famous names in British shipping, and a massive, vibrant industrial firm today.) After fitting out afloat, *Pathfinder* was completed on 18 July 1905.

She was to be the lead ship of the *Pathfinder* class of four pairs of scout cruisers. Scout cruisers were smaller, faster and more lightly armed than armoured cruisers and light cruisers. They were intended to range far ahead of the fleet, as the name suggests, scouting for the enemy but not engaging heavier vessels. A second group of seven scout cruisers was ordered under the 1907–1910 government shipbuilding programmes; these would be more heavily armed. Scout cruisers were however an evolutionary dead end, and although all these ships served during World War I, they quickly became obsolete as faster and more heavily armed classes of destroyers and light cruisers were developed.

Pathfinder displaced 2,940 tons fully loaded and was 385 feet long overall, with a beam of 38 feet 9 inches and a deep load draught of 15 feet 2 inches. She was driven by two screws that were powered by two 4-cylinder triple expansion engines – steam being generated by 12 water tube boilers. This gave her a top speed of 25 knots, fast at the time of her construction – but by the beginning of World War I, the new classes of light cruisers, destroyers and torpedo boats could make 27 knots. The scout cruisers were only marginally quicker than the battleships they were meant to scout for, which could make 21 knots, and the scout cruisers could be matched in speed by battlecruisers.

The three-funnel scout cruisers such as *Pathfinder* were also intended to operate as the lead ships of destroyer flotillas – but it was found in practice that the scout cruisers had poor range. They only carried 160 tons of bunker coal to feed their 12 boilers and power their two 4-cylinder triple expansion engines. With a limited range, and now being outrun by the newer classes of destroyers and light cruisers, they were relegated to secondary duties.

Scout cruisers were lightly armoured, with variable waterline amour thicknesses on different parts of the hull. *Pathfinder* had 2-inch-thick vertical armour covering her engine rooms, but the armour did not run the full length of her hull. She had a partial armoured deck ranging from 1.5 inches to 5/8 inch thick. Her conning tower had 3-inch armour.

When she was built, she was fitted out with ten quick firing (QF) 12-pounder guns and eight QF 3-pounder Hotchkiss light naval guns – and as was common with warships of this period, she was fitted with two submerged 18-inch torpedo tubes. Two further QF 12-pounder guns were subsequently fitted and the eight QF 3-pounder guns were replaced with six heavier 6-pounder guns.

In 1911–1912, in the run-up to World War I, her original but by now outdated 12-pounder guns were replaced by nine more powerful faster-loading QF 4-inch guns. A brand new design introduced in 1911, the new QF 4-inch light naval gun would become standard on most Royal Navy and British Empire destroyers during World War I.

Pathfinder spent the early part of her career with the Royal Navy Atlantic Fleet, before being transferred to the Channel Fleet, and then to the Home Fleet. As the opening shots of World War I were fired, she was attached to the 8th Destroyer Flotilla, based at Rosyth in the Firth of Forth.

Great Britain declared war on Germany on 4 August 1914, and Germany quickly scored some notable successes against Royal Navy warships with the laying of sea mines. HMS *Amphion*, one of the second *Active*-class group of improved scout cruisers, was sunk by a mine laid by the German auxiliary minelayer SMS *Königin Luise*, just two days into the war on 6 August 1914, off the Thames Estuary. The mine broke *Amphion*'s back and caused her forward magazine to explode with the loss of 132 crew. On 3 September 1914, the old torpedo gunboat HMS *Speedy*, built in 1893, and now converted into a minesweeper, hit a mine and sank in the North Sea, 30 miles off the Humber, whilst attempting to assist the minesweeper HMS *Linsdell*, a victim of the same minefield. But although there were losses to mines in the first month of the war, there had been no loss to a torpedo, and the Royal Navy did not fully understand, or accept, the threat to surface vessels from submarines.

As the war began, Britain began a naval blockade of Germany, intended to cut off her maritime war supplies and to prevent the Imperial German Navy from breaking out into the North Sea and Atlantic to attack British shipping. The only way Germany could blockade or interdict British supply shipping was by the new submarine weapon.

The German Navy was inferior to the Royal Navy in numbers of ships – and so, to reduce the numerical inferiority, Germany embarked on a submarine offensive intended to sink as many British warships as possible and even the playing field. Ten submarines were initially sent out to attack Royal Navy vessels.

The submarine campaign however did not go well for Germany at first. During the first six weeks of the war, two of her submarines were lost for little or no return in British shipping. But this was all about to change – and *Pathfinder* would have the misfortune of being the first British warship to be sunk by a locomotive torpedo during this submarine offensive.

The U 19-class submarine U 21 of III Flotilla and two other German submarines were tasked to raid British naval units in and around the Firth of Forth, where the major British naval base at Rosyth was established. The Firth of Forth is a wide expanse of water on the east coast of Scotland: Edinburgh and North Berwick sit on the southern shores of its narrower section as it opens out to the North Sea.

U 21 was under the command of the 29-year-old Leutnant zur See Otto Hersing, who would go on to sink 40 Allied ships, totalling almost 114,000 tons of shipping, as well as damaging two others. (After later sinking the pre-dreadnought British battleship HMS *Triumph* on 25 May 1915 and then the pre-dreadnought battleship HMS *Majestic* off Gallipoli two days later, on 27 May 1915, he became known as the Destroyer of Battleships by his colleagues. He would go on to survive the war, passing away in 1960.)

At the beginning of September, whilst approaching the Forth Rail Bridge in the Firth of Forth, the periscope of U 21 was spotted near the Carlingnose Battery, which opened fire without success. Hersing withdrew U 21 from the Forth and commenced a patrol in safer waters, from May Island southwards.

On the bright sunny morning of 5 September 1914, Hersing spotted HMS *Pathfinder* heading south-south-east, followed by elements of the 8th Destroyer Flotilla. At midday, the destroyers came about and began to head back towards May Island. Hersing watched as *Pathfinder* detached from them and continued her patrol to the south.

Later that afternoon, whilst at periscope depth, Hersing again spotted *Pathfinder* – this time she was returning to her base. With her endurance limited by her poor stocks of bunker coal, she was only making about 5 knots, to conserve her coal. A speeding warship was a very difficult target for any submarine to hit, but at this lumbering slow speed she presented a relatively easy and valuable target for Hersing.

At approximately 3.45 p.m., Hersing gave the command for a single torpedo to be fired.

Lookouts on *Pathfinder* spotted the torpedo track heading towards their starboard bow at a range of 2,000 yards. The officer of the watch, Lieutenant-Commander Favell, gave orders for the starboard engine to be put astern and the port engine to be set at full ahead with full helm. This should turn her bow to starboard as quickly as possible and allow her to comb the track of the torpedo, and avoid it.

The attempt to comb the track of the torpedo however failed – she was most likely unable to manoeuvre quickly enough given her initial slow speed of 5 knots. The torpedo closed at speed and then hit her just forward of the bridge. It is suspected that the torpedo blast may have ignited the silk bags of cordite propellant charges for *Pathfinder's* main battery guns and caused a flash, because there followed a second, massive explosion within the fore section of the ship, as the forward magazine blew up. Any crew below decks in the forward section were killed instantly. The foremast and No 1 funnel collapsed and toppled over the side.

The bow section of the ship, on the other side of the explosion, sheared off and sank like a stone. *Pathfinder* gave a heavy lurch forward and immediately took on an angle down by the bow of about 40 degrees. Water came swirling up the ship and quickly began to envelop the bridge and searchlight platform. The command was given to abandon ship, but the stricken ship was going down by the bow so quickly that there was no time to swing out the lifeboats.

As the water-filled forward part of the ship sank quickly into the sea, the stern lifted up out of the water and a massive pall of smoke rose into the air. Although the huge explosion in *Pathfinder* had happened well within sight of land and should have been seen and heard, in an effort to attract attention as she settled into the water, her captain ordered the stern gun to be fired. The gun mount perhaps had been damaged by the force of the explosion, because after firing a single round, the gun recoiled and toppled off its mounting. It rolled over the quarterdeck and then went over the stern, taking the gun crew with it. A short time later, the ship disappeared from sight below the surface, taking most of her crew down with her.

One of the few survivors later recounted how he had been below deck when the explosion occurred. He quickly got himself up on deck, only to slide down the sloping deck and become jammed beneath a gun. He was carried underwater as the ship went down but managed to free himself and swim to the surface.

Fishing boats from the port of Eyemouth were first to arrive at the scene of the disaster, only to find an expanse of sea that was littered with the scattered debris of a ship's passing and a slick of fuel oil. Clothing, bodies and parts of bodies floated on the surface amidst the debris.

In the distance, the two-funnel 350-ton destroyer HMS *Stag* and the 465-ton torpedo boat destroyer HMS *Express* both observed the plume of smoke from the explosion – and each capable of making 30 knots, they turned to steam for the scene. It is said that as one of the destroyers arrived on scene it had an engine problem, which turned out to have been caused by a dismembered leg in a sea boot blocking a seawater intake.

There were only 18 confirmed survivors from *Pathfinder's* crew.

At first, the British authorities attempted to cover up the true cause of the sinking, fearing to reveal just how vulnerable to torpedo attack British warships were. The loss of *Pathfinder* was therefore at first reported as being caused by a mine, the Admiralty having already reached an agreement with the Press Bureau that allowed for wartime censoring of all reports in the national interest.

Nevertheless, newspapers began to publish eyewitness accounts reflecting what had really happened, such as that of an Eyemouth fisherman who had assisted in the rescue, who confirmed rumours that a submarine had been responsible. The true story eventually came out, and the sinking of *Pathfinder* by a submarine made both sides in the conflict aware of the potential vulnerability of large ships to attack by submarines.

If further confirmation of the killing power of torpedoes fired from a submarine was needed, it came just a few weeks later. Early on the morning of 22 September 1914 in the North Sea, the three 12,000-ton *Cressy*-class cruisers *Aboukir*, *Hogue* and *Cressy* were sunk by a single submarine, U 9, under the command of Kapitänleutnant Otto Weddigen.

U 9 of I Flotilla had been tasked to patrol and attack British shipping at Ostend. At about 0600 on 22 September, U 9 spotted the three patrolling British cruisers and closed on her first target, *Aboukir*. U 9 then fired a torpedo from about 500 metres, which struck the British cruiser on the starboard side, flooding the engine room and causing the ship to slew to a stop.

The two cruisers *Hogue* and *Cressy*, initially believing that *Aboukir* had struck a mine, closed the stricken ship to rescue survivors. U 9 then fired two torpedoes at *Hogue* from a distance of about 300 metres. Both torpedoes were hits – she was mortally wounded, and capsized and sank within 10 minutes.

Shortly after, U 9 fired two torpedoes at *Cressy* from her stern tubes at a range of just under 1,000 metres. One torpedo missed – but the other hit the cruiser on her starboard side. U 9 then came about and fired her remaining bow torpedo at *Cressy*, striking her in the port beam. *Cressy* heeled over and capsized.

In this one action, three valuable 12,000-ton British armoured cruisers had been sent to the bottom of the North Sea, with the loss of 1,459 officers and men. Coming so soon after *Pathfinder*, it was another stunning success for the German submarine campaign.

The following month, on 15 October, the same submarine, U 9, sank the 7,770-ton protected cruiser HMS *Hawke* in the North Sea whilst on patrol off Aberdeen. Then the pre-dreadnought battleship HMS *Formidable* was torpedoed and sunk in the English Channel on 1 January 1915 by U 24. In all nine Royal Navy vessels had been sunk in the opening months of the war for the

The hand-thrown Lance bomb.

loss of five German submarines. If the German submarine threat had not been fully understood and feared by the Royal Navy at the beginning of the war, it certainly was now.

At the beginning of World War I, the Royal Navy had no effective means of detecting a submerged submarine and could only rely on physically sighting the periscope or its wake – and then firing on the periscope with their guns. Early anti-submarine weapons were rudimentary, like the hand-thrown Lance bomb, essentially a grenade on a stick that was hurled down by hand when the vessel was physically above or beside the submarine.

In the run-up to World War I, Britain had feared that foreign authorities might not allow its merchant ships to enter port if they were armed. But as the German submarine threat began to materialise, Britain began to arm its merchant ships with a single stern gun, equivalent to what a submarine might carry as a deck gun. Civilian captains were encouraged to use their greater speed to flee a surfaced submarine and shoot back from their more stable gun platform.

The first British merchant ship lost to a German submarine was the 866-ton British steamer SS *Glitra*, which was stopped by U 17 on 20 October 1914. In accordance with international maritime law, her crew were given time to launch their lifeboats and abandon ship before she was sunk. This pattern of giving crews time to abandon ship would prevail until the beginning of the following year.

On 5 February 1915, Germany published a formal Notice declaring all waters around Great Britain and Ireland a war zone. Then on 18 February 1915, she began a campaign of unrestricted submarine warfare within that zone against merchant ships: any shipping, including that of neutral countries, would be sunk without warning and without regard for the lives of the civilian crews. German submarines began to sink an average of 100,000 tons of shipping per month.

Unrestricted submarine warfare continued until September 1915, when it was temporarily abandoned after an international wave of condemnation and the intervention of U.S. President Woodrow Wilson, following the sinking of RMS *Lusitania* on 7 May 1915 and other ships carrying American civilians.

◆ ◆ ◆

HMS Pathfinder *was sunk by a torpedo fired from U 21 on 5 September 1914 and by a subsequent secondary explosion. Her wreck now lies in 64 metres of water in the Firth of Forth, off the Scottish east coast. Her damaged bow section sheared off and now lies about a mile away.*

The wreck of HMS *Pathfinder* was known in the 1970s to fishermen as a fastener or snag for their nets – and when she began to be dived in the 1980s, she was reported as sitting upright, festooned with nets. In the 1990s as the wreck began to be visited more easily by divers, ropes were still hanging from her lifeboat davits.

Pathfinder sits on an even keel in 64 metres of water in a deep channel in the middle of the Firth of Forth, which is so wide here that the land seems very distant – you feel almost as if you are in open water. She is in a depth that is well within the modern technical diving range. So I determined to dive her and see this fascinating piece of naval history for myself.

My regular dive buddy, Paul Haynes, and I booked ourselves onto a technical dive boat that runs out of Eyemouth, and with a fully laden jeep filled with two full sets of technical diving rig and two underwater scooters (diver propulsion vehicles – DPVs) we drove the three hours down from Stonehaven on a Friday evening to stay overnight locally in Eyemouth and be ready for an early ropes off the next morning to catch slack water – the Holy Grail of diving, the time when the tide would go slack on the wreck and there would be no current to fight against.

The next morning, we were up early for a full breakfast – I always like to stock up well first thing when I am going to be out at sea all day. Next came the laborious task of ferrying all our dive kit, rebreathers, weights, bailout cylinders and scooters along the jetty and onto the dive boat.

Finally, after working up a bit of a sweat, it was done, and it was time for ropes off. Our skipper skilfully took the boat away from the jetty and we moved slowly north-east out of the quaint, ancient fishing harbour. As we left the harbour, the mainland was to our left and local skerries to our right. To our north and east lay the North Sea.

Once in open water, we turned to the north-west and began to motor up towards the Firth of Forth – towards the last resting place of *Pathfinder*. It was a warm calm day, the early morning sunlight sparkling off the blue water and casting long shadows. We passed the rocky foreshore and cliffs of the famous St Abb's Head National Nature Reserve on our port beam, before leaving the land behind as we headed out into the open expanse of the Firth of Forth. Our destination lay far offshore.

As we neared the site, I popped into the wheelhouse and watched the echo sounder as the boat slowed on our approach to the site. On the first pass, the familiar multi-coloured silhouette of a wreck far below, rising a good 5–10 metres off the seabed, appeared on the sounder. We were in business – and the crew readied the shotline, a weighted line with a large buoy at its other end.

The UK has semi-diurnal tides, which means that the seawater flows in one direction, say south, for roughly six hours, before turning to move in the opposite direction, north, for another six hours. The current gets progressively stronger from the beginning of the six-hour period until midway through the cycle, after which the strength of the current begins to drop away and lessen towards the point when the tide begins to turn, at which point the water goes slack; there is little or no tidal flow.

The actual strength of the tide at any one time in the cycle depends on celestial mechanics and the alignment of the sun, earth and moon. There are two types of tides - the stronger are called spring tides, whilst the weaker are called neap tides.

Spring tides: When the sun, moon and earth are in a line and so there is a new or full moon, the gravitational pull of the sun on the earth's water adds to the gravitational pull on the water by the moon. This causes the water on the earth to bulge outwards towards the sun and moon. As the earth rotates, the bulge, locked towards the sun and moon, appears to sweep around the earth in the form of a long-period wave. We get the highest high tides and the lowest low tides, and the tidal flow each way is strong. Spring tides are nothing to do with spring or the seasons – they occur naturally twice each lunar month, all year long.

Neap tides: When the sun and the moon are at right angles to each other respective to the earth, the bulge of the ocean caused by the sun is partially cancelled out by the bulge of the ocean caused by the moon. We get weaker neap tides – with lower high tides and higher low tides. The tidal flow, and its rise and fall, are not as extreme as with spring tides – and just like spring tides, neap tides occur twice a lunar month, all year long.

At the moment when the tide turns to run in the opposite direction, the current, which relentlessly ebbs and floods in these six-hour cycles in UK waters, drops away and lessens to almost nothing as it swings around to begin to move in the opposite direction for the next six hours. It's the magical time called slack water.

Divers in tidal waters always aim to arrive on site well before slack water to give time to shot the wreck by dropping a line with a heavy weight tied to one end that has a buoy on the other end to keep it afloat. Sufficient time is always allowed for divers to get kitted up, everything being timed so that the water is just going slack as you enter the water to begin your dive. (In diving we say that you can never be too early for slack water. It will always come – but if you are too late for slack water, slack water won't come around for another six hours.) Divers descend down the shotline, often called the downline, and then for safety, at the end of a deep decompression dive or a dive in an exposed location, will tend to return to the downline to ascend.

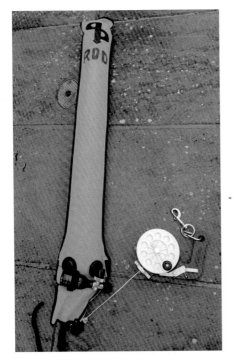

Above: Delayed surface marker buoy (DSMB) rigged for diving. It is clipped or stored somewhere convenient on the dive rig.

Left: The DSMB fully inflated on its reel. It is common to write the diver's name on the very top (which will protrude above the water) in large letters so those on the dive boat can identify who is below. © Bob Anderson

In the north-east of Scotland we get slack water of about 20 minutes at springs – and almost two hours at neaps. So, if we are diving a wreck on a spring tide, we aim to get that precious slack water whilst we are down on the wreck itself, in the knowledge that as we begin our ascent the tide will have turned and the current will be picking up.

But in the North Sea at springs we can get currents of 1–1.5 knots, and it is not feasible for a group of divers on ascent to all try to hang onto the shotline down to the wreck for perhaps an hour of decompression: it would be a rough hour with the water whipping past you at about one knot. (A knot – one nautical mile per hour – may not seem very fast, but when you're immersed in that water its force is considerable.)

As a result, technical divers ascending from moderate depths often carry out a free ascent, hanging on a reel under their red 6-foot-tall sausage-like delayed surface marker buoy (DSMB), which is inflated and sent to the surface as they ascend so that topside know where they are – in an hour of decompression in UK waters, divers will drift perhaps half a mile or more away from the dive boat. When the skipper of the dive boat sees DSMBs coming up, he knows to leave the fixed downline and shadow the DSMBs until the divers break the surface.

The alternative way of doing this sort of free decompression ascent in tidal waters is to deploy a free-drifting decompression station. This can be a decompression trapeze, or at its simplest, a weighted line, both of which get carabinered to the downline at 20–30 metres and have their own big surface buoy(s).

The trapeze is simply three long aluminium tubes that are horizontally secured to vertical ropes at either end of them, the tubes being positioned at depths of 12, 9 and 6 metres. The ropes at either side are tied off to their own large buoys, which suspend the whole contraption.

Either way, the trapeze or separate weighted buoy line can be laced with spare bailout cylinders of breathing gas at different depths to make sure everyone has enough gas if there is a problem. As rebreather divers, we all carry our own bailout cylinders under our arms, which hold sufficient breathing gas for us to do the whole dive open circuit if the rebreather malfunctions and we have to bail out off it onto our spare cylinders. So, in theory, no one should need any gas. But the unexpected often happens ... as divers we say you can never have too much gas underwater. But you can have too little – and then you are in big trouble.

The practice is that the trapeze is carabinered to the downline at a suitable depth with a transfer line – that is, a line that allows divers to transfer from the downline to the trapeze.

As the last diver comes up from depth at the end of the dive, when they arrive at the point where the trapeze or deco station is carabinered to the downline, the transfer line can be unclipped from the fixed downline. Everyone then goes for a drift, holding on to one of the trapeze bars. Drifting with the current in a fixed body of water, you now feel that you are stationary in the water – whereas, in reality, you are speeding over the seabed far below at anything up to a knot.

My group has a tag system to assist in knowing where everyone is. On the way down the shotline, at the beginning of the dive, we clip a plastic tag with our name on it onto a fixed ring on the shotline beside the trapeze carabiner that is to be unclipped to allow us to drift and ascend. On the way back up, each diver removes their name tag from the ring – so if your tag is the last one on the ring, you know everyone else is above you and that it is safe to unclip the trapeze and go drifting.

Like most technical divers, we also have a system that only red DSMBs are fired up on ascent if all is well. This tells topside boat cover that all is good. We also each carry a yellow DSMB and reel, which is only deployed to the surface to tell topside that there is a problem.

As a result of the area that *Pathfinder* lies in, although the underwater visibility in the shallows above the wreck can be quite good, the silty seabed can be stirred up as the tide runs over the seabed, and it is common to find that down on the wreck the particles in suspension filter out all light coming down from above. As a result, there is little or no ambient light – the wreck usually has the feeling of being very dark and moody. Divers are reliant on their torches, the rusty red brown metal of the ship being covered in the soft coral known as dead men's fingers, which flares white in the torch beams.

For UK technical diving on wrecks like *Pathfinder*, where you expect it to be pitch black with often poor, silty visibility in torch beams, each diver also carries a small strobe which is clipped to the downline a few metres above the wreck. The downline itself would be next to impossible to find without it, and doing a free ascent from great depth on a tidal wreck which is known to have many nets snagged on it is not the best idea. But 5–6 strobes flashing away in the darkness can be seen from a long way off. By the end of the bottom time, a diver's night vision will have kicked in and you often see a fuzzy halo of light from the strobes flashing well in the distance.

On this visit, the skipper having positioned his boat to take account of the tide, he then gave the command for the shotline to be deployed over the side of the boat, intentionally placing the shot on the seabed just off the wreck. Skippers are very sensitive to not dropping weighted shotlines on war graves – particularly on fully munitioned warships like *Pathfinder*.

Our group of divers had dressed into our drysuits some time before on the approach to the site; pee valves (or should I say, offboard urination devices) were already all connected up. With the wreck shotted and slack water approaching, we began to wriggle into our rebreather harness webbing, pulling on fins and mask, clipping on bailout cylinders under each arm, connecting suit inflation direct feeds and switching on our rebreather wrist computers to let them start going through their boot-up self-check menus. Finally, fully rigged, we simply sat still carrying out our rebreather final pre-breathe for a few minutes – if there is going to be an early problem with a rebreather, it's better it happens on the boat than in the water. All was good, we were ready to dive.

The skipper asked if Paul and I, being the most experienced, (what he meant, I suspect, was the oldest) if we would splash first and make sure the shot was near the wreck. We heavily stood up from the kitting-up benches on the dive deck and in the rather clumsy, ungainly gait of a fully rigged technical diver, carefully clumped our way over to the dive gate through the stern gunwale. At a signal from the skipper, it was one stride forward and we were splashing heavily into the water.

Righting myself, I dumped air from my buoyancy wings and drysuit and started to sink slowly. As the water closed over my head, I looked around and was surprised at how good the underwater visibility was. After an OK signal with Paul we started the descent down the line in about 20-metre visibility.

My optimism for such good visibility down on the wreck was abruptly smashed at about 40 metres down, when the water started to get rapidly murkier. By 50 metres down it was a silty brown with only about 5 metres visibility. This was most likely the result of the trawling in the channel that had been taking place up-current earlier.

We pressed on down into the gloom, our torches struggling to punch through it. At about 60 metres, the seabed began to materialise a few metres beneath me, at 64 metres. I shone my powerful torch around, up against the gentle current, and there at the limit of my vision was a brooding dark mass that seemed to be ominously rising up above me. Or at least that's what I thought I was seeing – most divers looking for a wreck in dark conditions are familiar with the feeling of thinking there's a dark silhouette out there, which recedes as you approach it; it's just an illusion.

We clipped a reel onto the downline and reeled out as we moved across what turned out to be a gap of 5–8 metres until we arrived at a solid wall of rusted steel. We had arrived at *Pathfinder's* starboard side, the hull disappearing down into the silty seabed. Shining my torch up the hull plating here, I could see where the wall of steel ended at the horizontal main deck above me.

We rose up this vertical wall of steel until we were able to pop over the bulwark onto the main deck at just under 60 metres, and here we tied off the reel line. The other divers wouldn't need to go all the way to the seabed and rack up unnecessary deco – they would just come down to the reel and then move straight across to the main deck. I looked up the downline and thought I could see the faintest trace of their torches far above us as they descended.

We appeared to have arrived halfway along the ship, between the bridge and the stern. We moved off slowly on our scooters, forward along the starboard side of the hull, past the open circles where her three smokestacks had stood on top of a slender superstructure that was one deck level high. Dotted along the starboard side of the deck were lifeboat davits – some of these still with the original ropes hanging from them despite more than 90 years on the bottom.

There is a pronounced rise at the back of the bridge superstructure: the hull rises up a deck level to the foc'sle deck and two rows of portholes were studded along the side of the ship here. The stump of the foremast rose up, directly abaft the bridge. It had been brought down by the force of the explosion in 1914, along with the foremost smokestack.

Moving up on top of the remaining bridge superstructure, we made out the circular outline of the conning tower. This wreck is a military war grave and British divers have shown great respect for it over the years; there has been no pilfering of artefacts that I am aware of. As a result, small personal items were still strewn about here in the bridge area – I spotted a brass sextant and brass cage lights and lanterns.

A number of brass 4-inch shell cartridges littered the ship here, and immediately beside the empty grooved circular mounts of her 4-inch guns, a number of non-ferrous boxes were stacked side by side. Each box still held six ready-use 4-inch shells – the circular bases of some of the shells had corroded away to expose the rods of spaghetti-like cordite propellant inside.

I left the bridge area and moved further forward and downwards, into the gloom. The foc'sle deck seemed to begin to slope downwards abruptly – and then it just ended, sheared clean across by the secondary magazine explosion. It looks as though the ship heaved upwards as the massive explosion blew the bow off, bending the leading edge here over and downwards.

Ancient large gauge heavy netting was snagged over the break. This may have been old commercial fishing net – or something more poignantly related to the loss. For after the sinking, the Royal Navy put a net over the vessel to catch bodies floating out of the ship. This was a common practice with Royal Navy vessels, and one that would be repeated during World War II with, for example, the sinking of the battleship HMS *Royal Oak* at Scapa Flow in 1939.

Paul and I turned the dive here at the sheared-off fo'c'sle deck. There was no point venturing out into free water here – we knew the bow section was missing and lay almost a mile away.

We moved aft down the port side of the wreck, past more empty lifeboat davits, the three funnel openings and the skeletal one-storey deckhouse from which they rose. As we moved aft we began to see the torch beams of the other divers moving here and there like light sabres, the divers themselves invisible in the darkness.

As we got to the very stern we found more scattered 4-inch shells beside an empty 4-inch gun mount. Was this the mount for the 4-inch gun which had been fired after the torpedo hit and had gone over the side taking its crew with it?

Moving round the stern, I shone my torch downwards and could see the three-bladed starboard prop in free water where the tide had created a scour pit round the stern of the ship. I traced the free section of shaft forward from its support bearing until it disappeared into its hull tube and forward to the engine room.

After 25 minutes exploring her remains, Paul and I called the dive and began to scooter back to the downline to ascend. The downline was easily found off the starboard side – a number of strobes were flashing away on it 5 metres off the wreck in the gloom. We retrieved our reel and wound in our line as we moved towards the downline and began to ascend.

As we rose above 50 metres, our surroundings began to get brighter again. We were rising out of the cocoon of darkness that shields *Pathfinder*. Then, at about 40 metres we seemed to pop out of the cloud of silty gloom into bright water. We suddenly had 20–30-metre visibility again.

We reached the transfer line and moved slowly across it towards the trapeze that we could see hanging in the water high above us. As we rose we started slowly going through our decompression stops, all the time moving towards the trapeze. As we got shallower, every now and then one of the other divers would appear from the gloom far below us, carefully carrying out their own deco stops.

Finally, the last diver up disconnected the transfer line and we all began to drift under the trapeze, moving slowly upwards as we carried out our deco stops at 12 and 9 metres before the long hang at the last stop, 6 metres. As it was getting a bit busy on the trapeze, Paul and I came off the trapeze and whiled away the deco time circling the other divers on our scooters.

Here at the end of the first dive, it is perhaps the right time to explain, in case you're new to this, a little about breathing gases and decompression, to start breaking you in gently!

The open-circuit (OC) divers in our group arriving at the deco station were breathing from standard diving regulators, where, as you breathe out, your exhaled breath is vented as bubbles from your regulator that rise up to the surface.

As the dive was deeper than the safe recommended limit for diving standard compressed air, they were using a helium-rich breathing gas for the deep part of the dive, known as *bottom mix*. As they ascended at the end of the dive and began their decompression stops at about 20 metres or shallower, they were able to switch over to a cylinder of *enriched air nitrox* (EAN) slung under their arm on their webbing and designed purely for use during decompression; it is called *deco mix*. Perhaps it is best if I also explain a little about diving gases and *accelerated decompression* at this early stage.

Basically, the more oxygen in your deco mix, the more you can shorten – or accelerate – your decompression stops. But there are certain depth limitations for different levels of oxygen in your deco mix, as these increased oxygen levels when you are diving can be dangerous at different depths.

The air you are breathing just now, reading this book on the surface, is comprised of 79 per cent nitrogen and about 21 per cent oxygen. Although largely inert on the surface, at high pressure levels nitrogen has a narcotic effect – the nasty diving problem called nitrogen narcosis. So both of the elements that make up ordinary air, nitrogen and oxygen, can become problematic when you are diving deep.

Nitrogen narcosis is a creeping (and at first largely unnoticeable) debilitating effect, which starts for me (when I'm diving on air) at a depth of about 30–35 metres. You need to know a little about the mechanics of diving to understand how it becomes a problem.

As a diver descends, the increasing weight of water surrounding them tries to compress internal air spaces such as their lungs, which are, simplistically, just bags of air. Imagine taking an air-filled crisp bag down underwater – it would very quickly be compressed to a fraction of its size by the surrounding water pressure. To avoid this eventually fatal effect happening to a diver's lungs, an aqualung (or breathing regulator) delivers increasing amounts of compressed air with each breath as they descend. The aqualung delicately and rather cleverly keeps the air pressure in the diver's lungs exactly equal to the increasing water pressure around the diver. The lungs stay the same size as topside, and no catastrophic collapse happens.

Once a diver has descended to a depth of 10 metres, the weight of the surrounding water in which they are immersed is conveniently exactly equal to the weight of the whole atmosphere that presses down upon us whilst we are standing on land at sea level. On the surface, the weight of the atmosphere (atmospheric pressure) is called one atmosphere or one bar. So, adding the 1 atmosphere weight of the atmosphere itself to the 1 atmosphere weight of water at 10 metres produces a pressure (water pressure) of 2 bar (or 2 atmospheres): at 10 metres, the water pressure is exactly double the air pressure we experience on the surface. The doubled weight of water and atmosphere above the diver will compress the volume of any air spaces such as lungs to half its normal size if an aqualung is not used.

To combat this 'squeeze' as the old hard-hat divers called it, at a depth of 10 metres a diver's aqualung feeds them air at twice atmospheric pressure, that is at 2 bar. The delicate equilibrium between the air pressure in the lungs and the surrounding water pressure is maintained.

At a depth of 40 metres the water pressure is five times atmospheric pressure – that is, 5 bar – and comprises the 1 bar (atmosphere) on the surface plus 1 bar (atmosphere) for each of the four 10 metres. Any air spaces such as lungs would be compressed to a fifth of the volume they would be on the surface – not good. So, the aqualung again cleverly feeds a diver air that is compressed to five times atmospheric pressure – 5 bar. Again, the air pressure in the diver's lungs is kept exactly the same as the surrounding water pressure – and the diver's lungs remain exactly the same size as on the surface.

Boyle's Law – the law of inverse proportions – governs this effect. When scientists were trying to work out what happened to air underwater, some brave, hardy men would sit in an upturned barrel cut in half, which was lowered into the water. As the barrel was taken below to predetermined depths, the air inside was compressed and the water level rose. Marks would be made on the side of the barrel at different depths. The depths and compression marks were correlated, and the law became clear.

If each breath the diver takes holds five times as much air as normal (compressed into the same volume), the diver is absorbing five times as much of the individual constituents. Therefore, in every breath the diver breathes in five times as much nitrogen, and five times as much oxygen.

Nitrogen is largely inert on the surface; the 79 per cent of nitrogen you are breathing right now as you read this is passing in and out of your body harmlessly. But the deeper you go, the higher are the volumes of compressed air breathed in each breath – and the more the increasing amounts of nitrogen in your body start to cause the debilitating effect known as nitrogen narcosis. Cousteau with typical flair called this effect the 'Raptures of the Depths'.

For me, breathing air at 50 metres is roughly the same as drinking four pints of beer. The narcosis strips away your ability to understand and rationalise situations – and robs you of the ability to deal with things when they go wrong. The 'narcs', as they are affectionately known, affect people in different ways. Some get euphoric – some get paranoid. Some people get tunnel vision; others lose control and panic when the simplest thing goes wrong – something that could easily be dealt with normally by the same person on the surface.

Rather than breathing compressed air at any depth greater than 40 metres, nowadays I always dive on a trimix diluent, which replaces a large element of the dangerous nitrogen in the breathing mix with helium, which has no discernable narcotic effect. Although nitrogen narcosis is no longer an issue for me, if you want to get an idea of what nitrogen narcosis can do, I recounted a hit I got in the chapter entitled 'Bail out on the *Cushendall*' in *The Darkness Below*. This was a 58-metre air dive in 3-metre visibility, in a current, on the wreck of the World War II casualty SS *Cushendall* which lies off north-east Scotland. Oh, the things we do when we are young …

Whereas oxygen is very therapeutic and beneficial in normal use, as the aqualung feeds a diver increased volumes of breathing gas on descending, this means that in addition to getting higher partial pressures (or concentrations) of nitrogen, the diver also gets increased volumes of oxygen.

Oxygen, the very stuff that keeps us alive on the surface (and of course underwater as well) becomes increasingly toxic in the larger volumes breathed by divers as they venture deeper. The risk of an oxygen toxicity hit becomes a very real danger. This starts off with twitching and spasms but rapidly develops to uncontrollable convulsions where a diver will amongst other things, rip off their mask and spit out the breathing regulator. In water, a hit nearly always results in drowning, unless the diver is wearing a full-face mask. A number of leading technical divers have sadly 'ox-toxed' over the years and died of the uncontrollable convulsions – so deadly underwater. Some had mistakenly breathed their shallow water oxygen-rich decompression gases at too great a depth, quickly bringing on a fatal oxygen toxicity hit.

The trick is to use a nitrox mix which has the right amount of oxygen to safely accelerate decompression – and to use it at the right depth where the nitrox does not become toxic. The consequences of getting it wrong can be fatal.

A commonly used enriched air nitrox (EAN) mix that is suitable to breathe and shorten decompression (compared to breathing standard compressed air all the way to the surface) from a depth of 20 metres upwards is EAN50, which comprises 50 per cent oxygen and 50 per cent nitrogen. The increased amount of oxygen and reduced amount of dangerous nitrogen shortens (or accelerates) the time needed for decompression before surfacing.

At a depth of 20 metres, the water pressure on your body is three times what the atmospheric pressure on your body is as you read this right now. So the aqualung feeds the diver three times as much compressed breathing gas to keep the pressure in the lungs exactly the same as the surrounding water pressure – and avoid a lung collapse. This means that in every breath the diver is breathing in three times as much oxygen as on the surface. If each breath is 50 per cent oxygen, or half of the total mix, we could say that at the surface that the partial pressure of oxygen (abbreviated to PO2) is 0.5. At 20 metres, breathing three times as much oxygen the partial pressure is 3 x 0.50 = PO2 of 1.5 bar.

Trials have shown that a PO2 of 1.4 is relatively safe, but above a PO2 of 1.6, you are entering an area where the oxygen concentration in your body is starting to become toxic – and if the levels increase or if that same level is breathed for more than a certain time, you risk an oxygen toxicity hit, convulsions and death. That's why we put a maximum depth limit on breathing EAN50 of 20 metres, where the PO2 is 1.5 bar.

But EAN50 has a fixed percentage of oxygen in it at all times – 50 per cent. Thus, at 10 metres, the PO2 is twice 0.5 = 1.0 bar. There's less therapeutic oxygen in the breathing mix compared to breathing, say, EAN80 with 80 per cent oxygen, where the PO2 is 1.6 bar. So, although EAN50 is good because you can start breathing it deeper, at 20 metres, and start reducing the level of nitrogen in your body early, in the shallows it is not giving you as much oxygen as you could safely breathe. You can breathe pure 100 per cent oxygen from 9 metres to the surface, which is extremely good at accelerating decompression. Thus, in the shallows EAN50 is not such an effective decompression gas.

Many divers do in fact use EAN80 (80 per cent oxygen and 20 per cent nitrogen) for decompression. This higher oxygen level is very beneficial for decompression, but can only be breathed from about 12 metres up to the surface. To breathe EAN80 deeper than 12 metres or to breathe EAN50 deeper than 20 metres, or EAN100 (100 per cent pure oxygen) deeper than 9 metres, risks a potentially fatal oxygen toxicity hit. Thus, every deco mix, be it EAN50, EAN80, EAN100 or whatever, all have their own depth limits where the amount of oxygen in the mix becomes toxic – and potentially fatal.

In a contrast to open-circuit diving, Paul and I, in common with the majority of technical divers, have for a long time been using closed-circuit rebreathers (CCRs).

Whereas in open-circuit diving the exhaled breathing gas is vented to the surface, a closed-circuit rebreather continuously recirculates the same breathing gas – there is no venting to the surface. One of the benefits of using a rebreather is that a diver can program their onboard computer to never let the PO2 in the breathing gas loop drop below a certain level.

As a diver rebreathes through a CCR, during each breathing cycle (that is, one inhale and one exhale) the diver's body metabolises some of the oxygen as it passes through the body, producing carbon dioxide (CO_2). The expired breathing gas thus contains less oxygen than the gas the diver inhaled. In a CCR, that expired gas is cleaned of the dangerous CO_2 in a scrubber canister filled with sofnalime and then analysed in a chamber in the rebreather by

Left: A modern rebreather, the A.P. Diving Inspiration Vision, popular with technical divers. The corrugated hose leading from the mouthpiece over the diver's right shoulder is the 'exhale' hose of the breathing loop. The corrugated hose leading over the left shoulder to the mouthpiece is the 'inhale' hose. The wrist-mounted computer handset is in the foreground. © Bob Anderson

Right: Rear view of a popular closed circuit rebreather (CCR).

The diver's exhaled breath moves from the mouth through the exhale hose that runs over the right shoulder and into the bottom of the central stack between the two cylinders. From there the exhaled breathing gas passes upwards through a canister holding the 'scrubber' sofnalime material, which strips the dangerous carbon dioxide out of the exhaled breathing gas.

After passing through the scrubber, the cleaned, exhaled gas passes into a chamber at the top of the stack, where three or more oxygen sensors analyse the resulting breathing gas to determine how much oxygen the diver has metabolised in the last breathing cycle. Two electronic controllers (essentially mini-computers) then trigger a solenoid (switch) that injects the correct amount of high-pressure oxygen into the breathing mix to raise the depleted oxygen level back up to the desired level (the PO2 'set point').

The cleaned, analysed and adjusted breathing gas then passes through the inhale hose that runs over the diver's left shoulder directly to the mouthpiece, and the breathing cycle repeats. No breathing gas is vented to the surface – it is continuously cleaned, analysed and corrected as it is rebreathed.

The right-hand cylinder holds high-pressure 100% oxygen. The left cylinder holds the 'diluent', the desired breathing gas – air or trimix. The small black cylinder on the left holds the diver's drysuit inflation gas. © Bob Anderson.

onboard oxygen sensors. The results trigger a solenoid switch to open and bleed just the right amount of oxygen into the breathing gas to keep the PO2 at the desired level of say 1.3 bar, no matter what depth the diver is at. So, on the ascent, all the way to the surface, the rebreather is trying to inject oxygen to keep the PO2 at say, 1.3 bar. At 20 metres, a CCR diver can be breathing a PO2 of 1.3 bar – but in contrast to breathing EAN50 on open circuit, at the final deco stop at 6 metres a CCR diver is breathing almost pure oxygen. The diver is getting the optimum amount of oxygen, so beneficial to decompression, at any point.

Of course, too much oxygen is also a problem. If something goes wrong, say the solenoid switch sticks open and the oxygen level in your breathing gas goes above that set level, audible alarms go off and red lights blink on the heads-up display (HUD) unit that is usually mounted on the corrugated hose breathing tube just below and off to one side of your mask in your peripheral vision. Too much or too little oxygen, and the normally green lights start flashing red warnings.

I generally use a PO2 of 1.3 bar, but with deep repeat dives I back it off to 1.1 bar just to stop racking up too high levels of oxygen over a period of days. I usually manually inject oxygen in my final decompression stops to keep the PO2 at 1.4 bar and shorten decompression.

Left: The wrist-mounted computer handset on my Inspiration Vision CCR. The top left figure reads 0.70 and confirms the pre-set PO2 set point being used. The three figures –in this picture all at0.81 – show the individual readings of the three oxygen monitoring cells that continuously analyse the breathing gas. The readings should be roughly consistent – if one figure differs wildly from the other two then it is an indicator that the cell is possibly malfunctioning.

The horizontal white rectangle at the top is the scrubber monitor: it displays how the scrubber in the back-mounted canister is performing. © Bob Anderson

Right: A fully rigged technical diver with a shallow bailout nitrox cylinder slung beneath the right arm on the 'oxygen' side. In this case the cylinder holds EAN50, which has a maximum breathing depth of 20 metres – and this is clearly marked on the cylinder, to avoid the wrong gas being breathed at the wrong depth, a standard tek diving practice. To breatheEAN 50 deeper than 20 metres for a prolonged time risks an oxygen toxicity hit with possible fatal convulsions. The mask strap is under the hood,to avoid it being kicked or knocked off.© Bob Anderson

2

HMS *AUDACIOUS*

27 October 1914 – the first British battleship of
World War I to be lost to enemy action

The 598-foot *King George V*-class battleship HMS *Audacious* is another important first in British naval history. She had the misfortune of being the first British battleship to be sunk by enemy action during World War I, on 27 October 1914, just two months into the war. She was also the only modern British dreadnought battleship to be sunk by enemy action in the war. The story of the loss of HMS *Audacious* also involves a famous White Star liner, RMS *Olympic*, which would carry out a dramatic rescue attempt.

The 23,400-ton King George V-*class dreadnought battleship HMS* Audacious–
the first British capital ship to be sunk by the enemy during WWI. (IWM)

Audacious was one of the four dreadnought battleships of the *King George V* class provided for under the 1910 building programme. Battleship design had taken a dramatic leap forward in 1906 with the launch of the revolutionary HMS *Dreadnought*, when the Royal Navy, under the charismatic leadership of the First Sea Lord, Admiral of the Fleet Sir John Fisher, boldly embraced a risky radical alteration of the prevailing balance of naval power with the creation of a revolutionary new type of battleship. HMS *Dreadnought* was such a quantum leap forward in battleship design that her name would be used to define the whole class of such new battleships – dreadnoughts. Almost overnight, the generation of battleships that had gone before her was rendered virtually obsolete; they became known as pre-dreadnoughts, and although they sailed with the respective fleets in World War I, they were relegated to the end of the battle line or given other rear echelon taskings. Soon, other major naval powers raced to build their own dreadnoughts.

The new dreadnoughts were some 10 per cent bigger than the pre-dreadnoughts; they were faster, carried better armour and were better compartmentalised internally. They also dispensed with much of the smaller calibre secondary armament of the pre-dreadnoughts, and gunnery on these new all big gun ships was radically improved.

The first of the new class of dreadnoughts were equipped with ten 12-inch guns set in five twin turrets, each gun being able to fire an 850lb shell 18,500 yards – more than 10 miles. The first British dreadnoughts had three of their five big gun turrets set on the centre line of the ship; A turret forward and two turrets, X and Y, aft. P turret was situated on the port side of the bridge superstructure, with Q turret on the starboard side in a staggered wing arrangement that allowed more space on the centreline of the vessel for boilers and machinery. The new dreadnoughts also had the latest 11-inch armour and faster new engines. They were indeed a revolution in naval warfare. Being the most important ships in the fleet, these battleships and the later battlecruiser evolution were called capital ships.

Before the dreadnought era, battleships and cruisers had no centralised fire control. Each gun was fired, independently of the others, from its respective turret. From 1906 onwards, battleships, and then battlecruisers, were fitted with the latest in range-finding techniques, sighting and fire control. Crucially, for the first time, all eight guns (and ten with later classes) in a broadside could be aimed and fired by one gunnery control officer positioned in an armoured chamber at the top of the conning tower just in front of the bridge – and also by a secondary gunnery control centre towards the stern of the ship. Officers in the spotting top – halfway up the foremast – observed the fall of shot, the splashes from shells landing beside the enemy ship far away in the distance, and could give suitable corrections to walk the guns in on their target.

The development of the dreadnought by Britain in 1906 could have been a colossal own goal – by destroying her traditional naval numerical supremacy in the balanced order of the time. But taking the calculated view that British shipyards could build more of the new dreadnoughts than could the shipyards of any rival countries, the Royal Navy gambled with the launch of HMS *Dreadnought*. They gambled – and won.

The dreadnought race stepped up in 1910 and 1911, with Germany laying down four capital ships in each of those years, and Britain laying down five. The British initially equipped their first dreadnoughts with 12-inch guns, which had a rate of fire of approximately 2 rounds per minute per gun. At long range, it was found that the latest version of this gun, which dated back to 1893 (but now had lengthened barrels), had accuracy problems.

To solve this, beginning with the *Orion* class of dreadnoughts of 1910/11, the Royal Navy quickly moved to the 13.5-inch gun. This larger gun allowed for a much larger shell, which gave improved penetration. The larger shell and increase in bore allowed a lower muzzle velocity, and this gave much greater accuracy and less barrel wear. The final development of the pre-war dreadnought was a 15-inch gun, which was reliable and accurate with a low muzzle velocity that gave outstanding barrel life. The first shipboard firing of such a gun took place in 1915.

Four *Orion*-class battleships were built for the Royal Navy between 1909 and 1912, and they were much larger than the earlier dreadnoughts. The next class, the *King George V*-class dreadnoughts such as *Audacious* were designed as an enlarged and improved evolution of the *Orion* class.

As Germany built up its own fleet of dreadnoughts, Britain responded by providing ten further super-dreadnoughts in the 1912 and 1913 budgets – the *Queen Elizabeth* and *Revenge* classes, which introduced further evolutions in armament, speed and protection. In contrast, Germany laid down only five battleships; she was now concentrating her resources on building up her ground forces. By the beginning of World War I in 1914, Britain had 22 of the new dreadnoughts in service compared to Germany's 15. Britain also had another 13 under construction compared to Germany's 5.

Battleships protected their most important and vulnerable parts inside an armoured box called the *citadel*, which ran from just in front of the forward gun turrets all the way back to aft of the stern gun turrets. Along the side of the citadel, on either side of the ship at the waterline, ran the main vertical armour belt, which was 11 inches thick in the first dreadnoughts but gradually got thicker with successive new classes of battleship.

In front of the forward gun turrets and aft of the stern gun turrets, a transverse armoured bulkhead ran athwartships, right across the ship from one side of the hull to the other. This transverse armour bulkhead connected the ends of the vertical main armour belts on both sides of the ship to form the rectangular framework of the citadel.

The deck over the smaller rapid fire casemate guns that lined either side of the beam of a dreadnought was armoured, and there was a further horizontal armour deck deep within the ship, designed to protect the machinery and magazines at the very bottom of the ship. In all, some 35–40 per cent of the weight of a battleship was made up of armour.

When the first generations of dreadnoughts were developed, the less powerful guns of the day fired in a relatively flat trajectory from relatively close range. Until 1905, normal battle range for capital ships was about 6,000 yards (3–4 miles) with long-range engagements perhaps out to 10,000 yards, or 6 miles. At both these ranges, the shell of a high-velocity gun would strike its target's side. For this reason, a capital ship's armour was concentrated on its vertical main belt along the hull side at the waterline and designed to protect the ship's vital areas, such as magazines, boilers and turbines.

The thickest part of the main belt ran from forward of the forward turrets to aft of the aftmost turrets, whilst thinner armour protected the hull forward and aft of the citadel. At short range, a horizontally fired shell would not be able to strike the deck of the enemy ship – and so, to save unnecessary weight, decks were more lightly armoured than the vertical side armour belt.

As battleship design developed, however, successive generations of new and improved big guns were able to hurl their shells further and further. Soon, shells were being fired with a range of 21,000 yards – some 12 miles. More powerful guns, firing from greater distances, increased the height of the shell's trajectory and produced a new phenomenon, 'plunging fire' or 'falling shot'. This was more likely to strike the lightly armoured deck of a battleship rather than the thick vertical side armour belt.

As the great naval arms race developed, *Audacious* was laid down at Cammell Laird's shipyard at Birkenhead, Merseyside on 23 March 1911. She was launched on 14 September 1912, and after fitting out afloat and the addition of her vertical armour belt plates, she was completed in August 1913. She was commissioned on 15 October 1913 and joined her sister ships in the 2nd Battle Squadron.

Audacious carried ten of the new Mk V 13.5-inch guns set in five twin turrets on her centre line: a super-firing forward pair called A and B turrets; a super-firing aft pair, X and Y turrets; and Q turret amidships. The staggered wing formation on earlier dreadnoughts, where P and Q turrets had been situated either side of the bridge superstructure allowing only 8 guns to fire in a broadside, had been abandoned – all turrets were now on the centre line and all 10 guns could now fire in a broadside. The new 13.5-inch gun could also fire an increased weight 1,400lb shell some 23,800 yards – about 13.5 miles. B turret was a super-firing turret, situated aft and above of A turret, whilst X turret was a super-firing turret forward and above the aftmost Y turret. The increased 1,400lb shell required four 106lb quarter charges of rod-based cordite. Each gun had its own magazine in the bowels of the ship that held 112 rounds per gun.

In addition to her main armament, *Audacious* was fitted with 16 breech-loading (BL) rapid fire Mark VII 4-inch secondary guns, set eight along either side in a mixture of casemate mounts and deckhouses, which were designed to target fast-moving torpedo boats that might close for a beam shot. These guns however proved to be ineffectual, being too light to deal with the newer and larger torpedo boats and destroyers and the increasing range of torpedoes. The casemates set in the forward superstructure were also found to be ineffectual in any kind of sea. The BL Mark VII 4-inch guns were removed in 1915 and substituted by 12 deck-mounted 4-inch guns. Three 21-inch submerged torpedo tubes were fitted, one in either beam and a third in the stern. She was protected by a 12-inch thick vertical waterline armour belt and an 8-inch upper belt.

The British Grand Fleet, formed in August 1914, was composed of the 1st Fleet and part of the 2nd Fleet; it comprised 35–40 capital ships (battleships and battlecruisers) along with supporting cruisers, destroyers and lighter naval units. It would be based in the great natural harbour of at Scapa Flow in the Orkney Islands, off the north of Scotland.

As the war began, German submarines initially had little success, but as we saw in the preceding chapter, things changed dramatically on 1 September 1914 with the sinking of HMS *Pathfinder* by a German submarine in the Forth. Admiral Sir John Jellicoe, in command of the Grand Fleet, became very concerned about the threat of submarine attack and the consequent safety of the Grand Fleet in Scapa Flow. The same day that *Pathfinder* was sunk, he ordered the Grand Fleet to weigh anchor and move out of Scapa Flow to sea. *Audacious* was at this point in HM Dockyard, Devonport, being refitted – she would rejoin the Grand Fleet at the beginning of October 1914.

The Grand Fleet began to move around the west coast of Scotland and the northern coast of Ireland, marking time until Scapa Flow could be made safe enough to take the fleet there.

Initially the fleet laid up in the alternative anchorage of Loch Ewe on Scotland's north-west coast for 17 days, before returning to Scapa Flow.

A month later, on 17 October 1914, the fleet put to sea again from Scapa Flow, but this time Loch Ewe was regarded as unsafe because a submarine had been reported near there 10 days earlier. The Grand Fleet thus retreated even further from the enemy, to Lough Swilly in the north of Ireland, where the 2nd Battle Squadron, including the recently refitted *Audacious*, would be based for some months.

As we saw in the preceding chapter, the loss of *Pathfinder* was quickly followed by the sinking of the three armoured cruisers *Aboukir*, *Hogue* and *Cressy*, with great loss of life by a single submarine, U 9, on 22 September 1914. Then, on 15 October 1914, the same German submarine, U 9, sank the British protected cruiser HMS *Hawke* with the loss of some 500 men.

By now, every report of a submarine was causing grave consternation. In Scapa Flow, the Grand Fleet had been thought safe from attack – but lookouts, now on full alert, began to see German submarines all around, and constant alarms were being raised.

Now fully aware of the potential of the submarine threat, when the Admiralty examined the anti-submarine defences at Scapa Flow, naval commanders were staggered to find just how poor the defences were for the fleet. The astonishing success of the German submarine would subsequently cause the First Lord of the Admiralty, Winston Churchill, to change his view about utilising submarines in the Royal Navy.

On 2 November 1914, Churchill issued a list of decisions taken by the Admiralty. In amongst a raft of war preparations it was provided that extra numbers of destroyers and armed merchant cruisers, along with 48 armed trawlers and three yachts with guns, would be sent to Scapa Flow. Attempts were made to fortify and block all but a few of the main sea entrances into the Flow. In addition to sea defences, coastal defence gun emplacements were installed at strategic locations covering the sounds, and powerful searchlights were installed that could sweep across the water.

In the water, impenetrable anti-submarine netting made from thick interwoven sections of wire cable was suspended on floating wooden booms strung across parts of Scapa Flow and the larger channels into the Flow such as Hoxa Sound, which were not going to be completely closed off. Any fast-moving enemy torpedo boat or destroyer would suffer extensive damage if it hit the boom, allowing shore batteries to fire on it. Moving sections of the boom, much like gates, were incorporated so that they could be opened and closed to allow British vessels to pass.

Because of the tidal race in the smaller sounds, mining was not feasible and it wasn't necessary to keep these channels open for navigation like the other larger channels. The water depths in the four sounds between the islands to the east of Scapa Flow and also in Burra Sound to the west, ranged up to maximum depths of about 15 metres at most – perfect to be blocked by intentionally scuttled sunken ships: Blockships.

These blockships were redundant, old or damaged vessels at the end of their lives that had no great commercial value – but which had great strategic value. They were stripped of anything valuable before being towed into position, their holds often filled with large boulders to make them sink quickly. Their hulls were then blasted open to the sea by explosives to finally sink them.

As the British Admiralty moved to make Scapa Flow safe and secure, German intelligence became aware of the deployment of the British 2nd Battle Squadron to Lough Swilly, and sent the converted liner *Berlin* to lay a 200-strong minefield in the shipping areas outside the lough. The North Channel of the Irish Sea lies between Northern Ireland and the west coast of Scotland, and was essentially a busy Atlantic highway for shipping moving through the Irish Sea to and from Liverpool for foreign ports. Whereas it would have been suicide for *Berlin* to actually sail through the North Channel into the Irish Sea, German Intelligence believed that a successful mining operation could be carried out in the open waters of the Atlantic to the west of the North Channel.

The first victim of the mines laid by *Berlin* was the freighter *Manchester Commerce*, sunk on 26 October 1914. The following day, 27 October 1914, the news of her loss had not yet reached the Admiralty – and no minefield was suspected so far west. The 2nd Battle Squadron super-dreadnoughts *King George V, Ajax, Centurion, Monarch, Thunderer, Orion* and *Audacious* left Lough Swilly with their escorts to conduct gunnery exercises at sea.

At 0840, in the middle of a turn, *Audacious* struck one of the *Berlin's* mines off Tory Island. The mine exploded under the ship at the rear of the port engine room, which soon flooded, along with the machine room, X turret shell room and the compartments below. The ship rapidly took on a list of 10–15 degrees to port. Thinking that the battleship had been torpedoed, the captain hoisted the submarine warning signal flag.

Audacious *lists to port as crew begin to abandon ship – other crew line the high starboard-side rail. (IWM)*

With the *Hogue, Aboukir* and *Cressy* tragedy a month earlier still very much in his thoughts – and no doubt fearing a similar torpedo attack on the other ships of the squadron – Admiral Jellicoe ordered the 2nd Battle Squadron to leave the area. The light cruiser HMS *Liverpool*, four 2nd flotilla destroyers and a number of lighter vessels would remain on the scene to assist the damaged battleship.

By deliberate counter-flooding of compartments on the opposite starboard side of *Audacious*, her list was successfully reduced. The central and starboard side engine rooms were still operating and with the ship still able to make 9 knots she headed for land on her centre shafts.

Water continued to flood the ship, however, such that at 1000 the central engine room had to be abandoned. Shortly afterwards, the starboard engine also had to be closed down and the room secured. *Audacious* now had no propulsion whatsoever.

At 1030, the captain of the light cruiser HMS *Liverpool* spotted the White Star liner RMS *Olympic* on a return crossing from New York, and ordered her to assist in the evacuation of the 900-strong crew of the *Audacious*. By 1100, as the immobile *Audacious* rolled with the swell, her port side main deck had begun to dip under the water. Two hours later, all but 250 of the battleship's crew had been taken off, and arrangements had been agreed to take the damaged battleship in tow to safety. The small and nimble destroyer HMS *Fury* set up a cable between *Audacious* and the larger and more powerful *Olympic* – and by 1400, the tow was secured and ready to begin.

Initially, progress was encouraging and the *Olympic* slowly began to make way, dragging the sluggish weight of *Audacious* westwards towards safety, flanked by other rescue vessels that were standing by. But when *Olympic* was required to alter course to south-south-east, to head towards Lough Swilly, things began to unravel. The seas were starting to rise and as the steering gear of *Audacious* was no longer operational, she became increasingly unmanageable. Eventually, she sheared off into the wind and the towline parted.

Another attempt at a tow was made at 1530, this time by HMS *Liverpool*. HMS *Fury* once again attached a cable, but after only 15 minutes, it became fouled in the cruiser's propellers, and it too parted.

By 1600, *Audacious* was well settled down into the water, with only 4 feet clear at the bow and one foot clear at the stern. HMS *Fury* took over a third tow cable for yet another attempt, but as this cable was being tightened, it broke. *Olympic* was ordered to stand by and be ready to make another attempt.

By 1700, the quarterdeck of *Audacious* was awash and the decision was made to evacuate the majority of the remaining crew. During their evacuation, due to the heavy weather and deteriorating conditions aboard *Audacious*, it was decided to abandon her completely until the next morning. By 1830, despite her heavy rolling, the remaining crew of the stricken battleship had been safely taken aboard *Olympic* and *Liverpool*. *Liverpool* stood by for the night, whilst the remainder of the ships departed for Lough Swilly.

Audacious is further down by the stern and her quarter deck
is now awash. The bulk of the remaining crew are now being
evacuated to small boats whilst three destroyers stand by. (IWM)

At 2055, *Audacious* capsized and turned turtle, floating upside down for a short period. At about 2100, a series of massive explosions in the vicinity of the forward shell rooms and magazines, which served A and B turrets, blew out her bow from about the bridge forward. Large sections of the ship were sent spiralling through the air. Within minutes, the battleship sank stern first.

Olympic had steamed back to Lough Swilly earlier that evening when *Audacious* was abandoned for the night, to disembark the rescued crew. For security reasons, *Olympic* was ordered to remain out of sight of the Grand Fleet vessels, so that none of her paying passengers, with perhaps pro-German sympathies, would be able to observe the fleet's activities. There were quite a number of German-born Americans aboard *Olympic* who had witnessed *Audacious* sinking – and it was felt that they could not be relied upon to keep quiet.

British military authorities then refused to permit *Olympic*'s civilian passengers to disembark and refused to allow the ship herself to leave Lough Swilly. The only people permitted off the ship were the rescued naval crew of the *Audacious* and *Olympic*'s chief surgeon Dr John Beaumont, who was being transferred to the SS *Celtic*.

The White Star Line was reluctant to risk moving its flagship, *Olympic*, whilst there was such danger at sea. But finally, on 2 November, after ship and her civilian passengers had been held aboard for six days, *Olympic* was allowed to leave Lough Swilly and complete her voyage – not to Greenock as originally planned, but to Belfast. She disembarked her passengers there the following day.

For security reasons, the Admiralty tried to cover up the sinking, but despite its best attempts, speculation about the possible sinking of the *Audacious* got into the public domain. In an effort to hide the disaster that had befallen a new dreadnought from a single mine, the Admiralty went as far as modifying the SS *Mountclan* to resemble the lost battleship and published her 'movements'. They also kept *Audacious* on the Grand Fleet's order of battle.

The British media kept largely quiet about the sinking to begin with – refraining from aiding the enemy. But the large number of witnesses to the sinking and the inevitable loose tongues made the task of keeping the secret all but impossible. It proved difficult enough to persuade the neutral passengers who had been aboard the *Olympic* during the attempts to save the battleship to keep silent – but some of the crew themselves also let the cat out of the bag.

The *Daily Mail* published a letter proclaiming that a masseur from the *Olympic* had openly boasted to his barber that he had seen *Audacious* sink – and that the authorities had ordered everyone to say nothing. The publication of this letter led to the Admiralty being deluged with enquiries from anxious relatives of the *Audacious*' crew. If the deception were to be maintained then the fears of the families would have to be assuaged.

None of the crew of *Audacious* had been lost during the sinking – so when an enquiry was received the Admiralty could reply with a reasonable degree of truth: 'According to the latest information, 85 is well and serving with the Fleet.'

All enquiries about *Audacious* herself were ignored.

As images of the stricken battleship taken by the *Olympic*'s passengers were published beyond the Empire and free from constraints placed on the British press, Germany knew by mid-November that *Audacious* had been sunk.

The only casualty during the entire momentous incident had been the unfortunate Petty Officer William Burgess on the cruiser HMS *Liverpool*. He was killed whilst standing on her crowded deck some 800 yards away, when he was hit by a 2ft × 3ft fragment of armour plate as *Audacious* blew up.

Audacious was the only British dreadnought battleship lost to enemy action during World War I. HMS *Vanguard* blew up at anchor in Scapa Flow from a magazine explosion in 1917, and the Royal Navy's other capital ship losses were either battlecruisers or pre-dreadnoughts.

Three days after the Armistice was called in November 1918, the Admiralty officially admitted the loss of *Audacious* in what it called 'a delayed announcement'.

◆　◆　◆

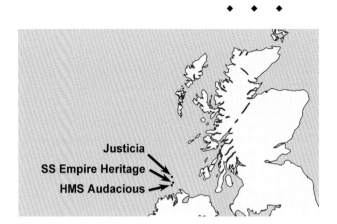

Location chart for the wreck of HMS Audacious. *Nearby are the famous wrecks of SS* Empire Heritage *and RMS* Justicia.

Today, *Audacious* lies far out from Malin Head into the Atlantic, and a dive on her requires careful planning because of her depth and because it is a very exposed site, where the weather can turn quickly.

The wreck lies in an area of water which has become renowned for its consistently crystal-clear underwater visibility. She lies in 67 metres of water, a lovely depth for today's technical divers that allows long bottom times – more than 30 minutes or so – down on the wreck for relatively modest decompression times.

Malin Head on the Donegal coast has become known as one of the world's hot spots for technical diving because, in addition to the crystal-clear Atlantic water, there are a number of classic tek dives that are on every tek diver's bucket list. Not far away from *Audacious* lies the large 512-foot long, 15,702grt SS *Empire Heritage*, which was torpedoed and sunk by U-482 on 8 September 1944. She is famous in diving circles for her deck cargo of tens of Sherman tanks that are spilled out onto the seabed.

A little further out to the north lies the wreck of the massive 32,234-ton White Star liner RMS *Justicia*, sunk by two German submarines on 19 July 1918 on a voyage from Belfast to New York. You may be aware that all White Star liners ended their name with 'ic', as in *Titanic*, *Britannic*, *Laurentic* etc. *Justicia* was to have been a Cunard liner; their ships' names largely ending with 'ia', as in *Campania*, *Carpathia*, *Aquitania*, *Mauretania* etc.

However, as Cunard didn't have a crew available, the British government handed the *Justicia* to the White Star Line to manage, as their crew of the newly sunk White Star liner *Britannic* were now available.

To add to these fine ships there are also the wrecks of the 14,892grt *Laurentic*, which sunk on 25 January 1917 after hitting two mines, along with the 13,580grt liner *Athenia*, sunk by a U-boat during World War II on a passage from Liverpool to Montreal.

In addition to these and countless other wrecks, at the end of World War II there were 156 German submarines surrendered to the Allies, of which 116 were scuttled during Operation Deadlight after the war. The U-boats were to be towed out, ostensibly to three defined areas about 100 miles north-west of Ireland where they would be scuttled. Many of the U-boats however were found to be in poor condition from a prolonged period waiting in exposed harbours for their fate to be determined – and this, allied to poor weather, meant that some 56 of them sank under tow before they reached the designated scuttling areas. Many of these have been relocated over the last 20 years or so, lying in perfect technical diving depths: pristine, virtually intact examples of several types of World War II U-boats. You can see why Malin Head is so popular with technical divers.

◆ ◆ ◆

About 20 miles offshore, above the grave of *Audacious*, I was about to dive another famous warship that was high on my wish list. Clad in my black drysuit, rebreather on my back, cylinders of deep and shallow bailout gases under either arm and with my underwater scooter clipped to my crotch D-ring and propped up on its nose, I stood at the dive gate through the gunwale, straining to support the 85kg of kit whilst I waited for the skipper to position his boat in the right place, directly beside and slightly up current of the shotline buoy. I was ready and eager to splash.

At the skipper's signal, I strode off the dive boat and dropped down into languid blue water. The sea was calm and the sun, already high in the sky, beat directly down. A lot of light would be pouring down onto the wreck far below.

Once in the water, I looked around me and, as ever at Malin Head, I was impressed by being able to see for at least 100 feet in any one direction. The visibility was fantastic, a stunning opposite to the dark, cloudy waters of my usual east coast dive sites. This wreck was going to be a joy to dive today.

My dive buddy and I dropped down slowly beside the shotline, peering below as we slowly descended. Finally, when we were some 35 metres down, the uniform deep blue beneath us started to acquire a form – blurred, indistinct, ragged lines began to materialise out of the darkness below. Something manmade lay beneath us.

We pressed on down, feeling the squeeze of the water pressure on our ears, on our body – our drysuits compressing and nipping at our skin until we bled some air into them to relieve the squeeze.

We eventually passed through a visibility horizon – one minute we were seeing blurry lines beneath us – the next, an upturned World War I dreadnought battleship lay beneath us. It looked magnificent: a massive manmade island set on an underwater desert of clean white sand and shale.

Our shotline had landed just off the wreck amidships – the wreck was so big I couldn't tell initially which way was forward and which way astern. So, picking one direction at random we gunned the motors of our underwater scooters and headed off. Soon, up ahead I could see the wreck beginning to lose its shape, and it became clear that we were heading towards the

The wreck of HMS Audacious *now lies upside down in 67 metres of water.*
The secondary explosion (forward) has destroyed her bow section. B turret lies
upside down with what is believed to be the base of the conning tower abaft.
The armoured barbette for B turret lies on the seabed nearby. A long section of
her starboard side runs outwards from the wreck to the bow, which still has two
anchors held in their hawses. Her four props remain on the wreck.

bow. I checked my depth gauge; it read 63 metres. In old money, that meant there was more than 200 feet of water above us – it was a long, long way back up to the surface.

As we made our way towards the bow, the upturned flat bottom of the battleship, lined with docking keels and with a bilge keel running down either side suddenly petered out – the whole bow section is missing, from the conning tower area forward.

The hull just stops abruptly in the vicinity of the conning tower and descends into a scattered debris field on the seabed. Parts of ship, winches, secondary casemate guns, cordite propellant charges and 13.5-inch shells for the main guns lie scattered around amidst sheared plates and sections of ship.

Some 100 feet of the bow section is missing – blown off in the magazine explosion that sank her as she hung upside down on the surface. The hull has been blown open, and the massively strong 12-inch thick vertical armour belt on either beam, is peeled back like a banana skin. The stem, the very tip of the bow, still with its two starboard anchors held snug in their hawses, now lies almost halfway down the wreck on the starboard side. It is staggering to think how seemingly effortlessly the 12-inch thick plates of her Krupp cemented armour have been blown apart.

I spotted what appeared to be the upside-down cylindrical base of the conning tower. On top lay a 4-inch barrel of one of her secondary guns, the barrel itself smoothly and apparently easily bent over the armoured base of the conning tower.

Further out forward of the conning tower, lying upside down and almost alone on the seabed, is a 13.5-inch gun turret with its massive twin barrels flat on the seabed. It is believed that this is B turret – and perhaps 30 feet away out to starboard and almost separate from the wreck itself, lies an upturned barbette for one of the main twin 13.5-inch gun turrets, most probably B turret barbette.

Barbettes are huge armoured cylinders that were integral to the structure of the ship, and ran down from the gun turret on the deck to the internal horizontal armour deck above the magazines and shell rooms. On *Audacious*, the cylindrical walls of the barbette were fashioned of 10-inch-thick Krupp cemented armour at their maximum, tapering to 5 inches or less where armoured decks gave some protection. The barbettes housed the ammunition hoists that lifted shells and propellant from the magazines below to the transfer room, directly beneath the turret itself. Whereas the barbette was fixed in position inside the structure of the ship, the ammunition hoists inside the barbette turned as the gun turret above turned.

If this was B turret and B turret barbette, there was no obvious sign of A turret and barbette in this area. It is believed that A turret fell downwards as the magazine explosion took place on the surface and that the ship has possibly come to rest upon it.

From B turret forward, the ship itself is largely missing. The massive explosion has split the ship open and the bow section has been blown back on itself. Scattered all around the seabed are dozens of her 13.5-inch shells, fallen from the forward shell rooms.

After exploring around the bow area for some time, we turned our scooters and headed aft. Past the upturned conning tower, the hull reformed to its full shape. The hull amidships is sagging – I suspect that it is being held up by the amidships Q turret barbette and turret. The 12-inch thick vertical armour belt of the citadel and the internal horizontal armour deck are

The stern of Audacious *still has both rudders upright and displays the aft submerged torpedo tube.* © *Barry McGill*

immensely strong and, allied to Q turret barbette, seem to be holding the wreck together here, as with the German World War I battleships at Scapa Flow.

The bottom of a battleship is unarmoured – just simple 1-inch-thick steel plating. It was so deep in the water that it was safe from any enemy shell or torpedo, the only danger seemingly being from running aground. Battleships were constructed with strong double bottom frames, the double bottom spaces holding oil and water.

As we sped aft down the upturned hull we soon arrived at perhaps the most visually stunning area of this wreck – the stern. *Audacious* has a small, almost delicate, stern with the upturned quarterdeck sitting flat on the sand. Both large rudders still stand upright, rising from the underside of the stern – and at the very stern itself is the aperture for her submerged stern torpedo tube.

The very aftmost section of the stern is broken off from the rest of the ship, leaving a small gap, and just forward of the gap here, on either side of the keel bar, are set her four high-speed propellers. The long sections of free propeller shaft run forward from their support bearings and disappear into the shaft tubes before running forward inside the wreck to the turbine rooms.

For a battleship weighing in at some 25,000 tons you'd think the props would be massive – the props on the far smaller 10,850-ton armoured cruiser *Hampshire* at Scapa Flow are large 43-ton affairs, which dwarf a diver. But the props on *Audacious* aren't of that scale – these were small high-speed propellers, designed for high revs.

All too soon, our 35-minute bottom time was up – and it was time to head back to the downline to ascend, rising up as we moved forward, the blink of our strobes easily visible far ahead in the beautiful visibility.

Postscript

The beautiful visibility off Malin Head can seduce divers into staying too long on the wreck. I know it did to me on an open-circuit trip back in 2003 before I had moved to rebreather diving. We were diving 60–75 metres every day for about 10 days, and on one occasion doing two 75-metre dives in one day. Even although every dive was carried out flawlessly using the prevailing decompression software of the day in our computers, I still got badly bent with decompression sickness after the very last dive of the trip. You can read about the whole episode in more depth in the chapter entitled 'Bent in the North Channel' in my prequel to this book, *The Darkness Below*.

3

HMS *HAMPSHIRE*

*Sunk by German mine off north-west Orkney on 5 June 1916
with the loss of the UK Secretary of State for War, Lord Kitchener*

The wreck of the 10,850-ton armoured cruiser HMS *Hampshire* lies 1.5 miles off the 200-foot sheer cliffs of Marwick Head at the north-west tip of the main island of Orkney. It is a very special and sensitive wreck for the people of Orkney – its memory deeply entwined in the fabric of Orkney itself. A total of 737 souls, including the UK Secretary of State for War, Lord Kitchener, and his staff, perished on the fateful night of 5 June 1916 as *Hampshire* sank quickly after striking a mine laid by a German submarine eight days earlier – part of German preparations for what would develop into the Battle of Jutland. There were only 12 survivors.

The 10,850-ton Devonshire-*class armoured cruiser HMS* Hampshire. *(IWM)*

Hampshire was laid down on 1 September 1902 by Armstrong Whitworth at its Elswick shipyard at Newcastle upon Tyne and launched on 24 September 1903. Fitting out afloat was completed on 15 July 1905. She was one of six such vessels in her class and displaced 10,850 long tons with a length overall of 473.5 feet, a beam of 68.5 feet and a deep loaded draught of 25.5 feet.

Hampshire was powered by two 4-cylinder triple expansion steam engines, each driving one of her two shafts and giving her a maximum speed of 22.4 knots. Her two manganese bronze propellers each weighed approximately 43 tons and had a diameter of almost 16 feet. Seventeen Yarrow and six cylindrical Scotch marine boilers provided the high-pressure steam for her two engines.

Hampshire's main armament consisted of four 45-calibre breech-loading (BL) 7.5-inch Vickers Mk I naval guns mounted in four single-gun turrets, one on the centre line of the foc'sle forward of the bridge, two set one on either side of the bridge and the fourth on the centre line towards her stern. These guns fired a 200lb (91 kg) shell to a range of about 12,600 metres – almost 8 miles.

Her secondary battery at the time of construction comprised six BL 6-inch Vickers Mk VII naval guns that fired a 100lb common Lyddite or high explosive (HE) shell with a maximum range of approximately 11,200 metres – almost 7 miles. These guns were arranged in a single casemate on either beam amidships, and a vertical double casemate on either beam towards the stern. The four lower guns were found to be of limited use, particularly in a poor sea, and were demounted in 1916, given gun shields and set on the upper platform deck – replacing four of the Hotchkiss 3-pounders, which were landed. The lower casemate openings were then plated over to improve seakeeping. *Hampshire* was also fitted at the time of her construction with two single 12-pounder 8cwt guns that could be dismounted for service ashore.

As built, 18 quick firing (QF) 3-pounder Hotchkiss guns were set nine along either side of the mid-section of her beam between main and foremasts. These reliable QF guns were in use with the Royal Navy between 1886 and the 1950s, and during WWI they fired a 3.3lb common Lyddite shell and had a rate of fire of 30 rounds per minute with a range of 4,000 yards. They were intended as a defence against fast enemy torpedo boats or torpedo boat destroyers attacking her beam.

Two lateral submerged 18-inch torpedo tubes were fitted one either side of the vessel just forward of the bridge. Torpedo hatch doors in the hull plating opened to allow a ram

Bow aspect of HMS Hampshire. *The top of the waterline vertical armour belt can be seen between the darker hull paintwork below and the lower row of portholes. The two upper foc'sle decks, each with a row of portholes, are unarmoured. (IWM)*

to project laterally from the vessel's beam for the full length of the torpedo, protecting the torpedo from the movement of the water down her side which could potentially jam the torpedo in the beam tube as it came out.

The ship's waterline main vertical armour belt ranged from a maximum thickness of 6 inches to 2 inches outwith the citadel, which was closed off at either end by 5-inch transverse bulkheads forward of the foremost 7.5-inch A turret and aft of the aftmost 7.5-inch Y turret. The horizontal deck armour ranged in thickness from 0.75 to 2 inches, whilst her conning tower, made of cast steel because of the complex shape, was 12 inches thick.

On completion in 1905, *Hampshire* was initially assigned to the 1st Cruiser Squadron of the Channel Fleet and later was assigned to the 6th Cruiser Squadron of the Mediterranean Fleet before being transferred to the China Station in 1912.

When World War I began in August 1914, she was in Wei Hai Wei, and was ordered south to the Dutch East Indies to search for the German light cruiser *Emden*, which was operating in the Indian Ocean. Ingeniously, the *Emden*'s captain had added a false fourth funnel en route as he passed through the neutral Dutch East Indies to make *Emden* look like a British light cruiser.

Emden sighted the *Hampshire* off Sumatra but managed to elude her and go on to sink a succession of Allied vessels before being tracked and destroyed by the Australian light cruiser *Sydney* on 9 November near the British Cocos Islands. Once *Emden* had been destroyed, *Hampshire* was released, and on her return escorted an ANZAC troop convoy through the Indian Ocean and Red Sea to Egypt. She then returned to Britain to join the Grand Fleet where, serving with the 2nd Cruiser Squadron, she saw action at the Battle of Jutland on 31 May and 1 June 1916.

The series of defeats which had overwhelmed Russia on the Eastern Front during 1915 had made it imperative for a high-ranking British minister to go there and examine the situation.

One of the famous World War I recruiting posters featuring Lord Kitchener's image.

The British Secretary of State for War, Lord Kitchener, the creator of Britain's new volunteer army and organiser of Western Front resistance, was chosen. Russia had demanded huge consignments of munitions, so the British Minster of Munitions and his staff would go as well – Kitchener had the experience to gauge how far Britain's munitions factories could assist.

Lord Kitchener had been the driving force behind Britain's recruitment campaign in the early years of World War I with his famous 'YOUR COUNTRY NEEDS YOU' poster. But by 1916, he was being openly criticised for his war tactics and beliefs. In the years following his death, a bitter controversy would rage about the sinking of the ship he had been on, the *Hampshire*. Was it really a mine, as per the official explanation – or was it a bomb planted by German, Irish or even British saboteurs? Great play was made of the fact that the Stromness lifeboat had not put to sea to pick up survivors, and that locals trying to get to the scene to help in a shore search were turned back at bayonet point.

At the beginning of June 1916, Kitchener travelled north up through Britain to the port of Thurso and on 5 June he crossed the stormy Pentland Firth from Thurso to Scapa Flow in the destroyer *Oak*. He was received aboard HMS *Iron Duke* by Admiral Jellicoe and the flag officers of the British Grand Fleet, and listened at lunch with interest as they recounted their exploits in the Battle of Jutland, which had taken place only a few days earlier.

The commander of the *Hampshire*, Captain Savill, had received his sailing orders the day before, on 4 June: *Hampshire* was to depart Scapa Flow on 5 June for Archangel in northern Russia – a journey of 1,649 nautical miles. She was to pass up the east side of Orkney on a route that was regularly swept for mines and to maintain a speed of not less than 18 knots.

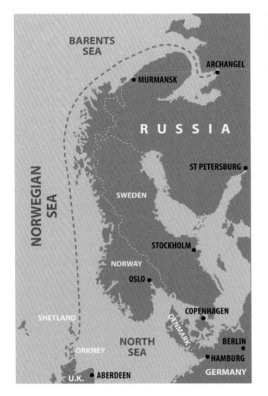

Above: Lord Kitchener, having arrived at Scapa Flow on 5 June 1916 aboard HMS Oak, *crosses at 1225 to HMS* Iron Duke *for lunch with Admiral Jellicoe and his officers. It is already wet and windy. (IWM)*

Left: Chart showing the proposed 1,649-nautical-mile route of the Hampshire *from Scapa Flow past Shetland, up the Norwegian coast round the North Cape to Archangel in the White Sea.*

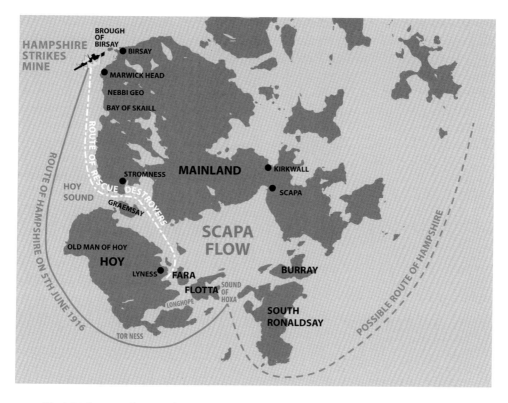

The initial proposed routing for Hampshire *from Scapa Flow was up the east coast of Orkney. But as a result of strong easterly winds and reports of German submarines operating to the east, that route was abandoned in favour of a route up the west coast.* Hampshire *struck a mine off the 200-foot high cliffs of Marwick Head near Birsay at 2040 on 5 June 1916. She sank within 15 minutes, with the loss of 737 souls. There were only 12 survivors.*

She was instructed to pass midway between the Shetlands and Orkney, and keep not less than 200 miles from the Norwegian coast on her journey north. She would have a protective screen of two destroyer escorts as far north as latitude 62°N, and from there on she would proceed alone at 18 knots, zigzagging to avoid torpedo attack.

On 5 June however, as final preparations were being made for the voyage, the weather worsened. By the afternoon, a gale was blowing from the north-east and a heavy sea was running along the east coast, which made minesweeping difficult. The Admiralty felt that the heavy sea would make it difficult for the *Hampshire*'s two destroyer escorts to keep up with the bigger and more powerful cruiser – and so the fateful decision was made to re-route *Hampshire* and send her along one of the routes up the west side of Orkney.

Of the two available west routes, it was decided to use the route set up in January 1916, which went past the western island of Hoy. This route was not regularly swept for mines, but it was thought that no German minelayer would dare to operate this close to the heavily protected main Grand Fleet base. It was believed that this route would give the two escort destroyers some shelter from the north-easterly gale and enable them to keep up with the *Hampshire*.

The fateful decision having been made, *Hampshire* slipped her mooring buoy and cleared the harbour at about 1640. She steamed south out of Scapa Flow through Hoxa Sound, and then turned westwards into the Pentland Firth to rendezvous with her escort destroyers, *Victor* and *Unity*, off Tor Ness on the south-west of Hoy. By 1745 she had picked up the two destroyer escorts, which fell into line astern of *Hampshire* at 18 knots.

The prevailing weather conditions had however been misinterpreted, for within an hour the storm centre had passed overhead and the wind backed sharply to the north-west and increased to a Force 9 severe gale.. The conditions now facing *Hampshire* and her escorts were exactly the opposite of what had been predicted.

At 1805, the smaller and less powerful destroyer, *Victor*, signalled that she could only maintain 15 knots.

At 1810, *Unity* then signalled that she could only maintain 12 knots, and shortly afterwards at 1818, signalled that she could only make 10 knots. At 1820, *Hampshire* signalled that *Unity* should return to base.

Shortly after this, *Victor* signalled that she could not maintain any speed greater than 12 knots, and so at 1830, *Hampshire* signalled that she should also return to base. Off the entrance to Hoy Sound, the two destroyers turned for home whilst *Hampshire* went on alone, fighting the fury of the Force 9 severe gale and its 7–10-metre-high swell.

Hampshire struggled to make progress up the west coast. Her bow dipped and crashed in the heavy seas and the bow splash billowed over her foc'sle – she was only able to make 13.5 knots.

At about 2040, when she was about 1.5 miles from shore between Marwick Head and the Brough of Birsay, a rumbling explosion suddenly shook the whole ship as she hit a mine. A hole was torn in her keel between her bows and the bridge, the helm jammed and the lights gradually went out as the power failed. With no power, she could not make radio contact with the shore to call for assistance.

The explosion seemed to have taken place on the port side, just forward of the bridge and according to survivors, seemed to tear the heart right out of the ship. Her bow immediately began to settle into the water and a cloud of brown, suffocating smoke poured up from the stokers' mess forward, making it difficult to see on the bridge.

Most of the crew had been down below decks and most of the hatches were battened down and shored up for the night. The crew began to knock out the wedges and proceed to their stations. The after-hatch to the quarterdeck was open, and as the crew streamed aft away from the explosion, an officer was heard to call out: 'Make way for Lord Kitchener.' He passed by, clad in his greatcoat, and went up the after-hatch, just in front of one of the few survivors. He was last seen standing on the quarter deck of the *Hampshire*.

The cruiser was settling quickly into the water by the bows, heeling to starboard. As all electric power was gone, none of the larger boom boats could be hoisted out. Those smaller boats that were lowered into the water on davits were smashed to pieces against the side of the *Hampshire* by the force of the gale. No survivor saw any boat get clear away from the ship. The Times of Friday 9 June 1916 reported that Kitchener's party were put in a boat that was subsequently swamped by the sea.

About 15 minutes after striking the mine, *Hampshire* was well down by the bows, heeling to starboard. Her stern lifted slowly out of the water and her propellers were seen clear of the water, still revolving slowly. She capsized to starboard and an explosion was reported as she went that brought smoke and flame belching from just behind the bridge. Then she sank from view.

Only three oval cork and wood Carley floats got away from the sinking ship. These rigid floats were made from a length of copper tubing divided into waterproof sections, bent into an oval ring, then surrounded by cork or kapok and covered with a layer of waterproofed canvas. The raft was rigid and could remain buoyant even if the waterproof outer skin of several individual compartments was punctured.

One Carley float had only six men in it and, faced with the severe conditions, it was flung over twice, jettisoning the men into the sea. Only two men were alive when it reached shore.

A second larger Carley float got away with 40 to 50 men on it. The men in the open rafts were drenched and badly affected by wind chill; most of them were soon suffering from exposure, losing consciousness or foaming slightly at the mouth. Those that lost consciousness never regained it. When the raft made the shore some four hours later at 0115, only four of its occupants had survived.

The third Carley float had about 40 men in it when it left the sinking ship, and another 30 were picked up from the water. Not all crew were wearing their life preservers and it is reported that as the raft couldn't hold the number of men now on it, an officer ordered those men wearing life preservers to enter the water and swim for shore. None survived. Almost four hours later, when the raft finally surged up on to the rocks, there were only six men left alive on it.

The subsequent search at sea in the days that followed located 13 mines in the vicinity of the wreck site, laid at a depth of 3 to 9 metres – deep enough to let smaller vessels such as fishing boats sail over the top of them and designed to catch only the bigger vessels. On 22 June 1916, a Royal Navy minesweeper, HM Drifter *Laurel Crown*, hit a mine in the same minefield as she was sweeping, and sank with the loss of nine of her crew.

It was later revealed that 34 mines had been laid by the German submarine U 75 on 29 May as part of German plans for what had developed into the Battle of Jutland. The German High Seas Fleet had put to sea to lure the British Battlecruiser Fleet out of its anchorage in the Firth of Forth. Anticipating that the main elements of the British Grand Fleet based at Scapa Flow would also put to sea, German submarines would be waiting for it. Three minelaying submarines, including U 75, were also sent out to mine the likely areas the British fleet would pass – and German intelligence was aware of the route that would tragically be used by the *Hampshire*. U 75 sailed from Germany two days before Jellicoe even knew of Lord Kitchener's proposed journey.

The Kitchener Memorial, a 48-foot-high stone tower, was erected by public subscription on Marwick Head, the closest land point to the scene of the disaster, and was unveiled in 1926 to remember Britain's Secretary of State for War, one of the men who died. No other names appeared on the tower however, so when Orkney Heritage Society came to restore the memorial for the 100th anniversary commemorations on 5 June 2016, an adjacent low arch-shaped wall was constructed and engraved with the names of all those lost on the night of 5 June 1916. The names of the nine crew lost when His Majesty's Drifter (HMD) *Laurel Crown* hit a mine in the same area were also inscribed upon it.

In 1933, reports of unofficial salvage work on the wreck of HMS *Hampshire* began to circulate. The *Singapore Free Press and Mercantile Advertiser* newspaper of 22 June

1933 reported that rumours of a secret salvage company formed to 'loot' the wreck were circulating in New York by a man called Charles Courtney who described himself as a 'master locksmith'.

In the 17 December 1933 edition of the British newspaper the *Daily News* it was subsequently reported that a German company was illegally salvaging the wreck of the *Hampshire* under the heading:

GERMANS SALVAGING HMS HAMPSHIRE
Kitchener's Death-Ship Secretly Raided

The report stated that a German vessel was secretly salvaging the *Hampshire* and attributed the story to the *Berliner Illustrate Zeitung*. The report narrated that salvage operations were unsuccessfully commenced in 1931 and were restarted in April 1933. The salvage vessel was alleged to have approached *Hampshire* in great secrecy, the captain taking a roundabout route from Kiel to avert suspicion and cruising along the Norwegian coast before crossing to the Orkney Islands.

A celebrated American locksmith called Charles Courtney was claimed to have been employed by the salvage consortium to dive to the wreck, and it was further claimed that £2,000,000 of gold to help fund the Russian war effort was situated in six safes in a small room beyond the captain's cabin.

Charles Courtney had his book *Unlocking Adventure* published in 1951 by Robert Hale Ltd, London, and it narrates a vivid, dramatised and possibly largely fictional account of the salvage attempt on the wreck that was located in '350 feet' of water. The wreck was said to have been entered 26 times and gold recovered, by opening the safes down on the wreck, as grabs couldn't reach them without dynamiting. Much of the dramatic account is unbelievable – such as when it is narrated that divers entered the room of the commander of the *Hampshire*: as the steel door was opened, the decomposed bodies of two British officers were said to have been found seated at a table in the airtight room. (The vessel is in fact upside down so this is incorrect.) As water swirled into the room, the bodies were said to have risen from chairs and, drawn by suction, floated past Courtney and vanished in the framework of the sunken ship. (Such a large compartment in a ship would never have remained airtight at that depth underwater for so long.)

It was claimed that divers worked by day and by night whilst the crew of the salvage vessel maintained a constant vigil lest the suspicions of passing vessels be aroused. It was claimed that using oxy-acetylene cutting apparatus, they raised £60,000 in gold along with personal papers relating to Lord Kitchener's Russian mission. (Oxy-acetylene cannot be used at depths of more than 30 feet, so this part of the account also appears incorrect.)

Courtney narrated that the wreck was largely covered in sand and that water lifts had to be used to clear access to it. But *Hampshire* sits on an area of clean shale and historic glacial deposits – the wreck is completely free of any mud, sand or silt deposits, and there is no mud bank in the vicinity so the report is incorrect in that respect too.

The report continued that when three explosive salvage charges were set off, one caused a secondary detonation of some of *Hampshire*'s munitions that hurled the divers into the mud and caused a mudslide. Courtney claimed to have been flung against the side of the wreck and pinned there by a raging current for an hour, suffering a broken wrist and injured ribs as a result – and that as a result of it being so traumatic an event, his hair had turned white. Two salvage divers were killed and another suffered a serious case of the bends. Courtney returned to New York where he claimed he underwent four operations for ruptures.

In 1977, 1979 and 1983 the wreck was dived by commercial consortiums who obtained a licence to survey and film it from the UK MOD, and the Aberdeen oil field diving support vessel, the *Stena Workhorse* was engaged in the 1983 survey.

In 1997, I obtained permission from the UK MOD to lead an expedition to dive *Hampshire* with a view to expanding my first book *Dive Scapa Flow* to cover the deeper wrecks such as this one, which had now become within reach of divers using the new technical diving techniques and breathing gases that had begun to develop in the UK in the mid-1990s. In 2000, I was able to lead a further expedition with MOD permission to revisit the wreck.

In 2002, *Hampshire*, along with many other famous British naval wrecks received protection by legislation. She was designated as a Controlled Site under the Protection of Military Remains Act 1986 – the higher of the two types of protection under the statute. This meant that no diving whatsoever was permitted on the wreck or within 300 metres of it. Some other naval wrecks were designated as Protected Places, which meant that divers could visit them but not enter, interfere or tamper with the wreck in any way.

The designation of *Hampshire* as a Controlled Site meant it was now off limits to divers – and no diving was permitted on it in the years following 2002.

4

HMS *HAMPSHIRE*

Explorers Club Flag #192 expedition on the 100th anniversary of its sinking

Notwithstanding that diving had been forbidden on the wreck of the *Hampshire* since 2002, in 2015 I was approached by Paul Haynes, and by Emily Turton and Ben Wade, the owners and skippers of the fine Scapa Flow dive boat, MV *Huskyan*. They had an idea about mounting an expedition to survey the wreck on 5 June 2016, the 100th anniversary of its loss. As I had previously worked my way through the corridors of power in 1997 and 2000 to get permission from the MOD to dive the wreck, they wondered if I would take on the role of expedition leader and make an application to the UK Secretary of State for Defence for a licence to dive the wreck.

At this point, I had thought since 2002 that I would never dive this particular wreck again. But the more I thought how historically important a wreck it was, the more I thought that it would be absolutely fitting to record the wreck for posterity at this important anniversary. Wrecks from both wars are now rapidly falling apart – it would never be in as good a condition again. We could record the wreck in detail as it was just now – information that would be made available for the public good and posterity.

On balance, I thought it was a great idea and agreed to take on the position of expedition leader. Paul Haynes, with his military and diving safety background would be the diving safety officer. Via a number of Skype video calls we agreed that a two-week expedition would be required to guarantee getting the results we wanted as it was foreseeable, given the exposed wreck site, that we could be blown out for 3–4 days. Sitting out to the north-west of Orkney, there is nothing for thousands of miles to the west until America, and great Atlantic gales and storms regularly sweep in from the west. We reviewed the tidal projections and thrashed out a mission plan: what results we wanted and how we would get them.

Armed with this rough framework, I contacted the authorities with the idea – more in hope than expectation. All my old MOD contacts from 1997 and 2000 were now gone, but I was passed on, and to my surprise I was told that the expedition plan was acceptable to them and that Navy Sec-3rd Sector would deal with the licence application. They naturally wanted to know who would be in the team, our backgrounds, the expedition aims, diving methodology and what new technology we would bring to recording the wreck. But in principle, if we could satisfy them in more detail, a licence would be granted.

With the first hurdle cleared, the four co-organisers then had to sit down and agree who would be invited to join the team. There would be 12 divers – and in addition to being seasoned deep mixed-gas rebreather divers, each would have to bring a specialist skill to the group to help us achieve our aims. There could be no passengers.

After throwing a lot of names into the hat we came up with a dream team of divers that we would like on the exped. There would be no massive egos, no difficult, abrasive, grand standing or needy characters – just good solid, safe, deep divers, each with a particular skill. It's fair to say that we ended up with at least two or three names for each of the slots.

We talked over our list of potential divers and whittled it down until we had a final group. The invitations went out, and aside from a couple of divers who couldn't make it due to work commitments, everyone else we asked jumped at the chance of being on such an expedition. The final expedition team pool was:

1. Rod Macdonald, expedition leader
2. Paul Haynes, diving safety officer
3. Emily Turton, expedition organiser, stills photography lighting support
4. Ben Wade, expedition organiser, survey diver and videographer
5. Brian Burnett, survey diver and videographer
6. Prof. Chris Rowland, survey diver and 3D imaging support
7. Gary Petrie, survey diver and diving support
8. Greg Booth, survey diver and diving support
9. Immi Wallin, survey diver and 3D photogrammetry imaging
10. Prof. Kari Hyttinen, survey diver and 3D photogrammetry imaging
11. Marjo Tynkkynen, survey diver and stills photography
12. Mick Watson, survey diver and diving support
13. Paul Toomer, survey diver and diving support.

A further chain of emails with Navy Sec-3rd Sector resulted in the Navy's legal department sending me a draught licence from the Secretary of State for Defence for approval. The draught licence was adjusted between us and approved – and then went for signature. A change in the legal team at the MOD however resulted in a tense wait, as the new legal team wanted to review what their predecessors had done before signing off. Could the expedition be killed at the very last moment? Thankfully the new team were happy to proceed.

After their review was completed, the signed Licence Ref No C/001/2016 was sent to me, granted under Section 4 of the Protection of Military Remains Act 1986. As expedition leader, I was appointed sole licensee and authorised, subject to conditions, to conduct a visual survey of the wreck over a specified period of 30 days between 30 May 2016 and 1 August 2016. The 30-day period straddled the actual day of the 100th anniversary – 5 June 2016 – and it was made clear to us that diving operations could not be conducted on 5 June itself as there would be a Royal Navy warship above the wreck for a wreath-laying remembrance ceremony.

A number of very reasonable conditions were imposed by the licence. The team must not:

a) recover any artefacts from the wreck site
b) tamper with, damage, move, remove or unearth any human remains
c) film or photograph any human remains
d) enter any hatch or other opening in the wreck.

It was also provided that although any film or photographic material taken during the dives would remain the property of me as licensee, it could not be used for any commercial purposes without the prior approval of the licence signatory, the military authorities.

Having received the licence, we fixed the dates for the two-week exped and reserved the *Huskyan* for the duration of the expedition. We then got around to sending out formal invitations and the necessary paperwork about insurance, liability and diving methodology to the selected divers.

Our general goal was to make this expedition the most advanced survey of a British warship that had ever been carried out. To achieve this we would be adopting and utilising the rapid advances that are currently being made in the development of underwater imaging technology and in particular 3D photogrammetry and virtual reality (VR). Specialist high-resolution video cameras would be used to capture suitable footage for the photogrammetry and VR, the video camera operator using two LED 100W video lights and a single LED 1000W specialist video light. The camera operator would be supported by two lighting assistants, each of whom would carry a 300W video light. 100W is roughly 10,000 lumens so in total 180,000 lumens would be used to capture the photogrammetry and VR footage.

In photogrammetry, the camera operator very slowly pans over sections of the wreck or an individual object. Each one of the hundreds of frames that make up the moving picture images would be taken from a slightly different angle. Once the underwater imagery was downloaded topside into powerful laptops, specialist computer software takes frame captures from the video footage and produces a basic point cloud within a few hours of processing. The point cloud image of the wreck begins to appear on the screen as literally thousands of points – but as the processing goes on, the points become more defined and the shape of the wreck begins to appear. Further computer processing of the point cloud raw data is then carried out whereby the software triangulates between recognisable points of data in each frame and is able to refine the raw image to give a lifelike 3D image that a viewer can 'fly' around on a computer and explore in detail. We aimed to make the 3D photogrammetry model available online for the public good so that maritime archaeologists, historians and other interested folk can study it in detail in the future, without having to physically dive it. I will be interested to see what information can be brought out by such specialists from our work in due course.

Going beyond 3D photogrammetry, we also planned to render the whole wreck on a 1:1 aspect ratio, that is at full size, in virtual reality. By putting on VR goggles, viewers would be immersed in the water, standing or floating beside a life-size image of the wreck. The wreck would tower some 50 feet above you from the seabed. Our plans were nothing if not ambitious.

In addition to photogrammetry and VR, hundreds of high-resolution underwater photographs would be taken and we would blitz the wreck with video cameras, getting as much imagery as we could of this never-to-be-repeated opportunity. We expected that some 100 hours of video footage on the wreck would be taken.

As we began to get going, sorting out the full logistics of the expedition, we began to get a distinct feeling that we were representing our sport, and that the expedition and our results would be closely studied from a number of angles. We believed that with our technical diving abilities and the underwater visualisation techniques we were employing, if we did a good job, the military authorities might realise just how good modern diving and underwater imaging techniques were. We hoped to bring results that the military themselves could not achieve – believing that this might open a door for better cooperation between military authorities and civilian divers on other projects.

There was little imagery of the wreck in existence before our expedition – just a few grainy still photographs of objects and a few bits of shaky underwater footage. Although I had dived the wreck several times in 1997 and 2000, anything could have happened to it since then. The current condition of the wreck was unknown – it was possible that it had totally collapsed.

We formalised the aims of the *Hampshire* 2016 Expedition as being:

1. To ascertain the present condition of the wreck
2. To undertake a detailed survey
3. To compile an extensive catalogue of stills and video imagery
4. To produce a survey expedition report for future historical reference
5. To raise public awareness of the historical significance of the sinking
6. To foster positive relations with government and shipwreck heritage bodies.

The Explorers Club is based in New York and is a multi-discipline club dedicated to promoting and encouraging exploration in all aspects. I was inducted into it in 2015 for my work with shipwrecks.

It was founded in 1905, and its members have a number of illustrious firsts in exploration. Robert Peary was a member when he was first to the North Pole in 1909. Roald Amundsen, was a member when he was first to the South Pole in 1911. Neil Armstrong and Buzz Aldrin, first to the moon in 1969. Sir Edmund Hillary and Sherpa Tensing Norgay, first to the summit of Everest were members, Thor Heyerdahl in *Kontiki* – the list of firsts for members goes on and on.

At The Explorers Club HQ in New York, there is a humble granite plaque which reads:

WORLD CENTER FOR EXPLORATION

First to the North Pole	1909
First to the South Pole	1911
First to the summit of Mt Everest	1953
First to the deepest point in the ocean	1960
First to the surface of the Moon	1969

Underneath the last entry there is a space – waiting for the first manned Mars landing.

Since 1918, whenever the Explorers Club believes that an expedition is going to be of scientific or special merit it awards an Explorers Club flag, which is then carried on the expedition. There are some 220 flags in total, and the flags are reused on successive expeditions in the field. Explorers Club flags have been carried to all the earth's continents, as well as to the deepest parts of the sea and the highest places on the land – and to the moon.

As at the date of my expedition, 850 explorers had carried the flag on 1,450 expeditions. A select few of the 222 flags have been retired and framed for display at the Club House in New York. These include the flags carried by Thor Heyerdahl on his raft *Kontiki* as he sailed across the Pacific, and the miniature flags carried aboard Apollo 8 and 15. Some special flags are of particular historic importance, such as the flag carried aboard Apollo 11 by Neil Armstrong and Buzz Aldrin to the surface of the moon.

The Explorers Club declared our *Hampshire* expedition to be a Flagged Expedition due to the historic importance of the shipwreck – and two weeks before the expedition was due to begin, an airmail package arrived with Flag #192 and the paperwork to go along with it, which included a list of the previous expeditions this very flag had been carried on.

Amos Burg	1968 Alaska Rivers Expedition
Dr. George V.B. Cochran	1974 North Baffin-Bylot Expedition
Dr. George V.B. Cochran	1972 Baffinland Arctic-Alpine Expedition
Dr. George V.B. Cochran	1973 Baffin-Kingnait Expedition
Peter Byrne	1975 Nepal Himalayan – Terai Mammals
Ralph Lenton	1970 Mt Ararat Expedition
Dr. I. Drummond Rennie	1973 American Dhaulagiri Expedition
William Isherwood	1971 Glaciological Survey
Bob Sparks	1975 Trans-Atlantic Solo Balloon Crossing
Bob Sparks	1976 Trans-Atlantic Balloon Flight.

The flag had been lost on expedition in the late 1970s – but had recently been found and returned to the Explorers Club shortly before my expedition. After a break of some 40 years, it was going on expedition again.

Our dates were now set in stone – and with all the acceptances now in from our team, we now had major commitments being made. Paul Haynes, in his capacity of dive safety officer, created a thorough 40-page Dive Brief, and this was emailed out to all the team members six months before the exped. This covered the basics of our planned diving methodology, such as the standardisation of rebreather trimix diluent gas of 15/50 across the team. This provided an oxygen partial pressure (PO2) of 1.2 bar at the deepest depth anticipated of 70 metres, and facilitated an effective rebreather diluent flush without the safety implications of using a 'lean' hypoxic gas, where a diver could black out. At the maximum depth of 70 metres, this trimix mixture would give divers an *equivalent narcotic depth* (END) of 25 metres. This means that at 70 metres the divers would only be experiencing the same nitrogen narcosis as a diver diving on air at 25 metres, next to negligible.

Each diver had to carry sufficient open-circuit bailout gas to independently support a full open-circuit decompression profile in the event of a catastrophic failure of the primary life support rebreather. As a minimum, divers were required to carry an 11-litre cylinder of

A diver tag in/out system was used for all dives during the expedition with named tags for all divers being supplied. The tags were clipped to a brass ring where the transfer line from the trapeze connected into the fixed downline. (Author's collection)

bailout 15/50 bottom gas under their left arm and an 11-litre cylinder of EAN 60 deco gas on their right side.

We would be using a decompression trapeze with horizontal bars at 6, 9 and 12 metres, and ropes leading up at either side to two large red buoys that would float it. We intended to lay two fixed downlines, one at the bow of the wreck and one at the stern. The trapeze would be secured to the bow or stern downline by a transfer line on a daily basis. Extra cylinders of bailout gas would be clipped to the downline and the trapeze in case of emergency.

A diver 'down / up' logging system using named tags was employed to monitor who had left bottom and ascended to the trapeze. Each diver was given a stainless steel shackle with a colour-coded plastic name tag on it, with their name. Individual divers clipped their named tags to a brass ring in the transfer line at a depth of 30 metres on the descent. Divers would remove their tag from the ring as they ascended at the end of the dive and moved along the transfer line to the trapeze for decompression. The last diving pair ascending would disconnect the trapeze from the downline before continuing their ascent up the trapeze transfer line. All 12 divers would then begin to drift with the current, which would be picking up as slack water passed, as they slowly ascended through the various levels of their decompression stops.

Once all 12 divers were on the trapeze and we had disconnected and begun to drift, the procedure would be that a single 6-foot-tall red delayed surface marker buoy (DSMB) would be sent up. If for any reason there was a separation event, and divers failed to return to the downline, the team would wait 20 minutes to give the lost divers a chance of finding their way back to the downline. If the divers had not arrived at the deco station by that time, the trapeze would be disconnected from the downline. With the tide picking up after slack water, it would be impossible for all the divers to carry out two hours of decompression stops with the trapeze still connected to the downline. It would be swept horizontal and possibly up to the surface. Once the trapeze was unclipped and was drifting with the current, the divers would feel that they were in comfortable stationary water – even though the whole mass of water they were suspended in was racing across the seabed at 1–2 knots.

If we had to disconnect with divers still on the wreck or doing a free ascent away from the downline, then we would send up a yellow DSMB. That would be the signal to the skipper topside that there had been a separation event and that he should keep his eyes peeled for DSMBs from free-drifting divers. With such a group of seasoned deep divers, each had lots of experience of carrying out free ascents under their own DSMB. It wouldn't be an alarming situation; we just wanted a way of telling the skipper topside that divers were separated and that he should look out for their DSMBs, as well as following the trapeze.

To keep the divers together in a loose single group on the trapeze for deco, we restricted bottom time to 35 minutes.

All divers were required to carry a minimum of one red DSMB with their first name or initials written in large black letters on the top of it, together with a whistle, hi-vis flag and yellow DSMB for emergency signalling. This was no place to be separated from the dive boat and not be seen.

The team would arrive in Orkney on Saturday 28 May and load kit onto the *Huskyan*, and once everyone was sorted out with cylinders filled and analysed, scrubbers filled with sofnalime, rebreathers all prepped and set up, we would have a briefing that night. Diving would start the next day, Sunday 29 May, with two shakedown dives on the deepest German World War I battleship in Scapa Flow, the upturned SMS *Markgraf* in 45 metres. The early morning dive would be a simple personal shakedown dive to reveal any problems that might have occurred in transit and so that people could make sure they were happy with their kit. The afternoon dive would be a full dress-rehearsal, deploying the trapeze, adding the extra bailout cylinders and everyone transferring from the wreck to it for disconnection from the downline and a free-drifting decompression.

Throughout Saturday 28 May 2016, our group of deep shipwreck divers began to arrive in Stromness from all points of the compass. The group consisted of ten British and three Finnish divers, many of whom had been travelling for days by road, sea and air to get here. The Finns, Marjo Tynkkynen, Kari Hyttinen and Immi Wallin, in particular brought highly specialist underwater stills and 3D photogrammetry expertise to the expedition, and collectively there was over 200 years of worldwide wreck diving experience between the group. However, despite the high level of technical diving and shipwreck knowledge, at this point many of the group had never met each other, let alone dived together before. Shaping this group of divers into a safe and effective deep shipwreck survey team would be the first expedition objective.

That night, the four co-organisers hosted a team briefing in our accommodation, the fine Divers Lodge owned by Ben and Emily. As expedition leader, it fell to me to give the welcoming address and expedition overview, including the legal restrictions by which we were bound. We felt it would be too much to brief on the wreck straight away on this, our first gathering, so we had decided to restrict this meeting to the basics and let everyone get to know each other. The wreck briefing itself would be done tomorrow after the shakedown dives on the *Markgraf* were completed.

To build upon the detailed expedition diving plan previously issued to all divers, my introduction was followed by a safety brief by Paul Haynes, wearing his hat as diving safety officer, the purpose being to instil an expedition diving safety culture from the very outset. This included confirming the safety policy, stating the expedition organisers' expectations, defining roles and responsibilities, and confirming the diving methodology, safety procedures and emergency protocols to be adhered to.

We wanted to stress that this was not a diving holiday – we were here to do a job. I emphasised to the team that the process of actually getting our licence had probably taken me about 20 months and it seemed unlikely that a licence would ever be granted again. We felt that a number of government bodies would be paying close attention to the expedition, our conduct and our results. We were representing our sport and if we did it right, other doors might open in the future for divers.

The HMS Hampshire Explorer's Club Flag No 192 expedition team in front of the starboard propeller of Hampshire at Lyness. The author (right) and Paul Haynes (left) hold the Explorers Club flag.

Left to right, back row: Ross Dowrie (crew), Russ Evans (skipper), Kevin Heath, Ben Wade, Brian Burnett, Marjo Tynkkynen, Kari Hyttinen, Mic Watson.

Front row: Paul Toomer, Gary Petrie, Immi Wallin, Emily Turton, Paul Haynes, Rod Macdonald, Greg Booth, Chris Rowland. © Marjo Tynkkynen

The next day, Sunday, was time for the full dress-rehearsal to confirm personal equipment functionality. This was no ordinary warm-up dive however – some divers in the team had never been to Scapa Flow before, and this was a chance to see first-hand one of the *König*-class battleships that fired at British Grand Fleet warships during the Battle of Jutland on 30 May/1 June 1916. It was a fitting start to the expedition, and helped shape the team's historical understanding of events leading up to the loss of *Hampshire*.

The first dive was uneventful, and following a suitable surface interval, a full team dive rehearsal was next. There was no time to explore *Markgraf* further; the afternoon was to be a carefully choreographed procedures dive. This included decompression station deployment, additional bailout gas staging, diver tagging procedures, simulated drifting decompression stops, emergency drop gas signalling and deployment, unconscious diver recovery, basic life support, oxygen administration and coastguard evacuation protocols – a very busy afternoon indeed.

With a limited window of opportunity to dive HMS *Hampshire*, spending a full day diving in the Flow with a group of such experienced divers, some of whom were technical diving instructor trainers and examiners, may have appeared unnecessary. But we felt that a group of divers is not necessarily a team – and the safe and efficient running of the expedition would be reliant on everyone aboard knowing their roles and responsibilities, the safety procedures and emergency protocols. The only way of truly confirming the operational viability of any procedure is to run through it in practice in the form of a real-time dress rehearsal. By the end of the day, everyone agreed that it was only at that point that we were collectively prepared and ready to turn west into the open Atlantic and safely start the expedition proper.

With the shakedown dives now safely behind us, we met again that night and I ran over what I knew about the ship from a historical perspective and what I knew about the wreck from my own knowledge gained from diving it a number of times 15–20 years previously, before it was closed off to divers.

As it was such a large site to survey, the team objective for the first dive was to gain a general orientation and appreciation of the site. Once we collectively had a feel for the lay of the site, individual survey tasks would then be allocated to each dive pair on a daily basis.

The next day, full of enthusiasm, we all rose at 0600, and after breakfast in the Divers Lodge, walked across the quay to the *Huskyan*, whose twin diesels were already turning over. We were soon all aboard, ropes were cast off and we were away – heading south out of Stromness harbour before turning to the west to head out through Hoy Sound to the Atlantic.

Once out of Scapa Flow, we turned our head to the north and started to run up the west coast of Orkney, retracing the route taken by the *Hampshire* 100 years earlier. Slack water would arrive about 1130, so we would be arriving on site well in advance of slack, ready to safely place a weighted shotline on the seabed beside the wreck, kit up and be ready to dive at slack – as I said before, you can never be too early for slack.

The passage up the west coast was beautiful on this first day. It was sunny, with little wind and the water seemed relatively smooth; it was however a little deceptive, as a languid Atlantic swell was still rolling in gently from the north-west, the boat slowly rising and falling a few metres as the swell passed beneath us.

As we arrived on site, we soon picked up the wreck on the echo sounder. The tall Kitchener Memorial Tower stood prominently just 1.5 miles away on the high cliffs of Marwick Head – very poignantly reminding us of the tragedy that had occurred in this very spot 100 years almost to the day.

We were aware from previous visits that the wreck lay in a roughly north-west/south-east attitude, with her bow to the north. We had decided that the first day's shot would be dropped on the seabed just off the stern, which was the most intact area.

The shotline would be floated initially with just a few rigid round fishermen's floats. As it was still an hour or two to go until slack water, we knew that these would be swept under by the tide – that was the idea – they would rise again as the tide dropped off towards slack water, an easy visual indicator of what was happening. If we had stuck a big danbuoy on the downline it would have remained on the surface, but likely would have been dragged down current by the tide, dragging the shot away from the wreck. There was no room for error.

Paul Haynes was excellent in his role as diving safety officer, a role he has played many times, in both civilian and military expeditions. He had the trapeze completely sorted out and rigged to self-deploy using his old parachuting knowledge.

The four expedition co-organisers had already divided the team into suitable dive pairs. Each pair had one diver who had a key role such as videography, stills photography, 3D photogrammetry etc., with the other supporting. Some of the pairings had been easy and natural – the well-known Finnish photojournalist Marjo Tynkkynen had been resident in Orkney for some time, diving with skipper Emily Turton off *Huskyan*. They knew and understood how each other dived and naturally fell to dive together, with Emily as lighting assistant and model for Marjo to shoot. Marjo's hi-res stills would be captured using a Canon 5DmkII camera in a Subal housing with 16-35mm LII and Sigma 15mm lenses. The camera strobes were Canon Speedlite 580exll. To light up larger sections of the wreck, two additional 300W LED Scubamafia Beast video lights were deployed by support divers.

Kari Hyttinen and Immi Wallin from Finland had worked together with 3D photogrammetry on a number of high-profile wrecks around the world, and so were another natural pairing.

To avoid congestion of the changing areas and the dive deck, to marshal all 12 divers, we subdivided them into two teams of six. Team 1 would get dressed in their thermal undersuits and drysuits in the covered dry changing area well in advance of slack water. They could then move aft outside onto *Huskyan*'s expansive dive deck and start prepping and getting into their rebreathers.

Team 2 would then get dressed in their drysuits in the changing area and would then assist the Team 1 divers, who were by now getting into their CCRs and clipping on bailout (stage) cylinders. Once slack water arrived and the Team 1 divers were beginning to jump into the water, Team 2 would be assisted by boat crew in getting into their own rebreathers and getting ready to splash. In this way, with the second wave of divers entering the water some 10 minutes after the first group, we managed to avoid 12 divers trampling all over each other and valuable kit. With bottom times down on the wreck of 35 minutes and run times inwater including trapeze decompression of about two hours, all the divers would be able to rendezvous on the trapeze for the final cast off and drifting deco hang.

Ben Wade and Greg Booth were to be the first to dive – their job was to make sure the shotline was on the seabed near the wreck and to secure it. They would be followed by Brian Burnett and Paul, who would take down the trapeze transfer line and connect it to the downline and add some spare cylinders of bailout gas. Then Gary Petrie and I would dive, our job being to add some more fixed bailout cylinders.

Dressed into my CCR and full rig, with my CCR safety pre-breathe done, I finally stood up heavily from the kitting-up bench and clumped gingerly to the dive gate in the gunwale. I could hardly believe that this moment had finally arrived.

Standing there waiting for the skipper to position the boat beside the downline, the familiar feeling of apprehension and excitement that I get before a big dive like this washed over me. I had been so consumed by the planning of the expedition over the last 18 months, securing the licence, writing to the Kirkwall police to advise of what we were doing, writing to advise the Coastguard and Orkney harbours of the licensed activity, the sheer logistics of getting everyone and all their kit to Orkney, the shakedown dives, the preparation …. And here, now, it was finally a reality – I was rigged in my CCR, bailout cylinders clipped under my arms, ready to jump. An unforgettable moment.

By the time I strode off the boat, Ben and Greg were already down on the wreck. The trapeze had been lowered into the water, and it self-deployed as Paul and Brian took the transfer line down and clipped it off to the downline. As I hit the water and the white froth of bubbles dissipated, I looked across to the downline which I could see dropping vertically down into the depths. The underwater visibility out here in the Atlantic was just as I remembered from my last expeditions 20 years earlier – astonishing for Scotland, at least 50 metres. I could see Paul and Brian below me; Ben and Greg were already out of sight below.

Gary and I moved over to the downline and started our descent. The water was absolutely slack; with no current at all, we could just freefall beside the downline.

As I reached 30 metres, where the transfer line from the trapeze had already been safely clipped in by Paul and Brian, Gary unclipped the spare cylinder of deep bailout he was porting and we clipped it off on the transfer line. It was set up so that when we recovered the trapeze and transfer line onto the boat after the dive, all the spare bailout gas would come out with it. Although the bow and stern downlines would be left for the duration of the exped, we wouldn't be leaving cylinders on them. Deep bailout gas clipped off, it was time for Gary and me to continue our descent.

Although it was very dark beneath us, the underwater visibility was still crystal clear. Looking down the downline, as my eyes traced its path down and slightly up-current, I was astonished to see the dim silhouette of the wreck far below us. The dim pinpoints of the four divers' torches, clustered in two pairs ahead of us, were visible at different points of the wreck. I could make out the upturned hull of the stern, and even see the long free section of the port prop shaft leading out from its tube to its circular bearing bracket, supported on struts connected to the main hull. This was the last memory I had from my dives on the wreck 20 years earlier – I'd never thought that I would be back here to see it again.

In the slack water, I was able to move away from the downline and make for the fantail of the wreck, which was lying upside down on the seabed. The seabed around the wreck was hard shale with scattered large Norwegian glacier melt boulders some several metres high. There is no silt and the wreck is clean, uncovered by sand.

Unlike the much larger capital ships of the day, *Hampshire* did not have a large elevated armoured superstructure, so when she capsized and hit the bottom, the lighter sections of her superstructure and her four smokestacks were crushed by her weight and momentum. The

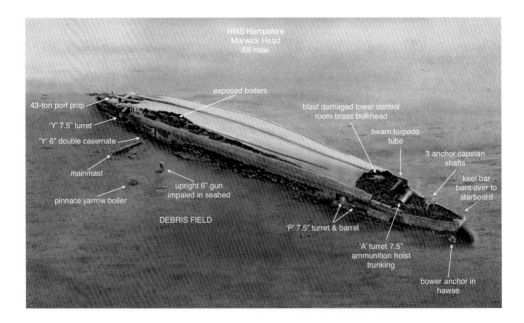

The wreck of HMS Hampshire *today lies in 68 metres of water.*

 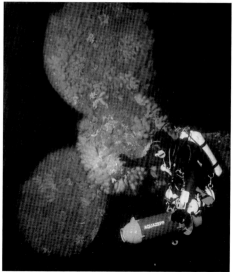

Left: The ship's name still rings around the fantail – now missing the HA. (Author's collection)

The port 43-ton propeller of HMS Hampshire. *© Ewan Rowell*

vessel came to rest almost completely upside down, but with a slight list to starboard, propped up by her 7.5-inch turrets and her conning tower.

I arrived at the stern at a depth of about 65 metres and Gary arrived soon beside me. With a quick exchange of OK hand signals, and a muffled 'Are you OK?' shouted through the mouthpiece of my rebreather in a squeaky helium Donald Duck voice, we turned to move forward along the port side of the wreck at seabed level on our first recce. I immediately started filming.

At the very stern, we could see how the two unarmoured upper deck levels had collapsed down and how the upside-down bulwark of the fantail was sitting a few feet aft of the more intact keel section of the stern. We could make out the large embossed letters of her name, *MPSHIRE*. The section of metal that would have held the *HA* was missing, having sprung somewhere as this section of the ship collapsed. The rudder lay fallen to the seabed nearby.

I moved forward, a few feet above a seabed that was littered with plating, spars and bits of ship. As I did so, the smooth intact steel of a large section of her keel began to rise up from the fantail and a gap began to appear between the seabed and this intact section of keel and hull. The keel swept upwards towards the vertical sternpost which would have held the rudder – and there just forward to port, and still supported on its bearing and struts, was the massive 43-ton manganese bronze, three-bladed prop – about 16 feet across according to the ship's drawings. Sections of the underside of the quarter deck lay flat on the seabed to port, and it appeared that the ship had sagged to starboard as the higher levels collapsed aeons ago.

The gap between the seabed and the intact section of the ship continued to increase – and then the reason for this became apparent. The large gunhouse of the 7.5-inch gun Y turret, situated on the centreline of the quarter deck, was resting upside down on the hard shale seabed. Rising up from its underside, the cylindrical armoured trunking that held the

The port side of the wreck aft has separated from the keel, allowing a glimpse of the 7.5-inch shell room. (Author's collection)

ammunition hoists extended all the way up to the underside of the keel bar. The ammunition hoists transported shells and cordite propellant charges up from the magazines and shell rooms, far below the surface in the bowels of the ship, to the gunhouse. Inside the ship, adjacent to the hoist trunking, masses of 6-inch shells for her secondary armament and QF 3-pounder shells had tumbled down from above to litter the underside of her main deck, now at seabed level. High up on the wreck, the keel plating had split open to expose the port 7.5-inch shell room, the large shells still neatly stacked in rows.

In the astonishing visibility, I continued to fin forward at a depth of just over 60 metres. Just forward of the aftmost Y turret, the two-storey port 6-inch gun casemate came into view, its curved armoured side projecting from the hull. With the ship upside down, the 6.8-metre-long barrel of the uppermost casemate now lay flat on the seabed, pointing aft. The lower (now uppermost) of the two 6-inch casemate guns had been demounted from the casemate in 1916 and moved to the upper deck in place of one of the original 3-pounder guns. The resulting vacant gun port had been plated over to keep the sea out – and the plate was still very evident on the wreck, its centre now corroded through.

As I looked at the 6.8-metre-long barrel on the seabed, I noticed the end of the barrel of a 3-pounder sticking up through the sand at its end. Tracing back towards the hull, this led me to the base of its pedestal, which was sticking up from under the sand just under the bulwark. Forward of the casemate gun we would go on to find several more of these now upside-down 3-pounder guns.

The main (aft) mast ran out at right angles to the wreck along the seabed, with thick old-fashioned electric cables running from the wreck up inside it. Just forward from it, a sturdy steel boom for a steam pinnace or boom boat lay on the seabed. As the ship sank, the boom boats could not be swung out and lowered, as all power on the ship had been lost; the boom boats were still secured on her as she turned turtle and went down.

As I swam out along the mainmast, I spotted a small triangular Yarrow boiler from a pinnace lying on the seabed just beyond its end. As the ship turned upside down, this Yarrow boiler, which provided steam for the pinnace engine, had fallen from its mounts straight through the wooden roof of the pinnace to the seabed. There was no sign near it of the engine or any other parts of the pinnace –presumably still lashed to the wreck and its boom.

As I looked further forward from the mast and boom, I spotted a large object standing upright on the seabed about 15 metres away from the wreck. I remembered seeing this in 2000 when I dived the wreck last – but at that time, on open-circuit trimix and limited bottom time on the wreck, I had not ventured out to go and see what it was.

This time, not having the same gas constraints, I swam out from the wreck towards it. Once I got to about 10 metres away, I realised that it was one of the 6-inch guns (similar to the 6.8-metre long gun I had just seen in its 2-storey casemate) that had been demounted from the casemates and installed on the upper deck. As the ship turned turtle on the surface, like the Yarrow boiler, this gun, which weighed more than 8 tons (excluding the casemate protection) had fallen from its mount and plunged down through the water column like a dart. At least 4–5 metres of the 7-metre-long barrel had impaled itself into the seabed – I

Starboard aft shot of Hampshire *showing the two-storey 6-inch gun casemate. The lower of these guns on both sides of the ship were demounted in 1916 and installed on the upper deck. (Author's collection)*

The two-storey casemate with the originally uppermost barrel lying on the seabed. The uppermost firing port has been plated over, the plate having now corroded in its centre. The main mast runs out on the seabed to right of shot. (Author's collection)

To the east, one of the two 6-inch gun barrels which have impaled themselves some 5 metres into the seabed as they fell off the ship as she capsized. A third gun was found lying flat on the seabed whilst the fourth is under the wreck. (Author's collection)

was looking at the last 1–2 metres of barrel and the breech block, all heavily encrusted in soft corals and dead man's fingers. In the days to come we would find another 6-inch gun impaled upright in the seabed not far away, and a third that had failed to penetrate the seabed and was lying flat. The fourth 6-inch gun was found under the wreck itself.

It was becoming clear as the dive went on, that lots of large items such as guns and boilers had fallen off the ship as she capsized – they were all lying in a debris field on the east or port side of the wreck as she now lay. This already confirmed wartime reports from the 12 survivors that she capsized to starboard on the surface.

I moved back towards the wreck and saw a row of portholes lying on the seabed along the side of the ship, in sections of hull plating. These portholes were originally situated in the unarmoured deck above the main waterline armour belt, and they had been still *in situ* in the ship's side when I dived her last in 2000. Since then, the weight of the non-ferrous portholes had triumphed over the rotting, unarmoured shell plating, and one by one they had fallen to the seabed, taking large rotted sections of shell plating with them. The structure of the ship remained – minus the shell plating with its row of portholes, leaving a seemingly black horizontal expanse, which ran fore and aft for about 150 feet, opening directly into the innards of the ship.

Looking under the inverted main deck, which was in places a metre or two off the seabed, we began to make out several more of the upside-down QF 3-pounder guns that had been ranged along either side of the ship. As built, there were nine of these along either beam, but during refit in 1916 a number of these were demounted and landed to make way for the two lower 6-inch casemate guns that had been removed from either beam and installed on the upper deck.

I continued to move forward along the port beam. As I approached the area where the bridge superstructure would have been, now largely crushed under the ship, the crumpled port side of the bridge projected out to the east. The collapse of the bridge and the rotting away of shell plating had exposed a row of several upside-down toilets that gleamed white in our torches – the ship's heads.

Above the crushed bridge superstructure, the armour belt plates were still pristine, although some had slipped from their mountings here and there, allowing a glimpse of their thickness. The end of the port 7.5-inch wing P turret barrel protruded from collapsed and fallen ship's plating.

At this point, as I looked up the port side of the armour belt, the shell plating of the bottom of the ship, which had been largely intact all the way from the stern to this point, abruptly stopped at the bottom of the armour belt. I began to fin upwards, moving towards the original bottom of the armour belt.

As I reached the top (originally the bottom) of the armour belt, in the amazing 50-metre visibility, I was greeted by a panorama of the innards of the ship. The complete bottom of the hull from the armour belt on this side, to the armour belt on the other was missing – from about Frame No 38 all the way forward to the bow. Moving from aft forward, the largely intact keel plating of the bottom of the hull just stopped at Frame No 38 and was gone all the way up to the bow. It was as though the keel of the ship had been sliced across and the bottom of the ship completely removed all the way to the bow, visible far in the distance. All 37 hull frames – all the stringers that connected the frames, the double bottoms and shell plating – everything was gone.

The scene in front of me was just as it had been when I had visited the wreck in 1997 and 2000 during previous surveys, except that the leading edge of the intact section of hull at

Above: Looking aft from near the bow reveals the extent of the damage to the wreck between bridge and bow before the hull reforms aft. The concave brass bulkhead of the lower control room can be seen, along with the starboard submerged torpedo tube. (Author's collection)

Left: On the starboard side where the keel reforms, keel plates have separated to reveal flashproof corrugated cordite propellant charge containers. (Author's collection)

Frame No 38 had sagged downwards. This was just natural degradation of the ship and the effects of the passage of time. The damage to the hull here at the bow was not from the single mine that had sunk her in 1916. That would have blown in a few compartments, but certainly had not produced this level of damage. This was commercial salvage work – it looked as though the keel had been grabbed out.

The keel plates where the hull reformed at Frame No 38 were coming apart at the joins as rivets turned to dust through differential corrosion, revealing ribbed boxes of cordite propellant underneath, inside the ship, on the port side.

As I hung in free water outside the ship beside the top of the armour belt plates and looked down into the exposed innards of the ship, initially a confused scene of jumbled devastation presented itself. The large cylindrical ammunition hoist trunking for the 7.5-inch gun of A turret, situated on the centreline of the fo'c'sle, lay on its side, its lowermost edge almost touching the far starboard side of the hull. To my left was a large transverse ribbed non-ferrous bulkhead – which was now concave from the effects of an explosion forward of it towards the bow. Across the ship on the far starboard side of the wreck I could see the long ribbed starboard beam 18-inch torpedo tube. In a later dive, I spotted the external torpedo hatch door lying on the seabed just off the wreck on the starboard side. There was, at this point, no apparent sign of the port 18-inch torpedo tube, which should have been almost right underneath me. Nearby, in the debris of the ship's innards, lay torpedo bodies and warheads.

I continued forward along the top of the armour belt plates on the port side on this, my first initial orientation dive. A little way forward of the A turret ammunition hoist trunking, three large anchor capstan axles projected upwards from the debris. Royal Navy vessels were fitted with two bower anchors, one on either side of the bow, and a third sheet, or emergency, anchor on the starboard side abaft the bower anchor – so they had two anchors to starboard and one to port. In contrast, German World War I warships carried two anchors on the port side and one on the starboard side.

At the top of the three projecting capstan axle shafts (originally at their bases), each had a circular gear that would have been driven by a small steam capstan engine that was visible

The mouthpiece of the starboard submerged torpedo tube. (Author's collection)

in the debris. The actual capstans themselves were originally situated on the fo'c'sle deck and were now hidden under the wreck.

The three anchor capstan axle shafts are not distressed, bent or damaged in any way as from the effects of a nearby mine explosion. So it looked like the mine that sank the ship did not explode in their immediate vicinity. I spotted several dozen ribbed brass cordite propellant storage boxes in this area, which showed evidence of pressure damage to the cordite boxes themselves but no signs of explosive damage. Survivors had reported seeing a small explosion take place forward as she made her final plunge, and smoke and flame belching from just behind the bridge. There had been speculation that this had been a secondary ammunition explosion, but from the evidence before me it appeared highly unlikely that any secondary ammunition explosion had occurred in the bow magazines, as such an event would have consumed all propellant in the boxes in the area.

As Gary and I moved forward, we spotted the large port bower anchor lying on the seabed on the port side of the wreck. We swam over for a closer look and found that its stock was still secured in its hawse pipe in a detached section of unarmoured hull plating that would originally have been above the armour belt. Running along the plating were a number of fixed ladder rungs for crew. There was no sighting of the two starboard anchors, which may be buried under the wreck.

Looking back at the wreck, it was clear that the bow section of the ship was resting on the vertical armour belt plates. The two unarmoured fo'c'sle deck levels, lined with portholes and originally above the armour belt, were now crushed beneath the armour belt. This is in contrast to the section of ship from the bridge aft, where the deck level originally above the armour belt is still there, albeit minus the portholes themselves which have fallen to the seabed.

Gary and I arrived at the bow, which rose up magnificently for about 10 metres from a deep pit around it on the seabed. The base of the stem was completely intact – so at least we know she didn't run bow first into the mine. The keel bar, one of the strongest parts of a ship, was still in place but bent smoothly over to starboard and angling down aft towards the seabed, where its severed tip rested on the shale about 20–30 metres aft of the stem.

By now, it was time for Gary and me to turn the dive and head back to the downline to ascend. To minimise decompression we finned up over the wreck until we were moving aft a few metres above the upturned flat bottom of the keel. We kept the video cameras running to record the less glamorous, but equally important, keel of the ship.

After a bottom time of about 35 minutes on this first dive, Gary and I arrived back at the stern downline. The other divers of the first wave were beginning to congregate around it, having kept to our agreed bottom times to keep us all loosely together. As we began to make our ascent up the downline we could see below us in the darkness, and further forward on the wreck, distant white pinpricks of the torches of the second wave of divers as they began to head back to the downline to begin their own ascents.

Gary and I rose up beside the downline and as we reached the transfer line at about 30 metres, we both removed our name tags before slowly beginning to cross over a seeming abyss towards the trapeze. Below us we could see the second wave of divers, now clustering around the base of the downline and beginning to silently rise up the shotline.

As the last divers reached the transfer line and removed the last name tags, satisfied that everyone was off the wreck, they disconnected the transfer line from the downline. The whole trapeze assembly now hung in free water, suspended from its own two large danbuoys on the surface. Slack water was long past, and the gentle current quickly began to drift us away from the fixed downline. As the downline disappeared from view up-current, we sent up a red DSMB on a reel to tell the skipper that all divers were up and decompressing on the trapeze – and that all was good.

We were disconnected and drifting, 12 divers clustered around the various bars of the trapeze, some hanging in free water just off it, to ease congestion. A long 90 minutes of uneventful decompression on the trapeze followed as we went through our decompression stops, culminating in long hangs at 9 metres and 6 metres.

As I finally finished my 6-metre decompression stop and began to move up one of the buoy lines that suspended the whole trapeze, I reflected on Day 1, Dive 1 of the exped, and what it had brought. We had already learned so much about the wreck on this first dive. What would the rest of the two-week expedition reveal?

Gary and I broke the surface after a run time for the dive of just over two hours, our heads spinning round until we spotted the attendant *Huskyan*. Once she turned towards us and started to close, now that it was clear that the crew had spotted us we let go of the trapeze buoy line. We rolled onto our backs and put our chests towards the gentle swell – this way we were facing into the waves and into the wind. We then kicked our fins gently and began to separate ourselves downwind from the trapeze buoys. We needed to be clear and downwind of the trapeze to give *Huskyan* plenty of room to come in close and pick us up with no risk of fouling the trapeze.

Once we had finned and drifted a good distance away from the trapeze, we stopped finning and just hung there in open water, two specks of humanity in the vastness of the Atlantic Ocean, waiting for *Huskyan* to make her pick-up approach.

After manoeuvring to get downwind of us, the *Huskyan*, with her lovely black and white bow, moved into the wind towards us. Very soon she was right beside us, the skipper, Russ, skilfully using her deadweight in the water to screen us from the seas and calm the water where we were. Russ then clicked the engines ahead to draw us down the starboard side of the vessel until we were just forward of the diver hoist. He then clicked the engines astern, to kill the water stream and stop with us dead in the water beside the lift gate. *Huskyan*'s spacious diver lift platform descended right beside us until it was deep enough in the water for us to swim onto it, one by one, and stand up.

Gary moved onto the lift platform first, as I held onto the grab line strung along the side of the vessel, waiting my turn. Once he was standing on the submerged platform, in water up to his chest, he marshalled all his cylinders, reels, torches and kit to avoid a snag before giving a nod of his head to crewman Ross Dowrie. The diver lift rose up from the water until the platform was at deck level, where Ross helped Gary and his 85kg of kit over the deck, and got him carefully seated on the kitting-up bench.

With Gary safely aboard, the process was repeated for me, and I was also soon on deck, being assisted to sit down in my heavy kit by Ross, who quickly whipped off my bailout cylinders, closed the valves and stowed them upright in the cylinder racks.

Once I was safely seated on the bench, I remained fully rigged and breathing from my rebreather, relaxing and breathing almost pure O2 through the rebreather for 3–4 minutes. I had learned the hard way after a bad exercise-induced bend in the North Channel off Ireland, that it's best to sit still and simply do nothing after a deep technical dive.

Safety period over, once I was comfortable and relaxed I pulled the gag strap over my head, dropped the CCR mouthpiece from my mouth, pulled my 10mm neoprene dive hood back and pulled my mask off. A steaming pint of tea was immediately stuck in my hand by Ross – it's something of a tradition on the *Huskyan*, and is much appreciated after a cold two-hour dive in 8°C water. As Gary did the same, we exploded into animated chatter about what we had just seen, the words tumbling out of our mouths like someone rapidly beating a drum.

'Did you see the pit around the bow? That's not a scour pit: she was 144 metres long and sunk by her bow in 70 metres,' I said. 'Looks like her bow hit the seabed whilst her stern was proud of the water – and then as she capsized to starboard her bow ground this pit in the seabed.'

'The keel bar is severed 20–30 metres away from the stem. It's the strongest part of the ship – so that might be where the mine hit?'

'Right, so if the keel bar was severed and she then ground on the seabed as she capsized to starboard, maybe that's why the keel bar is smoothly bent over to starboard and off the starboard side of the wreck.'

'Did you see the concave brass transverse bulkhead just forward of the conning tower? That's bent from a blast forward of it.'

'Did you see the 6-inch guns impaled upright into the seabed? There's all sorts of things in a large debris field that have fallen off the ship as she capsized out to the east – there's nothing on the seabed to the west.'

And so, the chatter went on as we sipped our tea – still in our full rigs. But very soon our initial thoughts and impressions had to stop, as other divers started to pop up to the surface after completing their own deco. We quickly wriggled out of our rebreather harnesses and were soon at the lift, as the *Huskyan* came in to pick up the next group of divers, who were now well away from the trapeze. Over at the trapeze, other divers were now beginning to surface, slowly starting to fin away and wait for their turn to be picked up.

As other divers came up the diver lift and heavily clomped down on the dive deck benches, the level of buzz and excitement escalated. Everyone was amazed at what they had just seen – each had spotted something unique. Whilst it was a simple joy to see such experienced divers clearly blown away by the experience, immediately I could see just how gifted a group of individuals they were.

Once we had all de-kitted and changed out of our drysuits into our dry clothes, we all gathered in the *Huskyan*'s spacious saloon, where even more pints of tea were served along with skipper Emily Turton's justly famous home bakes. You do get treated extremely well on the *Huskyan*!

In addition to *Huskyan*'s famous hospitality, Emily is also legendary for her fantastically detailed dive briefings and whiteboard drawings on her regular Scapa Flow dive trips. In advance of this expedition, she had had a huge whiteboard wall mounted in the saloon and as we all sipped tea and ate cake, she sketched out on it the upturned hull of the *Hampshire* on the seabed.

We had agreed to hold a debrief every day on the passage back south to Scapa Flow to capture everyone's memories in a formal way, before the days began to merge into one another and memories became muddled and lost. Once the basic outline was up on the board, we went around each of the divers one by one, asking them to take their turn at the whiteboard, saying what they saw and where. Emily then added the things they had seen, like the impaled 6-inch guns and the pinnace Yarrow boilers, in the right locations on the whiteboard. The process took about an hour, and it was clear that even after Day 1 we already had a good idea of the layout of the wreck.

The following day, it was reveille at 0600 for Dive 2. We were all aboard the *Huskyan* and ropes were being cast off by 0715. We headed south into Scapa Flow from Stromness before turning to the west to pass out through Hoy Sound. Once through the tidal and often very difficult waters of this sound, the *Huskyan* turned her head to the north for the run up the coast to the wreck site. The weather was beautiful again – the sky was a crisp clear blue, the sea calm, with a long rolling swell coming in from the Atlantic.

Whereas yesterday the task had been to establish a fixed downline near the stern of the wreck and explore it from there, today we would deploy a second shotline on the seabed near the bow and start our exploration from this area. The trapeze could then be deployed on either fixed shot as required each day – divers would know exactly where they would arrive at on the wreck and it would assist becoming familiar with the wreck.

As with the day before, we arrived on site a couple of hours before slack water. The buoys from the fixed shotline deployed at the stern the day before were still floating in position, marking where the wreck lay. Arriving well in advance of slack water like this gave ample time for Ben and Emily to get the boat positioned just off the bow and drop a second weighted shotline to the seabed. This was a fully munitioned warship as well as being a sensitive war grave, and we did not want to damage it in any way with a careless shot deployment. As with the placing of the shot on the seabed near the stern yesterday, Ben and Emily spent a considerable amount of time getting a feel for the exact positioning of the wreck far below before the signal was given to drop the shot.

As the shot weight went over the side, the coiled rope paid out quickly from the deck, only arresting its frantic deployment as the shot landed on the seabed. The rope had been precut to the length required and already had a couple of fisherman's floats attached to its end; they had insufficient buoyancy to drag the shot away from the wreck. The tide would drag them under until it went slack, when they would pop up to the surface again and make it clear it was time to dive. The first divers in would attach a large danbuoy to the shotline as they went in, to give buoyancy in case there was some sort of emergency during the dive itself. We all clustered in the saloon for our dive briefing and allocating of tasks and areas of operation for each pair of divers. Dive briefing over, it was time to start getting kitted up.

As with yesterday, Ben and Greg Booth would dive first to fix the shot near the wreck. Paul Haynes and Brian Burnett were next into the water, as Ross got the self-deploying trapeze into the water, taking spare gas and the transfer line down the shotline to clip it on at 30 metres. Next, Gary and I would splash.

As I righted myself after jumping off the boat into the water, I finned over to the downline. The trapeze was already hanging fully deployed in free water nearby – I could follow the transfer line from it all the way down into the depths to where Paul and Brian had already clipped it to the downline far below.

Gary and I had a round of OK hand signals and then started our descent into the beautiful crystal-clear water that surrounded us. We were hanging seemingly in the open expanse of the Atlantic – below me it was dark, and as yet there was no sign of the wreck far below.

The tide was now totally slack and so Gary and I let go of the downline and began to freefall deeper into the darkness. Gradually the darkness below took on a familiar form, unnatural straight lines began to coalesce to a point – the unmistakable upturned bow of HMS *Hampshire*. Far below in the darkness, I could see the shot sitting on the seabed just forward of the port side of the bow. There was no need for us to go over there, so we left the downline and headed over to the ship.

The ripped-open forward section of the keel at the bow, from bridge to stem, was right beside and below us. In the lovely visibility, I could see the full beam of the ship and how the two sides of tapered armour belt swept together towards the stem. The vertical armour belt plates protecting the most important parts of the ship, such as the engines, boilers and magazines amidships, were 6 inches thick, but these tapered towards stern and bow, outwith the citadel. The vertical armour plates beneath me here at the bow appeared to be about 2 inches thick. Inside the exposed innards of the ship I could see the now familiar cylindrical ammunition hoist trunking for A turret, the starboard beam torpedo tube abaft it – and the three capstan axles and circular gears nearby, ahead of it.

As I hung in free water above the wreck I studied this open area in more detail. There was still no trace of any of the keel frames, stringers or shell plating of the hull. Everything above the vertical armour belt plates of either side was gone. In the confused debris of ship's innards here I spotted a number of torpedo bodies, a number of separate torpedo warheads, shells for the 7.5-inch main guns and for the 6-inch casemate guns, and masses of corrugated rectangular brass tins holding cordite propellant charges for the guns. Cordite propellant was stored separately from shells in magazines well below the waterline of warships.

We spent the dive as planned around the bow, filming the debris area of the missing keel. I swam over to the starboard side of the wreck and spotted the beam torpedo tube mouthpiece lying on the seabed. Nearby a complete torpedo body lay parallel and up against the side of the ship, partly obscured by a fallen piece of plating. Why was this torpedo outside the ship on the seabed, unlike the others which were inside?

Whilst it was clear there was a rich debris field on the east side of the wreck facing towards Orkney, as I looked out over the seabed to the west, towards America, there appeared to be nothing at all lying on the seabed. To make sure I kicked my fins and ventured about 50 metres out over the seabed to the west, keeping the wreck in sight behind me in the glorious visibility. The seabed was clean shale with no debris at all to the west.

After another 35 minutes on the bottom, it was time for us to begin our ascent. After we and the other divers were all safely back aboard after long decompression hangs, Emily and Marjo Tynkkynen reported a stellar piece of work – they had spotted, just off the bow in the pit, a small circular artefact, about 8 inches across, that was green with verdigris and clearly non-ferrous. They had carefully photographed it with a ruler placed alongside it for scale. During our post-dive debrief, Emily and Marjo put the images of it up on the *Huskyan's* saloon screens. The central part of the object had an embossed rose that was surrounded by a garland of leaves that ran right around the outside of the object. There were four screw holes in its face. At first, we were all a bit non-plussed as to what it was, but the more we looked at it, the more it became clear that what we were looking at was a brass face plate for a tampion for one of the forward 7.5-inch main battery guns. These tampions were essentially leather-covered wooden plugs that were inserted into the end of the gun barrel when not in use to keep out sea water and the elements. They usually had a colourful decorative outer plate screwed to the tampion itself, carrying a motif personal to the ship. In this case, the rose surrounded by a crown or garland of leaves was the emblem of the county of Hampshire, after which the ship was named.

The tampion plate was lying off the ship – and not directly beside either the forward A turret 7.5-inch gun, which was under the upturned fo'c'sle deck, or the port P turret 7.5-inch gun, whose open barrel protruded from debris at the side of the ship some way away, near the bridge. We talked it through and surmised that as the ship turned turtle on the surface and then sank, increasing water pressure had perhaps compressed the air in the gun barrel, driving the wooden plug up the barrel a short way and forcing the tampion plate to pop off and fall to the seabed.

During the debrief we were able to add many more features to our whiteboard recreation of the wreck – it was already starting to become a busy whiteboard.

The next day, we gathered in the saloon of *Huskyan* as we ran up the coast once again to the wreck site. Now that we had covered and filmed the whole wreck in overview, now that there were fixed downlines at the bow and stern, it was time to start looking at particular features in detail.

Local diving historian Kevin Heath of Sula Diving in Orkney had carried out detailed side-scan sonar mapping of the wreck site in advance of our arrival. His preliminary work proved particularly useful in identifying large objects lying off the wreck in what had transpired to be the debris field of items that had dropped from the ship as she turned turtle on the surface. Each day, pairs of divers were assigned a particular task – and using Kevin's scans we could now take bearings from fixed points on the wreck to these objects out in the debris field, and send divers out to check them out.

Some of the divers were using diver propulsion vehicles (DPVs) and were able to cover large areas of the seabed quickly. There were some very big lumps on the seabed more than 200 metres off the wreck, and Paul Haynes and Brian Burnett were sent out on scooters to investigate those. These turned out to be large Norwegian glacial melt boulders, the size of an SUV.

Paul Toomer and Mic Watson were a very strong buddy pair who worked well together – they were tasked to go and devote a dive to filming in detail the upright 6-inch gun, impaled in the seabed, that was the furthest gun off the wreck. As they were doing this they noticed a dinner fork lying on the seabed beside the gun. Their videography was so good that when Kari Hyttinen worked on the 3D photogrammetry data processing that evening, as the gun materialised out of the point cloud data during processing, the fork could clearly be seen gleaming on the seabed beside it.

Gary and I were tasked on one dive to film the entire starboard side of the wreck – the 'low side'. The ship was canted over, propped up on her turrets such that her port side was slightly higher. Even although the hull on the low side was sunk well into the seabed, this dive turned out to be particularly interesting.

In 1983, the wreck was dived by a commercial consortium, who obtained a licence to survey and film it from the UK MOD, using the Aberdeen oil field diving support vessel, the *Stena Workhorse*. The 43-ton starboard propeller was stated to have been found lying on the seabed beside the wreck. The licence precluded removing items from the wreck – but the consortium believed it did not prevent them from recovering items lying on the seabed around it. The prop and shaft was lifted and the recovery reported to the Receiver of Wreck in Aberdeen. The prop and shaft were offloaded onto the pier at Peterhead when the vessel arrived there on completion of the works, and lay there for more than a year until it was sent to Orkney where it is now on display at the Scapa Flow Visitor Centre and Museum at Lyness on the island of Hoy. We were able to locate the shaft tube, where the prop shaft had broken off – or been cut off – just as it emerged from the shaft tunnel.

Kari Hyttinen and Immi Wallin spent their days filming the wreck slowly and meticulously in hi-res for photogrammetry with Prof Chris Rowland, the Director of the 3DVisLab at Dundee University, acting as supporting light. Chris is at the leading edge of underwater imaging with the company ADUS Deep Ocean, which was brought in to image the Deep Water Horizon in the Gulf of Mexico, and the *Costa Concordia*. Chris would assist with the photogrammetry and go on to do the virtual reality 1:1 aspect ratio, actual-size modelling of the wreck. Emily supported Marjo Tynkkynen in taking hundreds of hi-res still images and fully cataloguing the wreck. As the days went past, so our knowledge of the wreck increased – and so Emily's whiteboard became more and more full.

Week 2 of the expedition was soon upon us – and whereas the first week had been blessed with benign seas and awesome underwater visibility of up to 50 metres, during the second week the seas blew up and a plankton bloom closed the vis on the wreck down to a black 5 metres. This was frustrating but not a significant problem, as we had already filmed the wreck in detail and knew the wreck so well by then that we could still easily navigate our way around it to spend our time finding and mapping the smaller details.

The *Daring*-class Type 45 destroyer HMS *Duncan* was scheduled to be moored in Kirkwall for the 100th anniversary commemoration event above the site and the simultaneous ceremony at the Kitchener Memorial on Marwick Head. She is the sixth and final Type 45 destroyer to have joined the Royal Navy in 2010. She is 152 metres in length, just a little longer than the 144-metre long *Hampshire*. Despite being slightly longer, the unarmoured *Duncan* displaces 8,000 tons as opposed to the 10,800 tons displacement of *Hampshire*.

As the conditions of our licence prohibited us diving on the actual 100th anniversary of the sinking, 5 June 2016, the whole team was kindly invited for a tour of *Duncan* the night before. The four expedition co-organisers were also invited back for lunch aboard on the 100th anniversary itself by her commander, who warmly welcomed us and was very supportive of what we were trying to do. After a very pleasant lunch in his private rooms, we were able to show him some of our underwater footage and stills photographs, and explain how our buoys were laid out on the site; he would be going out to the site that evening for the ceremony.

That evening, 5 June 2016, the 100th anniversary commemoration event took place at the Kitchener Memorial atop Marwick Head at 2045, the exact time that the *Hampshire* hit the fateful mine. Our whole dive team attended the ceremony – and it was particularly moving for us to see offshore in the distance, silhouetted against the late summer's setting sun, HMS *Duncan* sitting above the wreck of the *Hampshire*. It was a powerful and moving image – and it was slightly strange to be in amongst so many interested people and officials to think that we would be diving down to the wreck the following day. Representatives of the Metropolitan Police from London were present as their man, Matthew McLoughlin, was Kitchener's personal body guard and was lost as the ship sunk. The Met would subsequently approach me to indicate that a suite of offices in their Royalty and Specialist Protection Command centre was going to be named after the late officer, who was the last Met officer to lose his life on protection duties. They asked for some imagery of the wreck to display in the new Matthew McLoughlin Suite. We were of course happy to oblige for such a worthy cause, and forwarded a number of stills. The suite was subsequently opened by the Princess Royal on 19 October 2016.

In the days following the 100th anniversary ceremony at Marwick Head, the commander of HMS *Duncan* sent me a note to say that the buoys had been very helpful in positioning his vessel at the correct site and in the correct orientation for the ceremony.

From our examination of the wreck, it became clear that with a length of 144 metres, as the *Hampshire* sank by the bow, her bow struck the seabed as her stern lifted out of the water 65 metres above. She then rolled to starboard and capsized on the surface. Everything that wasn't secured to her fell from the upside-down ship to create a debris field on the seabed to the east. Her four deck-mounted 6-inch secondary armament guns fell from their mounts and dropped through the water column, two impaling themselves like darts into the seabed.

Her two towering masts struck the seabed on the eastern side of the wreck and broke in several places. The small Yarrow boilers for her steam pinnaces fell through the pinnace roofs and landed to the east; the pinnaces themselves, still secured to the booms were pinned to the side of the wreck.

A drifting decompression on the trapeze on the final day was a chance to fly the Explorers Club flag inwater. Rod Macdonald on the left – Paul Haynes, right.

Over more than 100 years since her sinking, the wreck has sagged and collapsed in places, but she is very much recognisable for the fine ship she was. An armoured ship, strongly built, she has stood up well against time, tide and the fierce Atlantic storms.

As at the date of printing we have our 120-page-long Explorers Club Expedition Report almost finalised. It will be kept by the Explorers Club along with all the other reports of expeditions going right back to its genesis in the early 20th century. The report will also be circulated to other interested bodies such as local museums and national institutions such as the Imperial War Museum and the National Maritime Museum. The 3D photogrammetry and virtual reality modelling is well under way, but will take some time to finalise. I subsequently went down to the University of Dundee to visit Chris Rowland in the 3DVis Lab. Putting on the VR goggles, you are immediately transported to the wreck of the *Hampshire*, which at full size appears to tower 50 feet above you. The level of detail is incredible, and once the VR model is finalised I will be interested to hear what maritime archaeologists will say about being able to walk around the wreck of the *Hampshire*.

The wreck is designated as a Controlled Site under the Protection of Military Remains Act 1986 (Designation of Vessels and Controlled Sites) Order 2012 and no diving has been permitted on it or within 300 metres of it since 2002. With our survey under licence now completed, it is unlikely that another licence will be granted to survey the ship in the foreseeable future. I wonder what she will look like on the 200th anniversary of her sinking and how our 2016 results may be pored over then?

5

HMS VANGUARD

St Vincent-class British dreadnought battleship
Destroyed at anchor in Scapa Flow on 9 July 1917

On the evening of 9 July 1917, the British *St Vincent*-class battleship *Vanguard* lay at anchor in Scapa Flow, less than one nautical mile to the north of the island of Flotta. The *Revenge*-class battleship HMS *Royal Oak* lay at anchor nearby.

Without warning, at about 2320, a series of cataclysmic magazine explosions suddenly took place in *Vanguard's* magazine. She sank immediately, and all but three of the 845 men aboard her at the time were killed. The loss of life was greater than either of Orkney's other two famous war graves, HMS *Hampshire* lost in 1916 with 737 men, and the nearby *Royal Oak*, which would herself be lost in 1939 with 834 men.

Vanguard was laid down by Vickers Armstrong at Barrow-in Furness on 2 April 1908. She was the eighth ship to bear this name – a name that is enmeshed in the history of the Royal Navy. The ninth to bear the name *Vanguard* was launched in 1944, but only completed in 1947,

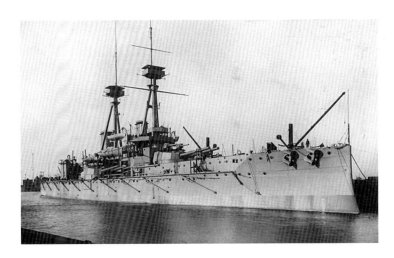

The 19,700-ton St-Vincent-class dreadnought battleship HMS Vanguard.

after the war had ended; she was the biggest and fastest British battleship ever constructed, with 15-inch guns and a speed of 30 knots. But the era of the battleship was over and when she was scrapped early after only 13 years' service in 1960, she was the last British battleship afloat. Today the eleventh *Vanguard* is the lead boat of the UK's Trident ballistic missile submarine fleet based at Faslane.

The eighth *Vanguard* was launched on 22 February 1909, and after fitting out afloat she was commissioned on 1 March 1910. She displaced 19,700 long tons standard and 22,800 tons deep load, and was 536 feet long with a beam of 84 feet.

Vanguard was fitted with ten breech-loading (BL) 12-inch Vickers Mk XI guns set in five twin turrets: the foremost, A turret, on the centreline forward of the bridge on the fo'c'sle deck; then P and Q turrets set one either side of the bridge superstructure; and two more aft on the centre line, X and Y turrets. The port wing turret was called P turret whilst the starboard wing turret was Q turret. These turrets had 11-inch face and side armour with 3-inch armour roofs.

These main battery 12-inch guns had a range of some 12 miles but suffered from bore erosion, short barrel life and poor accuracy due to inconsistent performance of the cordite propellant. The subsequent Mark XII evolution of these guns also suffered the same problems, and this led to the development of the 13.5-inch Mk V gun, which had much better performance.

Her secondary battery comprised 18 single Mk III BL 4-inch guns that were introduced in 1908 to deal with the threat of fast-moving, small and agile German torpedo boats. She carried four 3-pounder saluting guns and was fitted with three submerged 18-inch torpedo tubes.

Vanguard's main vertical waterline armour belt was 10-inch thick Krupp cemented armour – and above the main waterline belt was a strake of 8-inch armour. Her transverse bulkheads, linking the main waterline vertical armour belts on either side of the ship forward of A turret and aft of Y turret to form the citadel, were 5 and 8 inches thick. The P and Q 12-inch main battery wing turret barbettes abreast the bridge had 10-inch-thick outer face armour, whilst the three centreline barbettes, A, X and Y, had 9-inch armour above the main deck that reduced to 5-inch armour below decks. Her horizontal armoured decks varied from 1.5 to 3 inches thick.

Propulsion was delivered by 18 Babcock & Wilcox marine boilers that fed two sets of Parsons steam turbines and drove her four shafts to give her a speed of 21.7 knots. She carried a standard ship's complement of 823 officers and men – although at the time of her loss there were 845 men aboard.

Vanguard was initially based at Scapa Flow as part of the 1st Battle Squadron and when war broke out she began conducting North Sea sweeps and patrols from there before being attached, in April 1916, to the 4th Division of the 4th Battle Squadron just months before the Battle of Jutland.

During the Battle of Jutland on 31 May and 1 June 1916, no German capital ship came within range of her big guns – but she fired 42 rounds at the crippled light cruiser *Wiesbaden*, claiming several hits. She also engaged German destroyer flotillas with her main and secondary batteries. Although enemy shells landed near her she was not struck during the battle.

On the morning of 9 July 1917, *Vanguard* had moved from her anchorage, just north of the island of Flotta, north across the vast expanse of Scapa Flow towards the north shore of the

Flow as her crew practised 'abandon ship' training exercises. These were completed without incident, and after remaining at anchor to the north of Scapa Flow for the rest of the day, she weighed anchor at 1700 and headed back south across the Flow at 12 knots to her overnight anchorage, north of Flotta. On the way south, she practised deploying her minesweeping paravanes before anchoring off Flotta at 1830.

The evening went uneventfully until around 2320 when, without any previous warning, flames were seen coming up from below, just abaft her foremast. This was followed after a short interval by a heavy explosion deep within her. The flames greatly increased in intensity and wreckage was thrown up abaft the foremast in the vicinity of P and Q wing turrets, either side of the ship abaft the bridge.

This first explosion was followed after a short interval by a second, heavier, explosion that considerably increased the volume of flame and smoke. The ship was by now totally obscured by smoke and the exact location of this second explosion could not be determined.

When the huge cloud of smoke that had obscured the battleship drifted away in the gentle evening breeze, *Vanguard* was gone; 845 men had been aboard her at the time of the explosion – but only one officer and two ratings survived, one of whom subsequently died of injuries received. The total death toll of 843 included Commander Ito, an observer from the Imperial Japanese Navy – then an ally of Britain. Two Australian sailors from HMAS *Sydney* were locked in her cells when she went up and were also killed.

The bodies of her crew that could be recovered now rest in the naval cemetery at Lyness, and a memorial stands at the end of the gravestones, overlooking Scapa Flow where their destroyed dreadnought lies in the depths.

The subsequent Court of Inquiry took place on 30 July 1917 aboard the battleship HMS *Emperor of India* three weeks after *Vanguard* blew up. The court found that the likely cause of the explosion in either P or Q magazine was either (i) the ignition of cordite due to an avoidable cause or (ii) abnormal deterioration of a cordite charge subjected to abnormal treatment during its life.

Cordite is a smokeless propellant developed in the late 19th century to replace gunpowder in large military weapons such as tank guns, artillery and naval guns. High explosive gunpowder, used since the days of sail, produced a powerful detonation in the barrel that initially accelerated the projectile – but by the time the projectile was leaving the barrel, with the force of the explosion spent, the projectile was already decelerating. Gunpowder was very destructive of the gun barrel itself and produced a large quantity of black smoke.

In 1889, a new propellant consisting of nitroglycerine, gun cotton and petroleum jelly, was developed and manufactured in thin spaghetti-like rods. It was known initially as 'cord powder' – a name quickly abbreviated to 'cordite'. Cordite was not designed to be a high explosive such as gunpowder: it was developed to *deflagrate* – that is, to burn and produce high-temperature gases. It was the rapidly expanding gas inside the breech that accelerated the projectile up the barrel, to such an extent that the shell was still accelerating as it left the barrel, unlike gunpowder where the shell was decelerating from the moment of detonation. This expansion of cordite gas was much less destructive of the gun barrel than gunpowder.

Cordite was stored for protection in propellant magazines, deep in the ship below the waterline. The magazines for the big 12-inch guns were clustered around the barbettes and ammunition hoists.

During World War I, the British kept all their big gun cordite propellant in silk pouches stored in flashproof copper Clarkson cases in the magazines. These Clarkson cases were 5-foot-high flashproof brass or steel tubes (like large cigar cases) with a carrying handle on the side and a circular lid at one end. The top half of the cases opened longitudinally to receive and safely transport cordite in silk pouches from the magazine to the gunhouse above via the ammunition hoists. Cordite propellant charges for smaller calibre guns were housed in rectangular brass-ribbed flashproof cases with a removable lid.

The early versions of cordite required to be kept at a temperature of less than 50°F (or 10°C) by a cooling system lest it become unstable – so on all warships, the temperature of propellant magazines had to be monitored.

The Court of Inquiry on *Emperor of India* heard evidence that on *Vanguard* the temperatures of all 12-inch and 4-inch magazines were taken daily every morning by means of temperature tubes. Additionally, thermograph charts were inspected weekly by the gunnery officer.

There was however, at this time, no standardised Royal Navy procedure for taking magazine temperatures – and systems and procedures varied from ship to ship in the fleet. Some ships like *Vanguard* took the temperatures once a day – whilst others took the temperature three times a day.

In reaching its verdict, the court recommended that the taking of magazine temperatures should be standardised throughout the fleet. The monitoring procedure should be conducted at more frequent intervals and should be carried out under the direction of the gunnery officer by the gunner of the ship, who should physically enter the magazines two or three times a day and inspect them.

The phenomenon of 'hot pockets' in magazines was already known about, and it was further recommended that the readings of fixed-temperature tubes should not simply be accepted as the temperature of the whole magazine. It was noted that when cooling apparatus was in use, the difference between temperatures registered by the thermometers in different parts of the magazine became accentuated. It was suggested that the circulation of cold air in their immediate vicinity unduly affected temperature tubes in certain positions in the magazines.

Amongst a whole raft of findings and recommendations it was noted that when turned to the storage position in the magazines, the lids of the smaller calibre brass flashproof cordite cases were often found to be loose – and in some cases to have fallen off altogether.

It was further noted that in *Vanguard*, coal sacks were stowed in fuel spaces adjoining the P and Q turret handling rooms. These fuel spaces had no ventilation when the access hatch was closed – as was normally the case. One of the 3-inch thick bulkheads to these fuel spaces actually formed the bulkhead between it and a 4-inch cordite propellant magazine (which was being used as a 12-inch magazine at the time) and a 12-inch shell room. Here, favourable conditions for a spontaneous combustion were produced if the 3-inch thick bulkhead became heated to a dangerous degree unnoticed. The court recommended that in all ships arrangements should be made such that a considerable rise in temperature in any compartment adjoining a magazine or shell room must be discovered within two hours.

Captain R. F. Nichols, (who was in command of *Royal Oak* at the time she was torpedoed in the Flow in 1939), was a young midshipman on *Vanguard* that night. He lived to command the *Royal Oak* in World War II, because on the night *Vanguard* exploded he had been attending a concert party presented by *Royal Oak* sailors on the theatre ship *Gourko*. The show had lasted longer than intended, and he had missed his boat back to the doomed *Vanguard*.

Commercial salvage work was carried out on the *Vanguard* in the late 1950s and subsequently in the 1970s. When hard-hat salvage divers initially went to examine the wreck in the 1950s they found that the main battery turret tops had been blown off and all the 12-inch gun barrels were blown out of their trunnion mounts. One main battery 12-inch barrel, weighing 67 tons, was found standing upright some 150 feet away from the wreck, its barrel buried 15 feet down into the seabed in much the same way that the 6-inch guns from *Hampshire* had impaled themselves into the seabed by their barrels.

They then found A turret, complete with its barbette, standing some way away from the bow, with sections of the tripod foremast and spotting top beside it.

At the stern, the propeller shafts were bent, and one of the ship's propellers was found lying free of the ship and was lifted. The three other propellers were subsequently blown off and lifted to the surface.

The 10-inch-thick vertical main armour belt plates were very valuable and had been blown apart. This made them easy for the salvors to lift, in comparison to the German High Seas Fleet battleships nearby where the vertical armour belts were still firmly in place. On the German battleships, salvors had to blast their way into the ship through the unarmoured sections of hull bottom and get into the coal bunkers, which were directly behind the armour belt. Here, explosive charges were placed to blow the 25-ton plates off one by one, for stropping and lifting to the surface.

The 25-foot-long 28-ton condensers were blasted out and removed from *Vanguard's* turbine rooms. A number of valuable Weir pumps were also recovered. These large pumps stood vertically inside the ship and at the top of the pump was a cylinder that held a piston powered by steam from the boilers. Weir pumps were used for pumping many different fluids around the ship, such as oil, firemain (water for firefighting), condensate and bilge. Weir pumps also fed water into the boilers to make steam and power the turbines – the boilers had to be regularly topped up with water recycled from the turbines via the condensers.

The three submerged torpedo tubes were also recovered: two beam tubes and one through the stern. The three tubes are noted as still being in place with the sliding doors in the closed position by salvage diver Frank Lilleker in *Salvaging HMS Vanguard, 1958–59*. A hole was blown near the stern tube door to get access to the tube, but once that was done an inspection revealed a circular flange against which a roughly shaped piece of plate was bolted, as though the tube itself had been removed for maintenance. The tube was believed to still be inside the stern, but had not been located by the time he finished his salvage work there.

To enable the torpedo to be fired from the beam, when the ship was steaming ahead a ram was first run out to cut a path through the water and allow the torpedo to clear the ship's side without water pressure from the forward movement of the ship jamming the torpedo in the tube. These rams produced about 7 tons of gunmetal for the salvors when lifted and scrapped.

One of the ship's bells was also discovered still hanging in a tangled mess of wreckage. It was lifted to the surface and was subsequently returned to the shipbuilders.

Following on from the good relations developed with the MOD and Royal Navy in relation to the *Hampshire* expedition, Emily Turton applied to the UK Secretary of State for Defence for a diving licence to use the same techniques to survey the *Vanguard* on the approach of the 100th anniversary of the sinking on 9 July 2017.

The licence was granted on terms similar to the *Hampshire* licence, and over the course of a preliminary one week's diving the wreck during November 2016 and two further weeks diving during January/February 2017, Emily led a specialist team as they thoroughly surveyed and recorded the wreck with stunning atmospheric stills photography, video and 3D photogrammetry. As with the *Hampshire* imagery, once the photogrammetry results are ready they will be made publicly available for the common good. I was privileged to participate as a survey diver and videographer in the preliminary week of diving in November 2016.

◆ ◆ ◆

The wreck of this famous battleship lies in 30–35 metres of water less than one mile north of the tanker pier at Flotta to the south – the *Vanguard* east cardinal marker buoy swings nearby to the east. Although licensed salvage work was carried out on the wreck in the 1950s and 1970s, no diving has been permitted since the 1980s by virtue of Orkney Harbour Bye Laws and latterly by the Protection of Military Remains Act 1986. Now that I was part of a licensed survey team, after 35 years of diving in Scapa Flow but being unable to visit this wreck, I was now about to see this World War I dreadnought, hidden from sight for so long under the dark waters of Scapa Flow.

Preliminary sonar scans of the area revealed that the wreck lies with her bows to the north-east and her stern to the south-west. The two extreme sections of the wreck, the bow and stern, appeared to have survived largely intact. The foc'sle appeared to be sitting upright, detached from the rest of the wreck. The mid-section of the ship kept its ship shape on the sonar whilst the stern of the wreck appeared to be lying on its port side.

On Day 1 of the November 2016 expedition, the shotline was dropped to the seabed near the bow. After being aware of the history of this ship for so long, but never having dived it, I found it particularly moving to finally descend through the water column and see the majestic bow of this great dreadnought materialise in the depths below.

The bow section, from the stem back for some 60 feet, was sitting upright, with a least depth of about 25 metres at the top of the stem. The intact stem rose up from the seabed for about 11 metres but as I began to swim aft on the foc'sle deck, it quickly angled downwards towards the seabed where the ship has seemingly been cleaved across – just forward of where the barrels of A turret would have ended. The two large fairleads immediately abaft the stem (seen in the archive black and white photo) were still present, and portholes, still with their glass in them, lined either side of the foc'sle, interspersed by the two starboard anchor hawses and the single port hawse.

One of the three anchor capstans was sticking up out of the deck, exposing its axle – the collapsing of the deck from the stem aft has thrust it upwards from its original position on the deck. There are empty holes in the deck where the other two capstans have been blasted out of the ship as she blew up. Thick teak deck planks still lined the foc'sle deck above what was the officer's accommodation lit by a large centreline deck skylight that was still in place. A very different arrangement for officer accommodation from latter classes.

Just aft of the anchor hawse pipes, the sides of the ship flared out from the fo'c'sle, and one deck level down the upper deck begins, widening out to the full beam of the ship as you go aft. The sides of the ship here at the beginning of the upper deck, although still present, have been blown outwards and separated from the inner ship – the vertical armour belt plates on the starboard side are smoothly bent outwards by an incredible force.

The bow section just ends abruptly as the sloping deck reaches the seabed. The very end of the decking has a lip that angles abruptly downwards as a result of the centre of the ship lifting as she exploded. It appears that the bottom of the ship here at the bow has been blown out – and that the uppermost section of the bow has been detached and moved to end up sitting on the sand. The base of the stem is blown out allowing views inside through a sizeable hole.

Moving aft, as the bow section ends abruptly, it gives way to empty flat seabed that is scattered here and there with small sections of ship – the bow is seemingly isolated from the rest of the ship. Out at a 120-degree angle from the starboard side of the bow over scattered sticks of cordite there is an open expanse of seabed for some 20 metres before you arrive at the remains of A turret barbette, which lies on the seabed just as Frank Lilleker describes in *Salvaging HMS Vanguard, 1958–59*. The barbette lies on its side with the gunhouse deck to the north. The circular roller path on which the gunhouse turned is complete, but the gunhouse and barrels are missing.

Immediately aft of A turret barbette, and partly lying on top of it, is a section of tubular foremast along with the two tripod leg supports and the spotting top platform, which lies on its starboard side. The foremast leads down to an armoured chamber, and it is believed that most of the bridge is still here in the mass of structure in this area.

It appears that A turret barbette has been blown out of the ship – or that the ship around it has been totally destroyed. The barbette has landed on its side, whilst the lower sections of the bridge superstructure immediately abaft of it have been devastated and blown away, allowing the section of tripod mast and spotting top, high above it, to fall directly down.

After a long swim of about 50 metres out north-east, on the starboard side of the wreck what is believed to be the Q wing turret can be found – lying upside down and in isolation but amongst scattered small sections of ship.

The ship is largely gone here in the vicinity of P and Q turrets, which the Court of Inquiry appears to have correctly found to have been the centre of the explosion. There is a marked shallow depression in the seabed here, as though the seabed was excavated by the explosion. This may be ground zero, and is a similar effect to what I have seen when diving wrecks carrying munitions in Truk Lagoon that were catastrophically destroyed in a single secondary munitions explosion.

South of Q turret and the depression, the ship begins to reform – scattered large sections of plate and hull appear at first, before the tangled confusion of the innards of the battleship abaft P and Q turret appear. The sides of the ship with the vertical armour belt are gone – blown out and the armour plates salved. There is a large section of the port side of the ship, lined with a single row of portholes, which is angled back towards the stern and rests upright on the seabed.

Within the ragged outline of the ship as you move aft, the first of the sets of Babcock & Wilcox marine boilers start to be found. The boilers are more intact and stacked upon one another on the port side, whilst they are more distressed on the starboard side.

An upright bulkhead separates the boiler rooms from the turbine rooms. Of the two sets of Parsons steam turbines, the port side turbine is in good condition, barring the obvious scars of salvage work to free up the condensers. The turbines in the starboard set are shattered. This is the highest section of the mid part of the wreck, and moving out over free water to starboard, a long section of intact hull bottom leads aft over clean seabed towards the stern section. A number of 12-inch shells can be found on the seabed to starboard here.

Abaft the turbine rooms is the area where X and Y turrets were located. There are a large number of 5-foot-long flashproof brass Clarkson cases piled up together. Some are intact, whilst others are blown open and flattened by the magazine explosion.

The barbette and gunhouse floor of X turret sit bolt upright – the turret roof, walls and both 12-inch gun barrels are now gone whilst the massive cradles and trunnions for the 12-inch gun barrels are now empty. The shell room on the starboard side of X turret still has neatly stacked 12-inch shells in it.

The barbette for Y turret also stands upright, its gunhouse and barrels also gone. Between X and Y turrets, a single 12-inch gun barrel can be found low down, its end fractured as if by salvage blasting, and a chain is stropped around it as though being made ready for lifting by salvors.

Immediately abaft the aftmost Y turret, the stern section of the wreck reforms – lying on its port beam ends. The beginning of the stern section has the same lip of deck bent downwards from the quarterdeck as has the bow. It is as though the centre of the ship lifted as the explosion went off, breaking the bow and stern sections off and bending the decking downwards as she lifted and fractured athwartships. The bent-downwards section of deck has the semi-circular outline of the aft half of Y turret barbette formed in the deck.

Thick deck planks line the stern section, which remains in fine condition. A 3-pounder saluting gun still stands on its pedestal mount on the centre line – its barrel faces downwards to port. A number of large mushroom-type ventilators surround it, and further aft there is a large double hatch, hinged in the middle, which may have been used for loading torpedoes. A further saluting gun stands at the very stern amidst a tangle of snagged cables and debris. The stern comes to a narrow, almost pointed, fantail and the non-ferrous lettering of her name, *VANGUARD*, can still be made out ringing around it.

On the seabed, hard up against the quarter deck, can be found two lines of World War II anti-submarine boom net – thick circles of interwoven cable hoops with large circular steel buoys secured to large concrete block anchors. The boom net was laid over the remains of *Vanguard* during World War II and at war's end the steel floats were punctured and the boom allowed to sink to the seabed. The boom runs off into the distance along the seabed from the stern and continues forward on the port side of the wreck. The large rectangular concrete anchors with a steel eye on them for securing the boom net can be found in many places around the wreck.

The hull sweeps away under the pointed fantail to the large twin rudders, which are both still present, in position. The uppermost starboard side rudder hangs in free water whilst the lower port rudder is mostly buried in the seabed. The least depth down to her uppermost starboard rail at the stern is about 14 metres – much shallower than the bow.

After my week of diving in the preliminary survey, I was sadly unable to return for the full two-week survey in February 2017. The results they achieved, however, are spectacular and whilst processing all the data is still work in process, the knowledge gleaned from this work will add so much more to the archaeological record of this great ship and World War I.

On the 100th anniversary of the sinking of the ship itself, there was a commemoration event held in Orkney that was attended by officials and by relatives of the crew. The survey team assisted a military diving team in familiarising themselves with the wreck for the renewal of an ensign on the wreck as well as creating a number of display stands with information and underwater imagery for interested parties to see.

The wreck of HMS *Vanguard* is designated as a Controlled Site under the Protection of Military Remains Act 1986, and no diving is permitted on it or within 200 metres of it. Paragraph 33 of the Orkney Islands Council General Bye Laws prohibits diving within 100 metres of any of Her Majesty's ships or vessels.

With the survey completed, the wreck and the 845 men who lost their lives aboard it will now once again rest in peace, their sacrifice remembered.

6

THE BATTLE OF MAY ISLAND
31 JANUARY 1918

HMS/M K 4 and K 17

HMS/M K15 sporting the bulbous swan bow subsequently added to the class to try to improve seakeeping.

The Battle of May Island is the misnomer for a series of interconnected and tragic accidents that occurred in foggy conditions close to May Island in the Firth of Forth on Scotland's east coast during a Royal Navy fleet exercise codenamed Operation EC1 on 31 January 1918. It is a misnomer because there was in fact no battle at all – the events acquired the present-day nickname due to a sardonic touch of black humour.

The exercise called for a number of Royal Navy squadrons to sortie from the naval port of Rosyth, in the Firth of Forth, initially eastbound out of the Forth before slowly coming round to run north. Admiral Beatty would simultaneously sortie the main elements of the Grand Fleet from its base in Scapa Flow, and the plan was that the two forces would rendezvous in the

North Sea for the fleet exercise on the following night, of 1 February 1918. The exercise was ambitious in scale, and the entire British Grand Fleet – 26 battleships and battlecruisers, along with a multitude of cruisers, light cruisers, destroyers and submarines – would participate.

The ships sortieing from Rosyth included three battleships of the 5th Battle Squadron along with their destroyer escorts, the four battlecruisers of 2nd Battlecruiser Squadron and their destroyer escorts, two cruisers and two flotillas of the large steam-driven K-class submarines, each submarine flotilla being led by a light cruiser.

As the large force sortied from Rosyth in a spectacle of naval power, no one suspected that the exercise could go so badly wrong – and that 104 Royal Navy personnel would die that night without any involvement of the enemy whatsoever. But early in the run-up to the exercise, five collisions would take place involving eight of the vessels sortieing from Rosyth. The two submarines, K 4 and K 17 would be sunk and three other K-class submarines along with the light cruiser HMS Fearless would be damaged.

The subsequent Admiralty investigation into the disaster and the courts martial that followed were shrouded in wartime military secrecy – so much so that much of the information was only released some 70 years later in the 1990s.

Today, those two K-class submarines, K 4 and K 17, sunk in the Firth of Forth that night are popular technical dives, on the bucket list of most tek divers. To see these large submarines is to voyage back in time – to a time when the role of submarines was evolving. It is hard to believe now, but these submarines were powered by boilers and steam turbines.

The use of submarines by the Royal Navy in naval warfare was still in its infancy when the K-class submarines were conceived – and the role we ascribe to submarines today, of lone silent and potent ship killers, had not yet evolved fully. Naval thinking at the time was firmly focused on the battleship, and so every vessel in the fleet was expected to be able to keep up with the battleships – the fleet speed being 21 knots as determined by the design speed of HMS Dreadnought, launched in 1906. With this mindset in place, as war loomed in 1913 a new K-class of twin-screw submarines was designed that had to be fast enough to be able to scout ahead of the fleet, something which could only be done on the surface, submerging to attack if the enemy was spotted. In the run-up to World War I, there was only one form of propulsion that could allow a surfaced submarine to achieve those speeds – steam.

The first self-propelled locomotive torpedo had been invented just over 50 years previously in 1866 by British engineer Robert Whitehead, and had been adopted internationally. At the dawn of the 20th century, the seemingly invulnerable battleship was seen as the ultimate projection of sea power – and submerged and deck-mounted torpedo tubes began to be fitted to battleships, as well as to cruisers, torpedo boats, torpedo boat destroyers and other naval vessels.

Submarines that could fire torpedoes underwater were still quite a recent innovation in the years before World War I. The first submarine to incorporate torpedo launch tubes was built by Swedish inventor Thorsten Nordenfelt, in 1886 – and the submarine Nordenfelt III, launched in 1887, became the first submarine in history to fire a torpedo while submerged. French engineers built an innovative electrically powered submarine in 1893 – and in 1897, an Irish-born American engineer, John Holland, produced the first submarine to be fitted with electric motors for running submerged – and gasoline engines for running on the surface. The U.S. Navy purchased her in 1900 and commissioned her as the USS Holland.

As war in Europe loomed, two experimental prototypes of the new *K*-class design concept were ordered. The first, HMS *Nautilus*, was laid down in 1913 and launched on 16 December 1914. She was the largest submarine built for the Royal Navy at the time and the first to be given a name. Then HMS *Swordfish* was laid down on 28 February 1914 and launched on 18 March 1916.

The astonishing success of the German submarines with the sinkings of the cruisers *Pathfinder*, *Aboukir*, *Hogue* and *Cressy* in September 1914 had revealed the power of the submarine in naval warfare – and in October 1914, the First Lord of the Admiralty, Winston Churchill, pressed the Admiralty to come up with the largest possible programme of submarine boats to be delivered within 12–24 months. Admiral Sir John (Jackie) Fisher, the champion of the battlecruiser concept, was an early opponent of the steam-driven *K*-boats – and when in 1913 the class was proposed, he commented that it would be the 'most fatal error imaginable' to put steam engines in submarines. He did however believe that sea fighting would be governed by submarines – believing that a fast battle fleet which could be accompanied by submarines under all circumstances would possess an overwhelming fighting advantage.

Following trials of the first of the experimental boat, *Nautilus*, it was decided to proceed with a slightly smaller triple-screw variant, which was designated the *J*-class. By the middle of 1915 however, it had become clear that the *J*-class could not meet the design speed requirements as their triple-screw configuration only gave them a surface speed of 19 knots – too slow to keep up with the fleet. The larger twin-screw *K*-class design was resurrected.

At the time, only steam turbines could provide the surface speed necessary to allow a submarine to sweep ahead of the fleet speed of 21 knots – and so the age of the steam-powered submarine had arrived. The *K*-boats were given a surface speed of 24 knots – 3 knots faster than the fleet speed – and in August 1915, the Admiralty ordered 21 of the new *K*-boats in great secrecy.

The *K*-boats were a revolutionary design – and with their speed and hitting power they were essentially being built to fulfil the role of submersible destroyers, able to outrun and attack German battleships and most other vessels. They were the largest, heaviest and fastest submarines built anywhere in the world at that time – and were so fast that no British submarine of even World War II could have outrun them.

The *K*-class submarines were large boats for their time; at 339 feet long they displaced 1,980 tons surfaced and almost 2,600 tons submerged. Oil-fired Yarrow boilers powered their steam turbines and drove two 2.29-metre three-bladed props. Four 1,440hp electric motors gave them a submerged speed of 8 knots, and a diesel generator was able to charge their batteries.

The plumb stem of the *K*-boats was designed to slice through the water at speed like a ship. A 4-inch breech-loading (BL) Mk XI gun was positioned abaft the stem on the flush foredeck in the first pioneer units, whilst another 4-inch gun was situated abaft the long central superstructure. A 3-inch gun completed her armament. The hitting power of the *K*-class was four 18-inch bow tubes and four 18-inch beam tubes, similar to the beam tubes fitted on capital ships and cruisers. They were also fitted with another pair of 18-inch tubes on top of the superstructure for night use, but these were removed later as they were susceptible to damage in heavy seas.

Behind the streamlined conning tower was a long superstructure that carried a 3-inch gun and two squat retractable funnels, 5 feet high. Four mushroom boiler room ventilators, each 37 inches in diameter, were clustered between the two funnels. These ventilators were closed for diving by mushroom-type hatches that lowered onto rubber seats. She was fitted with twin 30-foot periscopes, the largest yet made in Britain, and carried two retractable wireless masts.

In addition to her eight torpedo tubes, there were in all twelve major openings in her hull, comprised of hatches, smokestack openings and boiler room ventilators. These, combined with innumerable valves, manholes and other openings in the hull, caused some submariners to observe that there were "too many damned holes".

K-boats were divided into nine compartments, each with a watertight door; the bow torpedo room, the officers' quarters, the control room which held a wireless cabin, the beam torpedo room for broadside-fired torpedoes, the boiler room, the turbine room, the diesel and electric motor room, the crew space and the steering compartment which also held further crew space. The boiler room split the submarine into two parts linked a by a narrow boiler room passage. There was no underwater escape apparatus.

The K-boats were double-hulled with a cylindrical pressure hull and an outer hull of light plating. The lower half of the space between the two hulls was divided into 20 main external ballast tanks – and along the bottom of the submarine within the pressure hull were further ballast tanks. Two keel-mounted 10-ton drop weights could be jettisoned in case of emergency to make the submarine positively buoyant.

The heavy plumb stem of the pioneer boats lacked any lifting buoyancy, and at 12 knots or more, even in a moderate sea, it was found that the bow would not rise as it met the seas. Instead the bow sliced through the waves throwing torrents of water over the foredeck, bridge and superstructure. In these conditions, it was found that the long, flat foredeck tended to want to dive and it became almost impossible for the K-boats to keep pace with the fleet, let alone take up a tactical position. It proved impossible to man the forward deck gun, as most of the time it was half-submerged. It became apparent that in a heavy sea the K-boats had to reduce speed, heave to, or dive.

To alleviate this, in later units a bulbous swan bow that rose 9 feet above the water was added (see image above), which also incorporated a 'quick blowing' ballast tank to improve handling. The forward 4-inch deck gun was moved aft and placed in an elevated position just in front of the conning tower.

The great length and beam of the K-boats made them pitch and roll unpleasantly, and in the boiler room stokers had to wear oilskins to protect them from the water that poured down the open mushroom ventilators. From time to time, a large wave would wash its way down the funnels causing the boilers to flash back as water hit them. Many a stoker lost his eyebrows to the flash. The K-boats were also just as vulnerable to heavy following seas; when waves were coming from astern they were easily pooped.

If the seaworthiness of the K-boats on the surface was alarming, their diving characteristics were even more alarming, their great length and weight giving a large moment of inertia, like a giant seesaw.

When a K-boat pointed her bow downwards in a dive, she was far more difficult to level off than a conventional submarine. If the diving angle was steep, the open expanse of the long foredeck tended to act as an extra hydroplane (diving plane), increasing downward momentum and making control difficult. Most of the *K*-boats nose-dived out of control to the seabed at some point.

Before a dive, a *K*-boat had to be carefully trimmed, taking into account variations in the density of the sea water and how much fuel, water, ordnance and stores were being carried at any one time. A *K*-boat displaced more than 2,500 tons fully submerged – and if she were heavy in the bows, the bow and stern hydroplanes allied to the ballast tanks might not be sufficient to correct her attitude. Because of this, and because the boats had an estimated diving depth of 200 feet (61 metres), captains were cautious about where they chose to dive: they only dived where they knew it was shallow and so there was a bottom to prevent an uncontrolled and fatal dive into the depths.

The way the *K*-boats carried their fuel oil caused another hazard. The bottom of the oil tanks was open to the sea – the oil actually floated on seawater and was drawn to the boilers by pumps at the top of the oil tanks. This was quite an ingenious way of dealing with buoyancy issues, for as the submarine used its oil, its place was taken by sea water.

This self-compensating system kept the weight of the submarine reasonably constant and in theory solved the issue of adjusting ballast.

Under stable conditions the system worked reasonably well – but when the boat rolled in heavy seas, the oil and water tended to emulsify. The resulting water and oil mixture would put the boiler fires out – a condition known as 'losing suction'.

The conning tower on the *K*-boats was a brass casting and was a small compartment within the larger bridge superstructure of the submarine. It was reached from the control room through a watertight hatch that opened upwards. The conning tower was oval shaped and was just 5 feet 6 inches long and 3 feet 6 inches at its widest. The aft portion of the tower was 4 feet 6 inches high and contained a hatch opening upward into the chart room above. The forward section of the tower was 3 feet 6 inches higher, at 8 feet high, and formed a dome, which had electric lighting. The compass was situated here, in this brass non-magnetic compartment, and so was beyond the magnetic influence of the steel of the main hull.

Of the 21 *K*-boats ordered in August 1915, as the first boats came into service, they were soon revealing their flaws. The low freeboard and great length made them difficult to control both on the surface and whilst submerged. With an estimated maximum diving depth of 200 feet (61 metres), this was less than their overall length of 339 feet (103 metres). Thus their bow could easily breach the maximum diving depth whilst their stern could still be on the surface. Their eight internal bulkheads were designed and tested to withstand a pressure equivalent to a depth of 20 metres – risking their collapse if the hull was compromised at a depth below this figure.

The procedure for diving the submarine was complex, requiring upwards of five minutes to secure the main engines, shift to battery motors for submerged running and get ready to dive. The boiler fires first had to be extinguished to prevent a build-up of noxious fumes whilst submerged. Then a complicated series of hydraulics and mechanical rods and levers lowered the twin funnels abaft the conning tower away from each other into a horizontal position in wells recessed into the superstructure. Hatches were simultaneously closed over the funnel uptakes. The four main intake boiler ventilators also had to be closed, along with seawater connections for the condensers and the boiler feed.

Stern view of HMS/M K13. She sank on 29 January 1917 in the Gareloch, Argyll, whilst diving,with the loss of 32 crew. She was subsequently raised, repaired and recommissioned as K22.

In all, about 16 different hatches needed to be secured before diving. In designing the *K*-class, naval architects had taken the view that with a speed of 24 knots, the *K*-boats could outmanoeuvre and outrun most surface threats, and thus a rapid crash dive would not be required. This was an evolutionary time in submarine design – and of course, the age of a threat from the air had not yet arrived.

The *K*-class submarines began to join the Grand Fleet in 1917 and quickly came to be dubbed the *Kalamity*-class due to many accidents that followed, with great loss of life.

Of the 17 *K*-boats completed and commissioned, none were lost to enemy action – but 6 were lost in accidents and many others had serious incidents. No class of modern warship in the Royal Navy, or possibly any other navy, has ever suffered so many incidents as the *K*-class. In all they were involved in 16 major accidents and countless other smaller mishaps. One *K*-boat sank on her trials, three others were lost after collision, a fifth just disappeared and another sank in harbour. The *K*-boats became known as the suicide club, and men went to extreme lengths to avoid serving in them.

For all the design work, construction, training and exercising, only one *K*-class submarine ever engaged an enemy vessel in their two years of war service – ramming a German submarine after hitting it with a torpedo amidships that failed to explode.

◆　◆　◆

As Operation ECI commenced in darkness around 1830 on 31 January 1918, a total of some 40 battleships, battlecruisers, cruisers, destroyers and submarines began to leave Rosyth on the north shore of the Firth of Forth, just to the west of the modern-day Forth Road Bridge. German submarine activity was suspected in the area, so orders had been issued to conceal external navigation lights and maintain strict radio silence.

Along with the three battleships and destroyer escorts of the 5th Battle Squadron, and the four battlecruisers and destroyer escorts of the 2nd Battlecruiser Squadron, the 14 ships of the 1st, 3rd and 4th Light Cruiser Squadrons and nine fleet submarines in two flotillas would be present. The 12th Submarine Flotilla comprised *K* 3, *K* 4, *K* 6 and *K* 7, and was led by the *Active*-class scout cruiser HMS *Fearless*. The 13th Submarine Flotilla was led by the 19,180-ton cruiser HMS *Courageous* and the flotilla leader HMS *Ithuriel*, and comprised *K* 11, *K* 12, *K* 14, *K* 17 and *K* 22.

The powerful naval force steamed north-eastwards out of the Forth in a single line astern that stretched out for 20–30 miles. In the vanguard, HMS *Courageous* and HMS *Ithuriel* led the 13th Submarine Flotilla, and then the 2nd Battlecruiser Squadron followed in line astern – comprising HMAS *Australia*, and HMS *New Zealand, Indomitable* and *Inflexible* with their screen of destroyers. After the battlecruisers came the 12th Submarine Flotilla led by *Fearless*, and finally the battleships of the 5th Battle Squadron.

To avoid attracting the attention of any prowling German submarines, particularly as one was suspected to be in the area, in the darkness each vessel showed only a dim stern light to the following vessel. All vessels maintained strict radio silence. As each group passed May Island at the mouth of the Firth of Forth they would increase to fleet speed of 20 knots.

As the first group of K-boats, those of the 13th Submarine Flotilla, passed May Island, lookouts on K 11 spotted navigation lights in the darkness that were thought to possibly be minesweeping naval trawlers putting to sea from the Fife port of Anstruther – on the north side of the firth – and approaching the single line of submarines. As conditions were getting foggy a reduction in speed and a turn to port was ordered to avoid closing on the approaching vessels.

As K 11 made her turn to port, the next submarine, K 17, followed K 11's manoeuvre. However the next submarine in line, K 14, wasn't aware in the poor visibility that K 17 had turned – and only realised the danger when two minesweepers emerged from the fog and were seen to be heading across her bow. Only then did the skipper of K 14 realise K 17 had turned, and in order to avoid a collision with the minesweepers he ordered full right rudder. This manoeuvre took K 14 clear of both minesweepers and also K 12, which was next in line and close behind – but K 14's helm chose this unfortunate moment to jam in the full right rudder position. As a result, she veered out of line.

Both K 14 and the boat behind her, K 12, turned on their navigation lights, and once K 14's helm was freed she began to manoeuvre to return to her position in the line. The next submarine in line however, K 22, had lost sight of the rest of the flotilla in the mist and was still running ahead at 20 knots.

Unknowingly, K 14 crossed, beam on, directly in front of K 22, leaving K 22 no time to take evasive manoeuvres. K 22's bow slammed into K 14's beam just aft of the forward torpedo room, her bow effortlessly slicing through the pressure hull into her innards.

With her pressure hull rent open, K 14 was in immediate danger of sinking, but this was stopped by the rapid closure of internal watertight doors. K 14 and K 22 however were now locked together – and sitting dead in the water directly in the path of the remainder of the battle line following on astern. Somewhere out there in the fog, the massive battlecruisers *Australia, New Zealand, Indomitable* and *Inflexible* were bearing directly down upon them at 20 knots. The two stricken K-class boats, whilst still observing radio silence, switched on their navigation lights and fired flares.

Although both submarines were now stopped in the water, the rest of the fleet, strung out in a line 20 miles long and operating in complete radio blackout, was unaware of what had happened and continued out to sea.

Fearing being run down, *K 22* abandoned radio silence and transmitted a coded signal to the cruiser leading the 13th Submarine Flotilla advising that she could reach port, but that *K 14* was crippled and sinking.

About 15 minutes later, three of the four large battlecruisers of the 2nd Battlecruiser Squadron passed May Island – and missed the two stationary submarines. But their luck ran out as the 20,700-ton battlecruiser *Inflexible*, following on at 20 knots, ran into *K 22*, striking her forward of her conning tower and smashing her forward bow section as the unstoppable momentum of the battlecruiser carried her right over the stricken submarine, driving the submarine under her keel.

Once over *K 22*, *Inflexible* continued on her way, fading into the mist as *K 22* resurfaced with the first 30 feet of her bows now at right angles to the rest of her hull and her ballast and fuel tanks wrecked. Her bow settled into the water until only the conning tower showed.

HMS *Ithuriel* received and decoded *K 22*'s signal about the first collision between *K 4* and *K 22* – and she turned back westwards towards the firth to render assistance, the submarines of the 13th Flotilla dutifully following her lead. This manoeuvre now put them on a possible collision course with the submarines of the 12th Flotilla, who were following on astern as they headed north-eastwards out of the firth.

As the submarines of the 13th Flotilla, in line astern behind *Ithuriel*, turned, the four battlecruisers of the 2nd Battle Squadron (one of which had already hit *K 22*), passed right through the line of submarines. It was only by a series of emergency manoeuvres by both groups of vessels that further collisions were narrowly avoided.

As the returning 13th Submarine Flotilla reached May Island, they encountered the outbound 12th Submarine Flotilla, which was led by the 4,000-ton scout cruiser *Fearless*. She had passed clear of May Island at 1954 and her captain, judging from initial radio reports, had estimated the position of the submarine collision as being 1.5 miles from the island. Believing that he had now passed the danger area he ordered the flotilla to increase to fleet speed of 21 knots. He wasn't aware that the vessels of the 13th Submarine Flotilla had come about and were now headed west, directly towards the north-eastward-bound 12th Submarine Flotilla. The scene was set for disaster.

Both flotillas met head-on some 13 miles east of May Island at 2032 as the 12th Submarine Flotilla leader, *Fearless*, ran into *K 17* of the 13th Flotilla. The cruiser's sleek bows sliced into the submarine's pressure hull on the port side just forward of the conning tower – shearing off a section of her pressure hull and allowing a massive influx of water to flood into the submarine. The lower section of the stem of *Fearless*, forward of the collision bulkhead, was also torn off – but the cruiser wasn't mortally wounded and would be able to return to port.

K 17 however was in mortal distress. With her bow ripped off, her buoyancy was fatally compromised and she began to settle by the bow. When *Fearless* came into view of those on the bridge of *K 17*, and when a collision seemed inevitable, the bridge ordered all watertight doors closed. Ten seconds later the two vessels collided – but this sharp command had saved many lives.

After the collision, the submarine's internal lights went out and clouds of chlorine gas came up from the batteries that were now flooded with sea water. The crew began to abandon her at speed, pressing up through hatches as quickly as they could, men popping out of hatches almost like corks, pushed on by the surge of humanity crowding around the ladders below decks.

Once it was confirmed that every man was on deck, the captain ordered everyone aft. The bow was now well down in the water and the stern slowly lifted out of the water. Men climbed on top of the superstructure, gun and funnels – but as she went down, they had to jump into the water or be washed off. Within eight minutes of being rammed, *K* 17 had sunk to the bottom of the firth.

The crew from *K* 17 found themselves in the cold winter waters of the North Sea, fighting for their lives in the pitch darkness of a January night. At least, with so many ships in the area they perhaps stood a good chance of being spotted and picked up.

K 4, which had been sailing closely behind *Fearless*, on witnessing her collision with *K* 17, now turned to port with a view to picking up survivors. *K* 3, sailing just behind *K* 4, followed *K* 4's lead, by turning to port and stopping some distance further on.

K 12 of the 13th Flotilla had already come about to head west to render assistance – and had already narrowly missed colliding with the outbound battlecruiser *Australia*. The vessels had passed so closely that crew on the larger vessel had reportedly been able to look down into the submarine's funnels and see the fires glowing below. *K* 12 had turned to get out of the way of *Australia* – and this manoeuvre put her on a collision path with *K* 6.

K 12's sudden appearance near the collision zone immediately caused alarm on board *K* 6, which was still heading eastward with the 12th Flotilla. *K* 6 made an emergency evasive manoeuvre to avoid colliding with *K* 12 – but in so doing she collided with *K* 4. *K* 4 was almost sliced in half.

Mortally wounded, *K* 4 immediately started to sink – but *K* 6 was still impaled in her and stuck firm. It appeared that *K* 6 would be dragged down with her – but putting her engines full astern, she was able to extricate herself from *K* 4. With the gap unplugged and minus *K* 6's buoyancy, *K* 4 rolled over and sank a few seconds later. There were no survivors.

K 7 arrived on scene and stopped nearby with her deck crew already stripped down and ready to assist in rescue efforts. Next in line eastbound however were the three battleships of the 5th Battle Squadron in line astern with their attendant destroyers. Moving at 21 knots, the massive capital ships passed through the scene of the unfolding tragedy – unaware of what had happened. Several of the destroyers surged right through the survivors from *K* 17 who were struggling in the water.

Two vessels from the 5th Battle Squadron narrowly missed *K* 3 – but as the wash of their wakes spread outwards, it swept across the deck casing of *K* 7, where crew were making ready to assist, washing some off her deck into the sea.

Only 9 of the 56 crew of *K* 17 were picked up from the water alive, and one of those died later. Within 75 minutes, the submarines *K* 17 and *K* 4 had been sunk, and *K* 6, *K* 7, *K* 14, *K* 22 and *Fearless* had all been damaged. In all, some 104 men were reported killed in the disaster: 55 from *K* 4, 47 from *K* 17 and 2 from *K* 14.

The British authorities, as with so many naval war tragedies, attempted to conceal the disaster from public scrutiny. The truth would only emerge long after the war was over.

The sensitive military war graves of *K* 4 and *K* 17 were designated as Protected Places under the Protection of Military Remain Act 1986 (Designation of Vessels and Controlled Sites) Order 2009. It is permitted to dive them, but forbidden to enter or interfere with them in any way.

◆　◆　◆

In 2014, I decided to jump on the well set up modern dive boat *Mako*, run by Shadow Marine Charters, that works out of the small fishing port of Anstruther on the north side of the Forth.

They had a dive going out to the *K*-boats, and as it's only a drive by car of just over an hour south from Stonehaven where I live, I really had no excuse for not investigating this unique maritime disaster, a famous incident in Britain's naval history.

The two *K*-class submarines sunk on that fateful night, relics of the Battle of May Island, lie in relatively close proximity to each other, in 55–60 metres of water about 20 miles off Fifeness on the northern side of the Firth of Forth. The area gets reasonably clear water with underwater visibility an average 10–20 metres.

Anstruther is a tidal harbour – that is, it dries out at low tide – so to be able to get out of the harbour and catch slack water on the wreck, ropes off would be very early the next morning.

So, rather than staying at home and getting up essentially before I went to bed the night before, Paul Haynes, Gary Petrie and I drove down from Stonehaven the evening before and checked into a small inexpensive local hotel. We had arranged to meet up with a couple of other fine divers from our neck of the woods, Brian Burnett and Mike Ferguson, who were also booked on the boat the next day. After a pleasant evening meal and a couple of drinks we hit the sack, ready for the off early the next morning.

At stupid o'clock we were down at the harbour, ferrying our heavy dive kit on our backs from the car park along a long pontoon out to the dive boat which was tied up at its end.

Finally, we were all loaded aboard, ropes were thrown off and the skipper took us out of the harbour, which was rapidly drying out. The boat's head was turned east-south-east and we began to run towards the site of the 'battle'. My first *K*-class dive would be on *K 4*.

After a pleasant run out to open sea, the boat slowed as we approached the site – and very soon the skipper was picking up the wreck on his echo sounder in a depth of about 56 metres. A weighted shotline was dropped just off the wreck and a large danbuoy clipped to its top. Spare decompression cylinders were attached to the line, and as slack water approached, our group of divers began the familiar routine of getting dressed to dive, strapping on fins, heaving bulky CCRs onto benches to wriggle into webbing, clipping on deep and decompression bailout tanks under either arm and booting up our wrist computers and letting the rebreathers go through their self-check menus. Finally, after a pre-breathe of a few minutes we were ready to splash.

On a signal from the skipper, I stood up and clumped in my fins to the dive gate in the gunwale. At a shouted command, I jumped from the stern through the gate and dropped heavily into the water.

As the explosion of bubbles from my entry dissipated, I looked down and could see the shotline running way down into the depths below me. The wreck lay almost 200 feet below so of course there was no glimpse of it from the surface – just the simple shotline running endlessly down into the darkness below.

With a round of OK signals with my buddies Paul Haynes and Gary Petrie, I dumped air from my drysuit and buoyancy wings, slowly becoming just negatively buoyant. I started to sink, righting myself into the head down position once I was a few metres down. Torches were switched on, and we started the descent.

The minutes ticked by slowly as we dropped down beside the shotline into the depths, my eyes straining to catch a first glimpse of this famous submarine. I passed through 20 metres in a minute or two, then 30 metres – still no sight of what lay below. Then, at about 40 metres down, I started to see the darkness below me begin to take on unnatural manmade straight lines as a huge brooding form materialised out of the gloom. I was arriving at the submarine – it was sitting upright on its keel.

As I got closer to the wreck below, the first thing that struck me was the sheer size of the submarine – it was very large. For some reason, when I think about World War I submarines, I tend to think of smaller German coastal U-boats – but this British submarine was massive. The beam was 26 feet 6 inches – that's the beam of a small coastal steamer of yesteryear and is wider than most old-fashioned deep-sea steam trawlers.

As I neared the deck I could now see right down a good 10 metres to the seabed. The draught alone was almost 21 feet – that's excluding the parts above the waterline. She dominates with her very size – and at 339 feet long, she is longer than many a steamship of the era. She is of course a complete steamship cleverly wrapped up inside the hull of a huge submarine.

The shot itself was intentionally lying on the seabed just a couple of metres off the port side of the submarine – but I couldn't tell at this point in the darkness whether we were fore or aft of the conning tower; despite the good visibility there was no sign of it. I clipped my strobe onto the shotline and set it flashing, so I could find it again in the gloom on my return. We headed off randomly to my right, and soon it became clear from hull features that we were heading aft.

Very quickly, we came to a large vertical gash in her port side where the powerful bows of *K* 6 had struck her beam. The pressure hull had been seemingly effortlessly sliced open to reveal the innards of the submarine itself. I could see internal walls covered with pipes, gauges and valves – and clusters of heavy-duty electric cabling hung down all around.

As both *K* 4 and *K* 17 are designated Protected Places under the Protection of Military Remains Act 1986 (Designation of Vessels and Controlled Sites) Order 2009, divers are not permitted to enter the wreck. We simply looked from outside before moving on.

When you research and write about the human tragedy of naval wrecks, as I have done over many years, it brings home the scale of the suffering that took place in these places. These wrecks are not just large lumps of rusted metal lying on the seabed; they were living, working vessels filled with life – and the remains of those that perished are often still inside them. You tend to form a mental connection with the vessel – and I almost see the vessel as it was. It always weighs heavily on me that I am looking directly into a place where many crew lost their lives.

Nowadays, divers as a general rule deeply respect these designated naval wrecks. I have never seen a British diver illegally entering one of our protected or controlled wrecks. Our UK legislation however does not apply to foreign nationals diving British warships in international waters – and there have been a number of well publicised incidents of divers entering our war graves and disturbing human remains.

People from time to time ask me about the rights and wrongs of diving war graves – and to try and let them understand, I liken the position directly to the situation on land where you can walk around a military cemetery and pay your respects. There would obviously be no question of tampering with any of the individual graves. People walk round the Flanders battlefields where countless thousands died in World War I – and are still missing today. The situation is exactly the same underwater.

Leaving the fatal gash in the pressure hull, I carried on exploring aft. The massive hull began to narrow as we approached the stern, and the deck started to drop deeper as it tapered towards the stern. I was particularly interested to finally see the stern, as from the photographs of her afloat, she seemed to have been constructed with surface seakeeping abilities well in mind. To allow her to sweep at speed ahead of the fleet, she had to be able to perform on the surface like a fast destroyer, and a schooner stern had been designed in.

The aft section of the boat began to narrow towards the stern, and I passed over the port aft hydroplane. As I moved on, the deck and stern just disappeared into the seabed. On this side, there was no sight of the large port propeller or her rudder– the prop was completely buried in the sandy seabed, the currents constantly piling up sand and silt – and then removing it.

I moved over the aft deck to the starboard side where there was more to see: the topmost tip of one of the three blades of her starboard prop was sticking up from the silt, and the delicate sweep of her schooner stern could just be made out above the very top of the rudder, which was peeking out from the sand. Her port and starboard hydroplanes were in the horizontal position, sticking out from either side of the stern like large ears.

I began to move forward along the starboard side of the hull, which began to fatten up again as I went forward. The aft deck was rising up and my depth began to decrease.

Very soon, I was in the area abaft the conning tower where, in between her two stubby funnels, I spotted the four 37-inch diameter boiler room ventilator mushroom hatches, above the circular openings directly into the hull onto which they sealed for diving. I had never seen this type of submarine mushroom valve before – they were in the raised position, the draw bars, used to pull the mushroom valves down onto rubber seats and seal up the circular openings, were visible running down below into the vessel. She had been running on the surface at the time of the accident and so these ventilators would have been in the open position. With no time to close them, water would have flooded into the boiler room below as she went down. The 3-inch deck gun abaft the conning tower was still in position with its tampion still in place in its barrel.

The K-boats were built with an almost circular wet deckhouse built over and around the small oval brass conning tower. This deckhouse was designed to provide a command bridge that gave officers shelter and navigational abilities whilst she was running at speed on the surface – just like a proper warship. The conning tower was a small compartment within the bridge superstructure of the submarine, reached from the control room below through a watertight hatch that opened upwards.

The bottom level, the integral brass conning tower itself, is still in place on the wreck with an open circular hatch from the main pressure hull leading into it. At 5 feet 6 inches long and 3 feet 6 inches at its widest, it is surprisingly small. The after portion of the tower was 4 feet 6 inches high and contained a hatch opening upward into the chart room. The forward dome section was 3 feet 6 inches higher and housed the submarine's projector compass in this non-magnetic compartment.

The top deckhouse was not part of the pressure hull of the submarine. It was designed only for use on the surface and, made of thin steel plating, it has now fallen off or been trawled from the wreck to lie on the seabed adjacent to the conning tower. It has a completely different arrangement from the conning towers of more modern submarines – in that as a deckhouse it has portholes and small square glass windows, although the glass is now gone. Two periscopes rise up from the pressure hull forward and aft of the small conning tower, but originally inside the deckhouse. Gauges and a telegraph lie around inside the topmost level of this deckhouse, the command bridge. On top of the deckhouse roof are the remnants of what appears to be a steam whistle.

I kicked my fins and moved around the outside of the deckhouse and was now able to look inside it. The internal lower section had two sets of fixed ladder rungs that led up from the small conning tower on one side, to two circular hatches into the upper chart room.

We pressed on forward from the conning tower – moving forward along the foredeck, the decking itself long gone to now reveal the skeletal lattice work of the deck gratings. Eventually the hull began to change shape again, beginning to rise as we approached her distinctive bow. Swimming down and around the bow, we located her four bow torpedo tubes.

By now we had spent some 30 minutes on the bottom, so it was time to be thinking about heading back to the shotline to ascend. We swam back down the port side, now completely familiar with the layout of the submarine and where we were on her. As I moved past the conning tower, with my eyes now dark adjusted, I could see the dim blinking of my strobe on the shotline, leading me back to the route to the surface.

◆　◆　◆

Although the other casualty of the Battle of May Island, K 17, is also a K-boat, a dive on her seems a completely different experience from K 4 in many ways.

As you move forward from the conning tower towards the bow, the pressure hull suddenly just stops, where a section of the bow was completely sheared off by HMS *Fearless* as she rammed into her at speed.

The pressure hull ends in an open circle that is cluttered with mangled sections of machinery, apparatus and electric cables. Those unfortunate crew in this area didn't stand a chance and would never have known what hit them. The bow section itself lies a little way off the main part of the submarine. The system of internal watertight doors however meant that the remainder of the submarine did not flood catastrophically. The submarine stayed afloat long enough for crew further aft to get up onto deck.

The damaged and torn metal of the hull here suggests that *Fearless* rammed her from the port side – the mass of tangled spars and steam pipes and the edges of her hull metal work on the port side are all bent inwards into the submarine.

Whilst the stern, rudder and props of K 4 were buried in the seabed, K 17's delicate schooner stern stands well clear of the seabed and both free sections of her shafts run out from the hull to their support brackets and to the large three-bladed screws. The large rudder dominates the area – seemingly too big for her delicate stern. Both diving planes are also horizontal and clearly visible above the seabed. Her 3-inch gun also remains on the wreck abaft the conning tower near to the boiler room ventilation mushroom valves.

7

UB 116

Type UB III coastal torpedo attack boat

The last naval vessel sunk in Scapa Flow during World War I – 28 October 1918
The last German submarine sunk in action during World War I

It is not as well known as it perhaps should be that the last naval vessel sunk in the Scapa Flow area in World War I was in fact the last German submarine to be sunk in action during that conflict. The wreck of the German coastal attack submarine UB 116 lies in Hoxa Sound to the south of Scapa Flow, sunk by a remotely detonated mine on 28 October 1918, just two weeks before the Armistice.

In the run-up to World War I, the German submarine was developed and improved to the extent that it became a potent offensive weapon during the war. German submarine warfare would account for the loss of some 5,000 Allied ships at a cost of 202 German submarines.

During the early years of the war, in 1914/15, a high percentage of these submarine losses took place around Britain's shores. But after the Battle of Jutland, on 31 May and 1 June 1916, British naval dominance of the North Sea became almost complete. In contrast to the early years of the war, it became extremely dangerous for German submarines to operate near Britain – and so they ventured far afield to other less well guarded but equally rewarding killing grounds. Germany lost 22 submarines in 1916 – and of those, only 5–6 were sunk in British waters.

Between September 1915 and February 1917, Germany adopted a policy of restricted submarine warfare. Her submarines would only sink a ship after surfacing, ordering the vessel to stop, giving a warning and allowing passengers and crew to abandon ship. In February 1917 however, the restricted submarine campaign was abandoned and unrestricted submarine warfare was once again unleashed – any ship could now be sunk without warning.

The unrestricted campaign brought immediate success: in the single month of April 1917, 1,091,000 tonnes of Allied shipping was sunk and German submarines were back in British coastal waters in numbers. British anti-submarine warfare (ASW) techniques had however developed by this time and the corresponding German submarine losses were much greater: some 65 submarines were lost in action during 1917, compared to 22 in 1916.

Bow shot of the Type UB III German coastal attack submarine UB 110 under repair in dry dock – the same type and build as UB 116. UB 116 was the last enemy casualty at Scapa Flow and the last U-boat sunk in action during WWI (Tyne & Wear Archives & Museums.

In 1918, as the war became desperate for Germany, 90 German submarines were lost in action or scuttled. Many of those were sunk in the English Channel, around the North Channel of the Irish Sea, on the east coast of Britain and around the Orkney Islands. The last German submarine lost in action (and not surrendered or scuttled), was UB 116, sunk on 28 October 1918 as she tried to break into Scapa Flow.

◆ ◆ ◆

After Britain declared war on Germany in August 1914, the Royal Navy moved to begin a distant naval blockade, a tried and tested tactic from the days of sail, in an attempt to cut off war supplies to Germany and starve the German population.

The Imperial German Navy had far fewer ships than the Royal Navy and so, to try and reduce the Royal Navy's numerical superiority on warships, Germany sent out 10 submarines. In the first six weeks of the war the strategy saw poor results: Germany lost two boats for little return.

But then things changed dramatically – and German submarines began to score important successes. Soon, nine Royal Navy warships and a submarine had been sunk by German submarines, and a Dutch battleship damaged. The first British loss was the cruiser HMS *Pathfinder* – to a torpedo from U 21 in the Firth of Forth on 5 September 1914. Then on 22 September 1914, the three old turn-of-the-century and now largely obsolete 12,000-ton cruisers *Aboukir*, *Hogue* and *Cressy* were sunk in the southern North Sea by U 9 under the command of Kapitänleutnant Otto Weddigen, with the loss of 1,450 British service personnel.

The armoured cruiser HMS *Palladia* was then sunk on 11 October 1914, by U 26, in the Gulf of Finland. Just four days later, on 15 October 1914, the old 7,350-ton cruiser HMS *Hawke* (launched in 1891) was sunk by U 9 in the North Sea with the loss of 526 men.

Then on 18 October 1914, the British submarine E3 was torpedoed and sunk by U 27 off the Ems Estuary. On 31 October 1914, the 5,600-ton seaplane carrier HMS *Hermes* was torpedoed and sunk by U 27 and on 11 November 1914, the minesweeper HMS *Niger* was sunk. The modern 22,289-ton Dutch dreadnought battleship *Jean Bart* was then torpedoed in the southern Adriatic, but remained afloat due to the modern system of dreadnought compartmentalisation.

The old pre-dreadnought British battleship HMS *Formidable* (1898) based in Sheerness was not so lucky – and not so able to withstand a modern torpedo attack. She was sunk by two torpedoes from U 24 on 1 January 1915, with the loss of 547 officers and men, 30 miles off Lyme Regis.

In return for these heavy losses to the Allies, five German submarines were lost during the same period.

However, even although Germany was beginning to erode the British numerical naval superiority, the Royal Navy still dominated the North Sea – and still was actively blockading German imports of food and materials. The only way Germany could reciprocate and blockade or degrade British supply shipping was by using her submarines.

In October 1914, Germany sent out 20 submarines to begin its own naval blockade and target British merchant supply shipping. These submarines began sinking merchant ships without warning in an unrestricted submarine warfare campaign. This policy was extremely effective, with some 100,000 tons of British shipping being sunk, each month.

German submarine warfare early in the war was particularly effective as the Royal Navy had no effective way of detecting a submerged submarine. British warships had to rely on sighting the submarine's periscope or its wake and then firing towards the periscopes with their guns.

British anti-submarine warfare (ASW) weaponry was at the beginning of the war very rudimentary. The hand-thrown Lance bomb, for example, was essentially a hi-explosive grenade on a spar that was issued to destroyers early in the war. A crewman literally hurled the Lance bomb by hand at a submarine below or alongside. It would take until 1916 for Britain to develop and deploy dropping mines, which became known later as depth charges. Hydrophones for naval sub-hunter vessels entered service in 1916. Merchant ships however at this time were largely unarmed and easy prey.

On 10 April 1915, a clearly marked Belgian relief ship, en route to America to collect food for starving civilians, was torpedoed without warning – and this enraged American feelings. Then, a month later, on 7 May 1915, the liner RMS *Lusitania* was torpedoed and sunk without warning south of Ireland with the loss of 1,198 persons – including 128 American civilians. This provoked further American outrage and was one of the factors that led to Germany abandoning her unrestricted submarine warfare policy in September 1915, in an attempt to avoid provoking America into entering the war.

Between September 1915 and February 1917, German submarines would only sink a ship after surfacing, ordering the vessel to stop, giving a warning and allowing passengers and crew to abandon ship. For small vessels, rather than using a valuable torpedo, the submarine would then sink the vessel by gunfire, or by a boarding party who would cross and scuttle her, or sink her by a grenade below the waterline.

Sometimes German submarine captains would tow lifeboats with crew and passengers close to land. But this kind act made the submarine vulnerable, particularly when Britain introduced Q ships – seemingly innocent civilian ships that were powerfully armed with concealed guns.

By the end of the war, many merchant ships were fitted with dropping mines (depth charges) and also had a large defensive gun equivalent to the deck gun of a submarine fitted aft that could fire (from its more stable platform) on a surfaced or just-submerged submarine as the ship used its speed to outrun it. Merchant ships became defensively equipped merchant ships (DEMS) and carried dedicated naval DEMS gunners.

◆　◆　◆

UB 116 was a Type UB III – one of some 96 boats of the UB III class commissioned during the Great War. She was ordered on 23 September 1916 to be built by the German shipbuilding and engineering company Blohm & Voss in Hamburg, as Baunummer (shipyard registration or yard number) 322. Blohm & Voss was founded in 1877 by Hermann Blohm and Ernst Voss and still is active today, building warships for the German Navy and for export. The company built a number of major German World War I warships such as the battlecruisers *Von der Tann*, *Derfflinger*, *Goeben*, *Moltke* and *Seydlitz*. Blohm & Voss built all the UB 111-class boats numbered UB 103–UB 117 between 1916 and 1918.

UB 116 was launched on 4 November 1917, and after fitting out afloat she was commissioned on 24 May 1918, just six months before the end of the war. She displaced 516 tons surfaced and 651 tons submerged, and had a height of 8.25 metres. She was 55.3 metres long overall (181 feet), with a beam of 5.8 metres (19 feet) and a draught of 3.7 metres (12.5 feet). Surface propulsion was provided by two AEG 6-cylinder diesel motors that developed 1,100 bhp and allowed her twin screws to push her to a surface speed of 13.6 knots. For submerged operations, she ran on two electric motors that developed 788 bhp and gave her a top submerged speed of 8 knots.

When she was submerged, running at 4 knots on her electric motors she had a range of 55 nautical miles. Surfaced and running on her diesels, she had a range of about 9,000 nautical miles at 6 knots. Her maximum operating depth was 75 metres (250 feet) and she was armed with five 19.7-inch torpedo tubes, one at the stern and four at the bow. She carried ten torpedoes but no mines. She was fitted with a single 88mm (3.4-inch) deck gun and had a crew of 34 officers and men.

After being commissioned on 24 May 1918, UB 116 was assigned to I Flotilla, based in Flanders, under the command of Oberleutnant zur See Erich Stephan, Iron Cross 2nd class.

The commander of UB 116,
Oberleutnant Hans Joachim
Emsmann, Iron Cross 2nd class.

After five months under his command, on 5 October 1918, just a month before the Armistice, UB 116 was transferred to the III Flotilla, under the command of Oberleutnant Hans Joachim Emsmann, Iron Cross 2nd class. He was an experienced submarine commander, having previously captained UB 10 and UB 40. Over the course of ten patrols, he had sunk 26 ships and damaged three others off the south-east coast of England. (During World War II, the 5th U-boat Flotilla was named Flotilla Emsmann in his honour.)

During her short career, UB 116 would carry out four patrols – without sinking any shipping. Her sea career was brought to an abrupt end three weeks after Emsmann assumed command, on 28 October 1918, in the dark waters of Scapa Flow.

By October 1918, it was clear that Germany had effectively lost the war and there was widespread near mutiny in her fleet. In this knowledge, German command planned to put a total of 24 submarines to sea with orders to sink as many Royal Navy vessels as possible in an attempt to weaken the British Grand Fleet, prior to a last-ditch German surface fleet operation. If the Royal Navy could be drastically reduced in numbers by these operations, Germany could perhaps secure a better bargaining position in the peace negotiations that now seemed destined to follow.

As part of this plan, UB 116 was tasked to penetrate the British naval defences of the southern entrance into Scapa Flow known as Hoxa Sound. Once inside she was to sink any British warships and merchant vessels found inside the Flow. Reports emerged many years after the war ended, suggesting that the main target for UB 116 was to be the super-dreadnought battleship HMS *Queen Elizabeth*. She was in fact in the Firth of Forth at the time but Emsmann and his crew were unaware of this.

UB 116 set off from her base at Heligoland on 25 October 1918 and headed towards the Orkney Islands. Emsmann reputedly told a colleague ashore as he left that he knew he would not return. German naval reconnaissance units had previously observed British vessels passing through Hoxa Sound, the main deep entrance into Scapa Flow from the south, and although they believed there were weaknesses in the British defences, they had incorrectly assessed the extent of the British defences.

This failure in German intelligence gathering would prove fatal for UB 116 and her crew – for there were extensive unseen British defences in place, including underwater hydrophones and detector (or indicator) loops. The latter were long lengths of wire cable laid along the seabed, which detected a shift in the earth's magnetic field caused by a steel hull, such as a submarine, passing over it. A 'swing' in the electrical current was displayed on an indicator loop galvanometer. Remotely controlled mines had been laid at predetermined locations – and these could be detonated from a shore station once the swing on the galvanometer revealed the presence of an enemy submarine close by.

In addition to these hidden defences, powerful searchlights had been set up to crisscross the Sound and shore battery guns with interlocking fields of fire covered the surface and were ranged in advance on certain set points.

A boom or anti-submarine net was strung across the Sound. This was a vertical wall of thick interlocking braided steel cables that was suspended on buoys and anchored to the bottom with heavy concrete blocks. A doorway was set in the boom net, which was opened and closed by boom defence vessels to allow Royal Navy units to pass. Other boom defence vessels were stationed in fixed positions along the boom.

As UB 116 tried to slip into Scapa Flow through Hoxa Sound on 28 October 1918, unaware of the submerged British defences, the noise generated by her motors at an unscheduled time was picked up by sensitive British hydrophone listening devices at about 2120. Once an enemy had been detected entering the Flow, all the British defences were put on full alert. A periscope was spotted about an hour later at 2230 – it was clear that Scapa Flow was under attack.

Just before midnight, the presence of UB 116 was picked up again on a detector loop that sent a signal to a galvanometer in the shore station indicating that the enemy submarine was now in the Hoxa Sound minefield. A shore-based operator in a hut flicked a switch – and a row of mines beside the detector loop exploded.

When daylight came the following day, it was found that oil and bubbles of air were rising up from the location of the underwater explosions. Two Royal Navy trawlers were able to locate the wreck with the combination of a wire sweep, and the new ASDIC system and a Royal Navy destroyer was called in to drop depth charges to finish her off. These brought debris and flotsam to the surface, including a jacket. There were no survivors from her crew of 34.

A Royal Navy diving team (known as the 'tin openers') led by Warrant Shipwright E. C. 'Dusty' Miller went down to the wreck that day – 29 October. After blasting open the conning tower hatch he entered the submarine – it was pitch black and his torch only lit a few feet around him. He found the drowned crew – all near the control tower – and all in officers' uniforms. He also found a stack of leather suitcases, and on opening several he found they were all filled with civilian clothes, suits, shirts and collars together with some sums of money. It was as if preparations were being made to surrender the boat after the operation. A few days later, on 4 November, they recovered UB 116's log book.

After the end of the war in 1919, the presence of wreck of UB 116 was deemed to be a hazard for navigation in the shipping lanes. The wreck was brought to the surface for salvage, but whilst under tow she foundered in Pan Hope, east of Quoyness, and sank in approximately 26 metres of water.

The wreck was relocated in 1940 by HMS *Challenger* and subsequently sold on to Metal Recoveries (Newhaven) Ltd on 4 March 1968 – but no salvage operations were begun on the wreck.

In 1974, the wreck was surveyed and reported to be standing 5.4 metres proud of the seabed. The following year, 1975, Royal Navy divers discovered that live torpedoes remained in her bow torpedo tubes. With the development of the new oil terminal at Flotta about to commence, this was a significant hazard for oilfield vessels.

The navy divers removed the remains of the German sailors and carried out a controlled explosion to disperse the torpedoes. This unfortunately resulted in the detonation of one or more warheads and catastrophic damage to the wreck. The Royal Navy vessel itself received some superficial damage, having drifted too close to the site of UB 116 just prior to the explosion. Windows, crockery and toilet bowls were smashed on the vessel – as were windows of nearby homes ashore.

Today the wreckage of UB 116 lies in about 26 metres of water on a soft white sandy bottom. This is a sheltered area of usually very clear water, and it is not uncommon to get visibility of 10–20 metres or more.

Her remains are well broken up as a result of the explosions in 1975 but are still a fine and interesting dive at a nice depth, a dive that is filled with lots to see – albeit that it can be a wee bit difficult to work out what you are looking at until you get your eye in, as she is well pulverised.

The bow itself is blown apart – it just peters out to the sandy seabed with scattered pieces of wreckage lying here and there in the distance, their dark rusted lines a stark contrast to the clean white sandy seabed. Several large compressed air cylinders can be seen lying inside the debris, deformed, having imploded.

Near the damaged bow area, about 25 metres off the wreck on the starboard side, at an angle of about 45 degrees from the wreck, can be found a one-half section of the topmost section of the conning tower with the complete top attached, facing back towards the U-boat. The semi-circular section of conning tower lies on its outside face with its leading edge facing in the direction of the bow – it is now half-filled with sand. The circular access hatch is open and the lid is missing – blown off by the tin openers in 1918. The hatch seems tiny and it is hard to think of World War I era salvage divers in their bulky standard dress getting down through it to enter the wreck after it was sunk. The large cowl for its attack and sky periscopes projects upwards immediately beside the hatch. By finning round to the other side (inside) of the conning tower you can see the small circular internal holes where the periscopes were located and rose up through the external cowl.

Finning back towards the boat, you arrive at a couple of very large pressure cylinders lying on the sand on the starboard side of the wreck hard up against a section of pressure hull. These are much bigger than those at the bow and presumably these held compressed air for ballast tanks or oxygen for life support.

UB 116 appears to have settled on her keel when she sunk for the second time – and the long mound of her remains rises up about 3 metres at most towards the centre of the wreck. Torn and collapsed sections of hull plating give way to exposed frames, curved sections of pressure hull, hatches, broken pieces of crockery that gleam white, warps of cable, masses of electric cabling, copper piping and spars – and here and there, pairs of verdigrised battery terminals can be spotted.

Amidst the debris, on the port side of the wreck, the sturdy turning pedestal for her 88mm deck gun can be spotted almost upside down, its base still attached to a section of deck and its higher section resting on the seabed. The gun itself is missing but some 88mm shells for it lie nearby.

Just forward of the stern, a half-section of the pressure hull has been turned upside down, and elsewhere towards the stern, away from the main site of the devastating explosion, larger sections of her pressure hull remain intact.

The hull wreckage stops abruptly towards the stern – the hull is sheared across and loses its height. A small detached section of stern with what looks like the aft torpedo hatch itself on top lies on the white sand a few metres just off the main body of the wreck.

The instantly recognisable skeletal remains of both aft hydroplanes extend out to either side of the stern section and lie flat on the seabed. The metal shell plating has largely rotted away to reveal the thick internal structure. The sturdy linkage and gearing to operate the hydroplanes is visible, with a small section of keel rising up from the centre of the two. A long metal spar runs forward from the central linkage that moved the hydroplanes.

BOOK TWO

THE PACIFIC

8

GUADALCANAL 1942

Operation Watchtower
Turning point of the Pacific War

I must be getting old. After a lifetime of diving 200–300 feet into the cold pitch blackness of the North Sea I have fallen in love with diving the World War II wrecks of the Pacific – seduced by the warm embrace of its waters, the palpable sense of history, the wrecks, the jungle and the people. Instead of 6°C North Sea water with underwater visibility at best of 50 feet – but more often about 10 feet – you get 29°C crystal-clear warm water where you can see some 200 feet around you underwater and see large parts of a shipwreck at a time. What's not to like about that?

I haven't gone completely soft – I still dive in the North Sea, hunting new wrecks and having fine adventures and craic with my mates – but I no longer jump in every puddle I can find or spend endless hours and endless days searching for every piece of rusted metal off our coasts that I can find. It's just that diving in the Pacific is just so … well … BRILLIANT!!

I first went out to Truk Lagoon in 1990 when I was a 31-year-old youngster – and visited Palau at the same time. After that first 1990 visit I always yearned to get back to Truk – but for a young lawyer struggling to make his way in the cut-throat Scottish legal profession, it was very expensive. Life, and the arrival of two gorgeous daughters, intervened, and I put all thoughts of returning to Truk to the back of my mind. It never occurred to me that 25 years later, life's rich tapestry would lead me to write the main guides to diving the wrecks of Truk and Palau, *Dive Truk Lagoon – the Japanese World War II Pacific Shipwrecks*, published in 2015, and *Dive Palau – the Shipwrecks*, published in 2016.

Whilst writing about Truk and Palau I found myself continually referring to the Guadalcanal Campaign – Allied codename Operation Watchtower – which comprised a number of land and sea battles between August 1942 and February 1943. The operation began with an amphibious assault by U.S. Marines on 7 August 1942, to seize the airfield that was under construction by the Japanese on the island of Guadalcanal, the principal island of the British Protectorate Solomon Islands chain. Guadalcanal and other smaller islands, such as Tulagi and the Florida Islands, had all been seized by Japan in May 1942.

The Japanese airfield on Guadalcanal and the Solomon Islands were strategically important, as from there Japanese long-range bombers would able to threaten Allied shipping moving between west coast America, Australia and New Zealand – and also directly threaten Australia itself.

The Allies had been on the back foot since Japan's surprise raid on Pearl Harbor on 7 December 1941 had crippled the American Pacific Fleet. The Guadalcanal Campaign would mark the turning point of the Pacific War, when the Allies moved from defending against the initial Japanese onslaught, to an offensive campaign, where they sought to retake territory seized by the Japanese.

Guadalcanal Province is some 85 miles in length and is the largest island and capital of the Solomon Islands archipelago – a chain of two roughly parallel north-west to south-east lines almost 900 miles long that sit to the north-east of the Solomon Sea, east of Papua New Guinea, and to the north-east of Australia and the Coral Sea. The Solomons comprise six major islands and some 900 minor islands, totalling some 11,000 square miles of land.

Guadalcanal sits amidst the southernmost main chain of the Solomon Islands, and the channel between it and the smaller Nggela Islands (also known as the Florida Islands) of the Central Province to the north is called New Georgia Sound. This sound came to be known as The Slot by the Allies during World War II.

The Nggela Islands themselves comprise two main islands – Nggela Sule to the north and Nggela Pile to the south – along with a number of other smaller islands such as Tulagi, Gavutu and Tanambogo. Such were the high losses of shipping and aircraft during World War II that the stretch of water here between Guadalcanal and the Florida Islands came to be known as Ironbottom Sound by the Allies during the campaign.

Simultaneously with the successful attack on Pearl Harbor on 7 December 1941, Japanese forces struck at American, British, Chinese and Dutch territories in the Pacific. Although they encountered stubborn resistance in the Philippines, Japan managed to establish bases in the New Guinea–Solomons area, allowing them to directly threaten Australia itself. On 3 May 1942, the Japanese occupied the small British Protectorate Solomon Islands of Tulagi, Gavutu and Tanambogo and began building a seaplane, ship refuelling and communications base. This would trigger the Battle of the Coral Sea of 4–8 May 1942, which became a strategic victory for the Allies and stopped the, until then, uninterrupted Japanese push southwards. Then came the Battle of Midway on 3–7 June 1942, one of the most decisive battles in naval history, in which the Japanese suffered crippling losses in aircraft carriers and which swung the balance of sea power in favour of the Allies. Japanese troops landed on Guadalcanal itself on 6 July 1942 and began constructing an airfield.

When U.S. reconnaissance in early July 1942 revealed that the Japanese had begun construction of a strategic airfield on Guadalcanal, American forces determined to embark on their first land offensive of the war, the Guadalcanal Campaign.

On 7 August 1942, just eight months after the raid on Pearl Harbor, supported by the South Pacific Force ships and aircraft, the 1st U.S. Marine Division carried out amphibious landings on Guadalcanal and Tulagi. The Allies wanted control of these strategic islands and use of the Japanese airfield, to support a proposed campaign to capture or destroy the major Japanese base at Rabaul in New Britain. The small island of Tulagi had a strategic and well-protected natural harbour – indeed, Admiral Jellicoe had visited the area during World War I

Beach landing of U.S. Marines during the early phase of Operation Watchtower. (National Archives).

and was so impressed by its naval potential that he proposed it as a base for the British Pacific naval forces.

For the initial Guadalcanal amphibious assaults of 7 August 1942, the U.S. landing forces split into two strike groups whilst Allied warships carried out a softening-up naval bombardment of the invasion beaches, and U.S. carrier aircraft bombed Japanese positions. One U.S. Marines strike force assaulted Guadalcanal Island itself, targeting control of the Japanese airfield then under construction and known by the Japanese as RXI. The other strike force assaulted and overwhelmed the numerically inferior Japanese garrisons on the strategically important Tulagi and other Florida Islands, despite strong opposition.

On the much larger Guadalcanal Island, the strike force of 11,000 U.S. Marines initially met limited opposition. By the afternoon of the second day, they had successfully seized control of the Japanese airfield and formed a defensive perimeter around it, a beachhead that was surrounded by Japanese forces. Work began immediately on completing the runway using captured Japanese construction hardware, and the airfield became the focus of all future operations in the area.

The American WWII airbase on Guadalcanal, Henderson Field – now the site of Honiara International Airport. (National Archives)

On 12 August, the airfield was named Henderson Field in honour of the U.S. Marine Corps aviator Major Lofton Henderson, who had been killed in combat on 4 June 1942 during the Battle of Midway as he led his squadron into attack Japanese carrier forces – despite much stronger enemy fighter protection.

Japanese reaction to the assaults was quick and powerful. In the early morning hours of 9 August, two days after the initial American landings, a strong Japanese force of cruisers and destroyers steamed down the gap between the two chains of the Solomon Islands – The Slot – and attacked the U.S. and Allied ships providing cover for Guadalcanal and the Florida Islands. The Japanese achieved complete surprise – the Battle of Savo Island had begun.

In less than an hour of battle, three U.S. heavy cruisers and an Australian heavy cruiser were sunk, with another heavy cruiser and two destroyers damaged. A third destroyer was also damaged – and was subsequently sunk after a follow-up Japanese air raid later the same day. The Battle of Savo Island was one of the worst defeats suffered by the U.S. Navy during the war.

From their advance bases, both the Americans and Japanese attempted to build up their strength on Guadalcanal, and a number of grim struggles on land, sea and in the air followed, that lasted six months. The Japanese made several subsequent attempts to retake Henderson Field between August and November 1942, ushering in three major land battles, seven major naval battles and daily aerial contacts that eventually culminated in the four-day-long decisive Naval Battle of Guadalcanal from 12 to 15 November 1942.

In this naval battle, a heavily protected Japanese transport convoy carrying 7,000 battle-hardened troops closed on Guadalcanal in an operation to attempt to retake Henderson Field. Japanese escort warships commenced a big gun naval bombardment of the airfield to destroy Allied aircraft that might attack the convoy. In response, American aircraft and warships attacked the Japanese convoy and naval forces in an attempt to try and prevent the Japanese ground troops reaching their objective – Guadalcanal.

Both sides lost many ships during the battle – but American naval forces successfully fought off the Japanese naval force, thwarted the naval bombardment, and went on to sink many of the Japanese troop transports. This battle was Japan's last attempt to oust American forces from Guadalcanal and was a decisive strategic victory – pivotal in the outcome of the conflict in the area.

But victory in the Guadalcanal Campaign had come at a high cost to U.S. and Allied naval forces. During the battle, between 7 August 1942 and 9 February 1943, the carriers *Hornet* and *Wasp* had been sunk along with the heavy cruisers *Astoria, Chicago, Northampton, Quincy, Vincennes*, RAN *Canberra* (Royal Australian Navy), the light cruisers *Atlanta* and *Juneau*, the destroyers *Barton, Benham, Blue, Cushing, De Haven, Duncan, Jarvis, Laffey, Meredith, Monssen, O'Brien, Porter, Preston* and *Walke*. The Motor Torpedo Boats PT-37, PT-43, PT-44, PT-111, PT-112 and PT-113 were lost along with the Transports *Colhoun, George F. Elliott, Gregory* and *Little,* and the fleet tug *Seminole.*

The list of U.S. and Allied naval vessels badly damaged during the campaign was even longer, and included the battleships *North Carolina* and *South Dakota*, the aircraft carriers *Enterprise* and *Saratoga*, and countless heavy and light cruisers, destroyers, minesweepers and transports.

The Imperial Japanese Navy lost two battleships, one light carrier, three heavy cruisers, one light cruiser, eleven destroyers, six submarines, thirteen transports and five cargo ships. It was little wonder that Ironbottom Sound acquired its name.

Following the battle, with U.S. forces now in undisputed command of Henderson Field and having secured air superiority, the Japanese were forced to resort to daring fast supply runs down The Slot to their beleaguered isolated garrisons, under cover of darkness. The Japanese supply campaign came to be known by the Allies as the Tokyo Express. With command of Guadalcanal now secured, the pre-dominantly American forces could now threaten the strategically important Japanese base of Rabaul.

Victory at Guadalcanal, together with the successful halting and repulse of the Japanese advance in south-eastern New Guinea, marked the turning point of the Pacific War. From this point onwards, following the earlier crucial Battles of the Coral Sea in May 1942 and the Battle of Midway in June 1942, Japan had lost the ability to win the war, and was forced into a defensive posture to try and slow the Allied advance and hold onto seized territory. The Japanese eventually evacuated Guadalcanal in February 1943.

To understand the Pacific War, you have to understand how crucially pivotal the turning point of Guadalcanal was to World War II itself – and as I strove to understand what took place as I wrote my Truk and Palau books, I found myself continuously writing about places like the Florida Islands, Tulagi, the Shortland Islands, Ironbottom Sound, The Slot and the Tokyo Express – but as I had never been there, I had no real comprehension of what these places actually looked like, or how they were so significant. They were but words in books – and I had always wanted to change that lack of knowledge.

In 2016, the organisers of OZTek 2017, the Australian Technical Diving Conference & Exhibition in Sydney, foolishly invited me once again to speak and this time to open their biennial conference. This would be the 3rd OZTek in succession that I would speak at.

I decided to speak about the Explorers Club Flag No 192 expedition that I had led to survey the historic and protected wreck of HMS *Hampshire* off north-west Orkney on the 100th anniversary of its sinking in June 2016. As with past OZTeks, I decided to have a bit of an adventure after the conference and this time to nip up to Guadalcanal and finally see the lay of the land. It's an easy internal hop from Sydney to Brisbane and then a few hours flight up from there to Honiara, the capital of the Solomons on Guadalcanal Island – in all it's about 5–6 hours of flying. You can easily see how Japan, in control of Guadalcanal, could directly threaten Australia itself.

On the flight up from Brisbane to Honiara I got chatting to a doctor who was working in country as part of efforts to try and combat the malaria problem and also the mosquito born dengue fever epidemic, which was spiralling out of control. He cheered me up no end by telling me that there had been 4,000 cases of the tropical mosquito-borne dengue fever in the last four months. It's a particularly serious disease – just one bite and you can be infected. It is also a particularly global problem: dengue is prevalent in more than 100 countries. Each year millions of people get infected by dengue, and it is estimated that 10–20,000 die each year from it. He advised me to wear long trousers and a long-sleeved shirt at night – and lastly added, don't get bitten! As a man who mosquitoes seem to love feasting on wherever I go, I was now a bit apprehensive about what I was letting myself in for.

Landing at Honiara International Airport, the plane doors opened to the familiar brilliant sunshine of the tropics. The sky was a dazzling blue – and the glare of sun-baked airport concrete, mixed with the oppressive heat of the tropics, overwhelmed me as I walked across the tarmac to the small terminal building. Standing in a long queue waiting for immigration checks in the humid arrivals hall, I was soon sweating.

I was quickly staggered to learn that the small Honiara International Airport I had arrived at is actually the former U.S. Henderson Field – the World War II airfield that I had written about in *Dive Truk Lagoon*. Interesting Fact No 1 learned – before I was even through immigration! I simply hadn't appreciated inbound that I'd be arriving at this famous airfield, a strategic objective for both Japanese and American forces during the Battle of Guadalcanal.

A hot, sticky, one-hour-long ride in an old beat-up car with no air conditioning, masquerading as a taxi, from the airport to the capital Honiara, was a series of wearisome delays as we crept along potholed roads that were lined with tumbledown shacks and stalls clumped in groups where hawkers were selling all sorts of local fruit and foodstuffs.

With the car being as hot as an oven, the driver and I had the windows open to try and get a cooling breeze. Clouds of dust were being thrown up by cars ahead of us, and soon a fine layer of dust covered my skin. As well as potholes, there were pools of dirty water to circumnavigate, and little in the way of lane discipline once the roads improved as we neared Honiara. On the flight in I had read that the probability of precipitation for my visit in March was that it would rain on 23 of the 31 days of the current month – no wonder the hills to the south on my left were thickly covered in the most dense and beautifully verdant green jungle I had ever seen.

I was disappointed at the amount of rubbish lying around as we drove in – there is no recycling or any attempt not to litter; everything seems just to be casually thrown away. There is litter everywhere – and the mosquitoes that carry malaria and dengue fever breed and prosper in the roadside pools of stagnant water, in the discarded roadside water bottles and empty drinks tins and soaking rubbish. They love the squalor of the city, where they find loads of places to breed, allied to a ready source of food – us. The doctor had told me that there is no dengue in the jungle as it is much cleaner; it's the squalor of the city they like. When I asked the taxi driver why there was so much rubbish around and why people were openly just throwing things on the ground beside me, he just replied with a shrug of his shoulders "It is the attitude of the people." My first impressions on the ride in from the airport were undeniably poor, and I was beginning to wonder if coming here was a good idea. It's no beautiful Palau, for sure.

There are only a few hotels for western tourists around in Honiara, despite it being the capital city. I'd chosen the grandly titled King Solomon Hotel, which is just a 10-minute walk away from the Tulagi Dive Centre, at the Honiara Point Cruz Yacht Club, that I was going to be diving with. The taxi pulled off the road into the hotel's private driveway; I offloaded myself and my kit, paid the driver and struggled into the vast ethnic reception area of the King Sol (as it's called). I was immediately engulfed in an oasis of calm, cool and serenity amidst the bustle of Honiara. A fresh drink in a coconut was being offered to me before I had even got to the check-in desk.

I soon learned how beautifully quirky a place the King Sol is – I love places like this. The accommodation is formed of rows of bedrooms that are built on timber posts on a steep hillside on either side of a small 2–3 person private cable car that takes you up the hill from inside Reception. There are steep wooden staircases that run up the hill on either side of the cable car – but I was maxed out for luggage with a 23kg main bag with my complete rebreather in it, a massive cabin bag with more dive kit stuffed in it, and an additional computer bag. There was no way I could climb up the hill, so after checking in I staggered with all my kit to the cable car and climbed in.

My room was on Level 3 – but the push button on the cable car panel for it was missing. There was just a hole where the button should have been. I knew this was going to be the case, as the helpful Reception staff had told me about it – and that I should just stick my finger in the hole up to the first finger joint and I would be able to manually press the internal button. After getting a bad electric shock as a kid, I don't like sticking my finger into anything electrical – so it was with much trepidation that I did so. But it all worked fine, and the cable car gave a little lurch and began to slowly climb up the hill.

I learned later, chatting at the bar, that the single cable car wire had snapped once, years ago, and that the cable car had ended up careering down the hill on its single rail. Depending on who you spoke to about the incident and how many of the local Solbrew beers they'd had, the cable car either burst through the bamboo screen wall at its base and ended up in Reception – or careered right through Reception and right onto the road outside. I love mythical stories like this!

The air conditioning had been off in my room during the day, and now in the early evening, as I finally opened the door and entered, it was like an oven. But at least I had arrived and was now safely ensconced in my spacious room halfway up the hill. I cranked on the AC and it started to try and put a dent in the humid temperature in the room. As I tried to cool down, I took a well-earned drink of water and looked out over the bustle of Honiara below through fixed mosquito window-mesh netting. The view was over rooftops to Ironbottom Sound – I could see right across the 25-mile-wide sound to what must be Tulagi and the Florida Islands in the distance.

Way up to the west, I could see the large the island of Savo. I soon learned that this is a volcanic island – essentially a big volcano that has regularly erupted throughout history every 150 years. The last eruption was between 1835 and 1850, and the eruption was so strong everyone on the island was killed. I know you've just done the maths: another eruption was long overdue. What would get me – dengue, malaria, electrocution, the cable car or a volcanic eruption? The possibility of a diving accident was far down the list!

First things first. I unpacked my rebreather and began to build it up so I would be ready to dive the next day. After an hour of fettling and getting all my kit ready I was as prepped as could be, so I walked down the hill to the bar for what I felt was a badly needed, well deserved, cold beer. The bar had just a couple of isolated western chaps sitting at it – one of them said hi and we started to chat as I got my beer in. He turned out to be a miner – as many westerners there were – and after a couple of beers he started explaining to me about the earthquakes in detail.

The two parallel chains of islands that make up the Solomons sit on the Pacific Ring of Fire – a 25,000-mile-long horseshoe shape that runs from New Zealand up through the Solomons and Papua New Guinea, up the east coast of Asia to Japan, across the Aleutian chain of islands south of the Bering Strait to Alaska, and then down the western seaboard of North and South America all the way down to the southern tip of Chile. It is a nearly continuous arc of oceanic trenches, volcanic belts, and plate movements – and some 90 per cent of all the world's earthquakes take place in this Ring. For the technically minded, the oceanic Nazca and Cocos Plates are being subducted beneath the westward-moving South American Plate, whilst a portion of the Pacific Plate is being subducted beneath the North American Plate. The Ring of Fire explains the presence of the Savo Island volcano nearby.

He continued … the reason our rooms were built on timber stakes was so they would withstand the fairly regular rattling from earthquakes. There are something like 80 recorded earthquakes in Guadalcanal each year, and countless minor tremors. I was told that the beds are on rollers so as the room shakes and moves on the stakes, my bed would seem to move back and forth across the room, although it was in fact staying largely in the same position – it was the room that was moving!

After a couple of Solbrews with this interesting chap, I made my excuses and jumped into the cable car. Hesitantly I stuck my finger in the hole for Level 3, crossed my fingers the cable didn't snap and headed up to my room. Entering it, I found the AC had done its job – the place was now like a freezer – so I switched it off for the night. I don't like sleeping on dive trips with the AC on in case I get a head cold. Hopefully the room would stay bearable most of the night? I drifted off to sleep that night with mosquitoes, dengue fever and earthquakes competing for my dreams. I woke up at 0230 covered in sweat in a room that was as hot as when I'd arrived – the AC got switched on again.

I rose for breakfast at 0600 the next morning and as agreed, bang on at 0715, a pickup truck arrived outside Reception to whisk me and my kit the short drive round to Tulagi Dive. I was warmly received by Neil Yates and Troy, who had a tub of sofnalime CO2 scrubber for my rebreather ready for me, along with 3-litre oxygen and diluent cylinders. I soon had gases analysed, my CCR fully rigged – and was ready to go diving.

Shakedown dives are always a good idea after you and your kit have done some rigorous travelling and been bashed around. They tend to root out what is missing, broken or goes pop, whiz, fizz or bang before you commit to a heavy-duty dive. The shakedown dives for me would be two wrecks that you dive from the shore, that were known locally as B1 and B2. The two wrecks lie a few hundred metres apart, where during World War II they were run ashore bow first onto the steeply shelving Bonegi Beach, which is about 40 minutes' ride by truck to the west of Honiara.

Hirokawa Maru and *Kinugawa Maru*

B1 turned out to be the Japanese World War II casualty *Hirokawa Maru*. She was a large 6,872grt 475-foot-long (145-metre) cargo freighter that was laid down in 1939, completed in October 1940 and then requisitioned for war service in February 1941. She had a central composite superstructure housing her bridge and engine rooms below abaft, flanked by two large foredeck holds and two aft holds. The word *Maru* is often attached to Japanese merchant ship names and means 'circle'. Thus, a ship called the *San Francisco Maru* would likely operate a circular route between Japan and the west coast of America; the *Rio de Janeiro Maru* operated between Japan and South America, and so on.

B2 is the local name given to *Kinugawa Maru*, a 6,937grt, 459-foot-long (140-metre) cargo vessel similar to *Hirokawa Maru* but slightly smaller.

Hirokawa Maru and *Kinugawa Maru* were both part of the Japanese Second Assault Convoy bound for Tassafaronga in what would become the Second Naval Battle of Guadalcanal. The assault force comprised 11 Japanese naval troop and supply transport ships protected by 12 Imperial Japanese Navy (IJN) escort vessels.

The Assault Convoy set off just before sunset on 13 November 1942 from the Shortland Islands, situated just to the south of the larger Bougainville Island, at the north-west of the

Solomon chain of islands. Some 7,000 troops of the Imperial Japanese Army (IJA) 38th Army Division and Special Landing Force were aboard.

Although the convoy escaped detection during the darkness of night, shortly after sunrise the large convoy was spotted passing down The Slot between New Georgia and Santa Isabel Islands, by two U.S. Navy reconnaissance Douglass Dauntless SBD dive bombers from USS *Enterprise.*

Throughout the day, U.S. aircraft attacked the Japanese ships relentlessly. Around 1300, 18 USN Douglass Dauntless dive bombers and seven Grumman Avenger TBF torpedo bombers attacked the convoy, sinking the *Canberra Maru*, hitting the *Nagara Maru* with an aerial torpedo, and damaging the *Sado Maru.*

Around 1430, 13 Douglass Dauntless dive bombers attacked the *Brisbane Maru* and set her on fire – she would later sink. Further attacks followed, during which the *Shinanogawa Maru* and *Arizona Maru* were hit by 1,000lb bombs and had to be abandoned. The *Naka Maru* was then attacked by fourteen dive bombers and three torpedo bombers and sunk. By the early hours of the following morning there were only four transports still afloat. At about 0100, the convoy commander was ordered to beach his remaining troop convoy ships at Tassafaronga.

Hirokawa Maru and *Kinugawa Maru* were run ashore bows first a few hundred metres apart at about 0400 on the shelving Bonegi Beach (where they remain today). *Yamaura Maru* was beached in Doma Cove and *Yamatsuki Maru* was beached at Aruligo Point.

By dawn, some 2,000 troops of the original 7,000 carried by the convoy had made it ashore. More than 4,800 IJA troops were rescued from the other stricken transports by the convoy escort destroyers.

Later that morning, the *Benson*-class destroyer USS *Meade* targeted the four beached Japanese transports for an hour between 1000 and 1100 with her 5-inch main battery and her 40mm anti-aircraft (AA guns), and set them on fire. Later that day they were attacked by USN dive bombers and torpedo bombers.

A Japanese auxiliary transport, run ashore during the early part of the Guadalcanal campaign. (National Archives)

◆ ◆ ◆

Back to the present

We loaded our gear into the back of a heavy-duty truck at Tulagi Dive and with a couple of local staff dive guides headed off to Bonegi Beach. The heavy traffic of Honiara soon gave way to a ribbon of small villages and shacks on each side of the road with dense verdant jungle behind. I've seen a lot of different jungles in my time but this is the densest, thickest jungle I have yet seen.

After a bouncy 40-minute drive west from Honiara along the north coast of Guadalcanal, on the southern side of Ironbottom Sound, the roads began to narrow as we neared Bonegi Beach. Either side of the road was thick, dense, seemingly impenetrable jungle. Already I was getting a feel for how difficult and tough the fighting conditions must have been during World War II.

As we arrived at Bonegi Beach, we turned off the main road onto a rutted sandy track and entered some light jungle that fronted the beach. Bonegi Beach was deserted apart from a few locals whose job it was to take payment of the beach entry fee – this was included in the dive package, so we drove right past them with a wave and they went back to attempting to stay out of the sun in the shade.

Once near the beachfront onto Ironbottom Sound, we turned to the east and drove along rutted tracks flanked by tall grasses until we arrived on the water's edge – we were literally just a stone's throw from the sea. We backed the truck up as far as we could to the beach and jumped out.

There was no sign of *Hirokawa Maru* even though I had seen the black and white archive photos of both vessels run ashore with their bows and much of the forward section of the ships towering out of the water during the war. I was briefed that the shallowest sections of the bow now came to just 5 metres from the surface and that her stern sat in about 60 metres.

The shallowest parts of the wreck had been salvaged in the 1960s and 70s – but most of the ship was still there, just under the water. I could see parts of the *Kinugawa Maru* projecting above the water, bow onto the beach, a few hundred metres to the west – she was a lot shallower wreck so we were doing the deeper *Hirokawa Maru* first. After spending so much time diving the countless *Maru* naval transports sunk at Truk and Palau, I was looking forward to this.

I got my CCR onto a convenient timber picnic table beside us and prepped it before getting into my 3mm full body wetsuit. The local guides were just diving in shorts and a T-shirt, but I have been stung too many times by invisible jellyfish stingers – and cut on sharp rotted metal. Nowadays I always take the basic precaution of wearing a full wetsuit.

Once we were ready to dive, I followed one of the guides as he strode down the beach with me and entered the water – as with Truk and Palau it was a warm 29°C, the same temperature as the atmosphere topside. We waded out through the surf zone then pulled our fins on and dropped our heads into the water. Straight away the white sand of the beach started to shelve away steeply in about 100-foot visibility.

We swam out until we got a bit of depth, then let the air out of our buoyancy wings and dropped down towards the bottom as we continued to swim away from shore and downwards.

Very quickly the rotted remains of the *Hirokawa Maru* appeared below me – the bow section was sitting upright, bows to the shore. The wreck sloped away dramatically downwards into the depths. We started to move downwards.

About a third of the way down the ship the vessel had broken in two – and the lower aft section was resting on her port beam ends. Although the ship was quite smashed up in the shallows, the deeper I went, the more intact and the more interesting the ship got.

At a depth of about 35 metres my guide, who was diving a single tank of air, indicated he wasn't going any further. We'd talked about maximum depths topside as we prepped to dive, and he'd told me that that was the maximum depth he would go to – but that it was OK for me to go on deeper if I wanted. In the good visibility, keeping an eye on him above me, I pressed on for a little way to get a feel for the ship – we were practically at the stern, with the guide on the starboard rail above me.

I reached the uppermost curve of the fantail of the stern at 45 metres and could see the sweep of the fantail plunging beneath me as the rounded stern returned under the port side to meet the seabed. In the crystal-clear visibility, I could still see the guide silhouetted above me holding on to the starboard gunwale. I was feeling very comfortable, but this was a shakedown dive and the guide didn't know me from Adam. I didn't want to freak him out on this first dive – so I turned the dive and began to swim back up the ship, picking him up as I gradually worked my way up the ship.

Although in the shallows it had been hard to understand the mangled ship quickly, now I'd been to the stern it all made more sense. She was a medium-sized steamship with a composite superstructure amidships holding her bridge with engine rooms below. There was no noticeable stern superstructure left – just a hatch down into the aftmost cargo hold, with kingposts forward of it, their derrick ends swung downwards.

Moving further forward I came upon the much larger rectangular hatch for Hold No 3 with much larger goalpost kingposts forward of it. Pressing forward and shallower, I arrived at the composite superstructure, which had completely collapsed to the seabed. Ships resting on their beam ends are very prone to collapse and don't stand the test of time underwater as well as ships that sit upright, as they were designed to be.

I spotted the smokestack below me and then the tops of the diesel engine cylinders poking out from underneath the debris – it looked as though the superstructure, which no doubt had projected above the water after the war, had been cut away. The wreck was progressively more damaged as we got shallower, until the break where the forward section of ship sat upright but well collapsed.

We continued to get shallower and I was able to move in and out of sections of the lower areas of the bow until we reached the very shallowest part of the forward section and it was time to head up to the surface again. This had, been a very pleasant shakedown dive – my CCR had perfumed faultlessly despite the rigours of baggage handlers at a number of international airports as I flew from Aberdeen to London, London to Sydney, Sydney to Brisbane and Brisbane to Honiara.

We had a pleasant lunch sitting at a wooden table in the shade on the waterfront and after a suitable surface interval, we jumped into the truck and drove the few hundred metres west along the beach to B2 – the *Kinugawa Maru*.

The 6,937grt Japanese auxiliary transport Kinugawa Maru *was run ashore at Bonegi Beach, Guadalcanal, on 14 November 1942 to allow the IJA troops she was carrying to land. Her wreck is now a popular shore dive.*
(National Archives)

Pulling on my 3mm wetsuit again, I propped my CCR up on the flat back of the truck and wriggled into it. As with the first morning dive, it was a short walk over the shingle beach and a wade out through the gentle surf to get enough depth to dive. In contrast to B1, of which nothing showed proud of the water, part of the rotted bow of *Kinugawa Maru* and some foredeck fittings were still sticking out of the water, marking her resting place. Once in about 5 metres of water we dived and finned across the clean white sand bottom to the wreck and had a pleasant scout around it down to a depth of about 28 metres. Being in shallower water, it is far less intact than B1.

IJN *I-1*

The next day's diving was to be two more shore dives on the wreck of the Japanese submarine *I-1* and the American B-17E bomber known locally as *Bessie the Jap Basher*. I was particularly looking forward to diving I-1, as she was a famous submarine that met her end in the most dramatic of fashions here in Guadalcanal.

I-1 was a 320-foot long (98-metre) Japanese submarine that had been commissioned in 1926. She had been positioned off Pearl Harbor, Hawaii, on 7 December 1941 when the infamous carrier air raid took place – tasked to attack any American warships that tried to escape the harbour. In the months after the raid, she shelled Hawaiian harbours on two subsequent occasions.

On 29 January 1943, whilst on a supply run from Rabaul along The Slot to the Japanese outpost at Kamimbo Bay, Guadalcanal, she surfaced in darkness at about 2030 in Kamimbo Bay in a heavy rain squall. She headed for the safety of the Japanese-held anchorage with her decks awash, but was detected in the darkness on ASDIC by the two New Zealand minesweeper corvettes HMNZS *Kiwi* and *Moa*. (ASDIC was a World War I era British, French and American invention pioneered by the Anti-Submarine Detection and Investigation Committee – the system was later called sonar).

The corvettes attacked with depth charges and *I-1* was forced to crash dive. The depth charging triggered several leaks of water into the pressure hull, and as seawater contacted her batteries, poisonous chlorine gas was released. The submarine's pumps had been damaged during the attack, her steering engine put out of action and her port propeller shaft disabled.

The loss of main electrics caused all the lights go out and the submarine was pitched into a 45-degree bow-down attitude as she began a seemingly uncontrollable plunge into the depths. In the darkness, her crew frantically tried to regain control of the boat by blowing the main ballast tanks and putting the remaining starboard shaft full astern. Amazingly, the desperate plunge into oblivion was halted just before she reached the incredible depth of almost 600 feet, well beyond her design crush depth.

As the descent slowed and then reversed, she then started to rise uncontrollably and broke the surface, down by the bow, some 2,000 yards away from *Kiwi*. *I-1* began to run on her remaining shaft in an attempt to make the shore, as hatches were thrown open and Japanese gunners rushed to man their forward deck gun and the 13.2mm conning tower machine gun.

Accurate fire from *Kiwi* with her 4-inch deck gun and 20mm Oerlikon bow gun killed most of the Japanese officers on her bridge as well as the crew of her deck gun. With no control from the bridge, the submarine started a slow turn to starboard.

A reserve deck gun crew was sent on deck, and Japanese officers, expecting a boarding attempt, rushed to get their *katana* swords. Rifles were passed out to the remaining crew for what was expected to soon become hand-to-hand fighting.

Unable to fatally wound the submarine's deck and conning tower armour with her deck gun, *Kiwi* swung in to ram the submarine at full speed, hitting her on the port side abaft the conning tower. She backed off and made another ramming attempt, this time hitting a forward diving plane as Japanese crew raked the corvette with small arms fire.

Kiwi made a third ramming run – this time holing a starboard ballast tank before riding up on top of the submarine's aft deck. As *Kiwi* withdrew, the submarine's list to starboard began to increase.

In a desperate situation, the submarine eventually ran onto a reef, 300 yards north of Kamimbo. The whole aft portion of the submarine was flooded, and as the stern settled the submarine slid back into deeper water to eventually leave only her bow sticking about 20 feet out of the water. Her crew abandoned the beleaguered submarine; 66 managed to reach the shore and join the Japanese garrison. *Moa* moved in to investigate the stricken submarine, capturing two survivors and killing one with machine gun fire, and recovering a codebook and nautical charts; 27 crew had been killed or were missing in action.

The next evening, after darkness had fallen, a Japanese officer and a number of crew and engineers return to the wrecked submarine in a Daihatsu barge and attached two depth charges and other explosive charges to the hull in an attempt to detonate the torpedoes aboard. Although this failed, the two depth charges caused enough damage to make salvage pointless.

A number of myths arose after the war about what exactly *I-1* was carrying, and in the early 1970s an Australian treasure hunter used a depth charge to open up the intact sealed section of the hull – and this caused one or more of the forward live torpedoes to detonate, destroying part of the forward section of the hull. The forward section now rests in 10 metres of water with the intact stern in 25 metres of water.

B-17E – *Bessie the Jap Basher*

The planned afternoon dive on the B-17E was also interesting. She had been shot down on 24 September 1942, attempting to return to Henderson Field after a mission to bomb Japanese shipping, when she was attacked and set on fire by Japanese fighters. Dropping to sea level as she sought safe refuge, she finally had to ditch in Domo Cove, which was occupied by the Japanese. Two of the crew appear to have made the shore but been executed. The remaining crew are still Missing In Action (MIA). The wreck of this substantial American bomber (minus its tail fuselage) sits in 15–20 metres, and was a type of aircraft I had never dived previously.

The night before the dive, however, the reason for the extremely thick green jungle on Guadalcanal was brought home to me with force. The heavens opened and there was torrential rain all night and into the morning – it was still pouring down at 0630 as I sat down to breakfast in the King Sol's vast and fine dining room, the roof of which internally is clad with bamboo and has long gaps between the uprights and the roof that are open for ventilation. The rain was hammering down past the roof ventilation gap and making quite a racket – I wasn't looking forward to the walk to Tulagi Dive.

I gathered my kit up, put on a waterproof and stepped into the tropical downpour – and was instantly soaked. By the time my 10-minute walk to Tulagi Dive was done there wasn't an inch of me left dry. The little creek that runs down the side of the Tulagi Dive and Honiara Yacht Club was now a raging torrent, carrying brown mud down to the sea; the water in front of the yacht club had turned an impenetrable brown.

Very quickly, the obvious decision was made that boat diving was out and that the inshore vis for shore diving would also be killed by the runoff from the land. The diving I was so looking forward to, understandably, had to be called off for the day. I had another 10-minute trudge through the deluge back to the King Sol.

The downpour petered out during the course of the morning and I took the chance in the afternoon to flag down a taxi in town and go up to the highest point overlooking Honiara to visit the Guadalcanal American Memorial, which honours American and Allied servicemen who lost their lives during the Guadalcanal Campaign. This unique memorial consists of a central pylon 4 feet square that rises 24 feet above its base. Four radiating directional walls point outwards from its base to the sites of major battles, and an account of the relevant battles is inscribed on the walls. The memorial is immaculately maintained by the American Battle Monuments Commission.

The next morning as I rose at 0600, it was as though the deluge had never happened – the sky was blue, the jungle seemed greener if that was possible, the heat was already intense and it was bone dry outside other than some large pools at the side of the road; and today, two boat dives were scheduled. My rebreather was wheel-barrowed down the wooden pier to the dive boat and there was a flurry of activity as divers and dive centre assistants loaded everything onto Tulagi Dive's fine spacious dive boat, powered by two 150hp Mercury outboard engines.

Soon we were ready, and it was time for ropes off. Neil Yates, the then owner of Tulagi Dive and a well-known and respected technical diver, was at the helm, and effortlessly guided the dive boat away from the pier as we started to motor north into Ironbottom Sound. Once we were into open water, Neil throttled up the engines, the boat surging forward, effortlessly and quickly riding up onto the plane. We started to scream directly across Ironbottom Sound at about 25 knots towards the small island of Tulagi on the north side of the Sound, about 24 nautical miles away.

The ride across the Sound took about an hour as we raced towards the jungle-clad island of Tulagi, which had been the capital of the British Solomon Islands Protectorate between 1896 and 1942. It was the quintessential colonial outpost, complete with its own cricket ground and post office. The Japanese had occupied Tulagi on 3 May 1942 intending to establish a seaplane base there and use its deep protected harbour for shipping. U.S. Marines seized the island on 7 August 1942, and after World War II, with the wartime destruction of much of Tulagi's infrastructure, the capital was then moved to Honiara, where it remains today.

USS *Kanawha*

Arriving at the location of the morning's wreck dive, in the crystal-clear water we had soon spotted the small white buoy that is permanently fixed to the bow section of the wreck. It was suspended just a few metres beneath the surface.

One of the boat crew took one end of the bow painter rope, jumped into the water, duck-dived and swam down to thread the rope through a loop on the buoy. He then swam back up and passed the bitter end to Neil. This was made fast on the bow cleat so that the rope was ready to slip when we were ready to depart. In a matter of just a few minutes, we were now tied into the famous World War II casualty, the American fleet oiler USS *Kanawha*, which lies in 61 metres of water in Tulagi harbour not far from a submerged reef that connects a small islet just offshore to Tulagi itself. It's just over 40 metres down to the deck of this huge vessel.

The American fleet oiler USS Kanawha *was bombed on 7 April 1943,and sank in TulagiHarbor the following day. Her wreck now rests upright in 61 metres.* (National Archives)

The *Kanawha* (AO-1) was the third ship to bear this name – and was the first oiler purpose-built for the U.S. Navy. Whilst tankers load fuel in one port and then transport it and offload it at another port, oilers are essentially tankers which are equipped for abeam refuelling of ships at sea, with special tanks, pumps and refuelling at sea (RAS) masts.

Kanawha was laid down in December 1913, launched on 11 July 1914 and commissioned into the U.S. Navy on 5 June 1915. She was 457 feet long with a beam of 56 feet and a full load displacement of 14,800 tons. She was armed with two 4-inch main defensive guns set on either side of the fantail at the very stern, and a number of anti-aircraft (AA) guns. During World War I she made repeated trans-Atlantic crossings carrying oil from Halifax, Nova Scotia, to Britain and France.

Fast forward to World War II. In late 1941, she entered Mare Island Naval Shipyard to the north of San Francisco in Vallejo, California, for refit. She was still there on 7 December 1941, when the shock Japanese carrier raid went in against Pearl Harbor. By this time her World War I era 4-inch guns had been replaced with more modern and more powerful 5-inch guns set one on either side aft where the 4-inch guns had been – but in enlarged gun sponsons that bulged out from the side of the hull at deck level. Four single-barrel 20mm Oerlikon AA guns and four 40mm guns set in lightly armoured emplacements called gun tubs were installed, one on the centreline of the fo'c'sle deck just abaft the stem and anchor capstans, one on the centreline at the stern in between the two wing 5-inch guns, two set amidships – one on either beam – and two more either side of the stern superstructure.

As the Pacific War began, *Kanawha* was initially tasked with carrying fuel from California to refuel the remaining units of the Pacific Fleet at Pearl Harbor. In the early part of 1943, she was engaged in refuelling ships at sea during the Solomon Islands campaign as American forces began their thrust westwards. Guadalcanal and Tulagi had been assaulted by American forces on 7 August 1942, and although the Battle of Guadalcanal itself had ended in November 1942, Japanese forces were not far away and still held many islands and airfields in the Pacific theatre. The Pacific War was still very much in the balance – and the threat of air attack in 1943 was constant.

On 7 April 1943, USS *Kanawha* was just getting under way in Tulagi harbour, as she waited to pick up naval escorts to take her back to her base at Pago Pago to refill her nearly empty tanks. She had refuelled American warships off Guadalcanal and then filled the fuel barge in Tulagi harbour.

Her escorts finally arrived, and she refuelled them before the group made ready to depart the harbour – just as reports came in of a large inbound Japanese force of aircraft. *Kanawha* was under way and moving to the mouth of the harbour at 1500 as the first aircraft appeared over Ironbottom Sound. This was a large Japanese raiding force comprising some 65 dive bombers and 110 escort fighters. The force had successfully evaded and penetrated the American air defences, and was now inbound to raid American shipping and positions on Guadalcanal.

A section of 18 Japanese Aichi D3A carrier-launched dive bombers (Allied reporting code name VAL) detached from the main flight and turned north to raid Tulagi. These single engine, manoeuvrable but rather slow dive bombers carried a crew of two – pilot and gunner – and could make about 240mph with a service celling of just over 9,000 metres (30,000 feet). They carried a single 550lb bomb mounted under the fuselage and two wing-mounted 132lb bombs.

Kanawha's naval escorts moved ahead of her and began to throw up a dense AA fire at the inbound aircraft – the gunners on *Kanawha* manned their 20mm Oerlikons and 40mm AA guns, waiting until the Japanese aircraft came into range.

Of the eighteen VALs that attacked Tulagi, five turned their attention to the lumbering and very valuable fleet oiler they spotted beneath them. The dive bombers began their bombing runs, diving straight down at breakneck speed towards the vulnerable oiler and scoring several hits with their 500lb bombs. One bomb hit a forward oil tank that extended under the bridge. A fire took hold that quickly spread along the deck. One or possibly two bombs hit her stern superstructure that housed the engine room below – the engine was wrecked and fires were started. The ship had been rendered unnavigable.

Several near-miss bombs exploded in the water beside her – shrapnel and the effects of the blast through incompressible water on her shell plating allowed water to begin to flood her hull. Her remaining fuel cargo was pumped into the sea to avoid it catching fire inside the ship, and with such dangerous fires raging the order was given for the crew to abandon ship.

As the Japanese attack ended and the aircraft disappeared, salvage and firefighting teams boarded the ship to try and extinguish the fires and save the valuable oiler. They managed to put the fires out in the forward section of the ship despite some ammo cooking off and exploding. The 190-foot long, 840-ton minesweeper USS *Rail* took *Kanawha* in tow to the west side of Tulagi, where around midnight she was beached with her bow onto the submerged sand reef that connects the small islet to Tulagi. Her stern remained afloat in deeper water – but at about 0400, the water flooding her innards overwhelmed her and she sank by the stern; the waterlogged weight of her stern dragged the bow off the reef and she slid down into deeper water.

She was completely submerged as dawn broke the next morning, 8 April: 19 of her crew had been lost in the attack.

◆　◆　◆

Present Day: The surface of the sea was a languid, oily calm – we were diving at slack water and there was no discernable current here in the harbour. One by one our party of divers rolled backwards off the dive boat, splashing heavily into the crystal-clear warm blue water. It was hard to believe that this idyllic location was the scene of such great tragedy in 1943, when 19 of her crew had perished – and that the large wreck of a World War II oiler was resting on the bottom 60 metres beneath us.

As I was about to embark on a mid-range dive of 60 metres, in addition to my back-mounted CCR I would be carrying two bailout tanks of additional breathing gas, slung one under either arm. The boat crew passed down my 11-litre aluminium (80cf) deep bailout of air with stainless steel carabiners banded onto it at top and bottom. The top clip was attached

Preparing for a deep wreck dive in Tulagi Harbor. (Author's collection)

to the D-ring on my harness on the left side of my chest, and the lower one was clipped to the D-ring on the lower left side of my buoyancy wings. I was then passed my shallow 11-litre deco bailout cylinder of EAN50, and clipped this to my harness and under my right arm in similar fashion. The standard practice amongst technical divers is that the oxygen-rich gases go under your right arm, and the more oxygen-lean deep bailout cylinders go under your left arm. This practice is repeated in onboard rebreather cylinders, where the oxygen side is your right side, and the breathing diluent of air or trimix is the left side.

Once we were all in the water, we started the descent – the wreck lay far below well out of sight in the darkness of the deep Pacific blue. Only the vertical coral-encrusted buoy line revealed the path we were to take into the depths.

Once I got to about 25 metres down, the darkness below me began to take form as the unmistakable outline of the forward section of a big ship sitting upright on its keel materialised out of the deep blue. We were falling down towards the foredeck, just in front of where the tall slender bridge superstructure would have been, positioned forward of amidships. The bridge itself seemed to have been well damaged by the fires from the oil tank here that was hit during the attack. The heat of the fires would no doubt have degraded and melted its structure, causing it to sag and lose much of its height. Her foremast in front of the bridge was still upright, and its two cargo booms were swung out at an angle over the starboard side of the ship, indicating that she had listed to starboard as she sank.

We moved up onto the fo'c'sle deck where the first 20mm Oerlikon in its gun tub position came into view. We then moved out into free water as we swam around the impressive bow, the vertical stem, iconic of the early 20th century, dropping straight down beneath me to the seabed far below.

After circumnavigating the bow, we moved aft along the starboard rail passing the dive-bombing damage, and the remains of the collapsed bridge, to the flat expanse of deck aft of the bridge, which was peppered by oil pipes and tank hatches. With the bottom time for the single-tank open-circuit divers now almost up, the dive was turned here, and we made our way back forward, rising up to meet the foremast and the downline. The deco trapeze suspended beneath the dive boat was already visible high above us in the beautiful visibility. Compared to the two-hour decos we sometimes do back home, shivering in 6°C water, it was only a pleasant 30 minutes of deco before I was hanging in the water on the surface beside the boat, unclipping my bailout cylinders from my harness webbing and passing them up to the waiting hands of crew and other divers.

Once we were all back aboard, Neil powered up the boat and took us into Tulagi Bay to Raiders Hotel and Dive Center. This is a beautiful, sympathetically designed and recently built, clean modern hotel and dive centre – seemingly surrounded by thick jungle on a shoreline lined with small wooden buildings. After a few cups of fine tea, we ate a lovely meal and rested up for a full three-hour surface interval before the afternoon dive.

Later in the week, as we had only seen the forward half of the ship, we returned to dive the stern section. The weather was perfect again – the jungle-clad shoreline and the underwater reef linking Tulagi to the islet seeming relatively close to our west.

We picked up the submerged stern buoy, and very quickly the crew dived, secured our boat's head rope through its eye and tied it off to the cleat on the boat. I busied myself switching my CCR on, letting the integral wrist computer go through its boot-up menu as it checked the three O2 cells, the two oxygen controllers, the internal batteries and the CO2 scrubber temperature stick that runs through the container holding the scrubber material and gives you a visual display on your handset as to how the scrubber is performing. The red and green visual displays on my heads-up display (HUD) clipped onto the mouthpiece hose just in front of my left eye blinked and went to a uniform green. The unit was ready – it was time to dive.

I rolled backwards off the boat into the water, and was passed down my two bailout AL80 cylinders and clipped them off under my arms. I moved away from the boat and as the other divers entered the water I just hung in free water on the surface, trying to film with the water level halfway up the lens of my underwater video camera, to catch them splashing into the water both above and below the surface in the same shot.

Once we were all ready, I dumped the air from my buoyancy wings and began to drift slowly down beside the downline. There was again no sight of the wreck below – all I could see was the familiar coral-encrusted buoy line descending straight down into the depths.

Like a skydiver I freefell down beside the buoy rope – adjusting and regulating my descent by bleeding air into my buoyancy wings when needed. Gradually the unmistakable form of the massive oiler swam into view far down below me.

The good underwater visibility revealed the large ship stretching as far as the eye could see in either direction – and we seemed to be coming down on the port side of the ship. Almost directly beneath me, just inboard from the port bulwark rail at the side of the ship, I could see a 20mm Oerlikon cannon in its tub. The expansive deck ran off towards the other side of the ship almost 60 feet away.

The free-swinging Oerlikon cannon was fitted in a flexible mount, being manually aimed by a gunner. The Oerlikon was designed in 1939 and began to be installed aboard U.S. Navy ships from 1942 onwards to replace the Browning M2 machine gun which had limited range and stopping power. The Oerlikon became an iconic sight aboard naval vessels during World War II, and in its role as an anti-aircraft (AA) gun it provided effective dense fire at around 300 rounds per minute (rpm) at short ranges of up to 1.5 kilometres, at which range heavier guns had difficulty tracking targets. Many versions of it are still in use by navies around the world today.

As the war progressed, as ranges to attacking aircraft increased and the Japanese turned to night attacks, it was found that the Oerlikon performed poorly in comparison to the 40mm Bofors autocannon. The Bofors could knock down an enemy aircraft at long range before it could release its weapon, whereas the Oerlikon could only knock down an aircraft when it was a lot closer and had possibly released its weapon. There was a saying in the U.S. Navy at the time, that when the 20mm Oerlikons opened fire, it was time to hit the deck. The Oerlikon was largely abandoned later in the war due its lack of stopping power against heavy Japanese aircraft and Japanese kamikaze attacks.

As Oerlikons were only fitted to U.S. ships from 1942 onwards, these had only been fitted to this old lady shortly before she met her demise in April 1943. This gun was pointing directly up to the sky and I initially thought it was frozen in time at the moment of the attack, firing against the attacking dive bombers. I later learned that these finely balanced guns returned to this upright position when not in operation, and that this made high elevation use simpler and more practical.

Immediately inboard beside the gun platform I could see the pitched roof of an engine room, its skylights all open. Oilers and tankers of this era always have their engine machinery

Stern defensive gun tub on USS Kanawha. *(Author's collection)*

aft of the oil tanks at the stern – so now I knew exactly where we were: on the port rail near the stern.

We swam down the port rail along the side of the ship towards the stern, and very soon the breech of a large 5-inch defensive gun, its barrel pointing dead astern, came into view in a curved sponson mount which projected out from the side of the ship. Inboard of it, a larger AA gun stood in its gun tub, its barrel also pointing up to the distant surface. The 5-inch gun was a major and powerful gun, and would have been devastating against any submarines that might try to close to a firing position on the surface or as the oiler outran the slower sub. With the great stability of this large oiler, this gun would have been much more accurate than the deck gun on a smaller, more mobile submarine. In the centre of the fantail directly at the guardrail was another AA gun, pointing upwards in its tub.

As I swam aft alongside the long 5-inch gun barrel, we started to drop down over the port side of the fantail where a single row of brass portholes was dotted around the sweep of the stern. Some 10 metres below me I could see the seabed, a slight silty haze at the bottom.

The shell plating of the stern was well corroded, and the heavy weight of one brass porthole had pulled a section of corroded shell plating off the hull at one of its ends. The section of plate had peeled off and swung outwards with the porthole embedded in it to rest at 90 degrees to the hull; the weaker rotted steel shell plating will soon lose the struggle with gravity and the porthole will fall to the seabed below at 60 metres.

Moving further round the stern I could see the ship's name, *KANAWHA*, in large embossed brass letters ringing around the fantail. Sadly, the porthole that had pulled off the section of shell plating seemed to be taking the initial *K* of the name with it.

I moved around the fantail and then started forward along the starboard bulwark rail, quickly approaching the end of the 7-metre-long barrel of the aft-facing starboard 5-inch gun in a mirror image of the port 5-inch gun set up. Moving forward, I could make out a number of ready-use 5-inch shells stacked beside it.

The open-circuit divers, diving a single AL80 tank, were now starting to move back towards the downline to ascend – making sure they had sufficient air left to reach the shallows safely. Unconstrained by open-circuit demands on my CCR, I signalled to the other divers that I was going forward. I'd told them topside that I would do so, so that they wouldn't be alarmed. I kicked my fins and began to swim forward along the starboard rail before moving over to the centre line of the ship. I soon relocated the pitched engine room roof sitting atop the collapsed single-storey stern superstructure with the Oerlikon tub beside the shotline to port, where the dive had started. Looking upwards, I could see a necklace of divers at various stages of ascent above me.

I moved further forward from the engine room roof, swimming over a scene of devastation – perhaps she had taken a bomb hit here. I spotted a large rectangular hatch used for lowering large engine and boiler room fitments, and peering down into it I could see engine room catwalks deep down inside the engine room. Tempting though it was, so near to the end of the dive and now solo, I didn't want to venture too deep and rack up massive deco when the others would be getting out of the water. So I continued to move forward from the engine access hatch and found the collapsed smokestack lying on its side, leading directly to its circular opening down to the boiler rooms below.

Glancing to port and starboard I noticed that a number of lifeboat davits here on the boat deck were in the swung-out position – the boats had had plenty of time to launch after the attack.

In complete solitary silence, with only the sound of my own breathing in the CCR breathing loop, I finned forward from the smokestack. The collapsed stern superstructure soon ended with what would have been the drop down to the main weather deck of the tanker. Forward of the stern superstructure the mainmast still rose vertically on the centre line, with a derrick cargo boom goosenecked to it and swung out to port, to rest over the port rail. The classic small raised deck hatches common to oilers and tankers were dotted about the deck, their lids missing and each allowing access to an oil tank directly below. Large fixed deck oil pipes ran here and there along the weather deck, designed for loading and unloading her oil cargo, and controlled by the large circular turn valves that were still in place.

I pressed on forward on my own in the eerie and complete silence of the depths. Diving on a rebreather is so silent compared to open circuit, where the regulator is noisy – as are the bubbles. I soon spotted the port side amidships AA gun tub, and in the distance across the ship on the starboard side I could see a similar starboard AA gun tub.

By now I had spent a good 30 minutes on this deepish wreck, and it was time to call the dive and return to the downline to ascend. I began to swim aft, retracing my steps from the amidships AA gun tubs over the smokestack opening and the pitched roof of the engine room. As I moved aft, a large shark swam out of the latticework of the collapsed stern superstructure and inquisitively swam near to me before giving way, turning and slowly swimming off into the distance. I moved over to the port bulwark rail, and very soon spotted the port aft Oerlikon tub and beside it, the downline leading up to the distant surface.

I started to move up the downline and towards my first decompression stop. Far above me I could see divers on the trapeze carrying out their own decompression. As I slowly made my way up the line, I reached the transfer line and followed it up and across to the deco trapeze where I carried out my deco as the other OC divers completed their longer deco stops.

You can follow this dive on my YouTube channel here:

Deco over, as I surfaced I unclipped my bailout tanks and passed them up to the boat crew, climbed up the ladder and got into the dive boat. There were still some OC divers in the water doing their own deco, so I started to chat about the wreck to the surfaced divers in the boat. As we did, from the direction of the tropical rain forests of Guadalcanal, the most amazing dark cumulonimbus clouds were forming, towers of cloud rising to incredible heights and beginning to come our way. Massive torrential rain showers are a feature of living beside these large islands – Guadalcanal itself is some 90 miles long and 25 miles wide and creates its own weather systems and regular tropical downpours. As the sun beats down on the land and sea there is significant evaporation and the pressure rises. Typically, tropical downpours are more intense in mountainous areas, like Guadalcanal and on the oceans, and small flat islands get less rain than large, mountainous islands like Guadalcanal.

We watched as the dark clouds began to obscure Guadalcanal itself – and then gravity won; the warm air became unable to support the moisture that had been raised, and the clouds began to discharge their moisture. It began to rain – and rain.

We looked towards Guadalcanal across Ironbottom Sound and just saw a wall of grey cloud and rain moving towards us, the rain battering the surface of the sea. Very soon it was upon us, the energy of the rain drops causing splashbacks several inches high as they hit the water – in Scotland we call it 'stottin down'. We all took such shelter from the deluge as we could under the boat's sun canopy, but still got pretty soaked. But within 20 minutes or so it was all over – just as the last divers, unknowing of what they had missed, got out of the water. We headed back over to Raiders Hotel in Tulagi for another of their fantastic lunches and copious amounts of tea before trying to rest up and pass a three-hour surface interval.

You can see what we got caught in on my YouTube channel here:

By about 1230, it was time to head off to the next dive site, a Japanese Kawanishi H6K flying boat – Allied reporting code name Mavis. It lay in 34 metres off the small Gavutu Island, just short of three miles east of Tulagi.

On 7 August 1942, the first day of the Battle of Guadalcanal, Tulagi with its wharf and seaplane slips was seized by U.S. Marines, along with the smaller islands such as Gavutu, where some 13 Japanese seaplanes and flying boats were based – this casualty was one of them. I had written about the Mavis for my other books, but had never seen one up close and personal, so this was going to be another special dive for me. There were reputedly more than 10 such Mavis wrecks on the bottom in this natural harbour – the one we were going to dive was one of the best preserved.

The Mavis was a large 84-foot-long, long-range flying boat that was deployed by the Japanese to the Pacific in 1938. The distinction between flying boat and seaplane is that a flying boat rests with its fuselage in the water, like a boat. A seaplane rests on wing floats and has its fuselage held out of and above the water.

Powered by four large Mitsubishi Kinsei 1,000hp wing-mounted air-cooled radial engines, the Mavis had a top speed of 210 mph. They had excellent endurance and could undertake 24-hour patrols with a long range of 4,100 miles. They could carry a 1,000kg (2,205lb) bomb load and were used for long-range bombing missions in South-east Asia and the south-west

Pacific. From bases in the Dutch East Indies they were able to range over a large section of Australia.

The H6K Mavis was well armed, with a 7.7mm machine gun in the nose, a 7.7mm machine gun in the spine, two more 7.7mm machine guns set one on either side of the fuselage in hull blisters, and a 20mm cannon in the tail turret. But the Mavis was a 1930s design – and as the war progressed it became vulnerable to the new breeds of fast and agile American fighters as the Allies retook Japanese-held islands and could base fighters there.

This particular Mavis was believed to have been sunk by U.S. Navy aircraft at its mooring on the first day of U.S. attacks, 7 August 1942. It had only been rediscovered by divers around 2001.

As I dropped through the water column, very quickly the lines of this famous flying boat started to materialise from below in slightly hazy but good visibility of about 25 metres.

We were descending beside a fixed line that was moored to a concrete weight placed well off the wreck, to protect it. As the aircraft came into view, I was able to leave the downline and swim over and down towards the nosecone that was pointing towards me. The Mavis was sitting perfectly upright, her wings extending at either side to rest on her wingtip floats on a gentle sandy slope.

I was immediately struck by the huge size of this lumbering brute of an aircraft – no wonder they became vulnerable to Allied fighters. The nose cone seemed huge, extending far out from the cockpit, such that it must have obscured the crew's visibility of what lay below; take-off and landing must have been challenging. Peering into the tight twin-seat cockpit, which still held its side-by-side seats, controls and instruments, I imagined what it must have been like to fly this huge plane.

The framework of the port wing was intact, the aluminium rotted away in places to reveal its basic but rugged box-like 1930s style air frame. Both port wing engines were still present, their propellers unbent, indicating that she sank at her moorings and didn't crash into the sea after flight. The innermost starboard engine had fallen from its mount and now rested on the aft part of the cockpit – the remainder of the starboard wing was gone.

As I moved aft, the size of the aircraft revealed itself fully – it was all there and it was possible to glimpse inside the fuselage through the hull machine gun blisters before moving aft to the iconic twin tailfin, aft of which was the tail gunner's position.

◆　◆　◆

The days were passing quickly now as I steadily racked up a number of dives on the famous World War II wrecks of Ironbottom Sound, thanks to Neil Yates, Tulagi Dive and the immaculately slick diving they laid on. The next day's dive would be on the wreck of the American *Gleaves*-class destroyer USS *Aaron Ward* (DD-483), which sits in about 70 metres of water less than 1,000 metres from Tinete Point of Nggela Sule in the Florida Islands on the north side of Ironbottom Sound.

Rising at the standard 0600, I breakfasted and walked round to Tulagi Dive for 0700 to quickly prep my CCR, analysing the gas in the 3-litre diluent and oxygen cylinders that I would use for the day. I'd replaced the used sofnalime scrubber material that forms most of the stack of the rebreather in the centre of my back, the night before after I'd finished the day's diving.

On a rebreather, when you exhale the exhaled gas passes over your right shoulder in a corrugated hose and is fed in at the bottom of your rebreather stack, which holds the scrubber canister.

The exhaled gas passes up through the stack, and the scrubber material – which resembles cat litter – strips the dangerous carbon dioxide (CO_2) by-product of your respiration from the exhaled gas.

The exhaled gas, now cleaned of the CO_2, then passes into a small chamber, where it is analysed by three oxygen sensors to determine how much oxygen you metabolised in that breathing cycle. Once that's calculated, the solenoid switch is triggered, and the correct amount of oxygen is injected into the breathing gas mix before the gas passes over your left shoulder on the inhale side of the loop.

A stack full of sofnalime scrubber on my Inspiration Vision rebreather lasts for about 180 minutes' diving. However, if I'm doing a deep dive I always like to have fresh, unused scrubber in my unit. A CO_2 hit is the last thing you want underwater. In the tropics, for mid-range diving, I change out my scrubber sofnalime every four dives.

The other divers for the day were beginning to congregate on the pier, and Neil soon had Tulagi Dive's boat loaded. We cast off the mooring ropes and in an instant were zipping across the familiar 24 miles of Ironbottom Sound to the Florida Islands.

Nggela Sule was garrisoned by the Japanese in April 1942 as they began to move towards establishing a seaplane base on neighbouring small island of Gavutu, where we had dived the Mavis flying boat the day before. On 7 August 1942, the Allies began their Guadalcanal Campaign with the 1st battalion of the 2nd U.S. Marine Regiment landing on the island to provide cover for the assault on neighbouring Tulagi Island.

The USS *Aaron Ward* is a famous ship, the second to bear the name of Rear Admiral Aaron Ward, who served with distinction in the United States Navy in the late 19th and early 20th century. He served in the short Spanish–American war of 1898, and died aged 66 in 1918.

The *Aaron Ward* was laid down in February 1941 in New Jersey, and launched on 22 November 1941 – she would have but a short sea career before she met her fate in Ironbottom Sound.

The 2,060-ton destroyer was 348 feet long with a beam of 36 feet. Powered by twin screws she could make 35 knots, and was fitted with four 5-inch dual-purpose (DP) guns set in single turrets: a super-firing pair forward and a super-firing pair aft. She also carried six 0.50-inch guns, four 40mm Bofors AA cannon, and five 20mm Oerlikon AA cannon. She

The Gleaves-class *destroyer USS Aaron Ward (DD-483) was bombed and sunk on 7 April 1943. She now rests upright in 70 metres. (National Archives)*

carried a quintuple 21-inch torpedo tube launcher set on a swivel mount between her two smokestacks – thus able to fire her torpedoes from either beam. She was fitted with six depth charge projectors and had two roll-off depth charge tracks leading to her stern.

As the Pacific War exploded in December 1941, the *Aaron Ward* formed part of the screen for Vice Admiral William S. Pye's Task Force 1, the core of which comprised the escort carrier *Long Island* and four battleships. Escort carriers were smaller and slower than fleet carriers, and carried fewer planes, and were less heavily armed. But they could be cheaply and quickly built as required when fleet carriers were scarce.

Task Force 1 steamed west from San Diego with *Aaron Ward* in the screen as the Battle of Midway developed from 4 June 1942, reaching a point 1,200 miles west of San Francisco. The Battle of Midway ended on 7 June 1942, allowing the escort carrier *Long Island* to be detached on 17 June – the *Aaron Ward* screened her on her voyage back to San Diego.

On 30 June 1942, the *Aaron Ward* was despatched to Hawaii and then to the Tonga Islands. Thereafter she was sent to Guadalcanal where she was involved in a number of contacts with the enemy that culminated with her being severely damaged by Japanese warships. She had to be taken in tow for temporary repairs at Tulagi before a return to Pearl Harbor for permanent repairs.

Aaron Ward was able to rejoin the fleet on 6 February 1943 and began convoy escort duties. On 7 April 1943, she was providing convoy escort bound for Tulagi when warnings of an impending air attack were received. *Aaron Ward* was ordered to detach from the convoy to cover the tank landing ship LST-449 off Togoma Point to the east of Honiara on Guadalcanal Island itself. Present on LST-449 was a certain Lieutenant John F. Kennedy (who would later become president of the USA) on his way to take command of the motor torpedo boat PT-109.

As the *Aaron Ward* rendezvoused with the tank landing ship, LST-449, lookouts on *Aaron Ward* observed a dogfight over Savo Island up to the west – and then spotted three enemy dive bombers attacking out of the sun. The destroyer moved to flank speed and opened fire with her 20mm Oerlikon and 40mm Bofors AA guns, and with her 5-inch main battery.

Japanese bombs scored a direct hit, along with several near misses. Near misses could be just as deadly as a direct hit – the force of the explosion carrying through incompressible water could blow in and tear the shell plating of ships, and cause flooding.

One near miss caused flooding of the forward section of the ship, whilst a second near miss burst shell plating to the engine room, disabling electrical power to the four main battery 5-inch guns and to the Bofors 40mm weapons. Gunners at the main battery turrets and the 40mm gun tubs moved to local fire control from their own positions.

A third near-miss bomb exploded in the water on the port side, holing the after engine room. The ship slewed to port as she lost power, and she was attacked by another flight of dive bombers, taking two further near misses.

The damage to her hull was now catastrophic – her buoyancy was fatally compromised and she began to sink. The minesweepers *Ortolan* and *Vireo* took her in tow and attempted to beach her on a shoal near Tinete Point off Nggela Sule. At about 2130 however she sank stern first into 70 metres of water, only 600 yards away from the shallow water shoal.

Her wreck was rediscovered by divers in 1994 and is now one of the most popular Guadalcanal dives.

Neil swung the dive boat to a stop as we approached the wreck site, and we were soon tied off to a submerged buoy. The sea was a flat oily calm, visibility was good, and although it was just after 0800, the jungle-clad hills of the islands nearby were a cacophony of noise.

We got kitted up and once I was ready I just sat still and pre-breathed my CCR for a few minutes watching the PO2 readouts on my wrist computer as I breathed in and out. A pre-breathe is a simple safety precaution to take with rebreathers – if your CCR is going to malfunction, or heaven forbid you've got the wrong gas in your cylinders, it's better to find out and have the incident while you're sitting safely in the boat rather than in 70 metres of water. Everything looked to be working smoothly, so I rolled backwards off the boat into the water.

My bailout deep AL80 cylinder and my bailout EAN50 deco cylinder were passed down to me as I floated immobile in the water beside the boat. The dive had been timed for slack water and there was no noticeable current. I clipped the cylinders onto my webbing harness under either arm. I was using a weak trimix as diluent today, to reduce nitrogen narcosis on the deep part of the dive.

Once all the divers were in the water, we collected at the downline and started the descent into the deep blue beneath. As usual there was no sign of the wreck below – just the white buoy line leading down into the darkness until it disappeared.

I pressed on down into the depths beside the downline. My surroundings got progressively darker and gloomier, but before long I started to make out blurred manmade straight lines far beneath me – Nature doesn't do straight lines underwater. Soon these blurry lines were morphing into the wreck of this famous World War II American destroyer. It was sitting upright in 70 metres of water with the deck at just over 60 metres.

The downline was tied off to the hull abaft the aftmost smokestack and just forward of the two aft main battery 5-inch guns. Even although I was still 10–15 metres above the wreck, now I had my bearings I could leave the downline and swim down the last way to the wreck. I arrived at the starboard bulwark beside a twin 40mm Bofors gun which had fallen on its side, the two large barrels projecting out over the bulwark. The Bofors seemed much more robust than the slender 20mm Oerlikon barrels seen in profusion on the *Kanawha*.

We began to swim forward on the starboard main deck in the space between the bulwark rail at the side of the ship and the long thin superstructure inboard, some of which was collapsing. We passed to starboard of the aftmost smokestack, the deck here strewn with ship's fittings and sections of plate that had fallen from above.

Immediately forward of the aftmost smokestack, between it and the forward smokestack, was the quintuple Mk 15 swivel 21-inch torpedo launcher. The launcher was secured fore and aft, and the starboard side outboard tube door was half-open whilst the other doors were closed. The length of the tubes was impressive – some 8 metres. The American Mk 15 contact torpedoes carried a 825lb warhead but were much inferior to the Japanese Long Lance torpedoes of the time. The Mk 15 had a range of 6,000 yards (3.5 miles) at 45 knots, and a maximum firing range of 15,000 yards (8.5 miles). The Japanese Long Lance torpedo had an effective firing range of 22,000 metres (13.6 miles) at 48–50 knots and a maximum range of 40,400 metres (25 miles) at 35 knots, and carried a larger 1,080lb warhead. Doors opened into the deckhouse beneath the launcher, and portholes were studded along its length.

As we moved further forward, I saw the foremost smokestack had fallen to starboard, with sections of it now lying on the seabed. The foremast had also fallen to starboard, and had come to rest on top of the smokestack. Collapsed standing rigging ran over the side of the ship to fixings high up the foremast. Two lifeboat davits just forward were in the swung-in position.

We continued swimming along the main deck, and very soon the bulwark swept up one deck level to the foc'sle deck, abreast the bridge superstructure. The top levels of this superstructure had collapsed down, although the walls, dotted with portholes, were more intact lower down.

Just in front of the bridge, the No 2 super-firing 5-inch gun turret could be found, its barrel pointing dead ahead over the lower No 1 gun further towards the bow on the foc'sle deck. U.S. Navy ships numbered their big guns starting from No 1 at the bow, aft. British Royal Navy ships called their big guns A and B turrets forward (A the foremost) and X and Y turrets aft, with Y turret being the aftmost.

As we moved forward, No 1 gun turret swung into view on the centre line of the foc'sle deck, its single 5-inch barrel pointing upwards at an angle of about 30 degrees. The armoured doors on either side of the turret were hanging open.

We pressed on forward, knowing that the bow was near. To my surprise the complete foc'sle deck forward of No 1 turret had sagged downwards for a few metres and then rose up again at quite a steep angle towards the stem. The bows of ships are some of the strongest parts of a ship, and the stem of this ship was fallen slightly back upon itself. The historical narrative records that the ship sank by the stern, so there is no way the ship could have righted herself, so that the bow could have contacted the seabed first. In any event it was unlikely a strongly built warship would suffer damage like this from such a short journey from the surface 70 metres above. So this could possibly be wartime damage from a near-miss bomb almost directly underneath the stem, or from the bow being held up on a slope as the rest of the ship settles. Down the side of the ship, the starboard anchor was still tight in its hawse.

At this point, given the depth, it was time to turn the dive. We retraced our steps to the downline to begin the slow ascent to the surface and complete our decompression before we could safely exit the water. It had been a stunning dive on a famous shipwreck.

You can watch this dive on my YouTube channel here:

Another lunch break at our familiar haunt of Raiders Hotel and Dive Center followed – a seeming oasis surrounded by the jungle of Tulagi. After our standard three-hour surface interval there, the second dive of the day would be on the World War II wreck of an American Consolidated PBY Catalina flying boat. After seeing a Japanese Kawanishi H6K Mavis flying boat the day before in fine condition, this would be another special treat – especially as it was only found a few years ago and remains in very fine condition.

The Catalina flying boats served extensively during World War II with America and the Allies – they were tasked with anti-submarine warfare, patrol bombing, search and rescue mission and convoy escort. They were so tough and reliable that they continued in use from the war right through until the 1980s. These remarkable craft had a wingspan of 104 feet and were powered by two Pratt & Whitney radial engines – unlike the Kawanishi H6K Mavis, which had four engines. The Catalina had a max speed comparable to the Mavis of 196 mph – but a shorter range of 2,500 miles compared to the 4,100-mile range of the Mavis.

Consolidated PBY
Catalina flying boat.
(National Archives)

The Catalina carried a crew of ten and was fitted with three 7.6mm machine guns, two in the nose turret and one in the ventral hatch at the tail, and two 12.7mm machine guns, one each in a blister on either side of the fuselage, aft of the wings. The Catalina could carry 4,000 lbs of bombs or depth charges.

In September 1943, the Catalina we were to dive was returning to Tulagi in the evening after recovering a downed airman, Lt Fred William Howard. As the Catalina touched down on the water of Tulagi harbour it struck a small boat that was travelling between Tulagi and Gavutu Islands. The Catalina somersaulted and began to sink – all the crew and Lt Howard were able to escape safely from the upside-down aircraft. The PBY righted itself as it sank and came to rest perfectly upright on its fuselage and wingtip floats in 34 metres of water on a sandy bottom.

We dropped over the side of the dive boat and began the familiar ritual of our descent. Very soon in the fine but slightly hazy visibility of about 30 metres, the PBY swam into view beneath us – the fixed buoy on the site was attached to a concrete block well off the nose cone of the wreck to protect it.

I left the downline and swam over and down towards the nose cone. Whereas the Mavis was a large aircraft with a massive bulky nosecone, the PBY was completely different. If the Mavis looked a clunky 1930s build, the PBY looked smaller, much sleeker and more modern.

I arrived at the armoured nose turret at the front of the nosecone – its twin 7.6mm machine guns (MG) were missing. Immediately abaft the turret was the two-seat cockpit, the perspex glass long gone. It was very close, just a few feet, behind the twin 7.6mm MG nose turret. The steel frames and armour back rests of the crew seats were still in place, along with the flight pedals, controls and instruments.

Immediately aft of the cockpit, the 104-foot-span wings were still *in situ* – seemingly massive in comparison to the remainder of the aircraft. The port radial engine had fallen from its mount to the seabed, but the starboard engine was still held in its mounts. The thin riveted aluminium sheeting of the wings was still present, and looked in remarkably good condition. There was no coral on it – corals detest the taste of aluminium and aircraft wrecks are always clean in comparisons to rusted steel shipwrecks.

I began to swim out the port wing and very soon came across the radar antenna, like a modern-day TV aerial, pointed dead ahead of the craft. I moved out to the end of the wing and found it stopped very abruptly as though sheared off above the float, which rested on the seabed. In flight, these floats retracted upwards to form the smooth outermost tip of the wing – very clever.

I swam round to the aft edge of the wing and moved back inboard towards the aft portion of the fuselage, which although suspended aloft in its active days, had now deteriorated, cracked and sagged to the seabed. The port waist blister was open, and the twin 12.7mm machine gun had fallen to the seabed whilst the machine gun with its armoured gun shield still remained in the starboard blister. Boxes of rounds for the machine guns were scattered around.

The fuselage ran aft along the seabed to the tail fin, and both horizontal stabilisers had sagged to rest their tips on the seabed; the vertical stabiliser was missing.

As I turned the dive and began to head back slowly up the aircraft towards the downline, I felt it had been another stunning dive – on an aircraft that seemed so modern and slender in comparison to the large, cumbersome Japanese Mavis.

You can watch this dive on my YouTube channel here:

After a week of hitting the stunning Ironbottom Sound wrecks suddenly my last day's diving was upon me – and after the morning wreck dive the group decided to do a coral and fish dive called the Tunnels – I don't know what was wrong with me! There were two circular holes about 3–4 metres wide in the reef flat at a depth of about 15 metres. The holes drop vertically through the reef, widening as they go until you bottom out at about 40 metres and exit onto the reef wall. There were a lot of sharks about, which came in for a good look at us.

For more adventurous and experienced divers, it is possible to dive the famous destroyer USS *Atlanta*, which was sunk by enemy action on 13 January 1943 and now lies in about 130 metres. This famous vessel was discovered in 1992 in an expedition led by Dr Robert Ballard (famous for finding the wreck of RMS *Titanic* and the *Bismarck*), using a remotely operated vehicle (ROV).

Diving it is a serious undertaking which needs a lot of planning, and sadly on this bounce week of mine this wreck would not be on the agenda. It was with a heavy heart that I stripped down my CCR and managed to get it and all my dive gear packed into my 23kg hold bag and cabin bag for the long trek home to Scotland via Brisbane, Sydney, Seoul and London to Aberdeen.

9

TRUK LAGOON 1944

Task Force 58 – Operation Hailstone
The sunken legacy

C huuk Lagoon (as Truk Lagoon has been known since 1990) is without exception, in my opinion, the greatest wreck diving location in the world. Although I covered the history, the wrecks and dive details in *Dive Truk Lagoon – the Japanese World War II Pacific Shipwrecks* published in 2014, a lot of people have asked me about the backstory to this book, how it was written and about the things that didn't make it into the final manuscript. There are many personal stories behind the writing of any book such as this – things that don't make it into my wreck manuals such as *Dive Truk Lagoon*, which by their very nature are very factual, and have to be an ordered review of the wrecks. So, here are some of the more personal tales that ended up on the cutting room floor – but first, I need to set the scene for those who have perhaps heard of Truk Lagoon but don't know the incredible story of how it became such a magnet for divers from all over the world.

Chuuk Lagoon is a coral atoll that rises up from the deep blue oceanic depths of the western Pacific and is part of Chuuk State, one of the Federated States of Micronesia, an independent sovereign island nation formed in 1979 that consists of four states, Yap, Chuuk, Pohnpei and Kosrae. These island states form part of the larger Caroline Islands group and comprise some 607 islands in total that are scattered over almost 1,700 miles just north of the equator to the north-east of New Guinea.

Chuuk Lagoon is situated within a roughly circular barrier reef that is about 40–50 miles in diameter and has a circumference of about 140 miles. There are only five passes or channels through the barrier reef that are big enough to be navigated by large vessels.

In the centre of the lagoon are a collection of large jungle-covered islands – with countless other smaller islands scattered elsewhere across the lagoon. Think of your idyllic iconic desert island, golden beaches fringed by palm trees – that's what the smaller Chuukese islands are like.

The outlying islands haven't really been developed much: only the main island of Weno (previously known as Moen) has electricity and its own water supply. All the other Chuukese islands have no electricity, and are dependent for water on natural springs and rain. The way of life on those islands hasn't changed that much in a very long time.

Diving in Chuuk Lagoon is a truly eye-opening experience, particularly for cold-water Scottish divers like myself. The water is 29°C and crystal clear, with visibility in some areas up to 200 feet or more. The clean white sandy seabed of the lagoon is littered with countless relics of World War II – more than 40 naval and merchant ships, a submarine, countless aircraft and several *kaiten* human torpedoes. In the main, all are the legacy of a two-day American fast carrier air raid by nine carriers of Task Force 58 on 17 and 18 February 1944. The raid was codenamed Operation Hailstone, and was intended to neutralise Truk as a naval and air threat to Allied operations in the Pacific.

When you enter Chuuk's warm water from a dive boat and start to descend to a wreck, you are leaving the 21st century and voyaging back in time – to a time when Chuuk Lagoon was known as Truk Lagoon and was the great Japanese forward naval stronghold and airbase of World War II.

At the start of World War II in 1939, Truk Lagoon became the Imperial Japanese Navy's (IJN) 4th Fleet Base. In 1942, it became the IJN's Combined Fleet base, acting as Japan's main forward naval base in the South Pacific.

As the war turned against Japan, and America pushed west across the Pacific in late 1943, assaulting Japanese island garrisons, Japanese commanders believed that an American amphibious assault on Truk would take place, just as it had done at Tarawa, Kwajalein and other outposts. To counter that threat, the Imperial Japanese Army (IJA) arrived in numbers in January 1944, to find that Truk was poorly equipped to defend itself. The IJA quickly established numerous coastal defence and anti-aircraft gun positions, and heavily fortified and defended Truk with a military infrastructure of roads, trenches, bunkers, caves, five airstrips, seaplane bases, a torpedo boat station, submarine repair centres, a communications centre and a radar station. The Japanese garrison grew to almost 28,000 IJN service personnel and almost 17,000 IJA service personnel. A significant portion of the Japanese fleet was based there at this time, and it was a focal point for supplying and resourcing the Japanese Greater Asia Prosperity Sphere islands and territories that had been seized during the initial phase of the war.

The five navigable passes through the barrier reef into the lagoon were heavily defended – flanked by large coastal defence gun emplacements set high on the mountainous islands either side of the pass. With the exception of North Pass and South Pass, which the Japanese would use, the other passes were closed off by mines.

The possible beach landing sites on the islands were made into killing zones with beach mines, obstacles, firing positions, artillery and mortar emplacements for short-range engagements. Any attempt to take the islands of Truk would cost the attackers a heavy toll in human life.

Heavily fortified, Truk Lagoon now served as a safe, sheltered and well protected forward base for the IJN main battle fleet. Super-battleships such as the *Yamato* and *Musashi*, as well as strategically vital aircraft carriers, cruisers, destroyers, tankers, tugs, gunboats, minesweepers, landing craft and submarines, all thronged her waters.

In addition to the frontline battle fleet, a large number of naval auxiliary transport ships, often converted former civilian passenger and cargo vessels, worked as tenders for the fleet and its submarines, carrying naval shells, ammunition, torpedoes, stores, spares and everything needed to keep a battle fleet in operation. Other naval auxiliaries constantly arrived, carrying munitions, tanks, trucks, land artillery, munitions, beach mines and the like, all destined to be landed to fortify Truk's land defences and to resupply troops there. Other vessels called in at Truk to victual, carrying similar cargoes onwards to other island garrisons. Landing craft were heavily used to ferry cargo from the huge auxiliaries to the shore.

Fortification of Truk Lagoon before the war had been carried out in utmost secrecy, with no foreigners being allowed near the islands. At the beginning of the war, the Allies *suspected* Truk was being used as a fortified anchorage but had little hard intelligence and no real idea of the scale of the Japanese operation.

When Japan entered the war in December 1941, the initial surprise of the Japanese attacks had allowed them to conquer quickly and easily vast swathes of Asia. Malaya fell, Singapore fell, the Philippines fell. But by the middle of 1942 Japan had started to lose significant battles such as the Battle of the Coral Sea and the Battle of Midway. Japan was forced to abandon its offensive strategy and concentrate on holding onto its most vital gains. Once the huge American war machine got going, the Allies started to take back the Japanese conquests one by one.

Guadalcanal was seized in late 1943 and then, between November 1943 and February 1944, American forces began the Gilbert and Marshall Islands Campaign, seizing Tarawa and Makin in the Gilbert Islands and Kwajalein, Eniwetok and Majuro in the Marshall Islands, the latter becoming an important base for the powerful U.S. Pacific Fleet. Even by this stage, the Allies still had no idea of the scale of what lay in Truk Lagoon – but with Truk now in range of reconnaissance aircraft, the first long-range overflight by two U.S. Navy Liberator reconnaissance aircraft took place on 4 February 1944. The sight that met American aviators' eyes was astonishing. Large elements of the Imperial Japanese Navy lay below – battleships, cruisers, submarines and carriers thronged its waters, along with a huge number of naval auxiliaries, merchant supply ships and tenders.

Although the two U.S. Navy reconnaissance aircraft had approached the lagoon undetected, once they were overflying the lagoon they were spotted and fired on by AA guns from shore batteries and from ships. Caught napping, Japanese fighters were scrambled to intercept – but the fast U.S. reconnaissance aircraft were able to outdistance the fighters and escape with their priceless reconnaissance photographs intact. When those were returned and analysed, U.S. military planners, now on the front foot in the Pacific War, immediately started planning a massive fast carrier raid.

U.S. Navy Liberator long range
reconnaissance aircraft. (National Archives)

The carriers of Task Force 58 in line astern. (National Archives)

Japanese commanders on Truk now knew their well-kept secret was out of the bag. The valuable heavy IJN warships and carriers immediately left the lagoon – some steaming to the relative safety of their western Pacific base at Palau. Others headed for Singapore or Japan.

Many smaller warships, destroyers, light cruisers, tugs and patrol boats stayed behind, along with a mass of naval auxiliaries, all busily engaged in offloading their war supplies – they could not suddenly leave with their supplies still on board. Their holds and decks were still packed with their cargoes of tanks, beach mines, land artillery, land vehicles, vital aircraft and spare parts, shells for the big land guns and for the warships, together with massed amounts of small arms ammunition – munitions all destined to be offloaded onto Truk to help fortify the islands against the U.S. amphibious assault Japan believed would soon follow.

Left: Douglas SBD Dauntless dive bomber. (National Archives)

Right: Grumman TBF Avenger torpedo bomber. (National Archives)

A U.S. naval assault force of nine aircraft carriers, with a screen of battleships, cruisers, destroyers and submarines, was immediately formed and designated Task Force 58. TF 58 was a fast carrier strike force that would become the main U.S. striking weapon in the Pacific War. The core of TF 58, the nine aircraft carriers, fielded more than 500 combat aircraft such as Grumman F6F Hellcat fighters, Grumman TBF Avenger torpedo bombers, and Douglass SBD Dauntless and Curtiss SB2C dive bombers. The nine carriers were split into three smaller task groups, and each task group was protected by its own independent screen of battleships, cruisers, destroyers and submarines.

Within a week of the reconnaissance overflight of Truk, Task Force 58 had been assembled and moved out west in total secrecy towards Truk Lagoon. Combat air patrols of fighters patrolled the skies above the task force, alertly looking for any Japanese reconnaissance aircraft that might reveal the presence of the powerful American striking force.

Despite the size of the strike group, the clandestine approach of Task Force 58 to its striking position 90 miles east of Truk was not detected by the Japanese. On the evening of 16 February 1944, TF 58 arrived in darkness at its holding position in total secrecy. The element of surprise was complete. The attack would begin early the next morning, codenamed Dog-Day Minus One.

Dog-Day Minus One

The following day, 17 February 1944, one hour before dawn, Operation Hailstone began in darkness around 0440 local time. In the skies above, as combat air patrols circled above the carriers, a total of 72 Grumman Hellcat fighters launched in darkness from the nine carriers to carry out the initial fighter sweep and establish air superiority.

As the groups of Hellcats launched from their individual carriers, they flew to one of three designated rendezvous points well away from the lagoon. The fighters formed up there into their combined strike groups before moving off towards Truk at their scheduled times, flying low at 1,000 feet to keep beneath Japanese radar.

Once the strike groups were 15 minutes' flying time from Truk, they started to rise up to their designated patrol altitudes. Whilst some strike groups attacked naval and ground

Left: A U.S. Navy Grumman F6F Hellcat fighter prepares to launch from its carrier. (National Archives)

Right: Japanese shipping on fire in the IJN Fourth Fleet anchorage. Nearly all these ships would be sunk during Operation Hailstone. (National Archives)

targets, other groups would patrol the altitude levels above, looking for any Japanese aircraft that might attempt to attack.

Between 0520 and 0530, Japanese radar based in Truk detected the approach of a large formation of aircraft – but although the highest state of alarm was ordered, the initial Japanese analysis of the radar reflections concluded that a large land-based bomber formation was approaching. Japanese commanders did not appreciate that such a large force of aircraft could be carrier-based.

After about 45 minutes of flight, the first of the 72 Hellcats swept over Truk Lagoon, making an unchallenged run around the whole lagoon before encountering any enemy fighters. The Hellcat fighter sweep was so swift and unexpected that, with uncanny parallels with the Japanese attack on Pearl Harbor, many of the Japanese aircraft were caught by surprise on the ground and destroyed. Others scrambled to get airborne, but were shot down as they lifted off. But soon, large numbers of Japanese fighters were rising into the air for what would become one of the largest aerial dogfights of World War II, as hundreds of fighters fought it out above the beautiful lagoon.

Whereas at the beginning of the war the Japanese Zero was almost untouchable by Allied fighters, being more manoeuvrable and with a rate of climb three times more rapid than any U.S. aircraft in theatre, the Zero (or Zeke) was now simply outclassed by the more modern Grumman F6F Hellcat. The Hellcat was better protected and faster, and packed a bigger punch than the now outdated Zero.

The great dogfight was quickly over and with U.S. air superiority established, throughout 17 February and the following day, 18 February (code name Dog-Day), U.S. carriers launched wave after wave of dive bombers and torpedo bombers to attack the now vulnerable shipping and land fortifications, each striking group escorted by a flight of Hellcat fighters. The strike groups met limited anti-aircraft fire from the lightly armed merchant ships below and from the island land defences. It was a one-sided battle – and more than 40 ships were sent to the bottom of the lagoon over the two days of Operation Hailstone.

The majority of the sunken vessels lay in water that was too deep for Japanese salvage divers and operations. The ships and their valuable cargoes were lost to the Japanese war effort, and simply left on the bottom to rust.

Seiko Maru is on fire and down by the stern in the centre of this combat shot, whilst a torpedo streaks towards the stern of Hokuyo Maru to right of shot. (National Archives)

After Japan surrendered in 1945, Truk was one of the six districts of the Trust Territory of the Pacific Islands that was administered by America under charter from the United Nations from the end of the Second World War until 1986. The world moved on and tried to rebuild, and the sunken ships of Truk Lagoon were forgotten about by the outside world.

The local Trukese islanders however could not forget the ships – they had to deal with the toxic legacy of a war they had never sought. Many of the ships held large cargoes of oil and aviation fuel, and these pollutants leaked from the submerged hulks in significant quantities right up to the 1970s and 1980s. Although the rate of leakage tailed off in the 1980s, several of the wrecks continued to leak smaller amounts of oil and fuel to the surface until the 1990s, causing skin burns to locals and divers. Nowadays the leakage seems to have largely diminished but on calm days you can still see droplets of oil breaking the surface above many of the wrecks and spreading out in a kaleidoscope of colour. There can on occasion be a noticeable smell of gasoline above some of the wrecks, as a rotted 55-gallon fuel drum from World War II finally releases its contents. From time to time, divers still get skin burns from contacting invisible aviation fuel leaching from oil drums.

The Japanese wrecks, still holding their valuable war cargoes, lay in deep water in a very remote location and were never deemed worthy of commercial salvage. They were simply left on the bottom of the lagoon, slowly rusting over the coming decades, untouched by Man. Nature took control, covering the wrecks in an explosion of life with a myriad of corals and sea creatures – the wrecks had become artificial reefs.

In 1969, the legendary French oceanographer Jacques Cousteau and his team mounted an expedition to Truk Lagoon. Many of the ship's locations and identities were unknown at this time – but armed with old charts and taking advantage of local knowledge from Trukese islanders, they began to locate and identify some of the wrecks. The resulting mesmeric and haunting television documentary 'Lagoon of Lost Ships' was an instant hit around the world and is still available today. Such was the power of Cousteau's name and the potency of the underwater images he broadcast that the diving world's attention focused on the wrecks of Truk Lagoon.

Divers started to visit the lagoon in increasing numbers, and in 1976 *National Geographic* carried a 40-page feature on Truk by Al Giddings. A local Trukese, Kimiuo Aisek, who had been a young man on the island when the U.S. attacks took place, opened the first dive shop in Truk Lagoon in the 1970s and went on to rediscover a large number of the lost ships in the lagoon; he became a deeply revered and pre-eminent figure in Truk Lagoon diving for many years. But even so, at this point only a fraction of the ships sunk had been rediscovered.

Klaus Lindemann – whose name would become synonymous with Truk Lagoon – joined Kimiuo later in the 1970s and together over several years from 1980 onwards they conducted extensive searches. In their first season, they found 16 new wrecks, and subsequently went on to locate even more. Collating much historical and first-hand information, Klaus Lindemann published the first edition of his definitive book, *Hailstorm Over Truk Lagoon*, in 1982, with an updated second edition in 1991.

You may wonder why Japan held islands such as the distant Pacific islands of Truk and Palau in the first place. These islands were not seized by Japan with the opening shots of World War II, but possession of them had come about during World War I, 30 years earlier.

It is a sad fact that the peaceful people of Truk and Palau have had to suffer being subjected to colonial power from several distant countries for hundreds of years. Spanish explorers reached what are now called the Caroline Islands around 1540, naming them Las Carolinas in honour of King Carlos II of Spain, and the Carolines became part of the Spanish Empire. The Spanish however did little to develop their distant island colonies.

In 1898, Spain and the United States went to war as a result of American intervention in the Cuban War of Independence. There had been revolts in Cuba against Spanish rule for some years and the USA was strongly behind Cuban independence. The trigger for war came on the night of 15 February 1898 when the American battleship *Maine* visited Havana harbour on a flag flying expedition – at a time when the Spanish regime was resisting an armed uprising by nationalist guerrillas.

Without warning the American battleship, safely at anchor in the harbour, suddenly blew up, killing 260 officers and men. The cause was immediately believed to be a Spanish mine – and seizing the moment, America sent Spain an ultimatum demanding it surrender control of Cuba. This ultimatum was duly rejected, and both sides declared war.

America attacked Spain's distant and vulnerable Pacific territories in a short and unequal war that only lasted 10 weeks and was settled by the 1898 Treaty of Paris, signed after the American annihilation of a Spanish fleet in Manila Bay in the Philippines.

The treaty gave America temporary control of Cuba, and ceded indefinite colonial power over Puerto Rico, Guam and the Philippine Islands from Spain. Spain decided to completely pull out of the Pacific, and the following year, 1899, she sold her holdings, including Truk and Palau, to Germany, who gave Palau its present name.

Despite these islands being under distant German ownership, in the coming years Japanese commercial traders managed to create a stranglehold in import and export around the islands. They expanded maritime freight and passenger services until they had established a virtual trade monopoly. Japan was becoming increasingly dependent on imported raw resources and the commodities its own home islands lacked. It wanted to develop an empire to rival the established colonial powers, and eyed covetously large parts of the Pacific that were rich in the natural resources she so badly needed.

When World War I began in 1914, Japan saw the opportunity to further expand its power and influence in the Pacific region. Honouring an Anglo-Japanese mutual aid military alliance dating from 1902, Japan declared war on Germany and joined British forces in an attack on the German-held colony of Tsingtao on the coast of China. (This was the required limit of Japan's support on the ground – the alliance only required her to assist Britain in operations in India and the Far East.) At sea however, the Imperial Japanese Navy went further and in 1917 sent several escort vessels to assist the hard-pressed Royal Navy with convoy escort duties in the Mediterranean.

Whilst ostensibly honouring the alliance provisions, Japan was in reality moving to protect its Pacific shipping routes, taking the opportunity to seize advance German bases such as Truk and Palau that would be strategically important in any future conflict with the USA. Special Japanese naval task forces, the South Seas Squadrons, were formed, and on 7 October 1914 the first landings were made in the Palaus at Koror. There was little German resistance.

Following the successful occupation of the German Pacific territories, Japan declared that it would not allow any foreign ships (including those of her allies) to enter the waters of its newly occupied territories. Japan established the Provisional South Seas Defence Force, and naval districts were set up at Palau, Yap, Saipan, Truk, Ponape and Jaluit under a command based at Truk. The Japanese navy took on immediate administration of the islands, issuing laws, promoting Japanese enterprises, instigating public works programmes and beginning to indoctrinate and educate the indigenous population in the Japanese way.

Whilst the Armistice of November 1918 halted the fighting, the terms of a final settlement would eventually be agreed with the Treaty of Versailles of 28 June 1919 in which the League of Nations was established by the victorious Allies. When the ex-German colonies in the Pacific were divided up amongst the Allies, the Japanese were mandated the islands they already controlled, such as the Marianas Islands, the Caroline Islands and most of the Marshall Islands. No open-door trade policy was put in place however, and Japan was able to effectively seal off the islands from the outside world.

The USA was deeply alarmed at the League of Nations policy on Japan, which it increasingly saw as a threat to its power and influence in the Pacific. President Woodrow Wilson refused to recognise the proposed Japanese mandate over the islands, insisting that the islands should be militarily neutral. The United States would not be part of the League of Nations.

The Versailles Peace Treaty provided that 'no military or naval bases shall be established, or fortifications erected in the territory'. A militaristic Japan, however, ignored this proviso and, intent on creating a Pacific empire to rival the main European powers, embarked on a programme of fortification of her South Seas island territories such as Truk and Palau.

Over the next two decades Japanese influence in the islands expanded – Japan controlled the infrastructure of schools, courts, hospitals, building, agriculture and mining. A process of making the islands Japanese was under way. Palau became the chief centre for Japanese South Seas commerce, shipping and air transport.

Realising that the creation of a Pacific empire would bring Japan into conflict with America, Japan's strategically important island territories were transformed into powerful forward battle stations, like unsinkable island aircraft carriers. The Truk islands and the sheltered lagoon were turned into a fortified harbour and resupply station. Truk became a key possession in the Japanese empire, whilst Palau, more than 1,000 miles to the west, became an important staging post and refuelling station for naval and merchant ships moving between the Japanese South Seas islands.

The first strikes of the Japanese offensive of December 1941 had been so successful – yet had been relatively cheap in casualties. The true weakness of American and British military power had been revealed by victories such as the assault on Pearl Harbor and the Fall of Singapore a few months later. Japanese commanders thus determined to embark on a second offensive aimed at seizing holdings in the Solomon Islands and Port Moresby on the southern tip of Papua New Guinea, to give Japan mastery of the air above the vital Coral Sea. Gaining control of these strategically important bases would prevent an Allied build-up of forces in Australia and would secure Japan's southern flank. The Japanese regarded the islands of Palau and the Marianas as forming the principal strong points in a chain of islands that were their last eastern line of defence.

If the assaults of this second offensive were successful, then in a second phase to the plan the Japanese Combined Fleet would cross the Pacific to annihilate the remains of the American Pacific Fleet at Pearl Harbor and capture Midway Island and the western Aleutian Islands. A ribbon defence anchored at Attu, Midway, Wake, the Marshall Islands and the Gilbert Islands would be set up, followed by the invasion of New Caledonia, Fiji and Samoa, to isolate Australia. If these conquests could be made impregnable, Japan hoped that, tiring of a futile war, America would negotiate a peace that would leave Japan as masters of the Pacific.

This second offensive, however, went badly wrong. In May 1942, Japan lost the significant Battle of the Coral Sea, where three of its carriers were damaged, and then in June Japan lost the Battle of Midway when four of its carriers and one cruiser were destroyed. Japan was forced to abandon its offensive strategy and concentrate on holding onto its most vital gains. Japanese planners had hoped to knock America out of the war quickly, having known from the outset that in a sustained war of attrition, Japan was doomed to be defeated by the massive resources of America.

The Pacific War would be a naval war, the greatest naval war in history, with mastery of the vast expanses of the Pacific the prize. Unknown to most, however, it was a time of great change in naval warfare. The end of the era of the battleship had already been heralded in December 1941 with the sinking, in one action, of the brand new British battleship HMS *Prince of Wales* and the battlecruiser HMS *Repulse* almost 200 miles north of Singapore by a massed attack by 85 Japanese torpedo and high-altitude bombers. Whereas in the past naval warfare had centred on the big guns of battleships, this Pacific war would be different – it would be an air war at sea. The Battle of the Coral Sea in May 1942 would be the first of these new-style actions, fought entirely between aircraft carriers, in which no ship sighted an enemy vessel.

Japanese commanders however failed to understand that their plans to carve out a Pacific empire depended on an adequate shipping supply system to support the distant perimeter – and on superior sea power to protect long lines of communication and supply shipping. Japan's merchant tonnage was insufficient and too inefficiently organised to meet the necessary sea supply requirements and she did not have the industrial capacity or manpower to create the additional merchant ships that would be required.

In addition, whilst Japan had initially displayed clear superiority numerically in aircraft and pilots, by April 1942 it had already lost 315 naval planes in combat with another 540 lost operationally. With unprotected fuel tanks, Japanese aircraft were very susceptible when hit, even by small arms fire. The fuel tanks would burst into flames, destroying the aircraft and killing the crew. In contrast, American aircraft had protected, self-sealing fuel tanks and armour to protect air crew. Whereas American pilots would often survive being shot down, Japanese air crew did not – and as experienced Japanese crew were lost, the quality of the crew replacements was noticeably lower.

The second offensive would fatally overextend Japanese military capabilities.

◆ ◆ ◆

When my good friend and regular dive buddy Paul Haynes and I were asked to present at OZTek 2013 in Sydney, we thought we might have a bit of a detour and come home to Scotland via Chuuk Lagoon. Now Chuuk isn't really on the way back home to Scotland from Australia at all – in fact it's completely the wrong way – but I'd been to Chuuk several times before, whereas Paul hadn't, and has had to suffer hearing all about it from me for years. So we decided to go.

I asked my good friend Ewan Rowell, who did most of the underwater photography for my early books, and who now lives in Perth, W.A., if he'd like to come to OZTek and then head up to Chuuk with us – and he agreed. And so the team of three musketeers was formed and after a whale of a time at OZTek in Sydney, the three of us headed up to Chuuk in March 2013.

I hadn't decided to write a book about Chuuk wreck diving at that stage, but once I'd got there, it became clear that although Chuuk is one of the world's great wreck diving locations, other than a couple of good but older books and some rudimentary line drawings of the wrecks done in the early 1990s, there was almost a complete lack of good hard diver information on the wrecks as they are today.

And so, on the long flight home - this time in the right direction via Guam, Seoul, London and Aberdeen – I decided to write *Dive Truk Lagoon – the Japanese World War II Shipwrecks*, and make my contribution to Chuuk wreck diving. Given the unparalleled number of large important wrecks at Chuuk, it turned out to be a particularly arduous and time-consuming project that involved a number of further visits to Chuuk.

Perhaps the most memorable was in March 2015 when Paul Haynes, Gary Petrie, Steve Pryor and I headed there. We flew into Seoul as normal from the UK, but as a result of a typhoon that had hit Guam, our flight down from Seoul to Guam was delayed and we were forced to take an overnight in Seoul.

We got a flight down from Seoul to Guam the next morning, but once we landed in Guam, on a Monday, we discovered that United Airlines had cancelled all the flights that day due to the typhoon. The typhoon had in fact now blown through (by this point we would, in Scotland, have called the wind a stiff breeze) but nevertheless for safety reasons all flights on from Guam that day were cancelled – including our onwards flight to Chuuk.

United Airlines kindly indicated that they could put us on the next available flight to Chuuk – which floored us when they told us it was five days later on the Friday. In disbelief, we did what we could to convince United Airlines, firstly to fly at once, but perhaps understandably they said no. There was another flight going out to Chuuk on Wednesday, but it was already full. In addition to booking us to fly to Chuuk on the Friday, United Airlines also put us on the standby list for the Wednesday flight, telling us optimistically that passengers often didn't turn up for these flights so we might well get to fly. We were told to arrive early on the Wednesday, check our bags in for the flight on our standby tickets, and then go through security and wait at the gate.

We checked into a hotel near the airport that day, and went to see Guam's sights. That didn't take long, and we ended up sitting on the windswept terrace of a beachfront hotel in blustery winds under a leaden grey sky drinking more beer than was probably good for us.

The next day, Tuesday, we went along to one of Guam's many gun ranges and got ourselves an hour's worth of shooting with a variety of weapons from a small Beretta through to a Colt 45 revolver. The owner was a particularly laid-back type of guy and gave us no instruction on the weapons before disappearing for an hour. We were left alone in the range – so Paul, who had been a small arms instructor during his time in the Royal Marines and Special Forces, stepped into the breach and sorted it out for us with some basic instruction. Whilst Paul was double-tapping the cardboard dummy at great speed, I found out that whilst I was good with the light and versatile Mk 16 rifle (famously used by U.S. troops in Vietnam) I couldn't hit a barn door at 10 feet with a pistol. We were given a single .45 round for the Colt 45 – when you fired that weapon you knew about it all right.

The next day, Wednesday, we were up very early in darkness for a taxi ride to the airport. Laboriously we got our bags checked in for the flight, always time-consuming when you've got a pile of technical diving equipment that raises suspicions. Once our bags were checked in, we went through Guam's tight U.S. security, suffering enormous delays in massive queues. But finally, we were through, and full of hope we walked along the tiled concourse to the gate.

Checking with the United Airlines officials at the gate, we learned that there were in fact four free spaces on the flight – so it looked like we would make the flight after all and only lose two days of our diving in Chuuk. Time ticked away slowly, as we clustered around the gate trying to befriend the staff so they might do us a turn, and mentally willing the gate to close so we would get the free spaces. Painfully slowly, the flight departure time approached. With 30 minutes to go until the flight it was looking good, the spaces were still free, we might get on.

Just as the gate was about to close, and staff were telling us we were about to be allowed to board, three Business Class, Gold card-carrying executives turned up in a last-minute fluster as standbys. Understandably they were given preference over us four travelling on economy tickets and were quickly boarded. That left only one seat for the four of us. We drew straws. Steve Pryor was in luck and would take the seat and get himself to Chuuk.

Paul, Gary and I resigned ourselves to waiting for the next available flight, which after all would be on Friday. Another two days of kicking our heels in Guam followed before we were able to fly down to Chuuk, after putting back our return flights to the UK so that we would not lose any diving there.

I had seen more than enough of Guam – but it was all forgotten about as our flight came in to land at Chuuk International Airport on the largest island of Weno. The approach to Weno airport is somewhat disconcerting for those of a nervous disposition. The plane comes in low, seemingly skimming the waves, to touch down on the extremity of the airstrip which had been extended to cater for modern aircraft, and which now juts straight out into the beautiful blue waters of the lagoon. It feels as though you are going to ditch in the water – like the Miracle on the Hudson. But it all went well, and after the guts of a week kicking our heels in Guam, we had finally arrived in Chuuk.

As the aircraft doors opened, the familiar tropical warmth wrapped around us as we walked the short distance from the aircraft across the concrete apron to Chuuk immigration. As we collected our gear – there is no baggage carousel – we were greeted by a smiling Cindy Hall who at that time was the mainstay at Truk Stop Dive Center and Hotel, where we would be staying and diving from. Whilst a number of fine liveaboard dive vessels work in the lagoon, there are only two land-based dive centres, Truk Stop and Blue Lagoon, both of which are set right on the edge of the lagoon and are only a few miles apart. Each provides accommodation in fine rooms, and has restaurants and bars. They each have a number of their own small fast dive boats bobbing at piers and pontoons, just a stone's throw from the rooms.

Chuuk is extremely well set up for divers – once you get there. Everything you need is on site, and other than doing a historical battlefield tour of land sites, divers tend to be out on the water all day and stay around the dive centre at night. Chuuk is quite a struggling state with high levels of unemployment – the roads aren't made up, there are no fancy stores or shops and no bars or restaurants that you would go out of the centre grounds to visit. Chuuk is about diving – period.

We loaded our kit into the back of the Truk Stop pickup and were soon bouncing our way along the dusty potholed roads through the main town and on to Truk Stop. The roads are hardly ever repaired and all the cars had to very painfully and slowly circumnavigate large potholes and pools of rainwater. There was one new section of tarmacadam roadway a few hundred metres long which had gone in since my last visit in 2013. Ironically, I learned it had been the source of a number of accidents, as drivers tended sped up on the good piece of road whilst the locals wandering across it were not expecting cars to be going that fast.

Our flight had got in about 1000 and so once at Truk Stop we checked in, showed our dive certifications and dive insurance, and then headed down with our dive kit to the wet dive area where Cindy had 3-litre cylinders of oxygen and air diluent ready for our rebreathers. Each of us was allocated our own drum of sofnalime CO_2 scrubber absorbent. We were also allocated a 7-litre bailout cylinder, which already had two stainless steel bands on it with large carabiner clips attached to them so we could sling it under our arm and attach it to suitable D-rings on our webbing harness.

We were each allocated a tall wet-gear locker that was right beside the plastic-covered prep tables used to build up your kit – and which in turn were literally about 6 feet from the water's edge. We soon had our rebreathers on the tables, building them up for the next day's diving.

Once our kit was prepped, we retired to the restaurant for a good bit of scoff and then sat in the open bamboo bar for a few beers as night fell and the inky blackness of a tropical night descended. As we finally crashed into our pits, at least we knew we were finally ready to dive Truk Lagoon the next day.

10

DIVING THE SHIPWRECKS OF TRUK LAGOON

Rio de Janeiro Maru, San Francisco Maru, Sankisan Maru
Shinkoku Maru, Aikoku Maru, Yamagiri Maru, Nippo
Maru, Hanakawa Maru and Katsuragisan Maru

W e rose at 0600 and headed down to the gear lockers, got our rebreathers out and did a final check over them before heading over to the restaurant for breakfast. Ropes off for our dive boat would be 0730. The practice in Chuuk is that, as most of the wrecks are at most about one hour away by boat (with many much closer), after the first morning dive – unless there is something special planned such as lunch on one of the desert islands – the dive boat comes back to the dive centre where you can top off cylinders with gas, change out sofnalime if necessary and have some time to relax, eat and rehydrate.

Once breakfast was done, we got kitted up into our wetsuits as dive centre staff trolleyed our kit to the dive boat. The Truk land-based dive boats are usually 25 feet long open skiffs with two massive outboard engines on them. Although they are open, a stainless steel-framed bimini covers the whole boat and keeps the harsh sun off guests – you simply cannot afford to be exposed to the sun out here for too long, so it's a case of hat, shades, wetsuit or T-shirt to travel in. Although it doesn't feel too hot once you are moving at speed in a fast dive boat, it is the tropics, and the sun is beating down on you at 32°C. Sunburn, heat exhaustion and dehydration are never far away from you, so shade is essential, as is covering up and having enough water to drink. Having a slash in your wetsuit whilst diving is de rigueur and an inevitable necessity.

Our favourite technical diving guide, Nuwa Paul, was allocated as our guide for the trip. It is Chuuk law that divers must be accompanied by a suitably qualified local dive guide who can show you round the wrecks but who also checks that nothing is being removed from them. Chuuk realises the value of their underwater museum, and although there has been some small-scale pilfering of the wrecks in the past by visiting and local divers alike, it is safe to say that most divers understand that it's a look but don't touch policy. The only thing you take is photos and memories.

I had dived with Nuwa on my last few visits to Chuuk – he was an extremely competent and knowledgeable diver, hard to beat. I shook him warmly by the hand and after a catch-up

141

chat, knowing that he liked to go deep, really deep, inside the wrecks, I told him that as this was our first dive of the trip I wanted him to go easy on us and not go wild inside the wreck we had chosen for the first dive.

Whilst it was a pleasure to be guided by Nuwa on this trip, sadly he would lose his life in a diving accident in Chuuk the following year.

Rio de Janeiro Maru

9,627grt passenger-cargo liner (1929)
IJN auxiliary transport (1940). IJN auxiliary submarine depot ship (1941)
IJN auxiliary transport (1943)

The wreck we had chosen for the first dive of the trip was the massive 9,627grt passenger-cargo liner *Rio de Janeiro Maru*, which lies on her starboard beam ends in 35 metres of water with a least depth down to her uppermost port side just short of 15 metres.

The *Rio* was 461 feet long with a beam of 62 feet and a draught of 26 feet, and could accommodate 1,140 passengers. Large cargo holds were set fore and aft of the long central superstructure. This elegant eight-deck passenger-cargo liner was built by Mitsubishi Zosenkaisha in Nagasaki in 1929, and is just one of the countless beautiful and largely intact wrecks at Truk Lagoon.

The *Rio de Janeiro Maru* was launched on 19 November 1929 and after fitting out afloat she was delivered to her new owners, one of the best-known Japanese shipping companies, the Osaka Shosen Kaisha Line (OSK) on 15 May 1930. The *Rio* had two screws that were powered by two 6-cylinder 2-stroke Mitsubishi Sulzer diesel engines, which gave her a cruising speed of 15 knots and a top speed of just over 17 knots.

The suffix *Maru* is found in the names of most Japanese merchant ships of the period and means 'circle'. Thus, as her name suggests, she was built to operate on a circular route from Japan via Hong Kong, Singapore and South Africa to South America, then on through the Panama Canal to the west coast of America before crossing the Pacific back to Japan.

In the run-up to war, the Imperial Japanese Navy requisitioned her on 8 October 1940 and converted her to an auxiliary transport – and then in 1941, to a submarine tender. Four 5.9-inch (150-mm) deck guns were installed, along with a range finder and anti-magnetic degaussing cables. She was attached to the Combined Fleet, and along with the light cruiser *Yura* and six submarines, she made up the 5th Submarine Squadron.

Port view of the 9,627grt passenger–cargo liner and submarine tender Rio de Janeiro Maru.

On 3 February 1944, filled with the munitions of war, she set off from Yokosuka in Japan, bound for Truk under escort by the *Mutsuki*-class destroyer *Yuzuki*. She arrived in Truk on 11 February 1944, just six days before Operation Hailstone.

As the dawn initial fighter sweep of 72 Hellcats burst over the skies above Truk on 17 February 1944, the *Rio* was at anchor in the southern sector of the 4th Fleet anchorage 400–500 yards to the east of Uman Island. She was struck by several 1,000lb bombs from U.S. aircraft during the first group strikes of the day, which caused severe damage and started fires aboard.

As the fires took hold around her fo'c'sle at the bow, some of the 5.9-inch shells for her defensive bow gun began to cook off – exploding and sending large chunks of shrapnel out through the shell hull plating of her hull. She began to settle slowly into the water, and took on a list to starboard.

She remained afloat throughout the remainder of the day – but just after midnight she finally succumbed and disappeared beneath the waves. When daylight came on 18 February, as American aircraft overflew the lagoon for Day 2 of the strike (code name Dog-Day) there was no sign of her.

◆ ◆ ◆

Listing to starboard as she sank, the *Rio de Janeiro Maru* landed on the bottom of the lagoon in 35 metres of water, on her starboard side, with her stern pointing to Uman Island. She was a big ship with a beam of some 20 metres, so her shallowest parts rise up to just 10–15 metres beneath the surface. At 461 feet in length she is one of the largest ships in the lagoon, and lying in such shallow water allows divers long bottom times with relatively little decompression penalty. She is a beautiful ship – and even today, more than 70 years later, although her superstructure is starting to collapse and fall downwards, her hull seems remarkably intact, the individual hull plates still easily discernable with thick degaussing cables running fore and aft along the hull just below the bulwark rail.

At the beginning of World War II, Germany developed a new type of magnetic mine that could detect the increase in the earth's magnetic field when the steel of a passing ship concentrates the earth's magnetic field above it – the steel hull of a ship is like a large floating magnet and has a large magnetic field surrounding it. As the ship moves through the water it either adds to or subtracts from the earth's magnetic field.

In November 1939, a German aerial magnetic mine was accidentally dropped at low tide from an aircraft onto the mud flats of the Thames estuary that were under direct control of the British Army, complete with a base and workshops nearby. British Admiralty experts were rushed from London – they already suspected that the Germans had developed magnetic sensors. Before approaching the mine, they carefully removed all metal items from their persons and used only brass tools, which had no magnetic signature.

The mine was duly disarmed and transported to Portsmouth, where the new German magnetic mechanism was finally uncovered and studied. The scientists discovered that the mine actually went off before the ship touched it – as with contact mines – the magnetic mine being set to explode at the midpoint of a ship passing overhead.

The firing mechanism, it was found, could be set to specific units of milligauss – the gauss being the unit of measurement of magnetic flux density (the strength of a magnetic field) and so named after the German mathematician and physicist Carl Friedrich Gauss.

The wreck of the Rio de Janeiro Maru lies on her starboard side in 35 metres of water.

Using the detector from the mine, the British scientists were able to study the effect of ships passing near to it. Once they understood the new weapon, the British scientists developed systems that induced a small 'N-pole up' magnetic field in ships, so that the net magnetic field was the same as the background. Thick steel cables were thus fixed to ships' hulls, running parallel with the main deck, around the whole length of the vessel. An electric current passed through the cables, neutralising the ship's magnetism, so the disturbance in the earth's magnetic field by the ship was cancelled out as nearly as possible.

The Germans used the gauss as the unit of the strength of a magnetic field in their mine trigger mechanism – and hence the Admiralty scientists started to call their magnetic mines countermeasure process 'degaussing', and the cables became known as degaussing cables. The Japanese had adopted the process, and distinctive degaussing cables can be seen running around the hulls of many of the shipwrecks in the lagoon.

The superstructure of this sleek elegant vessel has been collapsing in recent years, making the superstructure now quite dangerous to enter. In past years, when it was more intact, there were a number of entry points into the innards of this superstructure, which goes down (now horizontally) several deck levels – but the more recent collapsing has closed off many of these.

The *Rio* was built with a large composite superstructure, which rises up for four decks above the main weather deck. This held the navigation bridge at its highest levels to the front, and the engine rooms aft with passenger accommodation running aft along either side of the fireproof steel walls around the engine compartments – the engine casing.

Promenade deck walkways along the port side of the superstructure. Note the degaussing cables running along the hull below the bulwark. © Ewan Rowell

At maindeck level, rows of portholes line the sides of the superstructure leading back as far as the engine room. Promenade walkways on two decks run along either side of the long elegant superstructure, and passenger cabins, each with its own porthole, lead off these walkways – now entered through vertical doorways that lead to internal fore and aft corridors. The fires that raged throughout the ship consumed any wooden structures and decking.

The engine room itself can be entered forward and aft of the smokestack, and divers can find the Mitsubishi Sulzer diesel engines and bulkheads covered with switching panels, gauges and two telegraph repeaters.

The smokestack is still in place and still bears its OSK markings along with its steam whistle, running lights and fixed ladder. Several sets of lifeboat davits are located along the uppermost port side of the superstructure on the boat deck.

Notwithstanding my words to Nuwa to take it easy on this first dive, as we arrived down at the upwards facing port side of the hull he led us over the bulwark rail and down to a now horizontal door into the innards of the superstructure. He disappeared down the doorway, and Paul, Gary, Steve and I dutifully followed.

The swim down the corridor seemed to go on for about 50 feet before we entered into a wide-open area which was surrounded by a mangle of distressed catwalks that were bent out of shape – and steam pipes, large and small, ran all over the place. We were in the higher levels of the engine room, cocooned in a pitch blackness that was cut only by the beams of our dive torches, on which we were now totally reliant. It was disorienting to be deep inside such a large ship that is on its side. Horizontal doorways and corridors ran off in every direction, and staircases led from one deck to the next. I didn't want to lose Nuwa in here, so we stayed close on his heels.

Nuwa led us horizontally through a large space – the higher levels of the engine room – a maze of catwalks that were bent out of shape and ran at awkward angles. We swam aft over the internal section of the smokestack into another large space with more catwalks running at strange angles.

We were going aft and moving horizontally further down into the bowels of the ship, often squeezing through tight openings between pipes and fixtures where I had to get my chest right down to the base of the opening to allow the top of my CCR to squeeze through. It was pitch black in here, and the ship's interior was lined with fine silt. All the visible metal of her walls, roofs and decks was blackened by intense fires – there wasn't a single piece of wood; all had been burnt away.

As we moved aft and deeper into the ship, I spotted fractured ceramic mosaic flooring; most of the Japanese ships had this type of non-slip flooring in their galleys. Nuwa used his torch to light up a heavy steel door above us that had swung open and was hanging ajar down towards us. Below me lay a heavy metal sink that had tumbled out from above. He motioned with his torch beam for me to have a look inside the doorway, so I swam up to it and stuck my head and torch inside. It was the galley – the now vertical floor covered with mosaic non-slip flooring. High up above me were ominously large iron ranges and cooking stoves, which seemed to be hanging precariously and unnaturally on their sides. If one of those came loose right now and fell onto me I would be a gonner. It all looked so fragile inside there that I didn't venture further in. I let myself sink slowly downwards, out of the galley, making sure that I didn't knock anything that might fall down onto me.

We moved forward from the galley at the bottom of the ship, coming into another large space which had a number of white pressure gauges still in place beside large steam pipes, still wrapped in asbestos cladding. All exposed metal here was also thickly blackened from her wartime fires.

From here we swam along a metal catwalk, and as we arrived at a stairwell that led even further down to the bowels of the ship a now vertical white main switching panel gleamed in our torches, with some six sets of identical large switching gear, presumably one for each of the six cylinders of her Mitsubishi Sulzer diesel engine.

Nuwa turned and swam horizontally over a metal handrail and then down the tight stairwell. Gary followed him, his body with his rebreather on his back just able to make it, by a few inches, through the stairwell. There was no natural light from anywhere penetrating down to these levels – the engineers here would have been deep below the sea level outside, as they worked to keep the engines running smoothly. We were now far inside the bowls of this cavernous ocean-going passenger liner.

We began to carefully move forward – but very quickly we seemed to lose Nuwa. One minute he was there and the next he was gone.

As Gary, ahead of me, started to look around him, he caught my eye and I shouted through the breathing loop of my CCR "Where's Nuwa?" Gary replied ominously "I don't know."

We waited for a few minutes, expecting Nuwa to pop out of some corridor – but when there was no sign of him, I put my hand over my torch to blank out its light. I would never actually switch it off in these circumstances lest it choose that moment to fail and not come back on again.

Gary did the same and complete blackness consumed us. We calmly hung in mid-water inside the seemingly vast space of the engine room, staring in all different directions and slowly getting ourselves quite disorientated. We were so deep inside this massive superstructure that I thought we would have a hard time trying to find our way out ourselves. Corridors led everywhere; how would we know what was the right route? Although I was very familiar with ship layouts in general, corridors could have collapsed or be in the process of collapsing, doors could be closed. There was no straight exit from here right up the engine room to skylights – we were completely enclosed, deep inside this 75-year-old shipwreck.

A diver who enters a wreck that is not sitting on its keel must conceive of space differently than if simply walking around a ship topside. The *Rio* lies on her starboard side, so to try and understand where you are inside a wreck orientated like this you have to think in three dimensions. You look at what you're seeing – and then try in your mind to rotate it 90 degrees.

The starboard side bulkheads of rooms had become the floor of the spaces we were in. Decks were now impenetrable vertical sheets of blackened steel rising from below towards the port side of the compartments, which had now become roofs.

Normally, when you penetrate an unfamiliar wreck deeply, you lay a line in, so that you can follow it back out safely. But no laying of lines goes on in Truk Lagoon – the guides know the routes through the wrecks so well, you put your trust in them. But here, Nuwa was taking us into places so deep inside the wreck that he rarely visited them.

If you are not laying a line, you must remember everything you do – every little nuance of a turn in direction – for every movement you make has a consequence. A number of small movements can throw off your sense of direction and prevent you finding the way back out.

You remember every turn, every movement – up, down, along to the right, to the left. But we were so far inside the wreck and had made so many twists and turns, along corridors and down staircases, that there was no way we could remember all of this.

The scene unfolding before your eyes in a ship that lies on its side confuses your mind. It's hard to take it all in when your normal frames of reference are all skewed by 90 degrees. You try to memorise every obvious or recognisable piece of metal you see, to allow you to retrace your path through the twisted innards of the wreck to the illusive safety of clear open water outside. It may be safer outside – but you are still far beneath the surface of the water.

Serious wreck penetration requires ropes, reels and cave diving techniques. For those divers who don't reel in – and just wing it – danger lurks close at hand, as we were now finding out. Without ropes or reel, if you lose your bearings and sense of direction inside a wreck you will become disorientated, perhaps searching for the way out in the wrong direction. If your navigation slips … if your memory gets confused or falters … problems loom.

As soon as the worm turns and you think, 'Was it right here – or left?' you are in difficulty. One simple wrong turn takes you into an unrecognisable part of the ship, where you haven't been before. With nothing you recognise, it's simple to make yet another wrong turn, hopeful of seeing something familiar – but you just become even more lost, deep inside the rotting carcass of a ship that has lain at the bottom of the sea for 75 years. The futility of your situation flashes across your mind – the first flush of a panicked desperation courses through your body. You are lost inside the pitch darkness of a shipwreck.

A diver lost inside a shipwreck is in grave danger. Even when not lost, a diver is aware of a potential wave of panic lying just beneath the conscious. You may be in control, buoyancy nicely adjusted and all your equipment working – but you know that panic is never far away. And it just takes one small thing to start off a chain reaction that can lead to disaster. The mind, even whilst you are in control, plays an insidious game with you when you are lost in the bowels of a rotted shipwreck. In diving we say you are always only three breaths from death.

Once you start getting a bit paranoid inside a shipwreck it's easy to panic. Even thinking you're in trouble can cause unfortunate events to start to unfold. You worry about a myriad of potential problems such as entanglement in hanging electric cables or entrapment by some rotted bulkhead falling on you. The worm has turned – and you feel the first surge of panic rising. Suddenly your veneer of control seems wafer thin. You know the demon is there, waiting to snare you.

As panic sets in so your problems escalate – but even if you find your way out, the longer and the deeper you have been down the more the decompression time to surface stretches out. Gary and I were now in this danger zone – lost inside a huge wreck with no local guide.

After a few minutes of holding my hand over my dive torch to let my eyes adjust, down a corridor off to one side I saw the faintest chink of light from a torch beam – it had to be Nuwa. I motioned to Gary and together with Paul and Steve we swam along the corridor towards the light – finally meeting up with Nuwa. He told me later that he had become a bit disorientated as to where we were and had swum off to see if he could find the way out – perhaps the collapsing of the wreck had closed off one of his usual routes.

Very aware of the predicament I had found myself in, I was extremely relieved to meet up with him – the prospect of having to find my own way out from the bowels of the ship where corridors could be closed by collapsing was not appealing at all.

In the time we had been separated, he had managed to find a way out, and after navigating along more corridors and up staircases that were now on their side, I turned a corner to see a big, blue shaft of beautiful day light streaming in from outside the ship. We squeezed out of a small tear in the wreck's superstructure into open water after some 45 minutes inside the bowels of this great ship.

Undeterred by all this, we moved aft beyond the superstructure, and the accommodation gave way to the aft main deck and the two hatches for Holds Nos 4 and 5, which are separated by a large mast house from which the mainmast still projects horizontally. Hold No 4 contains coal and large circular artillery base mounts some 15 feet in diameter, which would be set in a hole dug in the ground that would then be infilled with concrete. The gun itself would then be set on this mount. Large artillery barrels, originally laid flat on the deck, now pointed vertically towards the port side of the hull above. Recoil chambers were scattered about – in all, a number of complete artillery guns were here in this hold.

Hold No 5 contains masses of bottles, most now loose and piled up on the lower side of the hold. Many are still stacked in their original wooden crates that are held between the ship's bottom frames and stringers.

A 5.9-inch deck gun is mounted on top of the poop deckhouse, its barrel pointing directly aft and looking down to the seabed here, ready-use shells are scattered underneath it. Near the very stern and directly above the rudder is the auxiliary steering position. The telegraph here has fallen over and is now held suspended upside down by its chains, flush with the vertical deck.

On the stern, the ship's name was easily legible in large non-ferrous letters. The *Rio* was a twin-screw vessel and both screws are still present, flanking the large rudder, another sign that salvors never worked these wrecks. Valuable non-ferrous props are the first things to be taken from a wreck, and are easy pickings. The large, uppermost, four-bladed port propeller dominated our group of divers as we clustered around it, seemingly small, insignificant specks of humanity beside it.

Two years previously, on my 2013 expedition with Paul Haynes and Ewan Rowell, as we swam around the wreck Nuwa had motioned for us to stop whilst near to one of the holds. He disappeared into the hold and a few minutes later reappeared tenderly holding a Japanese *katana* samurai sword. The sword had a thin film of verdigris on it but the steel was still pristine and it still had a point and a blade that could no doubt fulfil its intent today.

Samurai swords were greatly prized in Japanese society, and the art of making these swords appeared in Japan more than 1,000 years ago. Samurai swords have seen combat in many battlefields from the early days of the samurai warrior in mediaeval times to the Japanese invasion of China in 1937, when they were gleefully used, mostly on unarmed civilians. Japanese newspaper reports of the time carried photographs of the officers who had chalked up the highest numbers of beheadings of poor innocent Chinese civilians, such was the ancient hatred between Japan and China. In World War II, the swords were again used in battle in the South Pacific – and also for executing civilians and Allied POWs such as U.S. aircrew who had the misfortune to be shot down and captured.

During World War II, Imperial Japanese Army officers were allowed to take their family katana sword with them on military duty, the handle and scabbard being militarised. Those Japanese NCOs who did not have their own family swords or did not want to take their own sword into combat were provided with a machine-made sword, often in aluminium. Family swords often displayed the mark of the maker and their title on the tang. But the machine-made swords did not have such markings: their blades had a serial number stamped on the upper section followed by an arsenal stamp.

The katana in the *Rio* was not an aluminium forged sword, and was possibly a sword that was highly treasured and passed from one generation to the next. This sword may have been hundreds of years old and if made by one of the ancient famous sword makers would be worth many hundreds of thousands of dollars. I later heard that the sword was landed to avoid it being stolen from the wreck by other less scrupulous divers, Chuukese or visiting. I had heard that it had been buried – until a rumour reached me that it is now believed to be in use for cutting mangroves on an outlying island.

After having circumnavigated the aft portion of this huge wreck, we moved forward near the seabed towards the bow, passing the large superstructure amidships. The foremast loomed into view, still jutting out horizontally from a masthouse and winch platform on the deck in between the hatches for Holds Nos 1 and 2. Two cargo derricks ran forward and two aft from the foremast – these had swung down so that their ends rested on the seabed.

Moving into Hold No 2, we spotted more circular artillery base supports, destined for installation on the land, similar to the bases in the aft holds. Recoil chambers and a number of large bore artillery barrels can be found in the deeper recesses of the hold.

We passed the hatch for Hold No 1 and arrived at the now vertical fo'c'sle deck bulkhead. On the fo'c'sle deck itself, a 5.9-inch gun similar to the aft gun was mounted – its 24-foot-long barrel angled slightly down towards the seabed. The fo'c'sle spaces beneath the gun were used for storing ordnance for the gun and housed a hydraulic system to transfer shells up to the gun deck. The hull plating is cracked at the collision bulkhead, and the fo'c'sle appears to be at a different angle to the rest of the ship, with the decking and bulkheads aft of the bow gun torn and twisted. We were able to swim through the crack here into the innards of the fo'c'sle.

Near-miss bomb compression to the hull shell plating was visible on the upper port side of the fo'c'sle. It is believed that fire took hold here, weakening the structure of the ship, and that some of the 5.9-inch shells for the bow gun stacked in Hold No 1 cooked off from the heat of the fire and exploded, blasting fragments outwards from inside the ship. There are blown-out sections of shell plating on the lower starboard side here that are large enough for divers to swim through. On the upper port side, the hull is peppered with exit holes where shells have detonated inside the hold, sending shrapnel straight out through the 1-inch steel shell plating of the hull, curling the hull plates backwards like wet cardboard. Flooding through the large holes in her starboard side here may well have contributed to the starboard list as she sank. As with the engine room spaces, the walls, frames and stringers of Hold No 1 and the fo'c'sle compartments also show clear evidence of fire blackening.

We exited the fo'c'sle spaces and moved round the stem itself and up onto the higher shallower port side of the hull. The port anchor chain is run out through its hawse pipe over the bow and down to the seabed.

Several feet aft of the hawse, the name of the ship in large non-ferrous bronze letters can be made out in both two-foot-tall Roman letterscript and *kanji*, interspersed with portholes with their glass still intact. There are not many shipwrecks in the world where you can still find the non-ferrous ship's name still on them – mostly the valuable lettering, much prized by wreck divers of old, has been ripped from the ship. But with no salvage work carried out to the wrecks of Truk Lagoon, the ship's name still visible on the wrecks is a relatively common feature of diving here.

We finned slowly along the high port bulwark rail back towards the superstructure and the downline. It had been quite a dive for our first shakedown dive – a two-hour run time with 45 minutes inside the superstructure. But we were already off-gassing as we moved along the top of the wreck, essentially carrying out our decompression whilst exploring the higher sections of the wreck. By the time we were ready to ascend we had blown off a large chunk of our decompression.

You can watch this dive on video on my YouTube channel here:

◆   ◆   ◆

San Francisco Maru

5,831grt passenger-cargo vessel (1919)

IJA Transport (1941)

The 5,831grt *San Francisco Maru* is another of the world's greatest wrecks to be found in Truk Lagoon. She was launched on 1 March 1919 and was 385 feet long with a beam of 51 feet and a loaded draught of 27 feet.

Cargo was carried in four main holds, two forward and two aft of the split superstructure, with a smaller bunker, Hold No 3, set in between the bridge and engine room superstructures. Each main hold was divided into an upper 8-foot high tween deck and a larger, deeper lower main storage space.

After 20 years of civilian service, on the outbreak of war in the Pacific in December 1941, Japan suddenly had a pressing need for more cargo shipping. So although the *San Francisco Maru* was an old ship by then, she was requisitioned by the military.

After a couple of years of war duty, in January 1944 she departed Yokosuka, near Tokyo, in a supply convoy with a cargo of military hardware destined for the fortification of Truk against the anticipated U.S. assault. She carried a deck cargo of small Type 95 HA-GO light

The 5,831grt passenger-cargo vessel and naval auxiliary San Francisco Maru.

battle tanks, army trucks and bulldozers, whilst her holds were filled with staff cars, petrol tankers, hemispherical anti-invasion beach mines, fuel drums and crates of ammunition, aerial bombs, aircraft engines, Long Lance torpedoes and ordnance.

The supply convoy arrived safely in Truk on 5 February 1944, and *San Francisco Maru* anchored in the 4th Fleet anchorage, south-east of Dublon Island (now called Tonoas). She remained in the anchorage whilst the rest of the convoy departed Truk to resupply other garrisons on 12 February.

On 17 February 1944, Dog-Day Minus One, as Operation Hailstone began she was attacked by several U.S. aircraft at her 4th Fleet anchorage during the early morning group strikes.

The following day, Dog-Day, she is believed to have been hit by a number of 500lb bombs from USS *Essex* Grumman Avenger torpedo bombers, and was set on fire amidships. One bomb went straight through the starboard side of the hull close to Hold No 5, leaving a large gash in her side from her water level to the gunwale. The detonation of bomb caused the whole aft section of decking to sag down and collapse. Another bomb blew a hole in the port side of Hold No 4, deformed the shell plating and brought down the mainmast. With such catastrophic damage to her shell plating and hull, water flooded into her two aft holds and dragged her under by the stern.

◆　◆　◆

Today the *San Francisco Maru* is still packed full of ordnance and war cargo, earning her a long time ago the nickname of the Million-Dollar Wreck. She rests upright in 60–63 metres of water with a least depth to her bridge superstructure of about 45 metres. With the main deck at about 50 metres, she is one of the deeper popular wrecks in Chuuk. Her hull is in good condition, barring the bomb damage aft, but her main superstructure has heavily degraded. The wooden structures and fitments of the upper bridge levels were consumed by the fires that raged aboard her during the attack, leaving only the skeletal framework of the spars and struts of the upper levels and bridge wings. These too have largely disappeared in recent years, rotting and collapsing to leave only the steel rooms of the lower levels of the central structure and the structural framing of the side spaces.

After our standard 0600 rise and the routine fettling and prepping of our rebreathers, we headed into the cool of Truk Stop's restaurant for breakfast. As we ate, our gear was ferried down to the boat by dive crew, and once breakfast was done we were soon skimming south from our Weno Island base past the jungle-clad island of Tonoas (wartime Dublon), to the 4th Fleet anchorage. The water of the lagoon was a smooth deep blue.

None of the boats use GPS units in Truk – they are expensive to buy in the first place, and they don't cope well with the humid atmosphere and so become an unnecessary repair or replacement. The wrecks are simply found in the time-honoured way by lining up land points – transits. Using only distant transits passed from skipper to skipper, our crew guided us to the site of the sinking, and soon we had spotted the small white wreck buoy about 6 feet under the surface. Deep enough to let small island boats pass by without fouling their props.

Once we were dressed into our CCRs with bailout cylinders slung under our arms, we rolled backwards off the dive boat into the warm embrace of the 29°C lagoon water. The visibility where the wreck lies is nearly always, well … magnificent.

The wreck of the San Francisco Maru lies in 60–63 metres, still filled with her war cargo. Just abaft her bow gun platform, Hold No 1 contains hundreds of hemispherical beach mines whilst two tanker trucks are stored in Hold No 2. In front of the bridge superstructure are three deck cargo Type 95 HA-Go light battle tanks. Hold No 5 bears the scars of the fatal wound that sank her, the hold still filled with dozens of Long Lance torpedoes.

Inset: Type 95 HA-Go Japanese light battle tank

We righted ourselves and began the descent down beside the line to the wreck. The downline was tied off to the shallowest part of the wreck, the bridge superstructure, and as we descended the deep blue beneath us materialised into the famous shipwreck.

The buoy line was tied off on the port side of the bridge. Off to my right was the aft part of the ship, and to my left the bow section. As I arrived down at the wreck I could see just in front of the bridge superstructure on the port side, a deck cargo Mitsubishi Type 95 HA-GO light battle tank that was resting partly over the port bulwark rail, its barrel pointing forward and slightly depressed. These small manoeuvrable tanks were used for infantry support, and were not designed to take on the larger Allied tanks such as the American Sherman.

The Type 95 carried a crew of three men: a commander, a machine gunner and a driver. Only the commander was seated, in the cramped, hand-operated turret. He was responsible for loading, aiming and firing the 37mm main gun, the barrel of which was removable for transport and replacement and could fire two types of shell, high explosive and armour-piercing. (In contrast, the Sherman had a larger 75mm M3 gun or a 105mm Howitzer M4, and armour up to 7 inches thick.) Secondary armament on the HA-GO consisted of two 7.7mm light machine guns, one mounted in the hull and the other in the turret. As I looked over the port rail to the seabed far below I spotted a large steamroller lying on the seabed.

I dropped down to the main deck; there was no gunwale, just the rotted remains of guardrails. Hold No 2 has raised coaming and still had its hatch cover beams in place. Dropping in between the hatch beams I entered the hold itself; in the tween decks space are two tanker trucks and a staff car parked facing towards the bow. On the deck level below, 50lb aerial bombs were stacked, with their tailfins upmost, alongside more shells and a radial aircraft engine.

In Hold No 1, hundreds of hemispherical beach mines are stacked. © Ewan Rowell

A diver hangs above the bow gun, which is swung to port. Three boxes of ready-use shells are still neatly stacked behind it. © Ewan Rowell

I rose back out of Hold No 2 and continued moving forward towards the bow. In front of me, the foremast with its H frame base support still stood upright in between the hatches for Holds Nos 1 and 2, complete with its crosstree still in position and fixed ladder rungs running up it. Cargo winches were dotted fore and aft around the base of the mast for operating the derricks and working cargoes. The derricks appeared to have been made of wood – they have disappeared, although their goosenecks still remained on the mast.

Further forward, Hold No 1 also still had its hatch cover beams in place. The central space of the hold was an empty void that dropped all the way down to the bottom of the hold far below. The 8-foot-high tween decks space that ringed around the hold was packed with hundreds of stacked hemispherical beach mines, each with two grab handles welded on top, alongside boxes of their detonators, large shell casings and rectangular boxes of cordite. These beach mines were anti-invasion mines that would be buried in hundreds on beaches that the Allies would likely assault.

When I first visited Truk in 1990, the central void of this hold was packed right to the brim with these mines – there was no free space in the hold at all. Over the years however it is said that local Chuukese divers have been lifting the mines and robbing out the explosive for dynamite fishing. Some believe that some of the damage to the wrecks such as the collapse of the funnel and upper works of the *Fujikawa Maru* is due to dynamite fishing by locals. Today, divers can swim down several deck levels to the very bottom of the hold, where large numbers of mines can still be found.

A V-shaped breakwater was set on the deck in front of the bow gun. This was designed to divert any wash shipped over the bow away from the gun, the gun crew and Hold No 1. The large bow gun sits on its circular bandstand platform, pointing out to port high above the deck. Just behind the gun itself on the gun platform can be found three boxes of ready-use shells.

At the bow, a section of gunwale protects the flush-decked steamer – she has no fo'c'sle. Her plumb stem, iconic of the era of her construction, drops vertically from the main deck at 50 metres to the seabed at about 60+ metres. Anchor chains lead from her anchor windlass across the foredeck to disappear through hawse pipes. The starboard anchor is still held snug in its hawse whilst the port side anchor is run out and snakes away across the white sandy seabed into the distance.

Rounding the vertical stem of the bow, I finned back aft along the starboard side of the ship, passing the bow gun and Holds Nos 1 and 2. As I approached the bridge I spotted two more Type 95 HA-GO tanks sitting on the wide main deck, partly resting half over the starboard bulwark rail. It is not surprising that in the chaos of the sinking and plunge to the seabed these tanks on both sides of the deck, perhaps holding onto some of their buoyancy from the air trapped inside them, were moved about and that other large pieces such as the bulldozer on the port side ended up on the seabed nearby.

Immediately behind the tanks stands the well collapsed bridge superstructure. Along either side of the superstructure a covered walkway leads aft, its roofing long gone to leave just the skeleton of its framework. Portholes still with their glass in them are dotted along the outer starboard side of the deckhouse.

The *San Francisco Maru* had a split superstructure – that is, the bridge superstructure is separated by a section of open deck from the deckhouse above the engine and boiler rooms. Ships that have their bridge and engine room areas in the one central superstructure are said to have a composite superstructure. In between the bridge and engine room superstructures is the hatch for Hold No 3, originally designed to hold her bunker coal.

Aft of Hold No 3 is the deckhouse above the boiler room. The tall smokestack, again iconic of a coal-burning steamship of the early 20th century, has collapsed, its base section fallen aft, with a section of it lying at the starboard side of the boiler room deckhouse.

The boat deck, on top of the main section of engine room deckhouse, has lifeboat davits either side, still swung out as they were left when the crew abandoned ship as it sank. In the middle of the boat deck is the pitched roof of the engine room itself, with five opening skylights on either side of the pitch – some closed, others still propped open as they were for ventilation during the last moments of the attack – and which now allow access into her innards.

Head down, I carefully dropped in through an open skylight on the port side, and immediately, well beneath me, I could see the large triple expansion steam engine sitting fore and aft on the centreline, surrounded by catwalk gratings at different levels. The engine room dropped down to below seabed level at about 65 metres.

Retracing my path back out of the engine room through the same skylight, I continued to swim aft over a flat expanse of deck, which contains Holds Nos 4 and 5. The mainmast was broken off about 6 feet above the deck and lay fallen on the port side. Four small cargo-handling winches were set either side of the mast, two fore and two aft.

I swam down through the wide hatch into Hold No 4, where a large number of artillery shells in boxes could be found, along with more hemispherical beach mines, detonators, bombs, small arms ammunition and 55-gallon fuel drums stacked in the tween deck space and at the very bottom. On the port side of this hold, the shell plating was deformed, and a large gash went right through the hull, the catastrophic result of a bomb hit.

The main deck around the hatch for Hold No 5 has sagged downwards into the hold. The cause is evident, as there is a large bomb entry hole visible on starboard side, just forward of stern deckhouse. It looked like a delayed-fuze bomb had gone straight through the hull before detonating inside the hold, blowing the decking up, before it fell downwards again. This hold still contained dozens of 30-foot Type 93 Long Lance torpedo bodies and engines along with a large number of 55-gallon fuel drums and depth charges.

The earlier Type 91 torpedoes had used compressed air as the oxidiser with an 11-foot-long internal air cylinder charged to about 2,500-3000 psi (the same pressure as today's conventional scuba cylinders). Compressed air however left a noticeable bubble trail. The subsequent Type 93 Long Lance torpedo found in this hold used compressed oxygen as the fuel oxidiser in place of compressed air, with a wet-heater engine that burned a fuel such as methanol or ethanol to produce the driving force for the twin counter-rotating propellers. Compressed oxygen is dangerous to handle, but IJN engineers found that by starting the torpedo's engine with compressed air then gradually switching to oxygen they were able to overcome the sudden oxygen explosions that had blighted the torpedoes before. As a result of these explosions, Japanese crews were wary of the use of compressed oxygen, so to conceal the use of pure oxygen from the ship's crew, the Japanese called the oxygen tank the secondary air tank.

Since air is 21 per cent oxygen and 78 per cent nitrogen, pure 100 per cent oxygen provides five times as much oxidiser in the same tank volume, and this greatly increased torpedo range. The absence of inert nitrogen also resulted in the emission of much less exhaust gas, which now comprised only carbon dioxide and water vapour. CO_2 is significantly soluble in water, and the resulting exhaust gas mixture greatly reduced tell-tale bubbles in its track. The Japanese Type 93 torpedo had a long range, high speed and a heavy warhead, and this marked it as a quantum leap forward in torpedo development – it was far ahead of any Allied torpedo of the time.

Moving further aft past small stern deckhouses that held the docking bridge and auxiliary steering position above the steering gear, I reached the fantail – the section of stern that projects out aft from the rudder stern post. At the edge of the deck here on either side were two dropping mine holders – still, ominously, each with a depth charge nestling in it. These would be rolled out of their holders if the ship detected a submerged submarine. Looking over the very stern of the ship, I could see the propeller and rudder in place far below under the sweep of the stern.

Conscious of bottom time ticking away – and a lot of deco racking up – I moved back forwards along the port side of the ship towards the downline at the front of the superstructure. It had been an amazing dive on a wreck that was still packed full of her wartime deadly cargo.

You can watch this dive on video on my YouTube channel here:

Sankisan Maru (1942)

4,776grt passenger-cargo vessel (1942)
IJN auxiliary transport

The 4,776grt passenger-cargo vessel *Sankisan Maru* was built at Harima Dockyard, near Osaka in Japan, during 1941. She was launched in early 1942 and after fitting out afloat entered service in March 1942 with the Kaburagi Kisen Shipping Line. She was 367 feet long with a beam of 52 feet and a draught of 29 feet. Her single screw was driven by a coal-fired triple expansion steam engine that gave her a service speed of 12 knots.

Sankisan Maru was built with two holds on her forward well deck, and Hold No 3 set on the extended section of superstructure in front of the bridge. She was fitted with a composite central superstructure; immediately behind the bridge was the smokestack and engine room with lifeboats swung in davits on either side of the boat deck. Two further holds were set on the aft well deck before a sterncastle, which held the steering gear.

Such was the secrecy surrounding Japanese ship construction as the Pacific War gathered momentum throughout 1942, that the Allies did not know of the construction or launch of this large ship at the time. The now de-classified American Intelligence document *Japanese Merchant Ships Recognition Manual* (revised 1944) lists details of all the individual Japanese merchant ships known to American Intelligence at that time. Although most of the merchant ships sunk at Truk are listed, there is no mention of the *Sankisan Maru*.

On 31 January 1944, she departed Yokosuka Naval Arsenal in Japan for what would unknowingly be her final voyage down to the South Seas. She was bound for Truk, in a large convoy escorted by the subchasers CH-29 and CH-64, the auxiliary subchaser *Takunan Maru* No 6 and the minesweeper *Keinan Maru*. Her holds were filled with wooden cases of small arms ammunition, military trucks, 20mm AA shells, hundreds of depth charges, 4.7-inch artillery shells, ordnance and munitions. She carried more trucks as deck cargo.

The convoy arrived at the Japanese naval base at Chichi-Jima on 3 February 1944 and after pausing in safety there overnight, the convoy set off the following day, 4 February, for the last leg of the voyage from Chichi-Jima to Truk, with additional escort vessels being attached for this most dangerous leg of the voyage.

The 4,766grt passenger–cargo vessel and naval auxiliary Sankisan Maru.

An aerial torpedo strikes Amagisan Maru *on the starboard side forward. A second torpedo has run an erratic track to its left.* Sankisan Maru *is anchored just to her north. (National Archives)*

The convoy arrived safely in Truk Lagoon on 13 February, just four days before Operation Hailstone would take place. *Sankisan Maru* anchored off the western shore of Uman Island in the south part of the 6th Fleet anchorage, just to the north of the 7,623grt requisitioned passenger-cargo liner *Amagisan Maru*, which was now serving as a naval auxiliary transport.

On the first day of the Operation Hailstone group strikes, aircraft from the carrier USS *Bunker Hill* were tasked to attack shipping found in the anchorage between Fefan and Uman Islands in the lagoon. At 1250, five Curtis Helldiver bombers and four Grumman Avenger torpedo bombers attacked the largest ship present, the *Amagisan Maru*. As AA gunners and crew on *Sankisan Maru* nearby looked on, the Helldiver bombers scored a direct hit with a large 1,000lb bomb, and this was followed by an aerial torpedo attack from her starboard quarter. *Amagisan Maru* was hit by a torpedo just in front of her bridge on her starboard side, the torpedo explosion sending an expanding pillar of smoke and debris more than 100 feet into the air.

Amagisan Maru was carrying fuel and diesel in 55-gallon drums in her holds and this cargo ignited in the foredeck Hold No 2. As the plume of white smoke from the torpedo explosion dissipated, a large column of dense black smoke started to billow up from the ship as a second torpedo sped towards her stern. Within 15 minutes of the attack, the ship was burning fiercely and sinking by the bow. She disappeared shortly thereafter.

The *Sankisan Maru* was the second ship to be attacked in the anchorage by the *Bunker Hill* aircraft. She was strafed and bombed and, although the records are unclear (it may have been as a result of a bomb or torpedo hit or fire), the ordnance she was carrying in her aft holds detonated. The explosion was of such force that the whole aft section of the ship from abaft the bridge to the very stern was almost vaporised and completely dispersed. Sections of the ship were flung hundreds of yards across the lagoon, and a depression was instantly blasted out of the seabed underneath where the stern had been. All crew in that section of the ship were instantly killed. She sank immediately.

◆　◆　◆

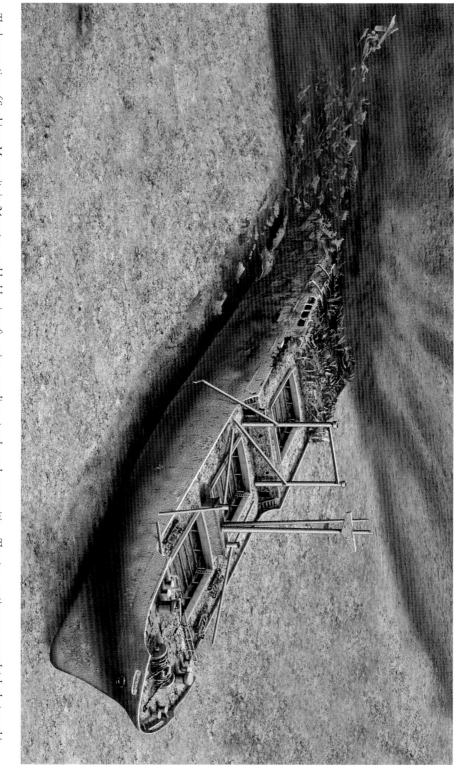

The bow section of Sankisan Maru sits in 24 metres and holds aircraft engines, cowlings, trucks and ammunition. The stern section was completely destroyed in a massive secondary munitions explosion. Scattered sections of ship lead down a slope to a depth of 45 metres where the rudder, prop and stern post sit in isolation.

As we swept towards the site on another flat calm, beautiful blue Chuuk Lagoon day, the skipper began to home in on the wreck by checking his transits. It is quite a skill in open waters such as the lagoon, where the land is far away – and before the days of the cheap GPS in boats this is how wrecks were found by divers around the world.

As soon as the submerged wreck buoy was spotted, the boat slewed to a stop beside it, and one of the local crew donned a mask, jumped over the side and duck-dived down to thread the boat's head rope through the eye on the buoy. We were tied off within seconds of arriving on site, and as the skipper switched off the outboards, complete silence enveloped us. As with most Truk Lagoon diving, because there are so many wrecks we again had a large and famous World War II wreck all to ourselves. She sits upright on a flat, gently sloping bottom in 24 metres of water at the bow.

Once we were kitted up, bailout tanks slung under our arms, and after a CCR pre-breathe sitting in the boat, we tumbled backwards over the gunwales into the welcome embrace of Chuuk's beautiful 29°C warm water. I righted myself and looked down; there was the foremast right beside me running straight down from just a few metres under the surface to the foredeck of the wreck below. The whole forward section of the wreck was clearly visible about 15–20 metres beneath me, the wreck surrounded by clean white sand with scattered pieces of wreckage and coral outcrops.

We began our descent. With no current here in the lagoon to worry about, we just dropped vertically, flat on our fronts like skydivers, down towards the wreck as our rebreathers automatically regulated our PO2, raising it from my first pre-programmed set point of 0.7 bar to 1.3 bar for the deeper part of the dive. As the pre-set PO2 set point changed, the HUD display in my peripheral vision on the left side of my mask blinked a reassuring green.

The impressive bow section dominates a flat shelving seabed that is peppered with coral outcrops and coral-covered pieces of wreckage. As we arrived down on the foredeck of the wreck I spotted the port anchor still held snug in its hawse; the starboard side anchor chain was run out across the seabed. Both anchor chains ran up through their hawse pipes to an anchor windlass set on the fo'c'sle deck that was heavily encrusted in coral.

Two large flat-topped forced-draught ventilators stood on the coral-covered fo'c'sle deck. The starboard side ventilator has been an impromptu rest for a 7.7mm machine gun and ammunition clips for the last 25 years or so – it was like that when I first visited Truk in 1990. Dropping down from the fo'c'sle deck to the well deck, two aft-facing open doors allowed entry into the fo'c'sle spaces.

Hold No 1 no longer has its hatch beams in place – these were presumably blown off with the expanding blast of the explosion. The hold is largely empty down to the keel frames at its lowest level, where a mass of 7.7mm AA ammunition, five-round infantry rifle clips and longer 30-round clips for heavy AA machine guns was dispersed amongst the frames, some loose, others still in their wooden boxes.

At maindeck level, on the port side of the well deck, the skeletal chassis of two deck cargo army trucks rested upside down half over the gunwale, complete with radiators, engine, drive systems and large chunky tyres. A third truck lay on the starboard side of the main deck.

In between the hatches for Holds Nos 1 and 2, the foremast rose up vertically towards the surface and had its crosstree in place. A jumbo cargo derrick was goosenecked to the bottom of the foremast, giving the appearance of a twin mast. Hold No 1 connected directly

Trucks are parked up on the tween deck of Hold No 2. © Ewan Rowell

to Hold No 2 at tween deck level, allowing me to swim below decks directly from Hold No 1 into Hold No 2, where aircraft engines and cowlings were neatly stacked along with a number of 1.5-ton Isuzu trucks that were parked up on the tween deck spaces on the port side, their chassis, steering wheels, gearboxes and twin sets of tyres still easily recognisable. Strewn about here were more aircraft engine cowlings, wheel assemblies, exhausts and, along the starboard tween decks space, three large radial aircraft engines.

Immediately aft of Hold No 3 was the bridge superstructure, which originally rose up some five deck levels, but of which however there is little left recognisable today. The superstructure has almost been severed right down to the level of the hatch for Hold No 3, and there is only a mass of bent, twisted and collapsed plating covered in coral, with a couple of solitary lifeboat davits hanging over the starboard side. The devastated superstructure started to slope off dramatically as I moved aft over it – and then the ship suddenly stopped. The whole aft part of the ship was missing; the hull plating at either side was peeled outwards with the expanding force of the wartime explosion as the aft part of the ship was almost vaporised.

We swam out aft from the ship into free water beyond the severed end of the mid-section of ship. Immediately the seabed dropped away dramatically – partly with a natural slope but partly into a depression gouged out of the seabed by the explosion. The water got much darker as Nuwa led us slowly down the slope.

Large sections of the ship's double bottoms holding several keel frames and hull plating were strewn all around on the white sandy seabed. From the depth of 24 metres to the seabed at the bow section, our depth rapidly increased: 30 metres, 35 metres, 40 metres and then to

162

The rudder, prop and sternpost sit in isolation at a depth of 45 metres. © Ewan Rowell

45 metres where the seabed levelled off. Breathing standard compressed air on this dive, I felt the familiar, almost nostalgic, warm wash of nitrogen narcosis sweeping over me.

We followed Nuwa out along the flat bottom at 45 metres until we were about 100 metres away from the devastated bridge area of the bow section. Sitting upright on their own, seemingly isolated at the bottom of the depression, were the rudder and propeller with a small section of the keel attached. Whilst the rest of the ship from here forward had been vaporised during the explosion, the strongly built stern post, rudder, prop and shaft had just fallen directly down to the seabed. It was amazing to think that such a large ship should be all around us just now – and that it had almost completely disappeared.

Shinkoku Maru

10,020-ton merchant tanker (1930)

***Shinkoku*-class auxiliary oiler (1941)**

The large 10,020-ton merchant tanker *Shinkoku Maru* was laid down in October 1938 in Kobe at Kawasaki Dockyard for the Kobe Sanbashi KK Line. She would be their main large ship, the others being tugs and tenders.

When launched in 1939 on the eve of war, *Shinkoku Maru* was 503 feet long with a beam of 65 feet, a draught of 29 feet and a cruiser stern. She was fitted with a single Kawasaki 8-cylinder double-acting diesel engine that gave her a service speed of 15 knots and a maximum speed of nearly 20 knots with a range of 18,500 miles at 15 knots.

The tankers of the early part of the 20th century were of a relatively simple construction – basically a long steel box divided into a series of compartments. The forward spaces were designed to carry water and dry cargo such as oil in drums. The after spaces held water, bunker fuel, cargo pumps and the ship's engines. Between these two end spaces, the rest of the tanker was divided into cargo compartments or tanks. This extensive subdivision gave tankers exceptional strength and stability: a tanker could take a number of hits from bombs or torpedoes but still remain afloat.

Each cargo tank could be filled and emptied independently of the others so that different types of oil could be loaded into separate tanks and discharged without being cross-contaminated. Numerous valves linked each cargo tank to a system of pipelines inside the ship that led to the ship's pumps. Another set of pipelines led up from the pumps onto the tanker's deck where they were conveniently located for connecting to shore pipelines for loading and discharging. The ship's pumps were primarily used for pumping the cargo out of the ship to shore storage tanks and for pumping ballast water in or out of the ship. Shore pumps were used for pumping the cargo aboard from the land.

The deck of a tanker was a continuous weather deck penetrated only by small raised cargo hatches, one for each tank. Rising above the weather deck were three superstructures: the fo'c'sle, the midships bridge superstructure and the poop or sterncastle.

The fo'c'sle spaces were used to store ship's equipment and held the chain locker and the lamp room etc. The midships superstructure held the bridge, chart room, radio room, store rooms and officers' accommodation. The stern deckhouse held the machinery and engines, which were surrounded by the fireproof engine casing.

A fully laden tanker would lie deep in the water, and in rough weather the weather deck would be continuously swept by moderate seas; the tanker would become a three-island ship with only its three superstructures visible. To allow crew to pass safely from each of the three islands when decks could be awash, an elevated catwalk walkway called a flying bridge was set about 8 feet above the deck, connecting all three superstructures.

On 25 July 1941, the USA banned the export to Japan of the oil and other materials that had been fuelling the Japanese war machine for years. (During the 1930s Japan had imported half its oil from America and by 1940–41 it was importing 80 per cent of its oil from America and 10 per cent from the East Indies.) Just one month after the final round of U.S. embargoes went into effect, on 18 August 1941, with war now decided upon, the Imperial Japanese Navy requisitioned *Shinkoku Maru* and converted her into an auxiliary oiler, equipped for abeam refuelling of naval ships at sea. A heavy 4.7-inch gun was fitted on a bandstand platform on her fo'c'sle deck, and another similar 4.7-inch gun at her stern. She went on to take part in a number of Japanese offensive operations in the Pacific before she entered Truk Lagoon for what would be the last time on 14 February, just three days before the surprise American carrier strikes. She transferred oil to the auxiliary oiler *Tonan Maru No 3*, and anchored in the Combined Fleet anchorage to the north of Fefan Island and west of Moen Island.

A valuable target, she was attacked on the first day of Operation Hailstone, and took a bomb hit amidships from Douglas Dauntless dive bombers from the carrier *Yorktown* – but remained afloat.

The following morning at about 0200, Grumman Avengers from the carrier *Enterprise* attacked her in a radar-guided night attack. A 500lb bomb with a 4-second delayed-fuze hit her on her port side at the stern, abaft the smoke stack and opening directly into the cavernous engine room. Water flooded unchecked into this massive space, which rises up several deck levels, and she began to sink by the stern, the weight of her water-filled stern pulling the rest of the ship under.

All the World War II tankers and oilers I have dived in the Pacific have been deliberately hit in the aft machinery spaces. Hits to the independent and sealed oil storage tanks were often not fatal; a tanker could take several hits and remain afloat. Consequently, American aviators and submariners deliberately aimed for the engine and boiler rooms at the stern. As well as the ship being disabled by a hit on the engine, these cavernous spaces, rising up for some 45 feet, could hold a vast amount of water – if they flooded, then a tanker would be dragged down by the stern. It was common in shallow anchorages to see tankers which had been hit in the stern, settle by the stern until they rested on the seabed, whilst the buoyancy of their forward tanks often kept the bow projecting above the water.

Shinkoku Maru settled on the bottom upright in about 40 metres of water. Given this depth – and her massive size – even as she sat on the lagoon bottom, the topmost sections of her two masts protruded above the surface. In subsequent years the top sections of her masts were cut away with explosives to minimise the hazard to shipping.

◆ ◆ ◆

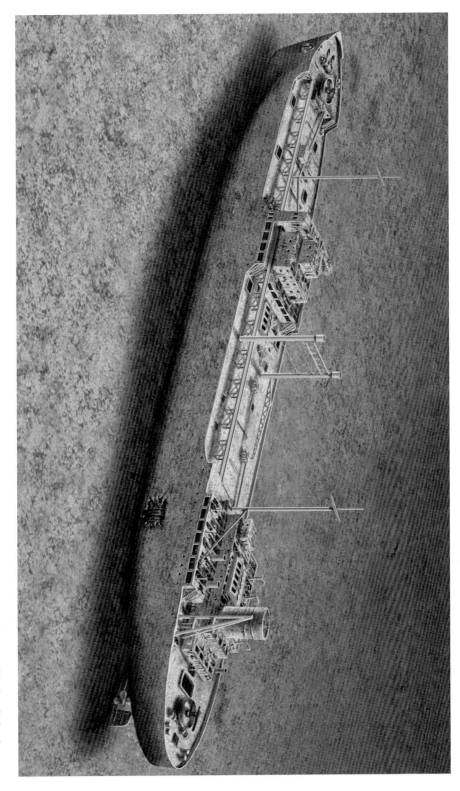

The 10,020-ton oiler Shinkoku Maru is one of the largest wrecks in the lagoon. She sits upright in 40 metres of water, showing the scar of the bomb that hit her in the stern, flooding her engine room and dragging her down. A flying bridge walkway 8 feet above the deck connects all three 'islands' on the port side.

Today the wreck of *Shinkoku Maru* sits upright on her keel in about 40 metres of water – but given her size, she has a least depth to the top of her bridge superstructure of only just over 10 metres. She is a massive ship – the second largest in the lagoon. Given her depth, a long dive starting at her deepest parts around the engine room at her stern and ending with her shallowest bridge area can be carried out with only minimal decompression.

On our 2013 expedition to Truk, *Shinkoku Maru* was the first dive of the trip – and I was diving with Nuwa, Ewan Rowell and Paul Haynes. Nuwa led us down the line in somewhat hazy, milky visibility to the deck of this great oiler and then over the port gunwale. We moved aft outside the hull, dropping deeper and deeper towards the seabed, the propeller and banded rudder visible a little distance further on.

Nuwa led us directly over to the bomb blast hole on her port side just a few metres above the sandy seabed – it's a sizeable hole, about 15 feet in diameter. I watched as Nuwa disappeared inside into what seemed like total blackness, followed by Ewan and then Paul. I followed, and we found ourselves immediately in a maze of tight corridors at the very bottom of the ship.

Entering the lower deck level of the engine room through the bomb hole in the port hull shell plating. © Ewan Rowell.

No sea life grows on the metal of shipwrecks in the pitch blackness of their innards. This oiler's steel shell plating was clean, rivets still holding her sturdy frames together – she looked strong, as though she would float today. Like in many other wrecks in the lagoon, most exposed internal steelwork was heavily blackened from the wartime fires that swept her after she was hit.

We moved forward along a grated walkway, up the port side of the lowest levels of her diesel engines. I squeezed past a long row of rockers, around the front of the engine cylinders, which ran fore and aft on the centreline, and then swam up a grated companionway staircase to the next level up, where we again circumnavigated the engines. In the darkness and tight corridors, I rapidly lost my sense of direction – it was eerily black and silent. Doors led off the corridors going further, seemingly endlessly, into the bowels of the ship.

Nuwa led us up another grated staircase and we entered into the cavernous cathedral-like space that is the top of the engine room,– directly above the eight cylinders of her Kawasaki double-acting diesel engine that we had been circumnavigating at lower levels. Each of these cylinders was at least 25 feet high, and they rose up from their mounts at the very base of the ship through the various deck levels that ringed around them. Each of the circular cylinder tops beneath me was about 4–5 feet across, and the lid was bolted down by some 14 large hexagonal cylinder head nuts, each about the size of a hand.

Divers can, with care, swim around the engines and rise up through several deck levels.
All steelwork is still blackened from the fires that engulfed her. © Ewan Rowell

The topmost level of the engine room is a cavernous space crisscrossed by catwalk gratings. The tops of the diesel engine cylinders can be seen; they drop down through several deck levels. The bright open skylights at the top of the image offer an easy route out – they can be seen on the wreck illustration, just forward of the smokestack.

Catwalks ran along either beam of the ship at different levels, along walls lined with piping, valves and gauges; and a couple of athwartships catwalks led across the cavernous open space high above. Far above at the very top of the roof, some 10 metres above me, light streamed in through the open skylights of the pitched engine room roof. The skylights were open, no doubt for ventilation, during her wartime days and offered a direct and easy means of getting out of the engine room, if any of our rebreathers chose that moment to malfunction. Far down below on the port side I could see shafts of blue light streaming into the darkness below from the bomb strike hole where we had entered.

We swam up and exited the engine room through the open skylights. Although we had incurred a significant decompression obligation by that time on the deepest part of the dive, *Shinkoku Maru* sits in such a perfect depth that we could now spend a further hour exploring the remainder of the ship whilst burning off our deco.

As I popped out through the skylight and looked aft, the banded smokestack rose high beside me and here on the port side, a large tripod used for supporting oil transfer rubber hoses rose almost as high as the smokestack itself. In the distance, the defensive stern gun stood on its bandstand platform, now well covered in coral, with depth charge roll-off racks nearby.

Moving forward from the aft deckhouse past the mainmast, we moved over a flat expanse of decking, over the oil tanks. Above us, the flying bridge elevated walkway about 8 feet above the deck led from the aft deckhouse to the bridge superstructure. A large goalpost pair of kingposts reared high above us, aft of the bridge superstructure.

The bridge superstructure rose up for four deck levels, the topmost level now well collapsed. The navigation bridge had long rectangular windows to its front, and just inside at the front there were three telegraphs: two close together, just forward of the helm and rudder direction indicator pedestal, and a third, likely the revolutions telegraph, towards the port wing. A compass binnacle was attached to the front wall of the deckhouse on the centre line.

I swam forward across the foredeck tanks past the tall foremast, beside a flying bridge walkway that connected the bridge superstructure to the fo'c'sle deck. The bow gun was still present on its platform, now heavily covered in coral. Chains led from the anchor windlass forward of the gun to hawse pipes on either side of the deck.

After a run time of two hours, our decompression was burnt off and we were free to rise slowly to the surface. It had been an amazing dive on another of Truk's stunning wrecks.

Aikoku Maru

10,500grt Passenger-cargo liner (1940)

IJN Armed Merchant Cruiser (1941)

IJN auxiliary transport (1943)

Such was the ferocity of the Operation Hailstone strikes that tens of thousands of Japanese navy and army personnel were killed, both on the land and at sea, during the two-day raid. Seeing human remains inside the shipwrecks of Truk Lagoon today is, as a result, not uncommon, once you start venturing into the deeper wrecks.

The 10,500grt passenger–cargo liner and naval auxiliary Aikoku Maru.

The 492-foot long 10,437grt, twin-screw passenger and cargo liner *Aikoku Maru* had been requisitioned for war use in 1941 and at the time of the Operation Hailstone she was acting as a naval auxiliary. Her forward holds were filled with a cargo of mines, munitions, bombs, high explosives and the ordnance for her forward gun. In the aft part of the ship she carried more than 629 infantry of the IJN 68th Guard Unit, housed in makeshift billets.

During the first morning's group strikes by U.S. aircraft, an aerial torpedo from a Grumman Avenger hit *Aikoku Maru* in Hold No 1, triggering a catastrophic secondary detonation of the munitions in her forward holds. The whole forward section of the ship from bow to abaft the bridge was vaporised in an instant – of the crew and the hundreds of infantry, there was only one survivor. Japanese sources report that 730 Japanese personnel were lost in the cataclysm.

In July 1984, with local government cooperation, an official delegation from Japan arrived to collect the accessible remains of the dead from the shipwrecks of Truk Lagoon. Followers of the Shinto religion, prevalent in Japan, believe that the souls of men who perished in battle are held in limbo – and only by recovering their remains and performing a religious ceremony can their souls be set free. The remains of approximately 400 men were recovered by Japanese divers from the tween decks and aft holds of *Aikoku Maru* at that time. The remains were ritually cremated on Truk and the ashes taken back to Tokyo, to be spread at sea following ceremonies at the Tomb of Unknown Soldier at the Japanese National Cemetery for War Dead.

These Japanese divers however could not sweep completely through every corridor and room of each of the countless wrecks in Truk and search every nook and cranny – particularly on the deeper wrecks, which were beyond their diving capability at the time. Such was the scale of loss of life on these Japanese ships that it is inevitable that some human remains remained in the wrecks.

When you dive shipwrecks a lot, you begin to see and understand more and more the human side to the tragedy of the sinkings. I am very conscious that I have dived more than a thousand wrecks and that these wrecks are the graves for tens of thousands of sailors – the enormity of what I have seen sometimes weighs on my mind, both when I am diving the wreck and at other moments of quiet reflection ashore. I sometimes imagine all the faces of the dead lining up in front of me, in black and white.

Although not every shipwreck took a toll in human life when it sank, many did. Diving shipwrecks, you become very aware that you are visiting a place where people just like you died. You treat the wreck and any remains you see with respect – just as you would behave when walking around a war cemetery or battlefield topside. Whilst diving shipwrecks around the world, I have infrequently seen human remains – but never in such numbers as I have seen at Truk. Whilst no diver goes looking for this sort of thing, if you venture deep inside the wrecks in Truk it is almost inevitable that you will see human remains, so be ready for it.

Most divers, certainly the ones I dive with, treat any such remains with respect. You look but never touch – and, personally, I never photograph any human remains, out of respect for the fallen. However, it is a sad fact that not everyone treats the remains with respect. Stories of human remains being interfered with by divers on wreck sites around the world are fairly common, some positioning human skulls – to be clear, that's people – just to get the particular gruesome shot they desire.

Back in the 1990s, certain local Chuukese dive guides had their own ways of giving visiting divers what they thought they wanted to see. On my first trip in 1990 as a young diver, never having seen any remains in a shipwreck before, I was shocked when our guide suddenly took out the concealed skull of some poor Japanese sailor that had been hidden behind a section of metal work inside a wreck. He brandished it with gusto towards me, as though that was what he thought I wanted to see. I just wasn't expecting that to happen – and I recall the diver I was diving with recoiling in horror at what had just happened.

Other divers, even to this day when the prevailing mores have changed, pick up human remains and move them about inside wrecks. There are many photos of Truk wrecks online which show, for example, rotted tables inside the wrecks with human bones stacked up on them by divers; there are photos of skulls that have been moved around and positioned with limb bones to recreate the Hollywood-style skull and cross bones pirate symbol. Some divers rearrange the bones so that they begin to resemble a complete skeleton – except with bones from different people. Why? I just don't know.

I find all this repulsive. These are the remains of human beings that fell in combat and should be treated as such – with dignity, no matter the rights and wrongs of the war. I deplore this interference in what is an archaeological site, just as I dislike the practice in Truk of lifting artefacts out of the wreck and setting them up on a section of open deck or the side of a ship (if it lies on its beam) so that divers can gawp at them, pick them up, interfere and degrade them. Once something is moved, it is out of context.

The passenger and cargo liner *Aikoku Maru* was built in 1939 at Tama Zosensho Shipyard in Tamano for the Osaka Shosen KK (Osaka Mercantile Steamship Co. Ltd) regular scheduled service from Japan to South America. She carried a crew of more than 130 and could carry up to 400 passengers in comfort. She had vast deep cargo holds forward and aft of the composite superstructure amidships that held her engine rooms below, with her passenger accommodation lining the engine casing abaft the bridge. She was launched on 25 April 1940 and completed, after fitting out afloat, 16 months later, on 31 August 1941 – just months before war in the Pacific broke out, on 7 December 1941.

The *Aikoku Maru* was powered by two Mitsui Burmeister & Wain diesel engines that allowed her two screws to push her to a service speed of 17 knots and a top speed of 21 knots – fast for the day, and easily able to outrun most merchant ships of the era. It was this design speed and the vast cargo-carrying potential of her foredeck and aft deck holds that would allow her to be converted for use as an auxiliary cruiser or fast transport, at a time when many enemy cargo vessels had a service speed of 10–12 knots.

On 31 August 1941, she was officially requisitioned by the Imperial Japanese Navy and converted to an armed merchant cruiser. Four older 5.9-inch main guns were fitted – most likely from the secondary armament of an old battleship or the primary armament of an old decommissioned cruiser from the time of the Russo-Japanese war of 1904/5. Two 88mm guns, two 76mm AA guns and four 13.2mm machine guns were fitted, along with two 54cm torpedo tubes and booms for loading and recovering Kawanishi Type 94 E7K twin-float Alf reconnaissance seaplanes.

On 15 October 1941, the *Aikoku Maru* was assigned to Cruiser Division 24, but in February 1942, Cruiser Division 24 was decommissioned and the raider was sent back to Kure Naval Shipyard where a refit and an armament modernisation programme began. The older 5.9-inch guns were removed, and eight more modern 5.5-inch guns added. One was set on an elevated circular platform on the fo'c'sle deck at the bow and another on a similar platform on the stern deckhouse; the remaining guns were set either side of the forward Holds Nos 2 and 3 and either side of the aft holds. Two twin 25mm AA auto cannons were added, and two more would be fitted later in August 1942 to give her four twin 25mm cannons high up on the boat deck, one either side of the searchlight platform (aft of the funnel) and the other two set a deck level higher, one either side of the bridge.

The Type 96 25mm AA cannon proved most effective when used at close ranges of 1,000 metres or less – but it was subsequently found in combat that elevation and traverse of these twin AA guns was slow, even with powered mounts, and that the sights were ineffective against high-speed targets such as the new wave of American combat aircraft. Fire at targets beyond 2,000 metres was found to be completely ineffective.

In January 1944, she was fitted out to house hundreds of troops of the 68th Naval Guard, who were to be carried to Brown Island and Rabaul. Her cabins and third-class passenger rooms, originally designed to carry 400 fare-paying passengers, were perfect troop-carrying accommodation. Additionally, special living quarters in makeshift billets had been created in the upper tween decks space of Hold No 4 to house more troops. She set off for Rabaul, with the Truk Fortress as a port of call en route.

Whilst she was en route for Truk, the U.S. Operation Flintlock began – the invasion of the Marshall Islands. As part of this, Task Force 58 landed the 4th Marine Division and the Army's 7th Infantry Division at Kwajalein, Roi-Namur and Majuro Atolls. As these landings were going in, the submarine USS *Trigger* attacked the *Aikoku*'s convoy 300 miles north-west of Truk. Although the minelayer *Nasami* was sunk, *Aikoku* escaped unscathed and entered Truk Lagoon safely on 1 February 1944. She soon departed with her troops and supplies for Brown Island as scheduled – but was forced to abandon the mission because of American air activity in support of Operation Flintlock. She returned to Truk Lagoon late in the afternoon of 16 February 1944 and anchored in the 4th Fleet anchorage to the east of Dublon Island. She immediately began offloading ammunition preparatory to departing for Rabaul with her troops.

On the first morning of Operation Hailstone, 17 February 1944, during the first group strikes immediately after the initial dawn Hellcat fighter sweep, *Aikoku Maru* was attacked by Douglas Dauntless dive bombers and Grumman Avenger torpedo bombers from the U.S. carriers *Intrepid* and *Essex*. She was struck by several 500lb bombs. The first bomb hit the officers' wardroom galley and started a fire that spread quickly. She then took three more bomb hits.

During the next group strike, at about 0830, an aerial torpedo from a Grumman Avenger hit her in Hold No 1 in her forward section, where the ordnance for her forward gun was

Combat photo showing the moment an aerial torpedo from a Grumman Avenger set off a secondary explosion of munitions stored in the forward holds, which completely destroyed the front section of the ship. Of the 945 IJA troops billeted in her aft holds and her crew, there was only 1 survivor. (National Archives)

stored, along with her cargo of mines, munitions, bombs and other high explosives. Moments later, there was a catastrophic massive secondary explosion. A huge pillar of smoke rose up from where *Aikoku* had been just moments before. Debris, parts of the ship and her cargo were scattered all around, raining down onto the waters of the lagoon, the large sections of ship producing enormous white splashes. The forward section of the ship from just in front of the smokestack was almost vaporised. The stern section from about the smokestack aft survived, and sunk immediately like a stone.

The troops that crammed her below-deck spaces at the time of the explosion didn't stand a chance. If the shock of the blast didn't kill them instantly, they were drowned. There was only one survivor, and Japanese sources report that 945 Japanese service personnel were lost.

◆ ◆ ◆

Today it is only the stern section of the *Aikoku Maru* that lies on the seabed. It is hard to believe that the forward part of such a large ship, from just in front of the smokestack to the bow, is completely gone – dispersed in a wide semi-circle around the stern section. The massive secondary explosion that sunk the ship has left a depression in the seabed directly underneath where the detonation took place.

This is one of the deeper dives in Truk Lagoon. The stern section sits on a relatively even keel in 65 metres of water – but there is no need to venture that deep. The least depth over the highest part of the wreck at the collapsed smokestack on the boat deck is around 40 metres, and as you swim the wreck you will drop progressively lower to the aft main deck at about 50–55 metres. In the good underwater visibility here, the seabed far below is usually visible from the boat deck.

The wreck is cut almost straight across just forward of the smokestack, and the severed distressed sections of deck plating, girders and spars forward of the funnel point almost directly down to the seabed. Sections of hull shell plating are bent completely back on themselves and are now under the stern section.

The boat deck is the shallowest part of the wreck, and consequently it is near here that a fixed downline to the surface is usually attached by local dive charters, allowing divers to start in the shallowest part and choose where to venture and to what depth from there.

The smokestack itself has now collapsed aft, leaving its circular deck opening from which a large exhaust muffler pipe (similar in shape to a rocket engine) points almost directly upwards, whilst another exhaust pipe lies at an oblique angle beneath it.

The stern section rests upright in 65 metres of water with a depth to her boat deck of just over 40 metres. Her smokestack has collapsed and on the boat deck below, two twin 25mm autocannon AA weapons still point skywards, flanking a searchlight platform. At the stern, her 5.5-inch defensive gun is swung to port .

One of the two twin 25mm AA auto cannon on the boat deck. © *Ewan Rowell.*

A few feet aft of the collapsed smokestack is the small, pitched roof of the engine room with its characteristic skylights, which allow access down into the engine room itself. The bottom of the cavernous engine room is at seabed level of 65 metres.

Moving aft from the boat deck over assorted debris and pieces of ship, past the collapsed smokestack, you encounter a drop of several metres down to the next deck level below. Here there are the stumps of forced-draught ventilator funnels, and in the middle a large, wide and tall searchlight platform mount. On either side of the searchlight platform is set a twin Type 96 25mm AA cannon, the starboard side gun being particularly photogenic, pointing upwards in the position it was during the attack. There would have been a gun crew in action clustered around this gun when the massive secondary explosion took place – I often wonder what happened to them and where they ended up.

Dropping off the aft end of this deck, the rectangular hatch for Hold No 4 at shelter deck level can be seen. Hold No 4 is formed from the extended section of the main bridge superstructure and is a deck level higher than the main deck on which the hatches for Holds Nos 5 and 6 are set. Hold No 4 is open, dark and brooding, with a single hatch cover beam bisecting the hatch – presumably the others were blown off in the attack. The goalpost kingposts for this hold are structurally very strong, and still stand tall with a horizontal connecting spar at the highest point and a second curved bracing spar just slightly lower.

When the wreck was located during Jacques Cousteau's expedition to Truk in 1969, his divers penetrated into the rooms holding the makeshift troop billets, and footage of hundreds of skeletons lying in the silt in these quarters was obtained and broadcast in the resultant documentary, *Lagoon of Lost Ships*. The force of the massive explosion would most likely have killed these soldiers instantly – and the bent and buckled bulkheads and structural beams in this area demonstrate the extreme force of that explosion. The unfortunate troops crowded into the cramped quarters, so close to such a devastating explosion, had no chance of survival and were killed *en masse*. The Japanese divers in 1984 recovered the remains of approximately 400 men from the tween decks and aft hold areas here.

Moving further aft across the shelter deck and Hold 4, divers arrive at the drop down to the main deck at just over 50 metres. Here the hatch for Hold No 5 can be seen – a vast, dark, cavernous void with two large booms fallen across it to starboard from the forward kingposts adjacent to Hold No 4 – these heavy-duty booms were used for handling the seaplanes.

At the aft end of Hatch No 5, another pair of goalpost kingposts again rise tall, braced by their horizontal connecting beams at the top – a feature unique to Japanese shipping.

Moving further aft towards the stern, you can find the much smaller hatch for Hold No 6. A hatch cover beam support bisects the hatch athwartships, and sections of the hatch cover itself, to fore and aft of the hold, are still in place. At the front end of the hatch, a small trapdoor is open, which would have allowed access down to the fixed internal ladder rungs that ran up the bulkhead beneath, without having to remove the complete hatch cover, a cumbersome procedure.

Near the very stern at about 49 metres, an impressive 5.5-inch gun is set on an elevated circular platform mount, much of which has rotted away to reveal the structural beams and girders. This dual-purpose gun had a rate of fire of about ten shells per minute and had an effective maximum ceiling against aircraft of 27,000 feet. The gun is still partially elevated to port – frozen forever in time as it fired on attacking American aircraft.

At the very stern, the auxiliary steering position is set on the docking bridge, which runs athwartships, level with the top of the stern deckhouse, its wings projecting out to port and starboard, and the aft section projecting dead astern well out over the rounded fantail of the stern. Looking out over the stern of the vessel the rudder, flanked by the twin screws, can be seen far below, half-buried in the seabed.

On one dive, as Paul Haynes and I descended to the deepest part of the wreck, the stern superstructure, Paul entered the wreck and swam along a corridor and into the 'heads' – the toilet block. Here there were the complete skeletons of three Japanese soldiers, still in their World War II uniforms, gently resting across the sinks. These unfortunate fellows had been killed either by the shock of the blast or were trapped and drowned as the ship sank quickly. Either way their bodies were taken to the bottom still trapped inside the heads.

The 5.5-inch defensive stern gun. © Ewan Rowell

After a few days in this warm tropical water their bodies would have started to decompose. Over time the bodies gassed up, eventually floating upwards and becoming trapped against the underside of the heads roof.

Putrefaction of the bodies and predation by scavenging sea life such as fish, crabs and by major scavengers such as sharks would have dismembered the corpses after just a few weeks. Within just one or two months in these waters, the bodies of these unfortunate Japanese soldiers would be largely skeletonised, although their uniforms would have remained intact. As the buoyant flesh rotted or was eaten away, at some point the bones would have become heavier than the buoyant effect of the bloated body. The remains would then have gently fallen downwards to land on the sinks – where they remain to this day, a stark reminder of the brutality of the two-day raid, almost 75 years ago.

You can follow a dive on this wreck on my YouTube channel here:

Yamagiri Maru

6,438grt passenger-cargo vessel (1938)

IJN auxiliary transport (1941)

The 6,438grt naval auxiliary *Yamagiri Maru* was laid down at the Mitsubishi Jukogyo KK Zosensho shipyard in Yokohama for the Yamashita Kisen Line as a commercial passenger-cargo liner on 6 December 1937. She was launched on 13 May 1938, and after fitting out afloat, she was completed on 2 July 1938 and registered in the port of Kobe, Japan. She was 439 feet long with a beam of 58 feet and a loaded draught of 26 feet. Powered by diesel engines and a single screw, she had a service speed of 14 knots and a top speed of 17 knots.

The *Yamagiri Maru* was built as a well deck vessel with a raised foc'sle and a composite central superstructure that housed the bridge, engine rooms and passenger accommodation. Forward and aft of the main superstructure was an extended section of superstructure, which held Holds Nos 3 (forward) and 4 (aft).

On 5 September 1941, after just three years of civilian service, she was requisitioned by the Imperial Japanese Navy, as war loomed, for use as an auxiliary transport. She was registered in the IJN on 20 September 1941 and conversion works started at the Mitsubishi Heavy Industries Shipyard in Yokohama, where she had been built. The works were completed by 15 October 1941 and she was attached as an auxiliary transport to the Sasebo Naval District.

As dawn broke on Dog-Day Minus One, 17 February 1944, as U.S. Hellcats were arriving at the lagoon for the initial fighter sweep, *Yamagiri Maru* lay at anchor in the repair anchorage, north of Fefan Island. Ships damaged near Truk could be taken to the repair anchorage, where IJN repair ships were stationed, fully equipped to make temporary repairs and get ships seaworthy again. Often, damaged ships were patched up here and made seaworthy enough to get back to Japanese shipyards for more permanent repairs.

The ships in the repair anchorage were attacked by dive bombers and torpedo bombers from the carrier *Yorktown*. *Yamagiri Maru* took a direct hit and several close misses, but remained afloat as night fell.

The following day, Dog-Day, four *Bunker Hill* dive bombers attacked her, dropping one 1,000lb and six 500lb bombs from 500 feet. The 1000lb bomb and one 500lb bomb hit her – one bomb going straight into Hold No 3 and blowing the bottom out. Another bomb hit and devastated the bridge superstructure forward of the smokestack, blowing it off almost down to the level of the extended superstructure of Hold No 3. Fires took hold, and a plume of

The 6,438grt passenger-cargo vessel and auxiliary transport vessel Yamagiri Maru.

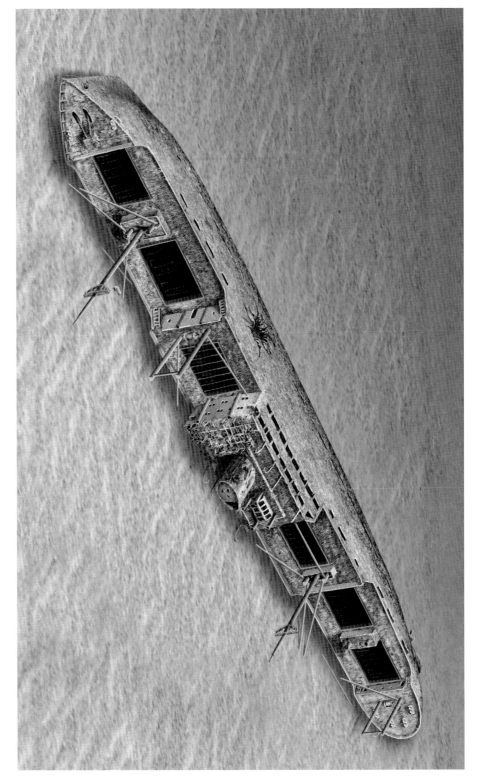

The wreck of Yamagiri Maru rests on her port side in 35 metres with a least depth of 15 metres.

smoke rose up for thousands of feet, followed by a series of secondary explosions as munitions cooked off and fuel ignited. As the group strikes of 18 February drew to a close there was no sign of her in the repair anchorage. Only a large slick of oil spreading out directly above where she had been moored, betrayed her presence below the surface of the lagoon.

◆ ◆ ◆

Today the large wreck of the *Yamagiri Maru* lies on her port side in 35 metres of water about one mile from the north-west shores of Fefan Island with its bow facing towards Weno Island. At 439 feet in length she is a big ship and yet with a beam of 49 feet, almost 20 metres, her shallowest starboard side is easily reached, just 15 metres beneath the surface. She is structurally intact, wonderfully preserved – and a favourite dive in the Lagoon.

The *Yamagiri Maru* was sunk at anchor – and her starboard anchor chain today is still run out through its hawse to drape over the stem and then hang vertically to the seabed. A large gun is mounted on the raised fo'c'sle deck and on the uppermost starboard side of the bow the ship's name can be seen in Roman and kanji characters.

Her foremast projects out horizontally from a small masthouse in between the hatches for Holds Nos 1 and 2 on the forward well deck, and still has its crosstree in place. Hold No 3 is set originally one deck higher, on the extended section of the bridge superstructure, and has its own goalpost-kingpost pair at its forward edge with derricks running to the front of the bridge superstructure and to the seabed. Looking through the hatch cover beams into the now horizontal and apparently empty hold, divers can see bright daylight through a gaping hole 30–40 feet in diameter where the bottom was blown out. On the outer higher starboard side of the hull there is a massive indentation of hull plating from a near miss.

Immediately aft of Hold No 3 is the composite superstructure with two large forced-draught ventilator funnels either side of it. The superstructure only rises up for a couple of its original deck levels – as the top levels have been obliterated by a bomb hit or from the fires. Walkways on two deck levels, with cabins off, run along the shallowest edge of the superstructure, bathed in light and covered in coral in just 15 metres of water. Empty lifeboat davits dot the edge of the boat deck.

The massive smoke stack is still in place aft of the bridge. On most World War II era shipwrecks around the world the funnels are long gone – made of light steel, they are usually some of the first structures to rust away and collapse. However here in the sheltered waters of the lagoon, with little current to bring oxygenated water coursing past it and accelerate rusting, the funnel remains intact, exhaust pipes projecting through its covered top. Either side of the funnel a large embossed Y can be found – the marking of the Yamashita Kisen Kaisha line. A large steam whistle is mounted on the forward side of the funnel, and immediately aft of the funnel is the pitched engine room roof with its skylights.

The aft section of the ship is something of a mirror image of the forward section. Hold No 4 is set on the extended section of aft superstructure before two holds in the well deck. Hold No 4 is empty, but it is possible to enter the engine room from the forward end of this hold, or through the engine room skylights.

The engine room is a large cavernous space, dominated by the now horizontal engine cylinders that are ringed by catwalk gratings. The internal bulkheads and decks and just about everything metal, is blackened from intense fires.

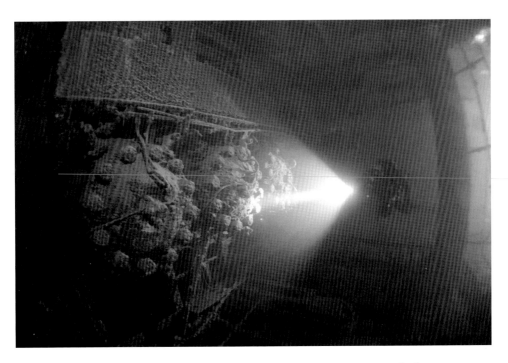

On penetrating the massive engine room, the tops of her diesel engine cylinders come into view, surrounded by grated walkways. © Ewan Rowell

Dozens of 14-inch shells for a Japanese capital ship are stored in her aft holds. © Ewan Rowell

Looking up to the upmost starboard side of the hull here, you can see a fire-blackened human skull, still in the remains of an IJA helmet, fused to the metalwork of the ship. A pile of bones lies on a shelf just below. This poor combatant was killed by the explosions or by drowning as the ship sank, his body becoming trapped in this compartment. Some time after the sinking, his body gassed up and became buoyant, floating upward to be pinned underneath the upmost starboard side. Over time, corals and marine growth fused his helmet and skull to the metal and as the flesh of his body rotted and was eaten away and the buoyancy was lost, the weight of the rest of his bones eventually caused them to fall downwards. From time to time in the Truk wrecks you will come across a similar grisly sight with a skull concreted to the underside of a roof or bulkhead and the rest of the bones nearby below.

The mainmast is set just aft of Hatch No 4 on the extended section of superstructure and there is a small deckhouse between Hatches Nos 5 and 6. It is perhaps the contents of Hold No 5 that make this wreck one of the best known in the lagoon. For in this hold are a large number of 5-foot-long 14-inch shells for the big guns of a battleship or battlecruiser. It is quite intimidating to enter this hold and be in the presence of so many of these powerful shells.

Nippo Maru

3,764grt passenger-cargo vessel (1939)
IJN water transport and auxiliary distilling ship (1941)

The 3,764grt Nippo Maru was a five-hold passenger-cargo vessel built in 1936 by Kawasaki Dockyard Co. Ltd in Kobe for Okazaki Honten Steamship Co. (who named all their ships with the letter N).

Nippo Maru was a classic three-island ship, 354 feet long with a beam of 50 feet and a draught of 23 feet. She had a raised fo'c'sle, two holds in her forward well deck and a third foredeck hold situated in the extended section of the main superstructure. Her composite superstructure held the bridge forward and, immediately behind, her engine room and machinery. Passenger cabins ran along either side of the engine casing, opening onto a covered walkway outboard that ran the full length of the superstructure. Her aft well deck held two further holds, before her sterncastle, which held her steering gear.

She was fitted with two coal-fired steam turbines that drove her single screw to give her a service speed of 12–14 knots and a maximum speed of 14–16 knots.

In August 1941, in the immediate run-up to war in the Pacific, she was requisitioned by the Imperial Japanese Navy and was fitted out as a water transport and auxiliary distilling

The 3,764grt passenger-cargo vessel and IJN water transport and auxiliary distilling ship Nippo Maru

ship, able to carry water container tanks to outlying Japanese island garrisons where water was scarce, as well as simultaneously supplying those garrisons with ordnance, ammunition and general supplies.

On 10 February 1944, just a week before the Operation Hailstone raids, the *Nippo Maru* arrived in convoy at Truk Lagoon, heavy with war supplies. Hold No 1 was filled with hemispherical anti-invasion beach mines, Hold No 2 held hundreds of shells and huge metal water tanks. Up on her foredeck she carried a deck cargo of light battle tanks and trucks, whilst a deck cargo of howitzers and larger artillery barrels were secured on the aft well deck. The bases and breeches for these large barrels were stored in Hold No 5 alongside the circular artillery base mounts, which would be set in an excavated hole that was then infilled with concrete. In amongst all this heavy-duty weaponry were the smaller essentials for the combat soldier such as bottles, gas masks and mess kits.

A week after arriving at Truk, on the morning of 17 February 1944, the *Nippo Maru* was anchored with her port anchor to the north of the 4th Fleet anchorage, east of Dublon Island, as the first waves of Grumman Avenger torpedo bombers from the carrier *Essex* swept over the lagoon. At about 0815, the Grumman Avengers scored three hits with 500lb bombs in the mid and aft sections of the ship. Much damage was caused and fires broke out – and within two hours, she had sunk from sight.

As she plunged through the waters of the lagoon she landed partly on a shelving underwater sandy slope. Her massive weight caused the slope to yield before her, and she slid down the slope for a short distance, carving out a large V in the hillside, before the slope bottomed out and she slithered to a stop, sitting upright on her keel with a slight list to port. The sand and debris she had dislodged during her passage down the slope followed on down the hill behind her, and partly engulfed her lower port quarter.

Today the wreck of *Nippo Maru* rests in 45–50 metres of water, with a pronounced list to port. The least depth to the wreck is 24 metres to the top of the bridge superstructure, which is where the surface buoy is usually attached. The *Nippo Maru* is not one of the largest wrecks in the lagoon, but her size and the pleasant depths to her superstructure and decks mean that it is possible to go down to the deeper sections first and explore the whole wreck, before returning to the shallower high parts of the wreck to burn off a substantial part of any decompression obligation before ascending.

At the bow, the port anchor is run out to the seabed whilst the starboard anchor is held tight in its hawse. Both chains go up through their hawse pipes to the foc'sle deck and run back to the anchor windlass. Immediately behind the windlass is the circular skeletal framework of the forward gun platform – the gun itself is now missing. Rotted guardrails ring around the top of the foc'sle deck, all now heavily encrusted with coral.

Moving aft from the foc'sle deck you find a drop down to the well deck and the forward cargo holds. On the port side of the deck beside Hold No 1, the skeleton of a truck, its tyres, frame and transmission, lies half over the side of the wreck, where it was swept as the ship sunk. Another similar truck lies on the seabed to port nearby. The foremast rises from a mast house between Holds Nos 1 and 2, and still has its crosstree in place.

Dropping into Hold 1, you encounter a large number of hemispherical beach mines, each with two handles on top – the same ones as are found in numbers in the foredeck holds of *San Francisco Maru*. These anti-invasion mines were destined to be deployed on

The 3,764grt passenger-cargo vessel and IJN water transport and auxiliary distilling ship Nippo Maru rests in 45–50 metres of water. She still has her deck cargo of howitzers on the starboard side of Hold No 4, and a Type 95 HA-GO light battle tank sits as deck cargo on the port side of Hold No 2 in front of the bridge superstructure

*Paul Haynes hangs motionless beside the Type 95 HA-Go deck cargo
tank just forward of the bridge on the port side. © Ewan Rowell*

beaches thought likely to be assaulted by the Allies. Boxes of detonators lie at the bottom of the hold.

The tween deck space of Hold No 2 still contains hundreds of artillery shells, whilst at the bottom level of the hold there are four large square water tanks. A huge pile of hundreds, or thousands, of beer bottles lies tumbled to port. On the port side of the main deck sits a Japanese Type 95 Ha-Go light battle tank – the same type as the deck cargo tanks on *San Francisco Maru*.

The Type 95 was fitted with a 37mm (1.45 inch) main gun, the barrel of which was removable for transport and replacement. Its secondary armament was two 7.7mm Type 97 light machine guns, one mounted in the hull and the other in the turret. The 37mm gun barrel on this tank is not apparent, and was most likely removed and stowed for transit inside the tank, which is now well sealed over by encrusting coral. These small, manoeuvrable tanks were used for infantry support and were not designed to go head to head in a fight with Allied tanks.

The large bridge superstructure rises up three deck levels above the extended superstructure that contains Hold No 3. The bottom and middle levels are studded with a row of portholes, all still with the glass in place. The top deck level has large rectangular windows along its full frontage through which it is possible to enter the navigating bridge, which still has its original teak deck planking in place. Here the telegraph still stands *in situ* with the telemotor for the helm just behind it. The wooden spokes of the helm have burnt or rotted away to leave just the circular band to which they were screwed.

Moving further aft on top of the composite superstructure, the boat deck has its empty lifeboat davits in the swung-in position at either side. It appears the crew did not have time to swing out and lower the lifeboats as the ship sank. The smokestack has collapsed to port, and immediately aft of its crumpled remains stands the pitched engine room roof with its skylights open and forced-draught mushroom ventilators studded around it. Enclosed walkways run down either side of the superstructure, off which passenger cabins were set, flanking the engine casing. Each cabin has its own porthole and white sink.

The superstructure then drops down to the aft well deck where Holds 4 and 5 are set. On the starboard side of the hatch for Hold No 4 can be found three light howitzers, which still have their tyres and splinter shields in place – two rest very close together and are iconic images of Truk Lagoon. These anti-tank guns could fire either an armour-piercing round or a standard high explosive round – which did not have the same penetration as the armour-piercing but could cause more damage to lightly protected targets.

The mainmast still has its crosstree in place and rises out of a small mast house with cargo winches set fore and aft of it. Nearby, the port side of Hold No 4 has been blown open to the sea by a 500lb bomb, a fatal hit that would have allowed huge amounts of sea water to enter. The hold appears largely empty but at tween deck level a massive pile of hundreds of sake and beer bottles lie strewn about, tumbled to port.

Hold No 5 contains a number of large cylindrical foundations for artillery base mounts. Once installed on the land, the turning section of the gun would then be located in the centre aperture. Three-barrelled recoil sections and breeches for the guns lie strewn about in the hold, whilst up on deck as starboard deck cargo, the large artillery barrels themselves are stashed, to complete the guns.

Howitzer deck cargo on the starboard side of Hold No 4. © *Ewan Rowell*

The sterncastle is ringed with portholes with their glass in place, and on the poop deck there is an anchor windlass, auxiliary steering gear and coiled hawsers. The circular skeletal framework of the empty aft gun platform is half-buried in the mass of sand that tumbled down the underwater slope as she sank, to engulf the port quarter of the ship.

Peering astern out into the blue from the starboard side of the fantail, you can see the white sandy hillside rising up towards the surface – still scarred with the large V carved out by her hull as she slid down the slope.

Follow a dive on this wreck here:

Hanakawa Maru

4,739grt passenger-cargo vessel (1943)
IJN Type 1B auxiliary transport

The 4,739grt Type 1B Standard passenger-cargo vessel *Hanakawa Maru* was built during 1942 and 1943 by Kawasaki Dockyard Co in Kobe. She was 370 feet in length, with a beam of 52 feet and a draught of 30 feet. She was built as one of 16 similar Type 1B standard ships to a standard design and specification – just one of a number of standard types that were operational towards the latter part of World War II. A well deck vessel, she had a raised fo'c'sle at the bow and four cargo holds separated by her split superstructure, the foremost bridge section rising up for several deck levels.

Before the war, in the 1930s, Japanese ships had been built to modern, fast designs. However, with its sea lanes enormously extended soon after the outbreak of war, and with the successful degradation of her existing shipping stock by U.S. submarines, Japan realised that it had to radically boost ship production. In 1942, work began on a number of new, modern standard ship designs, but as approximately two years was required to design and begin building new types of standard ship, actual construction of the newer designs of standard ships would not be able to start until early 1944.

In the intervening period, whilst the new styles of ship were being designed, desperately needing an immediate increase in ship numbers to supply its battle fleet and to service its far-flung Pacific garrisons, from 1941 Japan started a program of mass standard ship production using older, tried and tested, pre-war designs. Between December 1941 and July 1944 some 125 standard ships were built to a number of different standard designs.

Hanakawa Maru was a Type 1B standard ship. The number in the standard type refers to the year of construction, with Type 1 being a 1943 build, Type 2 being 1944 and Type 3 being 1945. The letter in the standard type refers to the actual type or specification of ship, and went from A, B, C etc. onwards. The standard Type 1B *Hanakawa Maru* had her engine in the split superstructure amidships and was for example, markedly different to the Type 1Ds, which had their engine machinery at the stern, like tankers. The design of the individual types varied from year to year.

The hull of the *Hanakawa Maru* was launched in Kobe on 31 August 1943, and after final fitting out, she entered service with the Imperial Japanese Navy on 25 October 1943. She would only have a short service career of four months, before Operation Hailstone would consign her to the bottom of Truk lagoon for eternity.

At 0700 on 25 January 1944, she departed Yokosuka in Japan for Truk in a convoy escorted by the IJN *Shimushu*-class *Kaibōkan* escort vessel *Hirado* and the sub-chaser CH-52. The convoy arrived at Truk on 7 February 1944.

Two days later, on 9 February 1944, *Hanakawa* departed Truk for Saipan – again in a convoy escorted by the IJN escort vessel *Hirado*. After a quick turnaround in Saipan she was soon back in Truk with a cargo of aviation fuel and fuel oil in 55-gallon drums packing her Holds. She moved to the fuelling dock on Tol Island, on the western periphery of the main group of Truk islands, to offload her cargo, unknowingly immediately before the opening day of Operation Hailstone, 17 February 1944, Dog-Day Minus One.

On Day 2 of the raid, Dog-Day, 18 February, as waves of U.S. aircraft swept across the lagoon unchallenged by any Japanese fighters *Hanakawa Maru* was spotted at anchor way out west at Tol Island, about 500 yards off the south-eastern shore , with her stern towards the island near the fuelling dock.

U.S. torpedo bombers from the carriers *Bunker Hill* and *Cowpens* had combined for a joint Strike 3A – and *Hanakawa Maru* was mistakenly identified as a particularly valuable target, a 12,000-ton oiler. Four torpedo bombers, flying in column, started their attack runs from the south on her starboard broadside.

A *Bunker Hill* Grumman Avenger torpedo bomber dropped the first torpedo – and scored a direct hit on the starboard side of the stationary *Hanakawa Maru*, between her bow and bridge superstructure. This first torpedo explosion caused a large burst of flame as her cargo of aviation fuel, densely stacked in 55-gallon drums in her foredeck holds, ignited. It was immediately clear that she had been dealt a mortal blow – but the other three torpedo bombers had already committed to their own attack runs, which would continue. Two of the other three torpedoes that were dropped were presumed hits whilst one torpedo ran erratically and hit land near the fuel dock on Tol Island itself.

Black fuel oil smoke started to immediately billow upwards from the forward section of the stricken ship and she started to go quickly down by the head. The damage was so severe that within 3–4 minutes *Hanakawa Maru* had sunk from sight, leaving only a burning slick on the surface. Burning debris floated ashore and reportedly started a fire in a mangrove swamp, which spread to some local buildings and a church.

Far out to the west in the lagoon, *Hanakawa Maru* is one of the less visited wrecks, but to survey it for *Dive Truk Lagoon* we had organised for a boat from Truk Stop Dive Center to take us out to Tol Island. It is the largest island to the extreme west of the main group of Chuuk islands and is quite a distance to run in a day boat; this distance, allied to its dangerous cargo, is why the wreck is rarely dived.

Truk Stop found that the usual Chuukese boat driver who we had had all week was not willing to take us out to Tol – he came from another island and would not be welcome on Tol. The islands are still fiercely insular, almost tribal, and there is still trouble between the various islands. However, Truk Stop were able to find a driver for us who came from Tol and knew the islands well.

After a passage of an hour or two west across the open expanse of Chuuk Lagoon from our dive centre on Weno, we started to approach the western group of islands, which are well separated from the central group. Very soon, our dive boat was speeding over flat calm waters, jinking between smaller green jungle-covered islands and through isolated channels between coral reefs that jutted out of the water – or lurked just beneath the surface. The route to the dive site on Tol was quite a maze and I could see why a local driver was needed.

The *Hanakawa Maru* lies to the south-east of Tol Island and as our dive boat approached the island a dull clanging of a metal bar striking a metal cylinder rang out, being repeated slowly. Dong … Dong …Dong … It may have been an entirely innocent coincidence, but I wondered if this was a warning to islanders that strangers were approaching their island.

Our boat slowed as we approached the last resting place of *Hanakawa Maru*, several hundred yards from shore near the southeast end of Tol Island. I tried to imagine the scene back in 1944 – the large passenger-cargo ship at anchor here in the oily calm waters of this sheltered spot, the sheer side of its hull rising high above our tiny boat. Her crew would have been busily working to offload her dangerous cargo of aviation fuel in 55-gallon drums, Daihatsu landing craft moving about, ferrying the drums ashore to the fuel station.

Suddenly the tropical calm would have been shattered by the noise of Grumman Avenger torpedo bombers dropping out of the brilliant blue skies as they started their attacking runs. Initial fear and shock as the attack began would disappear as gun crews readied their AA weapons and then began to fire as the Avengers closed. After releasing their torpedoes, the Avengers would bank away, the smooth splash as the torpedoes hit the water and the tell-tale track of exhaust bubbles speeding towards the ship spelling disaster. The torpedo hits – and then the fires … the bow settling into the sea as the blue skies turned black with the smoke from her burning cargo. The order to abandon ship, the struggle to survive in the water amidst slicks of burning fuel, and the swim to the shore 700 yards away. The whole scene played out in my mind in black and white.

As we chatted and began to get our dive kit ready, an open skiff with about 7–8 locals in it approached. I wondered whether there was about to be trouble – or whether we were going to be tapped for a 'local' tax, as happens, quite properly, on some of the smaller islands around the Pacific. But in the end it turned out that as the wreck is so infrequently dived, they were just fishing and were interested to meet us and see us and what we were doing. After a disjointed and stilted conversation, full of lengthy awkward silences, they went on their way and we began to finalise our dive preparations.

When she sank in 1944, she had a full cargo of aviation fuel and fuel oil in 55-gallon drums in her holds. As a result of corrosion, this dangerous cargo, largely unnoticeable to a diver's eyes, has leaked continuously to the surface since she went down. For or a long time the wreck was more or less off limits for diving – and was avoided by locals and visiting divers alike. Divers reported painful skin burns that left scars in addition to damaging expensive dive kit.

There was still a strong general smell of fuel above the wreck in the 1980s, but over more recent years these problems have been dissipating. Throughout the 1990s, small droplets of fuel still meandered slowly to the surface – and on occasion, even today, if the cargo has been disturbed or if corroded drums have finally released their contents, the smell of fuel still greets divers as they arrive topside. Divers today take great care in the cargo holds to avoid disturbing any fuel drums or dislodging sediment that is impregnated with fuel, by careless finning.

I couldn't detect any discernible smell of World War II fuel in the air as we began to get ready. Despite the pollution aspect, such is the clarity of water out here in the west – well away from rivers and human pollution – that we could easily see the shallowest parts of the wreck and the masts from the surface in our dive boat.

I rolled backwards off the dive boat into the warm water. Wearing a full body 3mm wetsuit I was largely protected from any fuel burns – but my follicly challenged head was as normal completely bare save for my mask.

I began my descent and as I dropped deeper the parts of the wreck, previously out of view, materialised from below. Although it was very clear on the surface, as I reached the wreck I found it to be in a layer of hazy water, quite common down near the seabed on Pacific wrecks that are located in enclosed bays or channels where a tide can stir the bottom up.

I arrived at the bow on the fo'c'sle deck where a twin anchor windlass still held the starboard anchor chain, which was run out to the seabed under tension. Guardrails ringed around the deck, now heavily covered with coral.

Dropping from the fo'c'sle deck to the well deck, I reached the hatch for Hold No 1, which was well filled with 55-gallon fuel drums – even after 75 years on the bottom, some of these corroded drums were still apparently intact and holding their contents. I stayed well above the hatch, wary of disturbing any of the dangerous cargo.

As I moved aft over Hold No 1, the foremast, with its large crosstree, rose up in front of me, all the way up to a depth of about 6 metres. Cargo winches and forced-draught ventilators were dotted around its base.

Abreast Hold No 2, on the starboard side, I spotted the fatal damage from the torpedo explosion and the secondary explosion as the fuel cargo had ignited. A large, gaping 25-foot-wide hole ran from the bottom of the hull almost to the top, and was fringed by torn and jagged metal. Cement bags and more 55-gallon fuel drums lay scattered about inside the hold, and others had tumbled outside to the seabed.

The bridge superstructure had largely collapsed, and a small coaling hatch for Hold No 3 was visible in the gap between it and the split superstructure abaft that held the engine and boiler rooms below.

A quadruple kingpost with ventilators was set immediately in front of this single-storey engine casing and passenger accommodation superstructure. I drifted along one of the walkways that ran down either side of this long superstructure, doors opening into the passenger and crew accommodation on either side of the engine casing. As I came to the aft end of this superstructure, I came to the galley with its mosaic flooring, heavy stoves and ovens, plates and bottles.

The smokestack had collapsed, but aft of the black hole within its circular rim, I arrived at the pitched roof of the engine room itself with more forced-draught ventilators dotted around. At the edge of this boat deck, the lifeboat davits were in the swung inboard position. Such was the speed she sank at, that the crew never had the opportunity to swing the boats out. With such a large explosion in the forward section of the ship, and with the potential for another secondary explosion of the volatile cargo in her aft holds, perhaps the crew were jumping into the water and swimming for shore – who knows? I entered the engine room through the open skylights of the small pitched roof and found the large reciprocating engine surrounded by catwalks, gauges and valves.

Aft of the superstructure, Holds Nos 4 and 5 are set in the main well deck, which, now at a depth of about 28 metres, has sagged and partially collapsed. The mainmast rises up between the two aft holds, which contain hundreds of 55-gallon fuel drums.

On the poop deck, at the stern, is set the circular defensive gun mount with a short barrel 4.7-inch gun used for AA and anti-submarine defence. This is pointing upwards towards the sky – frozen in action at the moment of the attack. The auxiliary steering position telegraph is still present but has fallen over. As I explored the rooms below the gun platform, I found ready-use artillery shells for the stern defensive gun, depth charges and the steering gear. Moving over to the fantail and peering over the rail, I could see the four-bladed propeller and the rudder beneath me.

After a pleasant 60-minute dive we headed back up to the surface, and after de-kitting inwater and passing our bailout cylinders up to crew, I climbed up the dive ladder and into the boat. Almost immediately Paul started to feel a burning sensation on his bare neck just above the collar of his wet suit. Very quickly the skin in this area began to blister, going red and puffing up. Within the space of 30 minutes the blister had turned brown and was in the process of going black and crusty. I had never seen an aviation fuel skin burn before – it was amazing just how quickly the area blistered, turned red, then black. During WII, aviators suffered horrendous burns from aviation fuel.

Aviation fuel is a clear liquid – you can't spot it under water and Paul wasn't conscious of having felt or seen anything down on the wreck. He had simply swum into an invisible stream of aviation fuel leaking from barrels on the wreck, and was now paying the price. Over the coming days the scab over the wound quickly fell off to leave pink new skin underneath. In small amounts, burns such as this are not serious – but it was a reminder, as if needed, of how toxic some of the cargoes in Chuuk still are.

Katsuragisan Maru

2,427grt cargo freighter (1925)
IJN Auxiliary Transport (1941)

On the last day of our 2015 trip we decided to go out and dive the 2,427grt, cargo freighter, *Katsuragisan Maru*, built in 1925 by Mitsui Bussan Zosensho in Tama, Tokyo. She is another wreck that lies well away from the main tourist wrecks, out towards Northeast Pass. She lies in 70 metres of water and is the deepest wreck in the lagoon – so she is perhaps the least visited of the Truk wrecks.

Katsuragisan Maru was constructed as a well deck steamer with a raised foc'sle and two foredeck holds before a composite superstructure amidships that had a tall narrow bridge superstructure forward and the engine casing superstructure aft. Two more holds were set in

The 2,427grt Katsuragisan Maru. Her wreck is the deepest dive in Truk Lagoon – and one of the most remote. She rests upright in 70 metres of water with 62 metres to the deck, well out from the central Chuukese islands at North East Pass.

the aft well deck before a raised stern deckhouse, which held the steering gear below. She was fitted with a traditional reciprocating triple expansion steam engine that gave her a service speed of 10 knots, standard for the older ships of the day, but slow in comparison to the new breed of ships fitted with diesel engines that were beginning to be built.

Katsuragisan Maru was almost 20 years old when, in December 1941, she was requisitioned by the Japanese Imperial Army and converted for use as an auxiliary transport. During conversion, a 3-inch defensive gun on a circular gun platform was added on top of the stern deckhouse.

Two years after her launch, on 20 December 1943, she departed Tokyo with a mixed cargo, southbound for Truk. In her holds were rolls of interlocking steel mesh matting ringed with hooks and slots for assembly using sledgehammers – a simple way to lay down and repair runways for aircraft on any ground, paved or unpaved, and extremely useful in the remote islands of the Pacific. Other holds contained military trucks and general cargo.

She arrived without incident outside the barrier reef that surrounds Truk Lagoon on 7 January 1944, and approached the Northeast Pass through the reef to enter the lagoon.

There are only five passes or channels through the 140-mile circumference of the coral barrier reef of the lagoon that are suitable for navigation by larger vessels. As part of their fortification of the lagoon, the Japanese had closed off and mined all but the heavily defended North Pass and South Pass – they were now the only channels open for navigation. Northeast Pass, which *Katsuragisan Maru* was now approaching, is a few hundred metres wide, and although it had been the main shipping channel prior to the war it had been closed off and heavily mined by the Japanese on the outbreak of hostilities, to prevent any Allied incursion by submarine or surface craft.

As a result of a breakdown in communication however somewhere along the line, *Katsuragisan Maru* inexplicably steamed into the Northeast Pass. She was unknowingly moving into great danger.

At about 0530, just inside the barrier reef of the lagoon, the inevitable happened – she struck one of the submerged mines with her starboard side just aft of the superstructure. The powerful explosion rocked the freighter and, fatally wounded, she sank quickly into 70 metres of water coming to rest on the bottom of the lagoon upright on her keel. Five of her crew had been killed in the sinking.

The inadvertent loss of such a valuable ship and its precious war cargo on the doorstep of one of their own bases was a bitter blow for the Japanese. Their investigation concluded that their own escort vessels, on entering the lagoon from afar, were not being sufficiently informed about the location of minefields and areas restricted to navigation.

The Japanese determined that all new captains and masters navigating the area for the first time should be made aware of the location of the minefields, and that up-to-date charts should be available. Formal notifications were sent out to the commanders of naval bases such as Saipan and Rabaul (from where ships were likely to come to Truk) as well as to the fleet commanders of the Combined Fleet and the China Area Fleet, stressing that the only channels into Truk Lagoon open to navigation were the North and South Channel; and advising that the sea area within the lagoon was dangerous for navigation for 4 kilometres in from the inner edge of the reef, except for navigators in possession of details of the minefields.

Today, lying in 70 metres of water, with a depth to her deck of 62 metres and a least depth to her superstructure and fo'c'sle deck of 55 metres, the *Katsuragisan Maru* is a wreck for technical divers only. Located out at the outer barrier reef, just inside Northeast Pass, she is so far away from the main islands of the lagoon that she is blessed with some of the best underwater visibility to be found on any of the Japanese wrecks, and is frequently visited by sharks.

The stem of her bow has the classic plumb stem so characteristic of ships built in the early part of the 20th century. Her fo'c'sle deck holds the anchor windlass, which still has two anchor chains running out from it to their hawse pipes. As she was under way when she sank, both anchors are still held snug in their hawses. Two aft-facing doors lead from the main deck into the fo'c'sle spaces.

In the well deck, the foremast, which rose up from in between the hatches for Holds Nos 1 and 2, has fallen forward and slightly diagonally to port across Hatch No 1, and now rests with its crosstree on the fo'c'sle. Venturing into Hold No 1 you will find tyres, gas masks and canisters – and the precious rolled-up steel mesh matting for airfield construction. Hold No 2 contains spare propeller blades, spare tyres, tracks, electrical equipment and rolls of hawser cable.

The superstructure amidships is a scene of chaos. A serious fire appears to have broken out following the mine explosion in the aft starboard part of the ship – and this raged through the bridge, destroying the wooden sections and weakening beams and girders. The bridge superstructure has collapsed and is now quite flat. The crew accommodation cabins outboard and either side of the engine casing have also collapsed, and this has exposed the triple expansion steam engine itself. The galley was situated at the aft end of this superstructure to starboard, and scattered china can be found here.

On the aft well deck, the mainmast that rose between the hatches for the two aft holds has broken and fallen forward to lie diagonally to port across the foremost hatch, its triangular crosstree resting on the port side of the deck.

The aftmost hold contains about half a dozen military trucks and an officer's car parked up in neat lines. The starboard side of the hull adjacent to the holds shows heavy structural damage from the mine explosion. The hull plating is bent over inwards from the contact, and the hull and main deck has collapsed down, almost splitting the ship in two. The force of the explosion blew the hatch cover beams into the air, and they have fallen to lie scattered amongst the trucks. The end of one hatch cover beam has gone straight through the windscreen of one truck as it fell down.

At the very stern, the 3-inch defensive gun still sits on its circular mount on top of the stern deckhouse, its barrel pointing slightly to port. The steering gear is housed in the spaces below.

We sped out from our base at Truk Stop, on the south-west side of the main Chuuk island of Weno, on another typically beautiful Chuuk dive day. The water was oily calm, a deep blue, and the sky was clear – and so the ride out of about an hour in our 11-metre-long open boat powered by two massive outboard engines was exhilarating and interesting. We sped past the runway for the airport, which sticks far out to sea at Weno's north-west corner, passing an old anchored freighter that was still apparently in use, but which was so corroded that in places above the water line you could see right through the shell plating of the hull. I suspected that it

Zipping out to North East Pass on a typical oily calm day in Chuuk Lagoon. (Author's collection)

wouldn't be afloat for much longer, and might be an addition to the wrecks of Chuuk Lagoon in the not too distant future. The sun was beating down, and I was glad of the shade from the bimini sun canopy that covered almost the entire boat from the helm aft.

The ride out was a high-speed dash north, skimming the west side of Weno on our right-hand side, before turning to the north-east and heading for Northeast Pass. As we sped over the shimmering millpond-flat waters of the lagoon, the chines of the hull threw out a delicate white spray of water to either side, creating a foaming wake that your eyes could follow astern, seemingly all the way back to where we had left.

As we rounded the airport runway, and as Weno began to recede into the distance astern, there was little to see ahead of us – just brilliant blue water running off into infinity to merge with the sky. But slowly, as we began to near the outer barrier reef of the lagoon, I began to see a line of breaking white water on the horizon, far in the distance.

As we sped on, we began to skim past scattered idyllic small desert islands – the sort of exotic paradise destinations you see on the TV. Small sandy beaches ringed around a copse of palm trees and jungle – the islands were too small to have any inhabitants. They were your classic idea of a desert island.

We sped on towards the outer reef and Northeast Pass. Very soon the line of breaking waves began to show a dark line of coral outcrops projecting out of the water. And then I began to see a gap on the line of breakers – we were nearing Northeast Pass. We roared on in our fast boat, closing in on the pass at speed – and then, well inside the actual opening of the pass itself, the boat began to slow. After a few moments of searching, we picked up the submerged buoy and tied off.

I had already had 10 days of serious repeat diving so far on this trip – and with my bad bend in the North Channel off Ireland in 2003 always in the back of my mind, I had decided

As the dive boat nears North East Pass it moves past scattered deserted islands. (Author's collection)

the night before not to push it and do a deep dive this day: I would stay topside and give surface cover. Paul Haynes would dive with Gary Petrie, and our dive centre guide would be diving, along with a couple of other visiting tech divers, one of whom was an open-circuit diver and would be diving twin aluminium 80L cylinders with a trimix bottom gas and carrying three other AL80 cylinders with various other gases for his deco.

There is little tide to worry about when diving in the central wrecks of Chuuk Lagoon. You can dive most of the wrecks most of the time. But we had been told that there would be a bit of tide on this wreck, as the passes through the barrier reef of the lagoon are the only places where the tide can bring in and extract water on the flood and the ebb. The dive had been timed for low water slack, when the tidal current would be almost nil – but it would rapidly pick up on the flood tide as the ascent from the wreck began.

We were tied off a few hundred metres inside the lagoon from Northeast Pass. We could now clearly see the two outermost sides of the pass, and could feel the body of water moving from oceanic depths outside the lagoon through the pass and into the lagoon. There was a gentle ripple of moving water running down the side of the dive boat from the tide.

The divers started getting dressed into their diving rigs. A deco trapeze of aluminium bars suspended on a rope from each end of the boat was lowered into the water, and emergency bailout cylinders of oxygen-rich nitrox breathing gas were clipped on to it to it, along with a separate bailout cylinder of pure oxygen at the 6-metre bar. Another AL80 cylinder of pure oxygen was carried aboard – this was no place to get a bend; there was no helicopter coming to get you. If there was a bend, we would self-treat with O2 until we could make it back to Weno, where there is a recompression chamber.

The plan was agreed that once down on the wreck, at the end of the bottom time phase of the dive, all divers would return to where the fixed downline was tied off to the wreck to simultaneously ascend. Because the tide would be starting to run by this time, it was agreed that once the divers had transferred from the downline to the trapeze, our dive boat would then cast off from the buoy line and drift free with the current – with all divers doing their deco on the trapeze beneath.

It is quite hard to hold onto a fixed downline from a wreck for an extended period of decompression of say an hour or more once the tide has picked up – the water can be moving past you at 1–2 knots. By untying the dive boat with the trapeze underneath, boat and divers drift with the tide, the divers comfortable in a fixed body of seemingly stationary water despite having a speed over the ground of 1–2 knots. The divers were briefed to deploy a tall red delayed surface marker buoy (DSMB) as they began their ascent, to let us topside know all was fine. If there was a problem, I could quickly go down with spare gas.

The divers had agreed a bottom time of 30–35 minutes down on the wreck. This would mean about 90 minutes of decompression and produce a total dive run time, including decompression, of just over two hours.

As the divers descended, large bloops of air and a fizz of smaller bubbles from the open-circuit divers breaking the oily calm surface revealed their presence below. As the minutes ticked by, I watched the bubbles starting to slowly move away from the boat as the divers began their exploration along the wreck far below.

The local Chuukese dive boat driver, thinking his duties temporarily over, promptly lay down for a snooze in the shade of the bimini. I was uncomfortable with this – I had once come back to my own RIB (rigid inflatable boat) far offshore off north-east Scotland to find seemingly no one in it. Getting alongside the boat and taking my mouthpiece out I shouted for the boat driver that day – but got no response. I began to worry that the boat driver had fallen overboard or taken ill, but eventually after a few minutes of shouting, a sleepy-eyed, yawning boat driver had peered over the side of the RIB to see what I was up to. If I had surfaced some distance away from the RIB after a free ascent away from the downline, there would have been no possibility of swimming back to the boat against our strong currents, and I wouldn't have been spotted until the boat driver had woken up. By then I could have been a mile, or even more, away from the boat and perhaps triggered a full-scale search and rescue. With a number of years' service as UK lifeboat crew, and perhaps wearing my old lifeboat crew hat, while the Chuukese boat driver nodded off I went to full alert, watching the progress of the dive from the bubble streams hitting the surface and keeping an eye out for any signs of trouble.

After about 25 minutes, I could see a line of diver bubbles streaming out down-current but slowly creeping back towards the downline. The current was running quite quickly now past the buoy line that we were tied to, making a little rippling wake on either side of it. Not a problem; my diver buddies were used to diving in the very tidal waters of our north-east coast of Scotland and would be well able to understand what was going on and cope with it. The boat driver slept on.

Hearing a louder whoosh of bubbles breaking the surface behind me, I turned around to see an isolated red DSMB break the surface about 50 metres away from the dive boat downstream – in the direction of main group of islands in the centre of the lagoon. One or more divers had become separated from the rest of the group and were doing a free ascent off the downline. As I stared at the DSMB I saw a tell-tale stream of bubbles downstream of it – it was one or more of the open-circuit divers and not one of my CCR dive buddies. Our boat driver snoozed on.

Even when not part of the dive plan, a free ascent away from the fixed downline isn't usually a problem; it isn't unusual, in our low vis North Sea diving off Scotland, to find a diver getting disorientated on a wreck in poor underwater visibility and be unable to get back to the downline to ascend. In really poor vis, it's common for divers to clip a reel onto the downline once they initially get down to the wreck and then reel off the downline – just so they can find their way back for the ascent.

But on this wreck in a remote part of the lagoon, the underwater visibility would be a crystal-clear 50–100 metres, so there was no prospect of not finding the downline if you really wanted to. It was possible however that, perhaps finding something of interest, one of the open-circuit divers had overstayed his bottom time well away from the downline and had elected to get shallow quickly by doing a free ascent, rather than incur higher decompression penalties by taking more time at depth to return to the downline. Or perhaps, there had been a problem; someone might be out of bottom gas. The possibilities were endless – but there was no immediate reason to panic or get too concerned.

I called out to the boat driver who was still lying down up at the bow, but there was no response; he was still asleep. I called out to him a bit louder, and then went and woke him up. His English wasn't that good – but after showing him the DSMB, he asked me what we should do, as none of the other deco bags were up yet. I knew that my guys Paul and Gary were used to this sort of deep deco diving and would follow the plan – and that they'd send up a yellow DSMB if there was a problem. I told him to cast off the buoy line and we would motor over to the drifting red DSMB and see what was going on. One possibility was that a diver had lost his grip on a DSMB whilst deploying it at depth, and that there was in fact no one hanging underneath it.

As we motored slowly over to the DSMB, I noticed that the bag wasn't fully inflated – only the top 1–2 feet of it was actually standing proud of the water. They are usually 2–3 metres long and normally would have a good metre or more sticking out of the water so they can be spotted by boat crew a long way off. There was clearly weight on the bag pulling it under; the line was taut. At least I had ruled out a drifting unattached free bag, so one possibility had been eliminated.

Our dive group's practice is to write the diver's first name or initials in big black permanent marker pen at the top of the DSMB so those topside can see who it is. The absence of a name or initials on this DSMB told me this wasn't one of my guys who had perhaps had to bailout off his rebreather and was breathing down his open-circuit bailout tanks.

The dive boat slowed to a stop beside the DSMB and I looked over the gunwale and peered down into the water. In the crystal-clear water, I could clearly see a diver holding the reel down at the bottom of the line, some 10–15 metres below the surface. It was the open-circuit diver who had gone in carrying five AL80 cylinders. He seemed relaxed and in no distress and when he saw me, peering down from above, he began giving me repeated OK hand signals. I acknowledged with an OK signal back to him.

As I looked back to the buoy about 50 metres away, the DSMBs from the rest of the group began to pop up beside the buoy as they began their ascent from the wreck. I counted them off – everyone else was there. So we had one diver drifting free and all the others on the downline. They would soon be looking for the trapeze and the dive boat above them, expecting to move from the fixed downline to the trapeze at about 12 metres. So, knowing that the solo diver was

OK, we motored back to the buoy and the boat driver nimbly tied off to it once again and then deployed the trapeze with the bailout gas over the side of the boat.

As we waited beside the buoy for our divers to get shallow enough to transfer over to the trapeze, I kept an eye on the solo diver's DSMB. We were a long way out from the main central islands here, and as there was little or no possibility of an emergency services air or sea search out here, we couldn't afford to lose sight of a diver. The flood tide was picking up noticeably in intensity and the solo diver's partly inflated DSMB was now receding towards the central islands at some speed.

With about an hour of deco still to go, as the minutes ticked by so the solo diver's DSMB became further away and increasingly difficult to see, its top only just showing proud of the surface.

I took a transit on the DSMB by lining it up with a distant hill peak on Weno so that at least I would have a direction to go look for him if we lost visual contact. We had to stay with the main group of divers ascending the buoy line, as any of them could have a problem of their own, and I knew that the solo diver had given an OK signal and seemed comfortable. All the spare bailout gas was attached to the trapeze.

I was just beginning to feel I was about to lose sight of the solo diver's DSMB in the distance when I noticed that it seemed to be getting bigger again. The DSMB was moving back in our general direction – but was well off towards our east. At first, I struggled to follow what was happening, as the tide had only just turned to the flood and wouldn't turn again for a number of hours.

In Stonehaven Bay, in my home waters, we have a local anomaly where at flood tide, when the tide is running south, the shape of the bay catches some of the flood tide and essentially creates a vortex in the bay. At the north end of the bay is Garron Point, a spur of rocks that sticks out to sea in a north-easterly direction from the rock foot just beneath the clifftop Stonehaven Golf Club. In that bay, despite a flood tide running from north to south, as a result of the layout of the shore the flood tide water of the vortex runs in a great clockwise semi-circle. Thus the water in the bay at the Garron actually runs in completely the opposite direction, from south to north. The local lifeboat crew know of this effect and have to factor it into their search patterns when looking for a casualty. I guessed this was what was happening here, too – the solo diver had been swept south into the lagoon from Northeast Pass by the flood tide but had entered a local eddy or anomaly which was taking him in completely the opposite direction, back up north.

The 1–2 feet of the top of his DSMB got steadily bigger until it moved past our dive boat about 100–200 metres off on our east side. He was now moving quite quickly and heading away from the centre of the lagoon towards the barrier reef.

I continued to check on the main group of divers coming up the buoy line, at the same time keeping an eye on the solo diver's DSMB which, having got smaller as it moved away south from us and then got bigger as it moved north past our boat, was now once again getting smaller as it moved at speed further north towards the reef.

Very soon I could barely see it in the glare of the sun on the surface of the water. I started taking transit fixes on it, lining it up with protruding sections of the distant barrier where white water was breaking. The glare was so bad that each time I checked the main group, when I turned back to look for the solo DSMB, at first I could never find it. Only by lining up my transit and staring hard and intently for several minutes was I able catch a glimpse of the errant and now distant DSMB, which now looked black against the dark blue of the sea.

As the main group of divers reached the shallows, they were able to transfer over to the trapeze and complete their decompression stops. After about two hours in water, the divers started popping their heads out of the water, ready to pass up their heavy bailout cylinders and get back into the boat.

Once they were all back in the boat, the dive guide immediately came up to me and asked if I had seen the solo diver – he said that they had all rendezvoused together at the bottom of the downline but as the group began the ascent, the solo diver had just waved to them and swam down-current, out into the blue. In the current, there was no way any of them could get to him without losing sight of the downline. They wouldn't have been able to work back to the downline against the strong current even if they had got to him. They'd had to let him go.

'He'll have gone that way,' said the guide, pointing south into the lagoon towards the distant central islands. 'We'd better go look for him.'

'You're not going to believe this,' I replied, 'but he went that way at first – but then he came back, passed us and is now heading off to the outer reef. He's gone 180 degrees in the other direction. I can barely see him now, but he's about a mile away and getting quite close to the reef over there.' I pointed towards the distant reef, the water seemingly featureless in the strong midday sun.

'Are you sure, Rod?'

'Yes – I've had a bead on him in line with the high point of that little outcrop over there. Every now and then I get a glimpse of his bag – it's not fully inflated; only the top 1–2 feet of it is sticking out of the water.'

The guide peered in the direction of my outstretched hand for a moment before replying, 'Well, I can't see it – we'd better go over and look.'

I stood beside the boat driver and dive guide, and using my arm as a pointer began to give directions on bearing as we motored over. There was still at first no sign of the DSMB, and I was beginning to think we might have a full-on separation incident beginning to take place, when I just caught the fleetest glimpse of the seemingly black tip of his DSMB, sticking up proud of the water about half a mile away.

'There he is!' I shouted, relieved.

'I still can't see him,' said the guide.

'Keep on this track – we've got him,' I said.

As we motored on towards the DSMB, it steadily grew in size until we were able to slow the boat to a stop beside it – we were very close to the outer reef by now and I wondered if the diver would already be seeing the bottom coming up. As we stopped, we peered over the side of the boat to get a clear view of the diver – he was looking up from below at 6 metres and giving us repeated OK signals.

After another 25 minutes, he finally surfaced and we hauled him and his kit in. He seemed completely oblivious to what had happened, to where he was now, or to the anxiety he had just caused. He just didn't appreciate how close he had been to a separation. He just went on about how good the dive was.

As the chatter subsided, I took him to one side and asked him why he had swum away from the main group in such a remote tidal location. He muttered some reason about enjoying the experience of a free ascent that I just didn't follow.

I explained to him in no uncertain terms where he had drifted and that on another day, he might not have been seen at all – and that we might still be searching for him to this day. To the best of my knowledge there is no organised local lifeboat service in Chuuk – certainly nothing similar to the Royal National Lifeboat Institution we have in the UK, with lifeboat stations dotted around our ports and coastline, ready to respond at a few minutes' notice. Micronesia comprises over 600 islands and with a lack of local resources, the U.S. Coast Guard Hawaii Pacific section regularly carries out the search and rescue operations and duties in these scattered islands. The U.S. Coast Guard Sector in Guam, some 650 nautical miles away, covers Chuuk. I think the penny finally dropped for this particular gentleman.

11

IJN *KAMIKAZE*-CLASS DESTROYER *OITE*

Truk Lagoon

Of all the wrecks lying at the bottom of Chuuk Lagoon, one of the most special I have dived is that of the sleek 1,400-ton destroyer *Oite* – yet another casualty of Operation Hailstone. She is a deeper dive than most in Chuuk Lagoon, in about 62 metres of water, and as she is a small destroyer that doesn't rise very high off the seabed, you will be not far above the bottom most of the time. *Oite* is therefore a wreck firmly in the realm of the technical diver using extended range diving techniques and trimix as bottom gas to eliminate dangerous nitrogen narcosis, whether in a rebreather or open circuit, and to shorten decompression times. If open circuit, then oxygen-rich breathing gases are carried in separate stage cylinders, which the diver will switch to for the decompression phase of the dive. One of the downsides to open-circuit deep diving using trimix in such a remote location is cost – it is very expensive to get hold of, and it is not uncommon to see open-circuit divers getting gas bills at the end of a deep week's diving of thousands of dollars. With rebreathers recirculating a small amount of trimix, gas bills are minimal.

IJN *Oite* is one of the more remote Chuuk wrecks, lying well away from the other wrecks way up north from Weno towards North Pass – one of the five navigable channels through the barrier reef that rings around the central islands. As she is so far away from the main islands, and from any runoff or pollution, the underwater visibility is usually crystal clear – the best in the lagoon with vis of 200 feet or more.

The 1,400-ton IJN Kamikaze-class destroyer Oite.

There was not much information available about diving *Oite* when I first visited it, as because of its depth and remoteness, like *Katsuragisan Maru*, it is not dived as regularly as the more popular shallower wrecks – but *Oite* is one of the wrecks in Chuuk that actually made me gasp with shock at what I saw.

IJN *Oite* was constructed in the 1920s – well before war in the Pacific was anticipated, and at a time when Japan was a World War I ally of Britain. She was laid down by the Uraga Dock Co Ltd in Tokyo on 16 March 1923 and launched 18 months later, on 27 November 1924. Fitting out afloat took just short of another year and she was signed off as completed on 30 October 1925. She displaced 1,400 tons standard load, with a full load displacement when filled with fuel, shells etc of 1,720 tons.

In the years following World War I, Japan began development of a new first-class type of destroyer – the *Minekaze*-class. In all, 36 first-class destroyers would be completed to the *Minekaze* basic design – and until the advent of the Special Type destroyers in 1929 these ships formed the core of the Japanese destroyer force.

The *Minekaze*-class was a hybrid of traditional British and German destroyer designs. The torpedo boat destroyer had been a very potent weapon of the Imperial German Navy during World War I, able to attack at speed, and with the potential to disable capital ships (battleships and battlecruisers) with a single torpedo. The Imperial Japanese Navy had been given five German destroyers after the war ended by way of war reparations, and had reverse-engineered their own version.

Japan wanted a destroyer that was larger and faster than the German World War I destroyers – a ship that would be able to operate in the rough waters of the Pacific, where they had dreams of creating their own empire to rival those of the European powers and to possibly confront America.

To give their new destroyer better seakeeping ability, Japanese naval architects altered the German design by moving the bridge further aft, out of the seas and spray that might sweep over the bow as it rose and plunged into heavy seas. The fo'c'sle was also lengthened, heightened and given a turtle back to further reduce the impact of heavy seas on the bridge – and a well deck was set in between the bridge and fo'c'sle. The new class was fitted with geared turbines that gave them a maximum speed of 39 knots.

A second group of nine *Minekaze*-class destroyers was ordered in 1921–22, designed to improve on the first group of 15 *Minekaze*-class vessels already built. Because of the differences in design, this second group was subsequently designated as a new class of destroyer – the *Kamikaze* class – even although the new ships were virtually identical to the last three ships of the first group of the *Minekaze* class.

The bridge structure itself was further modified and given an armoured, fixed steel covering in place of the previous canvas screen – these were the first Japanese destroyers to have such an armoured bridge. This extra weight, allied to a wider beam and deeper draught, increased the vessel's displacement and improved sea handling and stability – but reduced the top speed by 2 knots.

Oite was one of this second group of nine destroyers; she was 336 feet long overall with a beam of 30 feet and a draught of 10 feet. Her two propeller shafts were driven by Parsons geared turbines powered by four Kampon boilers that gave her a top speed of 37 knots – fast even by today's standards, almost 100 years later. Her name means 'Favourable Wind'. She had a range of 3,600 nautical miles at 14 knots and carried a crew of 148.

When she was first built, *Oite*, as with all the *Minekaze*-class destroyers, was fitted with four 120mm (4.7-inch) dual-purpose (DP) main deck guns in single mounts. DP guns could engage surface targets and also elevate to become AA guns with an altitude ceiling of 32,800 feet – just over six miles. The 120mm DP gun fired a 45lb base fuzed armour-piercing shell or nose-fuzed high explosive (HE) shell that had a range of 17,500 yards – almost ten miles.

One 120mm DP gun was set on the fo'c'sle, two on the centre line amidships and one abaft the mainmast. She was also fitted with three twin 21-inch torpedo mounts – one situated in the well deck in front of the bridge and the other two abaft the second smoke stack. She carried 18 depth charges on trolleys that could be deployed from two sets of tracks, one either side at the stern. She was also fitted with two single-sided Type 81 depth charge projectors.

Fast and powerful though she was at her launch, 20 years later, at the advent of World War II, the *Minekaze*-class and *Kamikaze*-class destroyers were considered old second-line units – more useful as destroyer transports and escorts than frontline surface warfare units.

At the time of construction in 1923/24, the threat to a warship from air attack had been negligible – and her original design was almost completely devoid of any anti-aircraft weaponry, with only two single 7.7mm machine guns, mounted one either side of the bridge.

As the threat to surface vessels from air attack became more potent in the years that followed her construction, it became clear that this class of destroyer was poorly protected against air attack, and modifications were carried out to make room for increased AA weaponry. One of her four 4.7-inch main guns, of little use against air attack, was removed, along with her aft bank of torpedoes. By World War II, her configuration was three main battery 4.7-inch guns, set one on the raised fo'c'sle at the bow, one in the amidships Q turret position between the two squat smokestacks, and the third situated towards the stern. She was also refitted with ten 25mm AA auto cannons in addition to her two original 7.7mm AA machine guns.

The standard Japanese Type 95 depth charge at the start of World War II carried a 220lb (100kg) explosive charge. Its fuze had a water inlet that detonated the charge when a certain amount of water had entered – and there were just two depth settings, 100 feet (30 metres) and 200 feet (60 metres). In the first few years of World War II, the Japanese were unaware that American submarines could dive to 300 feet or more, and were consequently setting the fuzes on their depth charges too shallow. That's why, in old black and white movies about the Pacific War, you sometimes hear the American submarine commander ordering the submarine to be taken deep; he was actually getting down deeper than the depth at which the depth charges would detonate. The deeper fuze setting of 200 feet (60 metres) was still well above the diving depth capability of an American submarine, and this shallow setting of depth charge fuzes allowed many American submarines to survive depth charging by running deep.

The Japanese only discovered from a chance public remark by a U.S. congressman that U.S. submarines could dive deeper than the Japanese had thought. Alerted by this unfortunate U.S. intelligence leak, they increased the explosive charge to 324lb (147kg) and added a 300-foot (90-metre) additional depth setting. American submarines were now very vulnerable to these depth charges – and many lives were subsequently lost as a result of the congressman's unfortunate slip.

The Japanese loaded depth charges on almost every ship that could carry them, and made heavy use of depth charge throwers. Most naval auxiliary transport vessels, the *Marus*, had single roll-off depth charge holders fitted one either side of the fantail at the stern. If the ship ran over a suspected submarine the depth charges could be dropped. Many of the *Marus* at Truk still carry these depth charge holders – each still with a deadly depth charge in it.

In December 1941, in the run-up to Japan's entry into World War II, *Oite* was assigned to Destroyer Division 29; she was then one of 12 destroyers in the South Seas Force. She took part in the initial unsuccessful Japanese invasion of Wake Island on 11 December 1941, where she was lightly damaged by gunfire from American coastal batteries. She operated with the second Wake Island invasion force that successfully seized the island on 23 December 1941. In January 1942, she was involved in the invasion of Rabaul and then Lae/Salamua in March 1942. During the Battle of the Coral Sea on 7/8 May 1942 she escorted the Port Moresby invasion convoy.

Operating initially out of Rabaul for the rest of 1942 and into 1943 (and latterly from Truk), she was heavily involved in transport and convoy escort duty between garrison islands such as Kwajalein, Rabaul, Saipan and Guadalcanal. On 21 September 1943, whilst escorting a convoy from Truk to Japan, she was hit by an American torpedo – which turned out to be a dud and caused only minor damage.

On 15 February 1944, *Oite* left Truk with Subchaser No 28, escorting the light cruiser *Agano* for Japan via Saipan. The U.S. submarine *Skate* detected the naval vessels en route approximately 160 nautical miles northwest of Truk. At sundown, *Skate* fired four torpedoes at *Agano* from a distance of 2,400 yards, scoring three hits out of the four. The damage to the lightly armoured cruiser from the three torpedo hits was substantial – she caught fire and started to slowly sink. *Oite* searched for the submarine fruitlessly and *Skate* was able to escape undetected.

Oite stayed with the stricken *Agano* throughout the night, receiving transfers of *Agano*'s fuel and more than 500 officers and men – 107 officers and men from *Agano* had been lost in the attack. *Oite* was then ordered to return to Truk Lagoon with the survivors – unaware of the approach of Task Force 58 and the impending Operation Hailstone raid.

During the initial fighter sweep early on the second day of the fast carrier air strikes on 18 February 1944, Hellcat fighters from the carriers *Bunker Hill* and *Monterey* spotted *Oite* entering the lagoon through the North Pass. They attacked and strafed her, killing the captain in his bridge and causing fires to break out aft of the smokestack. The rescued captain of the *Agano* assumed command of *Oite*.

Five Grumman Avenger torpedo bombers from *Bunker Hill* then joined in the attack. The new stand-in skipper of *Oite* threw his charge about in a desperate attempt to avoid the bombs and torpedoes of the U.S. aircraft – but whilst making a high-speed evasive turn to starboard, *Oite* was hit by a single torpedo aft of the bridge.

The effect of the torpedo on such a relatively small, lightly protected ship was catastrophic. The powerful engines were not immediately affected by the explosion and kept pushing her forward at her action speed of 35 knots as she turned to starboard. She broke her back, splitting into two roughly equal sections during the turn. The bow, free from the stern – which was still driving forward – slewed around to starboard, jack-knifing until the tip of the bow was almost level with the stern, in an inverted V.

Blown in half, she sank almost immediately. 172 of the *Oite's* crew and 522 crew of the *Agano* aboard her were all killed in this contact. Only about 20 men survived.

The wreck of *Oite* lay forgotten about and undisturbed on the bottom of the lagoon for more than 40 years, lying halfway out from the central Truk islands, towards North Pass and the barrier reef. She lay in deep water of almost 65 metres – too deep for safe conventional air diving. When Cousteau led his expedition to Truk to film *Lagoon of Lost Ships* in 1969, *Oite* had not yet been found. In 1986 however, enterprising divers rediscovered her – her two sections lying in close proximity on a flat clean white sandy bottom. She is now one of the most remote of Truk lagoon's wrecks, requiring a fast boat ride of about an hour north from Weno. With the seabed at 62 metres, her two sections rise up at most 5 metres from the seabed.

In 2015, Paul Haynes, Gary Petrie and I rose at 0545 and got down to Truk Stop Dive Center's gear lockers for 0600, hauling out our CCRs and building them up in the cool early morning half-light. Once the CCR was built up we ran through the standard positive and negative pressure checks of the breathing loop to see if it was holding pressure and that there were no leaks. After that we could relax and have some breakfast.

Once breakfast was done, we stretched ourselves into our 3mm wetsuits and strolled down the jetty as dive centre crew trolleyed our kit down to the boat. It was still only 0700 and we were about ready to go to sea. The sun had been up for an hour and even at this time of the morning the heat was beginning to build. Our guide for the day was long-time Truk Stop Dive Center stalwart Rob McGann – a well-known and respected American technical diver and cave diver.

Once we were all aboard, the ropes were cast off, and we turned our bow to the north and throttled up the powerful twin outboards. We were soon skipping over the oily calm waters of another magical Chuuk day at more than 20 knots.

As we closed on *Oite*, far out on the open northern expanse of the lagoon, it felt as though we were somewhere very remote. The central islands of Chuuk were astern of us, low down and beginning to look very small in the distance. In other parts of Chuuk Lagoon, you can be diving big ships, but still be relatively close to the islands. Out here towards North Channel, it was akin to blue water diving.

The dive boat powered down and came off the plane as we approached the wreck site – even at this distance from the land the skipper was using transits to close in on it.

Before long, the skipper had spotted the submerged buoy a few feet under the water, and his crewman had jumped over the side and threaded our head rope through the buoy eye and passed it back to the boat to be cleated off. The engines were switched off – and suddenly the silence was deafening; there was nothing else around way out here.

We started to get dressed into our CCRs, clipping our bailout tanks under our arms, pulling on fins, clipping on torches and video cameras and spitting in masks and rubbing the phlegm around to prevent any fogging of the lenses, before rinsing them in the sea. I powered up my CCR wrist-mounted computer and let it go through its boot-up self-check sequence.

Once all the self-checks had been done, my CCR was working beautifully and ready to dive. I stuck the mouthpiece of my rebreather into my mouth and slipped the mouthpiece-retaining strap over my head. Such straps have been around in military use since World War II but have not been universally adopted as standard by the present-day commercial CCR manufacturers – but you can buy them as an add-on. Underwater on a CCR you could lose consciousness for a number of reasons, such as carbon dioxide build-up, low oxygen levels, stroke, heart attack, the bends, nitrogen narcosis and many others. If you lose consciousness for any reason on a CCR and there is no one there to rescue you, then after a period of time your body will relax – the mouthpiece drops from your mouth and your lungs fill with water. The cause of death is inevitably drowning.

In recent years there has been a movement to get mouthpiece-retaining straps adopted by CCR manufacturers so they come fitted as standard with the CCR when you buy it. My dive buddy Paul Haynes has championed this cause – and has presented about the benefits of these straps at a number of international conferences. You can read one of his papers, 'Increasing the Probability of Surviving Loss of Consciousness Underwater When Using a Rebreather' in *Diving and Hyperbaric Medicine*, Volume 46 No 4, December 2016.

As a result of pressure and raising of awareness by Paul and like-minded experts, even although manufacturers have not yet adopted the strap as part of their standard CCR kit configuration, many CCR divers have bought their own straps and adopted the practice of wearing them as standard. I know my group certainly has – and I would feel very naked without using one nowadays. I shudder when I see CCR divers not using them – they are so cheap to buy, and yet are so effective.

In Paul's military days, on a long-submerged insertion in a swimmer delivery vehicle, it was fairly common for combat swimmers to have a short catnap of up to 15 minutes, whilst wearing a CCR with a mouthpiece-retaining strap, without incident. If a CCR diver loses consciousness for any reason and is wearing a retaining strap, the mouthpiece is kept in the mouth and the chances of the diver's lungs remaining dry and not flooding with water are greatly increased. They may well escape an otherwise almost inevitable death by drowning.

Once fully rigged, gag strap on, I sat on the gunwale of the dive boat pre-breathing my CCR for 3–5 minutes. Then, pre-breathe finished, I rolled over backwards into the water – and was immediately struck by the deep rich blue of the beautifully clear water. But even though I could see a long way down in the good visibility, the wreck, even in this amazing clarity of water, lay far below – well out of sight.

Hanging a couple of metres beneath the surface, I gave my dive buddies an OK hand signal, and after they had responded with the same signal we gave a simultaneous thumbs down signal to start the descent. I dumped what little residual air there was in my buoyancy wings and started to slowly sink.

I dropped down beside the line, equalising the pressure on my ears from time to time by pinching my nose and blowing out as some large black and white striped batfish came in for a look at the strange visitors to their realm. After having been momentarily distracted by them, when I returned my gaze downwards, the dark fuzzy outline of a large inverted V had materialised out of the gloom far below me – it was the first blurry sighting of *Oite*. I could see the downline from the buoy dropping away almost vertically down to the very stern on my left-hand side.

Once we got down to about 25 metres, our dive guide left the downline and started to fin gently and slowly across the open water between both sections, towards the bow section, which was now clearly visible, upside down in the distance. Looking beneath me to the stern section, I could see that it was sitting upright on its keel. The ship had a fine cruiser stern and as I traced her hull forward from the stern I could see a narrow central superstructure, one deck high, with one of her 4.7-inch guns at the aftmost end of it. Heavy-duty lifeboat davits dotted either side of the wreck in the distance, still in the swung-in position. The ship, still crammed with her own crew and the survivors of the *Agano*, appeared to have sunk so quickly that there hadn't been time to swing out and lower the lifeboats.

Whilst the two sections of ship are not far away from each other where she broke her back amidships, the gap between the fantail of the stern and the stem of the bow is about 70–80 metres – and we were swimming across that gap, high above the beautiful white sandy seabed, towards the tip of the bow. It looked as though the ship had split her back around the two smokestacks abaft the bridge whilst moving at great speed.

Finally, after a long free descent I arrived beside the bow just above the seabed at a depth of about 62 metres. The very tip of the fo'c'sle, from the chain locker forward, had cracked from the main upside-down bow section – and now lay on its starboard side, complete with both small anchors still held snug in their hawses. The damage didn't look consistent with wartime damage, and looked more as though a modern-day vessel had dragged its anchor through the wreck. Degaussing cables stretched from the bow across the open smashed debris of the tip of the fo'c'sle and wound their way round the bow section. Apart from the wreck itself, clear white sand ran out for as far as the eye could see all around me. The wreck was a dark stain on a beautiful underwater expanse of white sandy desolation.

I looked aft from the bow, over the fo'c'sle debris, down the wreck towards where the bridge would have been. I could easily see in the good underwater visibility where the upside-down hull reformed its wartime state – the hull was sheared athwartships in the well deck just in front of the bridge. Where it reformed, it had the look of an aircraft hangar on the land. We started finning aft towards where the hull reformed.

As we reached the intact section of hull, intent on filming the whole wreck I swam round the hull to the port side and began to move aft, filming the port side of the ship from the free water outside its hull. Very soon I could see the well deck rise up to the bridge superstructure. The hull rests on the small superstructure here and square windows, doors and portholes dotted its crumpled form. There is a large hole cut into the hull where the remains of many of her crew and the crew of the *Agano* were removed.

I kept moving aft – following the thick degaussing cables – and as I did so, the aft section of the wreck over to my left began to come into view, getting much closer here than at the bow.

As I approached where she had broken her back at seabed level, I spotted the barrel of her amidships 4.7-inch main gun (in the Q turret position) pointing out to port almost flush with the seabed. Immediately aft of the 4.7-inch gun, the hull ended up abruptly where it had been sheared completely across as she broke her back. Bent and distressed hull plates flanked the edges of her hull around a cavernous brooding dark interior.

I moved forward into the darkness of the hull, into a maze of sheared-off, torn and twisted pipes and cabling – then deeper into the darkness, into the boiler rooms whose walls and bulkheads were lined with steam pipes, electrical conduits, cabling and large circular steam valves. It seemed that the ship had broken her back immediately aft of the Q turret 4.7-inch gun, in between the two smokestacks.

Retreating out of the wreck the way I had come in, I turned and looked out aft across the expanse of seabed between the two sections of ship and spotted a large, blurred but seemingly rectangular object lying about 50 metres away on the clean white sand – totally detached and separate from anything else.

I swam away from the sheared-off bow section into the blue a few metres above the seabed. As I finned out towards the object it materialised into a twin 21-inch torpedo launcher with two parallel side by side torpedo tubes some 25–30 feet long. She was fitted with three such twin 21-inch swivel mounts when she was built – one in the forward well deck between the bridge and fo'c'sle, one abaft the smokestacks and the Q turret 4.7-inch gun mount, and a third towards the stern. The launchers could be swivelled to fire out from either side of the ship.

I was aware from research for *Dive Truk Lagoon* that many *Kamikaze*-class destroyers had had the aftmost 21-inch torpedo launcher removed, along with their aft 4.7-inch gun, to accommodate more 25mm AA autocannon positions. I felt it likely therefore that this twin torpedo launcher was her amidships launcher, and that as the ship broke her back in this area and the bow section capsized, it was sprung free and fell to the seabed. I ducked down and looked inside – to find that each tube had a live torpedo in it.

I was by now some 50 metres away from the wreck, so I turned from the torpedo launcher and started to fin back and across the gap to the crumpled outline of the sheared off stern section – which lay upright on its keel about 20 metres away from the sheared-off end of the upside-down bow section.

As I arrived at the stern section I rose up onto the main deck and began to fin aft along the deck. As soon as I did, I spotted the circular smokestack deck opening of her aftmost funnel – and this was followed immediately by an empty 4.7-inch gun mount wracking system. It looked as though this was for one of the guns removed during her pre-war modernisation in the 1930s. As I moved aft along the main deck, the gap between the two sections of ship began to open. At either side of the deck here, empty lifeboat davits in the swung-in position stood in silent testimony testament to the suddenness of her sinking. The crew hadn't had time to launch the boats.

I continued finning aft along the centre line of the ship, and two more pairs of swung-in lifeboat davits appeared, flanking a small deckhouse which had a 4.7-inch DP gun platform still with the large gun atop it, pointing directly ahead. There were two small doors into the deckhouse underneath the gun on the starboard side, and similar doors on the port side were wide open to reveal the heads (toilet block).

The port side of the ship here had collapsed inwards, leaving the thick degaussing cables stretched taut across the void where the hull had been, but now in free water. A 25mm AA autocannon sat on top of the aft part of deckhouse on the starboard side, its twin barrels still elevated, frozen in time as they were at the time of the attack.

Moving further aft towards the end of the long slender deckhouse and the beginning of the quarter deck, two sets of dual-barrelled 25mm AA cannons were mounted at the aft end, with a rectangular ready-use ammunition box sited in between. Both AA cannons pointed out to port. As I arrived at the end of the deckhouse, the aft-facing main battery 4.7-inch DP gun still sat in place atop it on the centre line. Along either side of the deckhouse there were rails used for moving torpedoes.

Finning over the flat expanse of the quarter deck, aft of the deckhouse, I arrived at her anti-submarine warfare (ASW) apparatus. Two sets of narrow-gauge railway tracks ran, one either side of the deck, from the ready-use depth charge loading stand to the very stern of the ship, where they projected a few metres aft of the fantail. In action, depth charges on small carriages could be rolled off these rails at speed, directly out over her stern.

Immediately forward of the depth charge loading stand stood a pair of coral-covered depth charge throwers with centrally located tail plug, ignition device and a pair of port-facing and starboard-facing projector tubes. Whilst the roll-off rails were only designed to allow depth charges to be dropped off the stern of the ship as it moved forward, the throwers could propel depth charges well away from the ship to either side and increase the chances of hitting the enemy submarine. A depth charge loading davit, used to lift and swing the charges from the loading stand to the throwers and the roll-off rails, stood just forward of the thrower pair.

Dropping over the side of the wreck, I gently descended down towards the seabed beside her cruiser stern. Underneath the stern, the rudder stood half-buried in the sand with its two large propellers set one either side, resting on the seabed. The free section of their shafts (outside the ship) ran forward from the screw itself to a circular support bearing that was firmly held to the hull by thick struts. From the support bearing, the shafts ran forward to the tubes where the shafts entered the hull and ran on forward towards the engine rooms.

I moved back up onto the main deck and moved forward along the port side of the slender central superstructure. Here, a collapsed doorway (or more likely a deck hatch) with an oval viewing port in it lay almost flat beside the deckhouse. I dropped down to the doorway and shone my torch inside the opening – and what my torch revealed made me recoil at the most macabre sight I have seen in wreck diving. There were at least four human skulls jammed close together right up beside the viewing port, amidst a forest of other human bones. It was immediately clear that I was looking at a scene of great human tragedy – a forgotten scene from World War II, preserved like a time capsule of horror.

The most likely scenario, I thought, was that when the ship was hit and broke her back these unfortunate fellows had been below decks. Possibly they were *Oite* crew at action stations, perhaps engine room crew – or perhaps they were some of the hundreds of *Agano* crew rescued by *Oite* who were billeted below decks.

As the attack took place, this doorway or hatch had possibly been dogged down. The ship was hit by an aerial torpedo and broke its back, well forward of the engine rooms. The ship was moving at full speed, her large propellers powering her through the water at more than 30 knots. As she broke her back, the engines may well not have been affected at first; they had kept turning her screws, driving her forward. The complete width of the ship was open to the sea at the break and would have flooded quickly with massive amounts of sea water, dragging the aft section of the ship under. With her screws still turning, and going down from forward, she would have essentially have driven herself underwater and down to the seabed. Her screws may well have still been turning as she hit the seabed.

These poor fellows, knowing she was going under, had possibly run up from below, cramming together at a door or hatch they couldn't get open in time. Perhaps they felt the ship hit the bottom when they still had air to breathe. Inevitably, remorselessly, the water had risen up and flooded where they huddled – struggling in panic and desperation to get out through this doorway.

The ship had ultimately flooded with water and they had all drowned in this small space that I was now looking at. It was a moment in time, a snapshot of the brutality of World War

II – a story of human sacrifice that had never been told. Their agony was clear to see in this scene, just one of countless thousands never before told and lost in the mists of time. Some of these men would have had wives, children, relatives who would have wondered for long after the war what had happened to their loved ones. They would never have found out – the loss would have been a pain that would have lasted for the rest of their lives.

I withdrew from looking at this scene and checked my CCR wrist computer. It revealed that I had already had a bottom time of 30 minutes down on the wreck. It had been a big dive, swimming the whole length of the bow section, then over 50 metres out to the twin torpedo tube launcher, before returning to the stern section and swimming the whole length of it and dropping down deeper again to see the props. We had agreed a 30-minute bottom time before we dived, so I turned now and headed over to the downline, which was tied off not far away at the very stern of the ship.

With a bottom time of 30 minutes, we would take well over an hour to ascend slowly to the surface, going through all the various levels of decompression stops. My CCR wrist computer was continuously monitoring my depth, and calculating my decompression obligations from my dive profile, the dive duration, the gases I had been breathing and what PO2 set points I had been using, and then scrolling out my TTS – the time to surface. This is the minimum time before you can safely reach the surface using a standard ascent rate and fulfilling all your decompression obligations. The computer also gives you your decompression ceiling – a continuously changing ceiling which you must not breach on the ascent. If you go through that ceiling and go too shallow, the green lights of the HUD, attached to your breathing hose in your peripheral vision, blink and turn an ominous red. It certainly gets your attention.

A long decompression on a trapeze after a deep dive on IJN Oite. (Author's collection)

As we arrived at our final 9-metre and 6-metre decompression stops, four of us were hanging on the trapeze with a few others hanging in free water nearby, when a large thresher shark swam slowly into view moving parallel to the trapeze about 5–10 metres away from us – just gazing slowly at us, before losing interest and swimming away.

As we finally broke the surface and began to get divers and gear back into the boat, although the dive had gone very well, and had been a mesmeric and fascinating wreck to dive, I couldn't help but feel sadness at the scene I had just witnessed. I had just visited a wreck on which 172 of her crew, and 522 of the *Agano* survivors, had been killed in action. The skeletons of the men trapped and drowned behind the doorway weighed heavily on my thoughts as our dive boat sped back to Weno – and they still do to this day.

You can watch this dive on my YouTube channel here:

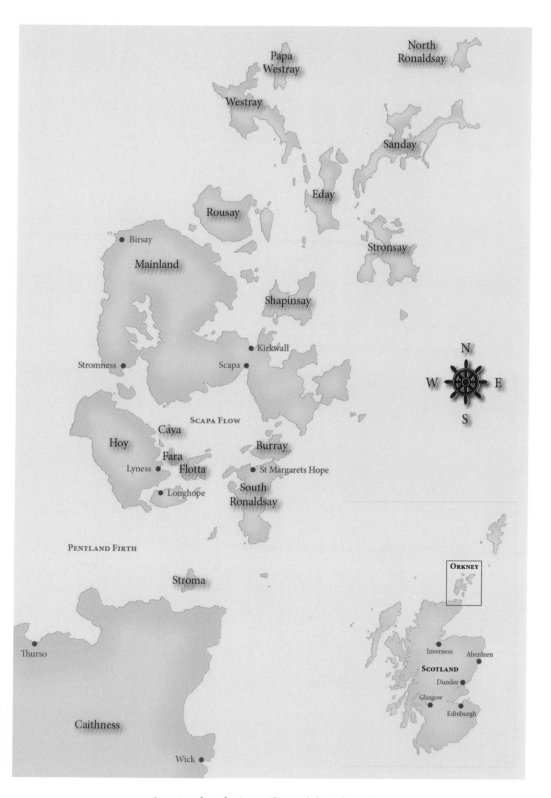

Location chart for Scapa Flow and the Orkney Isles.

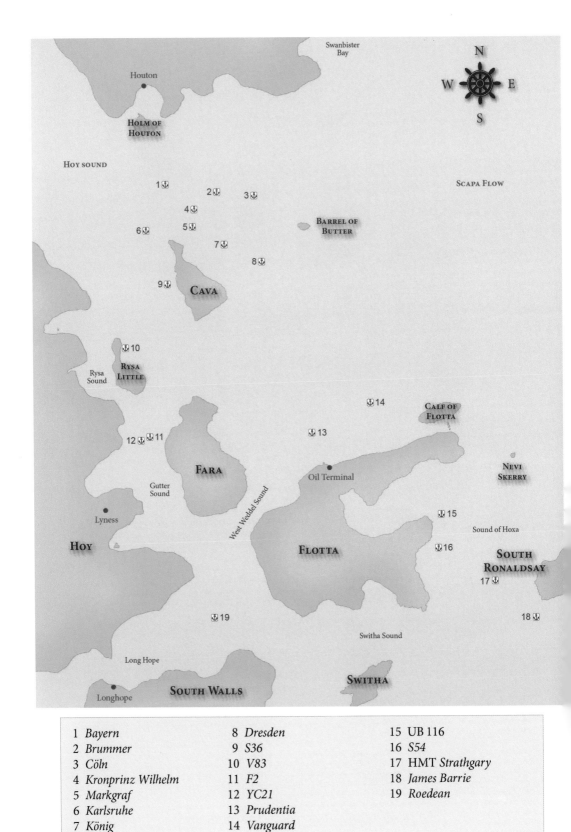

Swanbister
Bay

Houton

HOLM OF
HOUTON

HOY SOUND

SCAPA FLOW

1 ⚓   2 ⚓   3 ⚓

4 ⚓

6 ⚓   5 ⚓   BARREL OF
                 BUTTER

7 ⚓

8 ⚓

9 ⚓   CAVA

⚓ 10

RYSA
LITTLE

Rysa
Sound

⚓ 14   CALF OF
            FLOTTA

⚓ 13

12 ⚓ ⚓ 11   NEVI
                 SKERRY

FARA

Gutter
Sound   Oil Terminal

West Weddel Sound

⚓ 15

Lyness   Sound of Hoxa

HOY   ⚓ 16

FLOTTA   SOUTH
                   RONALDSAY

                   17 ⚓

⚓ 19   18 ⚓

Switha Sound

Long Hope

SWITHA

Longhope   SOUTH WALLS

1 *Bayern*	8 *Dresden*	15 UB 116
2 *Brummer*	9 *S36*	16 *S54*
3 *Cöln*	10 *V83*	17 HMT *Strathgary*
4 *Kronprinz Wilhelm*	11 *F2*	18 *James Barrie*
5 *Markgraf*	12 *YC21*	19 *Roedean*
6 *Karlsruhe*	13 *Prudentia*	
7 *König*	14 *Vanguard*	

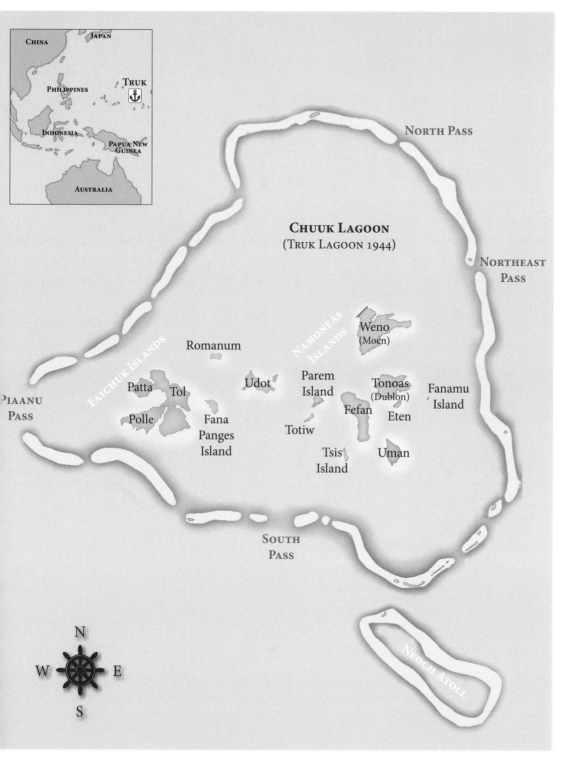

Above: Location chart of Truk Lagoon.

Opposite: Location chart of the wrecks of Scapa Flow.

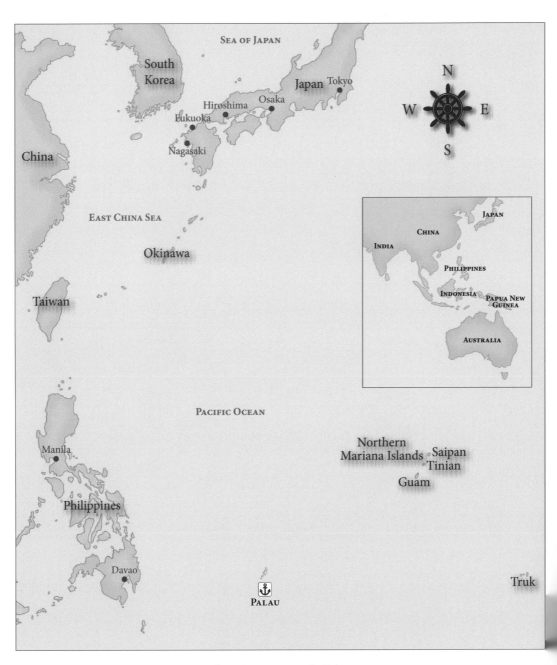

Above: Location map for Palau.

Opposite: The Palauan chain of islands. Although Babelthuap is the main island, most diving is based at Koror Island, on the north side of Malakal harbour. The small island of Peleliu, so bitterly fought over during World War II, lies towards the south of the island chain.

N
W E
S

Kossol passage

Toachel Mlengui
(West passage)   ●Bkulangrill

PACIFIC OCEAN

Karamadoo Bay

BABELTHUAP

Komebail
Lagoon

Kosabang
Harbour

Ngerchaol

Western   Ngeruktabel
Lagoon   **KOROR**

URUKTHAPEL Malakal Pass

MECHERCHAR

PELELIU

PACIFIC OCEAN

ANGAUR

The twin 13.5-inch guns of B turret HMS Audacious *in 67msw off Malin Head, Ireland. © Barry McGill*

Looking forward along the bottom of the starboard armour belt of HMS Hampshire *towards the bow. The three anchor capstan axles and circular gears project upwards. The keel bar runs aft from the stem, to rest its severed end on the seabed to starboard. (Author's collection)*

Above: About 25 metres off the forward side of the remains of UB 116 lies the top of the conning tower with its hatch and periscope tower. © Bob Anderson

Below: Paul Haynes carefully holds a katana *samurai sword found inside the* Rio de Janeiro Maru *in Truk Lagoon. © Ewan Rowell*

Above: The ship's name still rings around the stern of Rio de Janeiro Maru *in bronze lettering.* © *Ewan Rowell*

Below: Type 95 HA-GO light battle tank stacked as deck cargo on the port side of Hold No 2 just in front of the collapsing bridge superstructure of the San Francisco Maru, Truk Lagoon. © *Ewan Rowell*

Above: The galley of the Kensho Maru *in* Truk Lagoon *has mosaic non-slip flooring, cooking ranges and ovens adorned with pots, pans and bottles.* © Ewan Rowell

Below: Looking forward inside the Nippo Maru *command bridge in Truk Lagoon to the helm and telegraph (right). The wooden spokes of the helm have rotted or been burnt away to leave the circular reinforcing brass band.* © Ewan Rowell

Top: The compass binnacle of the Helmet Wreck, Palau, with white clinometer on its side. The face of the clinometer bears the legend D. McGregor & Co, Glasgow & Liverpool. The needle has corroded away from its fixing at the top, but the curved scale showing degrees of tilt can still be clearly seen. © Richard Barnden, Unique Dive Expeditions

Above: U.S. LVT Amtank (amphibious tank with 75mm howitzer) at the foot of Bloody Nose Ridge. (Author's collection)

Left: U.S. war memorial to the fallen near Orange Beach, Peleliu. (Author's collection)

Rod (right) and Paul Haynes (left) with the bell of the Creemuir. *(Author's collection)*

One of the four 15-inch gun turrets of the German WWI battleship SMS Bayern *lying on the bottom of Scapa Flow. The gunhouse and both barrels are buried in the seabed.* © *Bob Anderson*

Orcas in front of the hills of Hoy. (Author's collection)

A diver hangs beside one of the four props of HMS Audacious, the North Channel. © Barry McGill

12

PALAU 1944

Task Force 58 – Operation Desecrate 1
The sunken legacy

Six weeks after the brutal Operation Hailstone raid on Truk, an enlarged Task Force 58 reformed to neutralise the next great Japanese naval and air base west of Truk – Palau, some 1,100 nautical miles to the west.

Palau is part of Micronesia and the 250 or so islands that make up the western chain of the Caroline Islands. Japan seized the German Pacific colony islands in 1914 during World War I, and once that war ended, she was subsequently granted a mandate by the League of Nations to administer the former German colonies such as Palau. Japanese immigration to the South Seas increased substantially, and more shipping routes were established. Palau became a focal point for Japanese commercial shipping in the South Seas.

The Imperial Japanese Navy started initial preliminary surveys of the mandated South Seas islands for potential naval and air bases in 1933. Detailed surveys followed in 1936 to establish locations for airfields, coastal defence gun batteries and AA gun emplacements, naval anchorages, communications, fuel and ammunition storage facilities and radio and command facilities. The Caroline Islands were to be the first line of defence in the Pacific in the event of hostilities.

During 1937, tensions heightened between the USA and Japan, and the prospect of war loomed large. Using the 1936 survey findings, Japan embarked on a secret project to militarise the Palauan islands by building ports and fortifications, viewing the islands as unsinkable aircraft carriers. In 1939, Japan began to set up major airfields that would give long-range reconnaissance ability – as well as the potential for long-range air strikes against distant British and American holdings.

In 1940, the main body of the Imperial Japanese Navy arrived at Palau, and the rate of development of naval facilities increased to allow the islands to fulfil the role of an advance shipping and refuelling port. Barracks and additional shoreside facilities were built to handle fuel, ordnance and general naval supplies. Seaplane bases were constructed for long-range reconnaissance aircraft and for Zero variant seaplane fighters.

On 5 November 1941, just one month before Japan began her Pacific War, Palau, along with Truk and Ponape in the Caroline Islands, and other bases spread out throughout the South Seas in the Marshall and Mariana Islands, were formally approved as naval supply stations for Admiral Isoroku Yamamoto's Combined Fleet.

As Japan began her war on 7 December 1941, Admiral I. Takahashi's 3rd Fleet, an amphibious fleet unit of carriers, cruisers and destroyers, with the 2nd Fleet providing cover, staged from Palau for the invasion of the Philippines, and following successful offensive operations against the Philippines and Netherland East Indies, Palau assumed a vital role as a base for scouting and reconnaissance missions and for staging amphibious forces.

Admiral C. Nagumo's 1st Air Fleet was based in Palau, and its four carriers sortied from Palau to carry out a massive bombing raid on 19 February 1942 of Port Darwin in the Northern Territory of Australia, supported by the battleships and heavy cruisers of the 2nd Fleet. It was the largest raid mounted by Japan against mainland Australia.

Palau's importance as a convoy gathering point and refuelling hub grew as the war progressed. Great naval warships came and went whilst her anchorages thronged with merchant shipping of all shapes and sizes; some moving forward with men and supplies to the front at New Guinea and Rabaul, whilst others were returning to the Japanese home islands to collect further cargoes. Land-based aircraft from her new airfields, and seaplanes from her new seaplane bases, crisscrossed the skies and Palau became a major port and base for three naval Escort Squadrons of destroyers, coastal defence ships, minesweepers, sub-chasers and gunboats that provided convoy protection over the long distances between Japan and the Philippines, East Indies and Palau.

To American eyes, the Palau and Mariana Islands represented important military targets for several reasons: Palau was a powerful air and sea barrier to a U.S. assault on the Philippines. The Marianas gave the Japanese land-based air cover for naval operations, and conversely, if taken the Marianas would give the Americans air bases from where heavy bombers could mount bombing raids directly against the Japanese home islands.

With Japanese expansion being ended during 1942 by the Battle of the Coral Sea and the Battle of Midway, and with the strategic victory of the Battle of Guadalcanal in late 1942 giving U.S. forces air fields, anchorages and staging abilities in the Solomons, in the summer and latter part of 1943 U.S. forces began to assault Japanese possessions sequentially, securing first the Marianas and then Palau as they moved westwards to the Philippines.

The U.S. long-range reconnaissance overflight of Truk on 4 February 1944 had revealed to the Japanese that Truk was now vulnerable, and the commander-in-chief of the IJN Combined Fleet, Admiral Koga, determined to give up Truk as a major naval base. Most of the important IJN vessels in Truk fled 1,100 miles westwards towards the perceived safety of Palau. From being essentially a staging area well behind the front line, the Palau islands would now be in the front line.

On 10 February 1944, Admiral Koga left Truk in the battleship *Musashi* for Japan, and all the other major IJN vessels also left shortly afterwards, bound for Japan or Singapore. Those supply ships at Truk that could leave were ordered to Palau.

On 20 February 1944, the *Musashi* left Japan with Admiral Koga on board – southbound for Palau. Admiral Koga liked to base himself at a forward base so that he would be present whenever a fleet operation developed that required his attention – hence his earlier presence at Truk. As Truk became apparently vulnerable to long-range bombers, he withdrew to Palau, where he could remain close to the action.

The two battleships *Yamato* and *Nagato* came and went from Palau towards the end of February and early March 1944. The Japanese fleet maintained a high state of readiness and carried out training exercises inside the Palauan lagoon. Peleliu, the small island to the south of the main Palau island of Babeldaob, was already a powerful Japanese air base.

Palau was selected for the next U.S. fast carrier raid after the stunningly successful Operation Hailstone raid on Truk. The Palauan islands were only 700 miles northwest of Hollandia – which was the focus of an imminent U.S. naval operation. American strategic planners considered that if the use of Palau as a functioning Japanese air and naval base could be denied for a minimum of one month, Japan's ability to retaliate against the planned Hollandia operation would be greatly reduced.

The whole Palauan chain of islands was, much like Truk Lagoon, surrounded by a barrier reef with only three channels through it to its harbours and anchorages that were navigable by large vessels. If U.S. carrier aircraft could lay aerial mines in the shipping channels through the barrier reef and in the approaches to Palau and inside the lagoon, the harbours would be closed to shipping. The relatively shallow depths of the water and the narrow entrances to the Palauan lagoon were ideal for air-dropped mines.

The aerial mines would be laid in two phases. Initially mines would be air-dropped with parachutes from Grumman Avenger aircraft in the three main channels through the barrier reef concurrent with the first air strike on the islands. These were moored magnetic mines with short-delay arming periods of less than an hour that would prevent enemy shipping from escaping from the lagoon.

In the second phase, further minefields would be laid in the most important anchorages, channels and approaches to Palau, to close off the islands to the Japanese for 1–2 months after the air strikes. Mines for the second phase would be hard-to-detect ground mines with arming delay periods of 2–35 days. The Japanese would be prevented from clearing the channels completely for 35 days and would be uncertain of clearance for some considerable time thereafter.

Twelve U.S. submarines would patrol Palauan waters and intercept any Japanese fleet units or merchant ships that might try to escape from Palau during the initial approach of the Task Force 58 towards the Western Carolines, as well as any that subsequently tried to flee as the strikes went in. The date for the raid on Palau was set for 1 April 1944, and the operation was given the codename Desecrate 1.

Task Force 58, commanded by Admiral Marc Mitscher, comprised four task groups assembled from 5th Fleet ships based at Majuro Atoll (well to the east) and others operating elsewhere in the South Pacific. The operations plan produced by Admiral Spruance provided for three of the four task groups to attack Palau and the less important bases of Woleai, Yap and Ulithi.

Task Group 58.1 comprised the carriers *Enterprise*, *Cowpens* and *Belleau Wood*, along with the cruisers *Santa Fe*, *Mobile*, *Biloxi* and *Oakland* and a screen of destroyers.

Task Group 58.2 comprised the carriers *Bunker Hill*, *Monterey*, *Hornet* and *Cabot*, escorted by the battleships *Iowa* and *New Jersey*, the cruisers *Wichita*, *San Francisco*, *Minneapolis*, *New Orleans*, *Boston* and *Baltimore* and a destroyer screen.

Task Group 58.3 comprised the carriers *Yorktown*, *Princeton*, *Lexington* and *Langley* with the battleships *Massachusetts*, *North Carolina*, *South Dakota* and *Alabama*, along with the cruisers *Louisville*, *Portland*, *Indianapolis*, *Canberra* and *San Juan* and a destroyer screen.

The ships that had assembled at Majuro Atoll sortied on the 23 March 1944 and rendezvoused at sea with the other U.S. South Pacific naval forces on 26 and 27 March. Once assembled, the massive 12-carrier-strong task force began to move towards Palau – it would be refuelled en route by oilers and protected by combat air patrols (CAP) and anti-submarine patrols. Each of the 12 carriers maintained an eight-plane CAP and a four-plane anti-submarine patrol from sunrise at 0515 local time to sunset at 1806 local.

The Japanese were at first completely unaware of the clandestine approach of the carrier task force to Palau, and the Japanese Combined Fleet HQ was still completing the process of being relocated from Truk to Koror on Palau. (It would officially be installed there on 29 March 1944 – just one day before Desecrate 1.)

On 25 March however, approximately 700 miles from Truk, U.S. commanders believed that the task force had been spotted by a Japanese aircraft. Another Japanese reconnaissance aircraft was spotted the following day, 26 March, as the task force was being refuelled after rendezvous with fleet oilers. (But despite being in range of air bases on Truk, Woleai, Palau and Papua New Guinea, no Japanese air attack on the task force would be made until 29 March.)

Once it was clear that the task force had been detected, Admiral Spruance determined to strike immediately at Palau. The element of surprise had been lost and there was nothing to gain from the planned circuitous clandestine approach. He therefore brought forward the attack by two days from 1 April to 30 March, to allow the Japanese as little time as possible to prepare and reinforce. Task Force 58 would make a straight push directly towards Palau at an increased speed of 22 knots, so as to reach their planned launching position early on 30 March.

After the U.S. task force had been detected, Admiral Koga sent his main naval units out of Palau to the north to be held ready for a larger naval surface engagement – the 'decisive battle' so sought after by the Japanese. The battleship *Musashi* and units of the 2nd Fleet retired from Palau northwards on the evening of 29 March.

There were many Imperial Japanese Army (IJA) transport and supply ships and other requisitioned merchant vessels in Palau. The IJA vessels had problems with their communications, whilst other ships, in the midst of offloading war supplies, were not in a position to depart. Many Japanese ship's captains felt that they would be more vulnerable to attack in the open sea by U.S. aircraft, submarines and surface vessels, and chose to stay in Palau, nosing their vessels close to rocky cliffs in the hope that the island terrain would give them some protection from any raiding U.S. aircraft.

A large convoy of those able to depart was hastily made up, and on 26 March the convoy steamed north from the main anchorages and exited the lagoon through the western Toachel Mlengui Pass. The convoy managed to slip through the U.S. submarine patrols in a gap in the patrol formation left by the loss of the submarine USS *Tullibee*. She had been patrolling off Palau on 26 March when her own torpedo, which had run a circular course, struck and sunk her.

As no orders came from Japanese Army command, the IJA naval transports remained anchored in Palau. Most of the precious naval tankers and oilers present in the lagoon were damaged vessels brought in for repair by IJN repair ships, and would not in any event be able to escape.

Just after midday on 29 March, when the task force was still 300 miles from Palau, Japanese aircraft began approaching it from the Palau direction. Two long-range reconnaissance Betty bomber aircraft were visually spotted, one at a distance of about seven miles as it flew towards the TG 58.1 carrier *Enterprise*, almost skimming the waves at 100 feet – it was so low that it had avoided radar detection.

The *Enterprise* CAP of eight F6F Hellcat fighters split into two divisions and swooped down on the Betty from 6,000 feet. The Hellcats reached their top speed of 380 mph and after a chase of about three minutes attained shooting distance. The first division of four Hellcats bracketed the Betty, with two Hellcats approaching from the left and two from the right. The slower, less manoeuvrable Betty bomber could only weave from right to left.

As the fighters began their second run at the Betty, a ball of fire from its unprotected fuel tanks appeared on the starboard wing root and grew until the wing and part of the fuselage were on fire – American pilots had given the Bettys the nickname the 'flying cigar' due to the tendency of their unprotected fuel tanks to burst into flames when hit. The Betty crashed into the water in a fireball, its fuselage and wings disintegrating. The forward part of the fuselage continued to float for about 15 minutes and the smoke could be seen from the distant *Enterprise*. The other Betty was shot down after managing to strafe a U.S. ship.

Four Hellcats from *Cabot*'s CAP were radar-vectored 45 miles out to a large radar echo approaching rapidly – the contact turned out to be eight Nakajima B6N Jill torpedo bombers and a Kawasaki Ki-61 Tony fighter. All were shot down.

At sundown, just as the CAP was being recovered to the carriers for the night, a flight of Japanese aircraft attacked. The U.S. ships returned AA fire and drove off the attackers with no casualties. An unlucky fighter pilot on *Cowpens* was swept overboard when the retractable wing of a Hellcat suddenly swung open during a sharp turn on deck. He could not be found and was listed Missing presumed dead. The Japanese aircraft had disappeared from U.S. radars by 2000 local time. Meantime, Intelligence reports were being received that Japanese warships were fleeing Palau.

At 1837 local time, TG58.3 was attacked by six aircraft coming up from the south-east that were detected by radar 25 miles out. The Japanese formation split into two, with aircraft approaching the task group from both port and starboard. The battleships, cruisers and destroyers of the screen opened AA fire at 1850, and within one minute one plane caught fire and crashed starboard of the group. Three minutes later a second plane was shot down.

By 0300 local time on 30 March, the U.S. task groups had arrived at their designated holding points between 70 and 120 miles south of Palau. The carriers immediately turned into the wind and assumed cruising formation to begin launchings. Day 1 of the attack had been given the codename *K*-Day.

K-Day

Following the template used during Operation Hailstone at Truk, CAP night fighters were initially launched to guard the task force during the early morning launches of 72 Hellcats for a dawn initial fighter sweep of the Palaus designed to wipe out Japanese air power. The fighter sweep would be followed by successive waves of Grumman Avenger torpedo bombers and Douglas Dauntless dive bombers, escorted by more Hellcats. The Japanese airfield on the southern Palauan island of Peleliu was high on the list of targets, along with the two seaplane bases on Arakabesan to the north of Koror.

With the CAP patrolling above, at 0435 local time, the Hellcats began to launch from the carriers, the launch being timed so that the Hellcats would be arriving over Palau just before local sunrise at 0600 after a flight of around 70 minutes.

The battle-hardened TG58.1 *Enterprise* Hellcats had been selected for low cover and ground attack assignments – they would be in the thick of the battle whilst other air groups kept the intermediate and high altitudes above them clear.

As the Hellcats arrived at the Palaus, they dived to strafe Peleliu airfield – where they found many Betty bombers parked up, but none of the expected Japanese fighters. It was assumed that knowing that TF 58 aircraft were approaching, the Japanese fighters had already taken to the skies. The *Enterprise* Hellcats made several strafing runs and shot up the Bettys, which burst into flames when hit. The Hellcats received limited AA fire from the ground.

After the attack runs on Peleliu, one division of *Enterprise* Hellcats swung north over Urukthapel (just to the south of Koror Island) and reported some 15 freighters, one oiler, one destroyer and a hospital ship in anchorages amongst the myriad of Palau's jungle islands below. On their return south to Peleliu, they encountered some of the missing Japanese fighters – 17 Zeke (Zero) fighters and the Zero floatplane fighter variant, Allied reporting name Hamp. The American aviators reported the Zekes to be extremely manoeuvrable, but that their tactics were to shy away from a pitched battle with the Hellcats – the Zekes seemed to prefer to attack single or damaged U.S. aircraft. Many of the Japanese aircraft at Peleliu air base were well dispersed and camouflaged, and it became clear that a substantial number had not been destroyed by the initial fighter sweep.

Meantime, the other division of *Enterprise* Hellcats was dog-fighting with Zekes and strafing ground targets. Further north, on Babelthuap, an oil storage facility near a barrack was set on fire; the phosphate plant on Angaur Island was strafed and began to smoke. Japanese AA fire from land-based batteries was poor and largely ineffective. An old Japanese destroyer was attacked in open water 20 miles off the western Toachel Mlengui Pass.

In total, during the initial fighter sweep, some 35 ships were reported in the various Palauan anchorages; 35 Japanese aircraft were reported shot down whilst two Hellcats were shot down and three others damaged by AA ground fire and fire from Japanese aircraft.

As the initial fighter sweep was going in, behind them on the carriers the second U.S. group strike was being launched at 0532 local time. Hellcat fighters launched ahead of the Avenger torpedo bombers and Dauntless dive bombers they were to escort, their primary objective being to destroy Japanese shipping. Once formed up in the air, the flights of dive bomber and torpedo bomber strike aircraft proceeded in formation to their designated areas of operation.

A large Japanese convoy, PATA-07, had formed up in the Western Lagoon to try to flee Palau on the evening of 29 March 1944, before the anticipated imminent U.S. strike, and escape to Takao, Formosa. The convoy included the 1941-built transport *Kibi Maru*, along with the fleet oiler *Akebono Maru*, the auxiliary transport *Goshu Maru*, the IJN requisitioned Standard Type 1C steamers *Raizan Maru* and *Ryuko Maru*, and the IJA transports *Teshio*

Maru and *Hokutai Maru*. The convoy was escorted by Patrol Boat 31, the IJN second-class destroyer *Wakatake* and the auxiliary subchaser *Cha-26* and several picket boats. At the far southern end of the convoy, several other freighters were congregating, waiting their turn to join.

Although the convoy had been scheduled to leave the Western Lagoon on the evening of 29 March, there were problems in organising such a large convoy so quickly. Departure was delayed until first light at 0500 the next morning, when simultaneously, 70 miles to the south, the first initial fighter strike groups of Grumman F6F Hellcats were lifting off from their carriers and forming up into their strike groups to head north towards Palau. At this point, Convoy PATA-07 and the initial fighter sweep Hellcats were completely unaware of each other.

As the first rays of light filtered over the eastern horizon, the ships of the convoy had started to leave the anchorages of the Western Lagoon. In line astern, they moved north up the west side of the main Palauan island of Babelthuap in the main narrow deep-water channel that leads up towards Toachel Mlengui – the West Passage through the fringing barrier reef. On either side of the channel, light green/brown coral reef flats just a few metres deep flanked the azure blue waters of the deep shipping channel. There is little room to manoeuvre for a large ship in the channel.

As the *Lexington, Bunker Hill* and *Monterey* F6F Hellcats swept at speed over the southern Palauan islands, they all spotted the northbound convoy. Such valuable targets were given priority and the U.S. pilots recognised the first speeding warship, which had already left the lagoon in the vanguard of the convoy, as an old destroyer, *Patrol Boat 31*, and immediately began strafing runs to silence her AA fire.

The Dauntlesses split into two divisions, and the first began dive-bombing runs on the destroyer. One 1,000lb bomb was a near miss at the bow, which lifted the bow up in the water – the others were further off. One of the Dauntlesses made a perfect dive on the ship but didn't pull out of the dive as expected and continued until it impacted into the water and disintegrated – the aircraft surely hit by AA fire. Another Dauntless took small calibre AA fire hits to its engine, which started to smoke. On the way back to the carrier, the plane started to lose altitude and it had to be ditched 20 miles south-west of Angaur. The crew got off safely and were picked up three hours later by a U.S. destroyer.

More dive bombers continued the attack after the first division's bombs were spent. One bomb was a hit at the stern, and the ship immediately slowed drastically from its high speed to about 8 knots, desperately making for a rainsquall in the distance that might cloak its position. After further attacks the destroyer began to move in circles – a classic indication of a jammed rudder. Six Grumman Avengers began to attack her, with a hit about midships erupting in a huge white geyser that reached 20–30 metres into the air. The old destroyer finally succumbed, broke in two and sunk.

Bunker Hill's Avenger torpedo bombers swept in to attack the lead ships in the convoy as F6F Hellcats from *Lexington* strafed and met limited AA fire from the ships' own defences. Meantime other Grumman Avengers started air-dropping mines in the shipping channel in West Passage to block it and seal the convoy ships in the lagoon.

As the TF58 aircraft started to attack the convoy, the Japanese ships began to take evasive manoeuvres, and having no doubt seen the mines being air-dropped and the West Passage effectively sealed off, the convoy dissolved and the ships scattered. But with little room to manoeuvre in such a narrow channel, during the contact *Kibi Maru* ran aground on the western side of the channel whilst *Teshio Maru* grounded on the eastern side. The *Hokutai Maru* successfully came about and headed back south towards Malakal harbour. All the merchant ships of PATA-07 would be sunk over the two days of the air raid, as would the escort destroyer *Wakatake*, which was sunk west of Babelthuap in Karamadoo Bay near West Passage.

Grumman Avengers loaded with bombs attacked the air bases at Koror and Arakabesan. The seaplane base on the western side of Arakabesan was peppered with bombs from four aircraft, and direct hits were scored on repair and shore facilities which caused fires to break out. Two Type 95 Nakajima E8N reconnaissance float planes (Allied reporting name Dave) were sunk, along with two Zero variant Rufe fighter float planes.

At about 0808, 12 *Enterprise* Hellcats launched to escort 11 dive bombers (armed with 1,000lb bombs) and Avenger torpedo bombers (armed with 500lb GP bombs) tasked to attack targets of opportunity. The strike group headed for a point ten miles east of Babelthuap where a possible battleship had been reported by a previous strike. The flight arrived in the location at 0900 but there was no battleship to be seen – so after a brief search the bombers split up to attack the previously identified 15 freighters, oilers and cargo ships anchored in Malakal harbour and amongst the small islands of Urukthapel anchorage. Many ships were anchored close inshore and alongside the steep cliffs of the jungle-clad islands seeking protection from bombing runs.

At Malakal anchorage, the dive bombers and torpedo bombers bombed and strafed the repair ship *Akashi* and other merchantmen – and attacked others in open water west of Peleliu along with several other small ships at Koror. There was little AA fire, and no airborne aircraft were encountered. The Avengers dived at an angle of 50–60 degrees from a height of 8,000 feet, swooping down to 2,000 feet as they attacked.

Meantime, eight Hellcats and six Avengers had been launched from *Belleau Wood* although only six Hellcats went to the assigned target as two were detached for a search mission with a cruiser's floatplane, looking for a downed U.S. aircraft. The six Hellcats arrived at the Toachel Mlengui Pass and started strafing runs on a freighter from the convoy attacked earlier and which was now grounded on a reef on the east side of the pass, setting it on fire. They then joined the other aircraft attacking shipping at the Urukthapel anchorage.

By 0939, with the Americans now having total air superiority, the *Enterprise* and *Belleau Wood* Dauntlesses and Avengers were able to attack targets of opportunity at will, with escorting Hellcats able to break off to strafe ground targets. The Peleliu airfield was strafed again, along with two freighters near Angaur. Ten Hellcats and eight Dauntless dive bombers from *Enterprise* combined with eight Hellcats and two Avengers from *Belleau Wood* for another attack on Peleliu airfield – its aircraft, buildings and hangars soon ablaze with large fires. The Dauntlesses and Avengers then flew to the Malakal and Urukthapel anchorages to attack shipping, making a direct hit on a large oiler. Hits were also scored on a medium tanker outside the claws of the Malakal anchorage, and another medium freighter.

At 1145, six escort Hellcats rose into the air from *Enterprise* followed by their charge of ten Dauntless dive bombers and six Avenger torpedo bombers, and a further eight *Belleau Wood* Hellcats and six Avengers. The combined strike group strafed Peleliu airfield before moving north and strafing the ships in the western anchorages and knocking out a lighthouse high on a mountain plateau on Babelthuap near Toachel Mlengui Pass, as well as a radio station and a beached freighter south of the pass off Karamado Bay. The large freighter *Nagisan Maru* was attacked and three hits scored, one in the bridge and two at the stern. As the flight broke off the attacks about 20 minutes later, she was seen to be smouldering and going down by the stern.

For the fifth group strike of K-Day, Strike 2E, *Enterprise* again launched Avengers, Dauntlesses and Hellcats, several of which were heavily loaded with 1,000lb bombs fuzed with delays of several hours. These would be dropped on Peleliu airfield to deny the Japanese the opportunity of repairing it overnight.

Fifteen Hellcats launched from *Belleau Wood*, with eight Avengers loaded with four 500lb bombs each. The group was joined by eight Hellcats from *Cowpens*, tasked to make subsequent attacks on shipping in the Malakal anchorage, where a freighter and an oiler were hit along with smaller vessels. Two large ships anchored either side of the northern tip of Urukthapel were attacked.

Two of the Hellcats had a 45-minute duel with a Nakajima Ki-27 Nate, a small old monoplane that ducked in and out of clouds as it frantically tried to outmanoeuvre the two far faster and more heavily armed American fighters. Eventually it was shot down, but as the pilot made to bail out, his parachute caught the tail assembly of the Nate and he was taken down with his plane to crash below.

Task Group 58.2 had positioned itself about 74 miles south of Angaur Island on the morning of 30 March. The launching of her twelve Hellcats for the initial fighter sweep began in darkness at 0430 local time along with the launch of Mining Group No 1 of four Hellcats and three Grumman Avengers.

The Avengers were heavy with their large mines for their mission – to lay a minefield in the southern arm of the main shipping channel that leads to the Toachel Mlengui Pass. The mines would be parachute-dropped from 200 feet at a speed of 180 knots off the seaward end of Malakal Pass to prevent ships in that anchorage escaping. These mines would prevent the escape of ships from the Palauan lagoon during the early phase of the raid.

Fifteen Hellcats, twelve dive bombers and six Avengers launched from *Bunker Hill* at 1115 for Strike 1D and were soon followed by similar aircraft from *Hornet*, *Monterey* and *Cabot*, loaded with 1,000lb GP bombs and rockets tasked to hit shipping in the anchorages and to further strafe Peleliu airfield. The final minelaying and Group Strikes 1E and 1F against shipping and land installations were launched at 1500 local time.

Task Group 58.3 had assumed a holding position 119 miles south of Palau. Its Hellcats were tasked to patrol the intermediate level of 10–15,000 feet. As with the other two task groups, its strike aircraft carried out group strikes throughout the day against shipping and land targets and also carried out a number of mining group strikes. Six group attacks were flown to destroy shipping and ground installations, a total of 454 sorties.

Combat air patrols of eight Hellcats had flown routinely throughout the day above the carriers in case of attack: four planes circling the carriers at 5,000 feet and four more at 10,000 feet. Around 1700 they were ordered to intercept an unidentified contact about 50 miles distant from the carriers.

As they closed the contact, they spotted 10–12 Japanese aircraft, identified as Nakajima B6N torpedo bombers (Allied reporting name Jill) or Yokosuka D4Y dive bombers (Allied reporting name Judy). All but one of the aircraft were quickly shot down – but the one surviving aircraft, a Judy, continued to head towards the task force at speed.

Two of the Hellcats, capable of a top speed of 380mph, turned to chase after the dangerous Judy – which had a fast top speed for a dive bomber of 342mph. The Judy had closed to within six miles of the task force by the time the two faster and more agile Hellcats were close enough to engage. The Judy was quickly hit and exploded. As with most Japanese aircraft the Judy had sacrificed armour and fuel protection for speed.

As the two Hellcats turned to head back to their carrier they spotted two more Judy dive bombers hugging the waves as they closed on the task group. Two more Hellcats soon joined the chase, and one was able to open fire at extreme range of 1,000 metres. This caused the Judys to drop their heavy bombs and leave the contact unscathed.

In all, more than 30 Japanese aircraft had been damaged or destroyed on the ground on Peleliu airfield and Arakabesan Island Seaplane Base during the initial fighter sweep – with an additional 28 aircraft reported destroyed throughout the day by the strike groups. Only a few serviceable Japanese aircraft remained.

As a result of the heavy losses, reinforcements of Japanese aircraft were rushed to Palau with some 12 Betty bombers from Saipan arriving in the late afternoon. After refuelling, they immediately took off to attack the U.S. task force, but scored little success due to the intense AA fire thrown at them by the U.S. screen of battleships, cruisers, destroyers and the carriers themselves. None of the task force ships were damaged. More than 50 Japanese fighters arrived at Peleliu from Saipan in the evening. The scene was set for a mass aerial fighter duel the following morning.

As the last American air raids of the day drew to a conclusion, with Japanese air cover destroyed and most of the shipping sunk or badly damaged, at 1830 Task Group 58.1 was detached from the task force and sent to Yap to launch aircraft against the small island and against Ulithi. *Enterprise* had flown 221 sorties claiming 5 enemy aircraft shot down, 1 oiler, 1 large transport and 3 medium freighters sunk, and 9 freighters, 3 destroyers and 1 minelayer damaged.

Task Groups 58.2 and 58.3 would attack the Palaus again the following day – *K-Day Plus One*.

K-Day Plus One

As with *K*-Day, an initial fighter sweep of the remaining 60 Hellcats was launched in darkness – again timed to arrive over Palau at first light. The groups of strike aircraft from the remaining Task Groups 58.2 and 58.3 carriers moved to rendezvous en route at 7,000 feet and by 0545, the flight of 60 Hellcat fighters was over Palau. The high-altitude patrol of Hellcats at 20,000 feet spotted six Japanese aircraft circling below at the top of a cloud layer at about 6,000 feet – and dived down to attack. Reports were coming in from other pilots of a total of 60 Japanese fighters airborne during the initial fighter sweep. These were the fighters that had arrived from Saipan the evening before, along with the few serviceable aircraft that had survived the previous day's attacks. In a massive aerial dogfight, 53 of them were reported shot down.

As the initial fighter sweep was going in, Strike 1A-2 from TG 58.2 carrier *Bunker Hill* launched an air target observer aircraft to identify targets for subsequent attack by dive and torpedo bombers. The observer found that there were few ships left in fair condition, most being already damaged or disabled in some way. The shipping would be attacked again – and then most aircraft in the strike would bomb land installations before flying south again to attack Peleliu airfield en route back to the carriers in their southern holding position.

At 0540, the first mining mission of the day launched. Five Avengers escorted by eight Hellcats, took off from *Hornet*, each carrying a single Mark 25 ground mine with delayed arming of 2–35 days.

A second mining mission was later launched from *Hornet*, targeting the shipping channel between Babelthuap and Koror. When this mission was successfully completed and the aircraft had returned safely to the carrier, TG 58.2 air operations against Palau ceased. After a total of some 161 sorties flown against Palau, TG58.2 moved off towards Woleai at sunset, and air operations began there at 0646 ship's time (+2hrs local) on 01 April with 193 sorties being flown. The raid on this small Japanese island would be called off after the third strike for lack of targets.

Strike 3A-2 from Task Group 58.3 carriers *Yorktown* and *Lexington* launched just after 0600 and comprised 46 aircraft: 20 Hellcats, 14 Dauntlesses and 12 Avengers. Strike 3B-2 launched at 0810 from *Lexington*, with 22 aircraft.

As Japanese AA fire had now been largely suppressed, it was decided to arm the Hellcats for these missions with 500lb and 1,000lb bombs. The powerful aircraft could easily carrier-launch with such a payload, and it gave the strike groups more hitting power. Ten of the Hellcats would carry a 500lb GP bomb with a short 4–5 second delay fuze to allow a masthead attack. Twelve Douglas Dauntless dive bombers would carry the more powerful 1,000lb bomb.

Strike 3C-2 launched 39 aircraft from *Lexington* as Desecrate 1 was drawing to a finale for the penultimate strike. Nine Hellcats again carried 500lb bombs, the Dauntlesses 1,000lb bombs and the Avengers each carrying a mine.

Strike 3D-2 launched from *Lexington* at 1210 and was the last strike of the day. Long-delay-fuzed bombs were dropped on Peleliu airfield to deny the airstrip to the Japanese. Landing of returning carrier aircraft began at 1532 and had finished by 1554, by which time TG58.3 was already speeding away from Palau, bound for Woleai.

During Desecrate 1, more than 40 Japanese ships were sunk or damaged. The ex-Momi-class destroyer *Patrol Boat No 31*, and the destroyer *Wakatake* had been sent to the bottom, as had at least eight IJN subchasers, auxiliary subchasers and picket boats. The valuable tankers *Iro*, *Sata*, *Ose*, *Akebono Maru*, *Amatsu Maru*, *Asashio Maru* and *Unyu Maru No 2* had all been sunk, and the tanker *Hishi Maru No 2* damaged. The loss of so many tankers at Palau was a crippling blow to the Combined Fleet – and to Japan's ability to sustain her naval war effort. The shortage of tankers after Desecrate 1, coming so soon after the loss of the tankers *Fujisan Maru*, *Hoyo Maru* and *Shinkoku Maru* at Truk six weeks before, severely limited the range of the fleet and degraded Japan's ability to transport oil from the Netherlands East Indies to the empire.

In total, U.S. pilots claimed 110 Japanese aircraft shot down over Palau, and U.S. ships claimed four Japanese aircraft shot down with AA fire. U.S. figures claimed a total of 214 Japanese aircraft destroyed or severely damaged on the ground, although these figures have never been formally agreed.

The Palauan sea approaches and exit routes for shipping had been successfully mined. Palau harbour was completely blocked to naval shipping until it could be swept – and sweeping was made difficult by the extensive use of ground mines, which self-activated at irregular intervals. The underwater terrain made it impossible to successfully sweep for ground mines.

The American task force anti-aircraft screen had proven very effective against Japanese air attacks, in particular the feared night torpedo attack. The principle of the initial fighter sweep had again been proved sound, successfully eliminating air opposition over the target as had been done at Truk and Saipan before it.

The fighter escort for the vulnerable minelaying Avengers was crucial to the successful mine drop. Japanese AA fire was intense, but had been successfully suppressed by repeated strafing by Hellcats as the Avengers made their vulnerable low-speed low-altitude drops from 200 feet.

Seven U.S. aircraft had been lost in combat and others lost operationally to landing accidents and forced ditchings. Eight U.S. pilots and 10 crewmen were killed or reported missing in action.

The war moved onwards – northwest towards Japan.

13

Diving Palau's shipwrecks

The Helmet Wreck (Nissho Maru No 5?), IJN Sata, Showa Maru No 5?,
exploring Peleliu, unidentified auxiliary subchaser, IJN Iro

Amongst Palau's famous Rock Islands. (Author's collection)

Although much has been written about the shipwrecks of Truk Lagoon, there had been relatively little written about Palau's shipwrecks since the great era of wreck location and exploration in Palau pioneered by Klaus Lindemann, Dan Bailey and local diver Francis Toribiong, who in the early 1970s opened Palau's first dive shop, Fish 'n' Fins in Koror.

In the 1980s, Francis dived with Klaus Lindemann – whose name is also synonymous with Truk Lagoon – finding and documenting the lost Japanese shipwrecks of Desecrate 1. Klaus Lindemann published the first edition of his definitive book, *Desecrate 1*, in 1988, with an updated second edition being published in 1991.

The other great name in literature about Truk Lagoon and Palau's wartime legacy is that of Dan E. Bailey, who published World War II Wrecks of Palau in 1991 – it is a triumph of original first-hand detective work and primary research. In the intervening years since then, however, the wrecks have almost been overlooked in favour of the beautiful scenic diving that Palau offers.

I had first dived in Palau in 1990 and it was too long a gap before I was able to return once again in 2015 after OZTek – the Australian Technical Diving Conference and Exhibition that is held once every two years in Sydney – with the idea of writing a diver guide to the Palau shipwrecks. I managed to persuade my long-suffering dive buddy Paul Haynes to accompany me – lubricating the idea with several pints of Guinness. My good friend, fellow Scottish technical diver Gary Petrie also came along, and we were joined by the legendary skipper of the Truk Lagoon dive boat *Odyssey*, Mike Gerken.

Paul, Gary and Mike were great company, each with a good technical knowledge of diving and shipwrecks. They were a great help to me, picking up on the points I'd missed. If there were things I needed specifically to check up on, I'd brief them before the dive about what I needed. We are never happier than when we're measuring the beams of ships, engine cylinder head sizes and the like.

We spent about two hours underwater on each of the 20 wrecks we dived in the ten-day trip. Back ashore, after every dive we'd huddle together in a group over a coffee for a debrief so I could download as much information from their brains as I could before the memories were lost. All the dives were working dives – but working or not, the craic was as brilliant as ever on one of our Most Excellent Adventures.

In Palau, we based ourselves with Sam's Tours in Koror – just a few minutes' ride by boat from several of the Japanese wrecks. Sam's Tours has a fantastic setup for tek divers such as us, and went out of their way to give us the specialist equipment we needed. They allocated us our own fast spacious powerboat and driver, allowing us to cover large distances effortlessly. They were flexible, allowing us to choose what particular wreck we wanted to dive, and when.

The author (right) during the 2015 Palau wreck survey expedition with Paul Haynes (left) and Gary Petrie (centre). (Author's collection)

Paul Collins from Sam's Tours looked after us brilliantly, sorting out what we needed by way of 3-litre rebreather cylinders, banded and clipped stage cylinders, O2 and sofnalime.

Paul Collins came out and dived with us, going out of his way to show us the sort of things we needed to see, like Japanese World War II gun emplacements and burnt-out fuel dumps in caves. He also took us onto two very special wrecks – only found in the last six months or so before our arrival – that were still unidentified, and undived since those initial discovery dives.

Richard Barnden lives on Koror and is getting known for his classy underwater photography. He came out with us most days and kindly allowed me to use some of his shots in my subsequent book, *Dive Palau – the Shipwrecks*, that was launched at Sam's Tours the following year.

The founder of Sam's Tours, Sam himself, also came out diving with us on a few occasions just for the craic. One of the original pioneers of Palau diving, he is still very interested in its shipwrecks, and took the time to make us feel very welcome.

The mysterious Helmet Wreck

The wreck of an unknown Japanese auxiliary transport was discovered in the east part of Malakal harbour just months before my first visit to Palau in 1990 – and I was lucky to dive it at that time. But despite more than 25 years passing since it was located, its identity had never been established. It has variously been known locally as the Depth Charge wreck, X-1 and the Helmet Wreck – the latter name has stuck and with its identity unknown, that is how this famous shipwreck is still known today.

Whilst researching and writing *Dive Palau – the Shipwrecks*, I surveyed the wreck and measured its length and beam and the cylinder head sizes as best I could. As a result of my research I came to the conclusion that this mysterious wreck is in fact the coastal freighter *Nissho Maru No 5*, which although known to have been present in Palau during Desecrate 1, had until now been believed to have been sunk some distance away outside Malakal harbour and to have been salvaged and scrapped in the 1950s. The records on which this premise was based were very spartan, and although there was a seabed debris field in the proposed area, nothing had ever been found to conclusively confirm whether the debris field was the *Nissho Maru No 5* or not.

Trying to establish the identity of the mystery wreck led me on one of my longest, wildest wreck identification adventures to date – I spent days researching Japanese World War II losses and checked the details of every single listed Japanese auxiliary transport vessel in a variety of formats both on the internet and the old-fashioned way, by poring over countless old reference books. Although I suspect the wreck is that of *Nissho Maru No 5*, as nothing definitive has ever been found on the wreck that ID is by no means certain – it is just my best guess. I look forward to the day when something conclusive is found on the wreck that will confirm its identity one way or the other. I do however add one caveat to this ID; more of that later.

The Helmet Wreck – so called because of several stacks of Imperial Japanese Army helmets in the aft hold – was rediscovered for sport diving in about 1990 by a group of divers, led by Dan Bailey, who were searching for two shipwrecks known from U.S. aerial combat photos to have been attacked in the area. The search threw up this unknown wreck – they had found a virgin shipwreck, untouched since World War II, that still carried its cargo and was filled with artefacts.

The mysterious unidentified wreck quickly became a 'must' for anyone diving in Palau. The wreck today is one of the most popular in Palau and is only a 10-minute boat ride from most of the dive centres in Koror.

Despite the wreck apparently having lain untouched by divers and salvors since World War II, there were no easy clues to its identity immediately forthcoming. No bell was found – perhaps the wreck had been visited by local divers in the past and it had been removed, or perhaps it had been lost in the attack. There was no lettering on the bow or stern, and no maker's plate has been found. The abundant crockery was standard issue, the sort to be found on many other wrecks in Palau, Kwajalein and Truk.

More than 25 years after its discovery, the identity of this wreck still remains a mystery; it is a testament to the chaos of war that such a ship, filled with its wartime cargo of depth charges and aircraft parts, can be lost so easily – and that once found, official records are largely silent about its identity.

The Helmet Wreck I had always estimated as being just short of 200 feet long, with a beam of about 30 feet and a tonnage of 1,000 grt or less. She is a small well deck coastal cargo steamship, which sits on her keel on a sloping bottom that runs down from a depth of 15 metres at the stern to about 30 metres at the bow.

At the bow, she has a raised fo'c'sle with a double anchor windlass from which both chains run out to their hawse pipes. The port anchor is run out and the chain wraps around the stem; it is piled up on the seabed on the starboard side. There is a dent in the stem bar just above where the chain wraps round the stem – this is where the chain went tight as she sank. The starboard anchor is still in its hawse.

The ship was built with an old-fashioned plumb stem, reminiscent of the beginning of the last century – however as her shell plates are welded and not riveted, she isn't that old; labour-intensive riveting started to be overtaken by welding only in the 1930s, so her construction

Crockery on the Helmet Wreck bears generic markings of an eagle on top of a globe. (Author's collection)

The wreck known as the Helmet wreck has remained unidentified since her discovery in the late 1980s. The author believes she is the wreck of the auxiliary netlayer Nissho Maru No 5, which records show was fitted with a single 80mm deck gun and two depth charge racks, and carried 24 depth charges. The aft hold of the Helmet Wreck is still filled with depth charges.

dates her from about the 1930s onwards. As Japan rapidly built vessels in the 1930s with possible wartime use in mind, it used old-fashioned tried and tested designs, so even though this ship looks old, it perhaps dates from just before the war.

There are two cargo holds set in the forward well deck, which has a high gunwale and large rectangular vertically-barred scuttles. The foremast is set on the section of well deck in between the cargo hatches and is flanked fore and aft by sturdy winches. A gooseneck on the mast held a single cargo boom forward and a single cargo boom aft, which rested on a cradle just in front of the bridge. The booms themselves are missing and were presumably wooden.

The forward Hold No 1 contains several rotary aircraft engines. There are numerous large ceramic containers here, and lots of beer bottles and ceramic sake containers scattered about – many Japanese wrecks at Truk hold large quantities of beer and sake bottles, designed to ease the rigours of life in such hot climates.

Hold No 2 holds depth charges, and still has a couple of its hatch cover beams in place. There are two Lewis-type machine guns – possibly originally mounted atop the bridge superstructure but which have now collapsed down into the hold. A searchlight has also fallen down into the hold from its mount atop the bridge superstructure. The aft bulkhead of this hold has rotted away, and divers can now get glimpses into the coal bunker underneath the bridge superstructure.

The composite superstructure amidships held the bridge forward and, immediately abaft, the engine and boiler rooms, with lifeboats swung in davits on the boat deck either side of a tall smokestack, so characteristic of a coal-burning vessel. The lower levels of the front of the superstructure are studded with two rows of portholes, with two open forward-facing doorways set one either side of the bridge superstructure at well deck level. Sets of steps lead up outboard of these doors on either side of the well deck to the walkways that run through the base of the bridge wings and then along the boat deck on top of either side of the main section of superstructure. The teak deck planking of the boat deck floor either side of the engine casing has been burnt away to reveal a latticework of structural beams and views down into the corridors. The lifeboat davits on either side of the boat deck are in the swung-out position, indicating that the crew had time to abandon ship.

The uppermost forward levels of this superstructure held the navigating bridge and chart room, but these decks, made largely of wood, are now almost completely gone, apparently consumed by fire to leave only the skeletal inner steel box of the room underneath.

The slightly raised outline of the engine casing, flanked by the lattice work of the boat deck, runs from the back of the bridge to the aftmost edge of the superstructure, and accommodates the engine and boiler rooms below.

On top of the raised engine casing can be found the pitched engine room roof with skylights and the remains of four forced-draught ventilators, dotted one at each corner. Outboard of the engine casing were originally situated cabins, storage rooms, heads and the like. The tall smokestack has collapsed and fallen to the seabed on the starboard side of the wreck – leaving only a gaping black hole where it once stood with 2–3 inches of ragged steel around it.

The engine room holds a vertical triple expansion steam engine. Penetration into the engine room is tight but possible – involving a bit of a wriggle along tight corridors before a turn into the engine room itself. The engine sits fore and aft on the centre line of the vessel, surrounded by catwalks. The walls are covered with pipework, and there is a large wall-mounted pressure gauge on the port side of the forward doorway to the boiler room. The smaller high-pressure cylinder of the engine is at the front, nearer the boiler room. Each of the three cylinders has on its top a circular turn valve. Steps lead up from this level to a room aft that is studded with portholes and where more machinery and pipework is located.

The aft well deck has a single large hold with the mainmast set aft of it, rising up through the well deck, hard in front of the aft deckhouse and flanked on either side by open doorways into the sterncastle and fixed steps outboard leading up to the poop deck. The mainmast rises up a long way although its topmast section is missing. It still has a gooseneck attached to it lower down – however the wooden derrick boom itself is missing.

The aft hold is filled with a large number of depth charges, neatly stacked up on the port side from the bottom level of the hold to the very top at its foremost corner. None of the depth charges has a detonator fitted – that would have been far too dangerous for transport.

The starboard side of the hold has a massive gash in it. The cause of this ship's loss is unmistakable: a bomb came into the hold, apparently from the port direction, and exploded against the starboard side of the hull. The blast blew out a large section of her starboard shell plating, almost right down to her keel. A large section of her hull plating, complete with gunwale and scuppers, has been ripped from her frames, folded almost right back on itself to aft and angled downwards to reach the seabed. The steel deck from the starboard side of the hold has been blown upwards and bent back on itself so that its end now reaches, and is level with, the aft gun platform.

The depth charges immediately adjacent to the damaged starboard side of the hull have been thrown about and tumbled on top of each other. Initially I wondered why the bomb did not set off a secondary explosion of the munitions, but I suspect that by a quirk of fate the bomb just missed a direct impact with the depth charge cargo and struck the starboard inner side of the hull, the full explosive force venting out through the starboard side of the ship. The bomb was not a direct hit on any of the depth charges. Whilst the depth charges on the port side of the hold escaped any disturbance and are still neatly stacked in rows, the depth charges on the starboard side are jumbled up, with some having spilled out through the huge gash onto the seabed.

In the tween deck of the aft hold are the famous stacks of IJA infantry helmets that have given the wreck her name, along with a mixture of other general cargo such as rifles, ammunition, belts, shoes, bowls and gas masks.

A stern defensive 80mm deck gun had been fitted on a platform on top of the poop deckhouse when she was converted for military use; the platform is now a skeletal structure well covered in coral. The 80mm gun has fallen from its mount and lies on the platform, its barrel pointing out to port. Three boxes of ready-use ammunition sit nearby, and open hatches beneath the platform no doubt allowed for the transfer of shells from storage below to the gun platform.

There are two depth charge release boxes built into the guard railing either side of the fantail at the stern. When the ship was first found, each box had a depth charge still inside it, but these were removed in 2013/14 for diver safety. The auxiliary steering position and rudderpost are mounted on the deck just forward of the fantail, with position slots laid out in a quadrant shape on the deck below. An open hatch gave access to the steering compartment below deck. The ship had a counter stern with a square-topped rudder and a single screw.

The plumb stem and her coal-fired triple expansion engine mark her design as being from the early part of the 20th century; however the use of welding for her hull plating marks her as a post-1930s vessel built to an old design. It has never been known how this vessel came to be in Palau, but it was thought that she was probably a captured vessel, possibly a war prize.

This vessel was anchored not far from another vessel in the east part of Malakal harbour, and both vessels were attacked and sunk during the Desecrate 1 air raids. It appears that the second vessel was salved post-war, as no trace of it remains. Somehow the commercial salvors never found the Helmet Wreck, or else decided that it was of little commercial value and not worth scrapping, as they went after more valuable ships. Its propeller – the first, most valuable and easiest item to salve from a shipwreck – was still visible on the wreck when it was found in 1990 but is now completely buried in the seabed.

When diving the wreck in 2015, researching for *Dive Palau – the Shipwrecks*, I noticed a top section of the compass binnacle in the bridge area. It was a large round brass section of the pedestal about 2 feet in diameter, which formerly supported the now missing compass head.

When I looked at the binnacle closely I saw that there was a glass-fronted clinometer with a white face on it. Marine clinometers are used to measure the list of a ship in still water, and the roll of the ship in rough water. They can have a simple pointer or can have a liquid-filled curved tube with an air bubble in it that works in much the same way as a spirit level. It is an important tool for a loading officer – or the captain – to see how the ship is lying in the water in port as cargo is being loaded.

When I examined the white face of the clinometer I noted the needle was gone but that the curved scale was still there at the bottom. The legend on it identifying the marine instrument maker was still visible – and read:

D. MCGREGOR & CO., GLASGOW AND LIVERPOOL

I had always gone on the assumption that the Helmet Wreck was a Japanese ship – a small *Maru*. But D. McGregor & Co. was a Scottish company that began manufacturing marine instruments in the 19th century in Glasgow, before going on to open offices in Liverpool and London and become marine navigation instrument makers for the British Admiralty.

To find Scottish-built marine navigation instruments in the bridge of a Japanese vessel wasn't that unusual; at the beginning of the 20th century something like three quarters of all the ships built in the world were built on the Clyde. It is well known that quite a number of vessels were made on the Clyde for Japanese interests – from three-masted sailing ships to modern steamers and Imperial Japanese Navy vessels such as the pre-dreadnought battleship *Asahi* launched in 1900 when Japan was an ally of Britain.

I speculated that the Helmet Wreck could perhaps be a vessel built on the Clyde for a Japanese owner, and perhaps requisitioned into the Japanese merchant fleet as the war started. Alternatively, it could be that in the decades before the war a Japanese company had purchased an older ship built on the Clyde in the ordinary course of commerce, and that the ship had subsequently been requisitioned in the run-up to war.

Another possibility, just as likely, was that the marine instruments had been taken from an older Scottish ship perhaps being broken down for scrap, and subsequently fitted to a newer Japanese ship.

The possibilities were endless – but could it be that this mystery wreck, that has intrigued people for so long, was a Scottish-built ship? The clinometer clue certainly merited further investigation: it would perhaps be fitting if it was a Scotsman who identified a Scottish-built ship sunk by an American aircraft in Palau. This rather romantic idea set me off on a bit of a dead-end quest that consumed an inordinate amount of my time. (Sadly, when I subsequently visited Palau in 2016 and dived the wreck once more, I found that some idiot had taken a knife to the face of the clinometer and, perhaps trying to get at and remove the white face, had completely obliterated and destroyed it, such that the legend can no longer be seen. Why any diver would do such a thing is beyond me. This clinometer is a historic artefact and should be cherished – but at least the legend has been recorded for posterity.)

Of all the endless possibilities, applying Occam's razor (the simplest explanation is usually the right one), I decided to research Scottish-built ships owned or operated by Japan pre-war. If a ship was being built in Scotland, it was likely in those days that it would be fitted with marine instruments sourced locally.

I started to research, scrolling through endless website and online images of ships, and soon came to a website, www.clydesite.co.uk, that covered ships built on the Clyde for, or owned by, Japanese concerns. A list of ships and images appeared on my screen, and I scrolled down through the list of ships and corresponding photos, discounting immediately ships of the wrong shape or with more than one funnel. I had estimated that the Helmet Wreck was less than 1,000 grt, so I discounted all ships of greater than 1,500 grt. A photograph of one ship jumped right out of the list – a ship built on the Clyde in 1899, called the SS *Josephina*. The site had a bow photo of the *Josephina* aground in 1917 – and she certainly looked the spit of the Helmet Wreck.

I read that the 1,192grt steamship *Josephina* was built by Robert Duncan & Co., shipbuilders in Port Glasgow and her dimensions were 233.1 feet long with a beam of 34.7 feet. She was fitted with a steam triple expansion engine built by Hall-Brown, Buttery & Co. of Glasgow, and she was listed as 'Sunk 1944' – the year of Operation Desecrate 1 – but no date or further details were given. That seemed to fit the bill; the plot thickened. I conveniently ignored that she was built before welding of ship's plates appeared and that she seemed slightly too big a ship.

I read further: Holland Gulf Scheepvaart Maats of Rotterdam had acquired her in 1902 and then she had gone through a succession of other owners, from being involved in World War I with the British Royal Navy, to post-war owners in Bremerhaven, Panama and Shanghai.

On 7 December 1941, the day the Pearl Harbor raid began the Pacific War, she had sailed from the Indo-Chinese Port of Campha for Shanghai with a cargo of coal – but arrived in Hongay on 13 December 1941 under French guard. With the fall of France to the Nazis there was little to stop the Nazis' Axis partner, Japan, seizing a French ship, and by 22 December 1941 she was under Japanese guard and being sent to Haiphong and Saigon.

In December 1942, she was condemned in the Sasebo Prize Court in Japan, which had convened to consider whether or not the ship had been lawfully captured or seized. A ship being 'condemned' is a legal use of the word – and not quite what you might imagine at first sight. A Prize Court decree of condemnation was required to convey a clear title to a seized vessel and its cargo to its new owners and settle the matter. *Josephina* now belonged to Japan.

The website concluded that she was subsequently reported as a war loss in the South Seas, which would fit. It also commented that there were other reports that she had been broken up at Hong Kong in 1945 – that most definitely did not fit.

I searched further with Lloyd's Register of Shipping, and found that the *Josephina* had been built with one deck and deep framing. She had been renamed several times, which was not uncommon, and had been called in her time *Grahamland* (1915), *Pollcrea* (1922), *Isabel Harrison* (1924), *Amanda* (1925), *Sturmsee* (1937) and *Essi* (1942) – after which the trail went cold. Her dimensions – 233.1 feet long with a beam of 34.7 feet – were in the right ball park – but if anything, were slightly too large. The bores of her triple expansion engine were 18½, 30 and 49 inches.

There was very little other information available on the *Josephina*, so I did some more digging around, searching against each of the *Josephina's* various other later names. When I searched for the *Pollcrea* I got a hit with the well-respected shipwreck information site www.wrecksite.eu, which had the *Pollcrea* as being under the control of the Japanese government from 1942 to 1945 and having been renamed *Ejri Maru*. At last I had a possible Japanese name for this vessel.

Nearly all my searches through the internet and all my Japanese reference books failed to turn up any more information on *Ejri Maru*. However, www.wrecksite.eu had a stern shot of the *Pollcrea* at the time of her grounding in 1917, and when I looked at this, my spirits sank. It showed that there were two aft deck holds with the mainmast positioned in between them. But the Helmet Wreck has only a single aft hold, with the mainmast positioned hard against the forward bulkhead of the sterncastle and rising through the main deck from its mount. This was a serious ID problem – it was unlikely that the Japanese government had gone to the cost of reworking the aft deck layout and mast position to allow her to carry larger cargoes. This just didn't fit.

Then I noticed on reviewing my underwater video footage that the rudder was the wrong shape. The Helmet Wreck rudder has a squared-off horizontal top, compared to the black and white stern photo of *Pollcrea*, which shows a graceful, slender, almost delicate curved rudder. Perhaps the topmost section had been damaged, or become detached and fallen away, squaring it off – or alternatively it may have been a replacement rudder. It slowly dawned on me that I was trying too hard to make this ship fit the bill.

On my 2015 trip to Palau, Gary Petrie and I measured the beam of the Helmet Wreck and got it as 30 feet 7 inches across the foredeck immediately in front of the bridge. Dan Bailey had also measured the beam and noted it in *World War II Wrecks of Palau* as being 31 feet 4 inches, so we are in fairly close agreement that it's around 31 feet, give or take. But the beam of the *Josephina* as listed at Lloyd's is 34.7 feet – the discrepancy was just too much.

The discrepancy in the beam, the problem with the aft hold layout, the lack of riveting and the shape of the rudder finally forced me to face the truth. From trying to make a round peg fit a square hole, I had to conclude that the *Josephina* was not the Helmet Wreck. I had wasted all my time – it was back to the drawing board.

Reluctantly I started researching from the beginning again – this time I went through the records for every Japanese *Maru* of World War II in my reference books and looked at each of the many classes of *zatsuyosen* – converted auxiliary transports. In all there were hundreds of transports, divided up into about 130 classes dependent on their tonnages and cargo-carrying abilities.

After hours of monotonous, tedious … oh, so, so tedious … tedious checking, I eventually spotted the name of a vessel that I was aware had been sunk at Palau but had believed to have been salvaged by Fujita Salvage in the 1950s and had discounted as a possible ID for the wreck – IJN *Nissho Maru No 5*.

Starting to look at other sources again, I noticed that Fujita Salvage did have a preliminary salvage document that listed *Nissho Maru No 5* as being a candidate for salvage in 28 metres of water in the 'Palau Harbor' area. When I checked Dan Bailey's book, he had taken the view that the *Nissho Maru No 5* was the minesweeper reported as dismantled by Fujita Salvage Company in the 1950s, some 150 yards west of the wreck of the large auxiliary transport *Ryuko Maru* on the north side of Ngargol Island, the northern claw of Malakal harbour. An extensive debris field from salvage work, in 30–80 feet of water was present – but nothing was found to conclusively establish the identity of the ship that Fujita had scrapped there.

After a bit of detective work, I managed to trace a photo online of *Nissho Maru No 5*. When I clicked on it to open it, the exact image of the Helmet Wreck jumped out of my screen – I almost spilled my coffee. Like the Helmet Wreck, this vessel had a raised fo'c'sle with no gunwale other than a small section right at the bow – she had a guardrail. She had two foredeck holds with her foremast in between. The composite superstructure seemed right, with a tall coal-burner smokestack – and she had a single hold aft with her mainmast set hard up against the bulkhead of the sterncastle and a single derrick extending over the hatch. The rudder shape also looked correct.

The *Nissho Maru No 5* had a gross tonnage of 783 grt, which also seemed right. She had a length of 180.4 feet with a beam of 31.2 feet. That was pretty close to Dan Bailey's 31 feet 4 inches and not far away from my own 30 feet 7 inches. She had been built in 1935 by Ohara Zosen Tekkosho – again right, welded plates – and was requisitioned as a netlayer at the beginning of the war.

Nissho Maru No 5 was listed as being fitted with one 80mm deck gun and two depth charge racks carrying 24 depth charges. All these features fit with what is seen on the Helmet Wreck – aka the Depth Charge Wreck.

My best guess for the identity of the Helmet Wreck therefore is *Nissho Maru No 5* – it nearly all fits, and perhaps Fujita didn't salvage her after all; they don't make any specific reference in their records to her other than listing her as a candidate for salvage.

Nissho Maru No 5 – is this the HelmetWreck revealed?

But there is one apparent discrepancy; it is potentially major – but I think can be disregarded.

The Helmet Wreck has a triple expansion steam engine whereas Lloyd's Register of Shipping simply states that *Nissho Maru No 5* was fitted with 'Oil Engines'.

Normally with Lloyd's entries about diesel engines there is a lot of information given – about the number of cylinders, who built the engines, whether they were two-stroke, what horsepower they developed etc. But as tensions heightened between the USA, Britain and Japan in the 1930s, to conceal the true nature of its war shipbuilding programme, Japan banned Lloyd's agents from about 1934–35. Without access to official sources, their agents were reliant on gleaning informally what information they could from builders' yards. It is known that Lloyd's information about Japanese ships of this period needs to be treated with a certain amount of caution.

Thus, it is a feature of Lloyd's entries for late 1930s-built Japanese ships that the usual level of information is not given, and the two simple words 'Oil Engines' are stated. Given the climate in the run-up to war it is perhaps understandable if the usual level of detail is not given – and indeed if incorrect information given. It looks to me that Lloyd's here did not have the correct information and just made an assumption. Its two-word 'Oil Engines' is thus not a deal breaker.

In favour of my ID, in the authoritative online resource www.combinedfleet.com it is stated that *Nissho Maru No 5* was fitted with one triple expansion reciprocating steam engine that developed 490 bhp. That fits with the archive picture of her, which clearly shows the tall smokestack of a coal-burner belching a black cloud of coal smoke, and thus contradicts the Lloyd's statement. Hayashi's 11-volume set, *Senji Nippon Senmeiroku*, lists *Nissho Maru No 5* as being triple expansion steam, again also contradicting the Lloyd's entry.

Now I had a possible ID, I could research the vessel itself. The 783grt cargo vessel *Nissho Maru No 5* was laid down in Osaka at the Ohara Zosen Tekkosho KK shipyard on 1 October 1934. She was launched and named on 25 January 1935 and completed on 1 March 1935.

After six years of civilian duties, *Nissho Maru No 5* was requisitioned by the Imperial Japanese Navy on 26 August 1941 in the immediate run-up to Japan's Pacific War. She was registered in the Imperial Japanese Navy as an auxiliary netlayer attached to the Kure Naval District. On 15 October 1941, her conversion to military duty at Osaka was completed at Namura Zosensho KK shipyard, and the same day she was assigned to the Kii Defence Corps.

The standard armament for netlayers was one 80mm deck gun, one depth charge launcher, two depth charge racks, 24 depth charges, two catching nets and one K-type hydrophone.

On the opening day of the war, 8 December 1941, she was assigned to sea defence forces under the Osaka Guard District, and was soon engaged in minelaying duties and ferry duties, working out of Yura through the early part of 1942.

On 28 September 1943, work began to convert her to an auxiliary transport attached to the Kure Naval District. She was reclassified as such on 1 October 1943, and on 1 January 1944 she was assigned to the Combined Fleet as an auxiliary transport, and was soon involved in carrying troops to New Guinea.

On 21 February, she departed Yokohama as command ship of a fishing boat fleet that was being repositioned south to Saipan, each of the fishing boats carrying a small amount of ammunition for the garrison there. The convoy arrived at Saipan on 7 March and from there

Nissho Maru No 5 moved south to Palau – arriving there on 24 March as, unknown to the Japanese, U.S. naval forces gathered far to the east for their strike against Palau.

On 31 March 1944, she was bombed and sunk 'at Palau by TF58 aircraft', taking hits to her bridge area and to her hull. She sank quickly, and was removed from the Navy List on 10 May 1944.

This wreck has been regularly dived now for 27 years and resting so close to the Koror dive centres, it is surprising that her identity is still unclear. At some point, something will be found on her which will conclusively establish her identity. I look forward to finding out if my best guess about her identity is correct – or not!

IJN *Sata*

15,450-ton *Shiretoko*-class fleet oiler (1921)

The *Shiretoko*-class fleet oiler IJN *Sata* was laid down on 7 March 1920 at the Yokohama Dock KK shipyard, which also built her sister *Shiretoko*-class oiler *Shiriya*. *Sata* was 470 feet 8 inches long at the waterline with a beam of 58 feet and a draught of 26.5 feet. She was one of a class of ten oilers built during 1920–1924, which included the *Shiretoko, Notoro, Erimo, Tsurumi, Ondo, Hayamoto, Naruto, Shiriya* and the famous Palau shipwreck *Iro*.

Oilers were very important to the Japanese during World War II from the very beginning, when the Japanese aircraft carriers that hit Pearl Harbor on 7 December 1941 were refuelled en route at sea by oilers that sortied from Palau. Being naval fleet oilers, they did not carry the suffix *Maru* that requisitioned civilian vessels often carried.

Sata was launched on 28 October 1921 and after fitting out afloat, she was completed on 24 February 1922 and was registered in the Sasebo Naval District. She was equipped to carry 8,000 tons of oil and was powered by a vertical triple expansion engine and a single screw that gave her a service speed of 9 knots and a maximum speed of 14 knots.

Sata was built with a raised fo'c'sle and a foremast flanked by goalpost kingposts on her foredeck, above her oil cargo tanks. A slender bridge superstructure forward of amidships rose up four deck levels, with an inner structural steel core of deckhouses flanked by extended bridge wings made largely of wood on a skeletal steel structure.

Abaft her superstructure, the vast hull space was given over to further oil cargo tanks, with another goalpost-kingpost pair in the middle. At the bottom of the cargo tanks, a system of heating coils was installed through which steam was passed if the cargo was heavy grade oil that required heating to enable it to be pumped. As with all oilers and tankers, her machinery,

The 15,450grt fleet oiler IJN Sata

along with the boiler room, engine room and steering gear, were all situated at the stern. This allowed the main central part of the ship to be used for oil storage and avoided the need to have a long section of prop shaft running from an engine amidships through the oil tanks to the stern.

Sata was fitted with two 140mm (5.5-inch) low-angle guns, set one at the bow on a bandstand-type platform on her fo'c'sle and the other on a similar platform at her stern. She also carried two 80mm (3-inch) high-angle AA guns.

On 28 January 1944, Sata arrived at Palau carrying 8,000 tons of fuel oil in her tanks. After a few days there, on 31 January she set off for Truk, arriving there on 7 February, where she transferred 1,150 tons of fuel oil to the passenger-cargo vessel Asaka Maru on 8 February 1944.

On 10 February, as a direct result of the long-range U.S. reconnaissance overflight of Truk Lagoon on 4 February, Admiral Koga began to scatter the valuable naval units present at Truk. On 12 February, Sata departed Truk in a convoy consisting of the oiler Hishi Maru No 2, the ammunition ship Nichiro Maru and the cargo ships Kamikaze Maru and Kitagami Maru. The convoy was escorted by the destroyer Hamanami, the subchaser Ch 30 and the auxiliary subchasers Takunan Maru No 2 and Shonan Maru No 5.

At about 2200, on the moonlit night of 17 February, as darkness brought the first day's air strikes of Operation Hailstone to a close at Truk, the American submarine USS Sargo intercepted the Japanese convoy about 150 miles north-east of Palau and in a surface attack fired eight torpedoes at one of the most valuable targets, the oiler Sata. One of the torpedoes struck Sata and disabled her.

Several minutes later USS Sargo fired two more torpedoes at the ammunition ship Nichiro Maru, one of which set off a massive secondary explosion that caused her to sink immediately with great loss of life.

On 19 February, the ammunition ship Aratama Maru rendezvoused with the convoy and took the beleaguered Sata under tow for repair at Palau. Aratama Maru and Sata safely reached Palau the following day, carefully entering the Western Lagoon through the narrow West Passage before turning to head south down towards the sheltered anchorages of Kosabang harbour. With her potentially dangerous cargo of oil, Sata was moored for repair – well away from other ships – in the bay south and west of Ngeruktabel, the southern claw of Malakal harbour. On 29 February 1944, repairs were started.

One month later, on 23 March, the crew on Sata watched as their sister Shiretoko-class fleet oiler, Iro, limped into the same bay and anchored half a mile away. Iro had been hit in the bow by a torpedo from USS Tunny the day before, 22 March.

Both Sata and Iro were still under repair on 30 March as the first strikes of Operation Desecrate 1 began. The two ships swung at anchor, their bows pointing eastwards into the bay towards shore, Sata thus presenting her port side to the open expanse of sea to the west, from where any torpedo attack run would be made.

Just after 0500 on 30 March, for the first bombing strike of the day, Strike 1A, a total of 38 Helldiver dive bombers, Grumman Avenger torpedo bombers and escort Hellcats, lifted off from TG 58.2 carrier Hornet and sped towards the lagoon – following on after the initial fighter sweep.

At around 0630, two Strike 1A Grumman Avengers swooped down from the west on attacking runs at Sata. She was hit by an aerial torpedo on the port side just forward of her

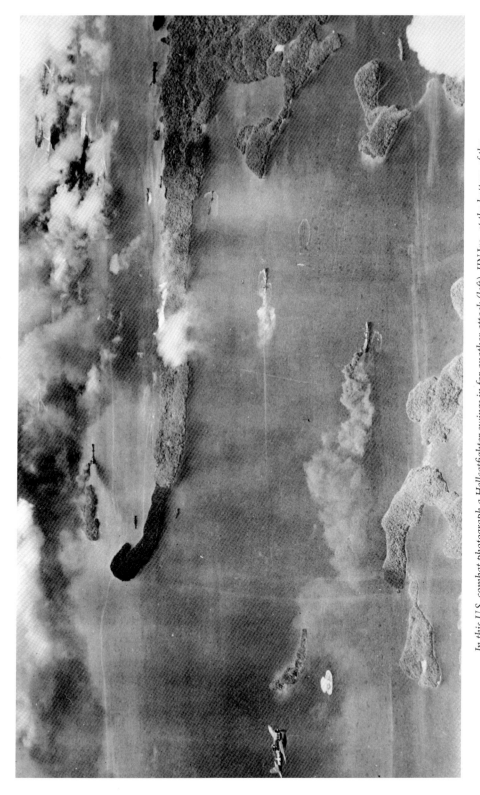

In this U.S. combat photograph a Hellcat fighter swings in for another attack (left). IJN Iro, at the bottom of the shot, is already ablaze and billowing clouds of black smoke from her stern, and has just taken a near miss on her starboard beam. IJN Sata, in the centre of the shot, is down by the stern and taking near misses. (National Archives).

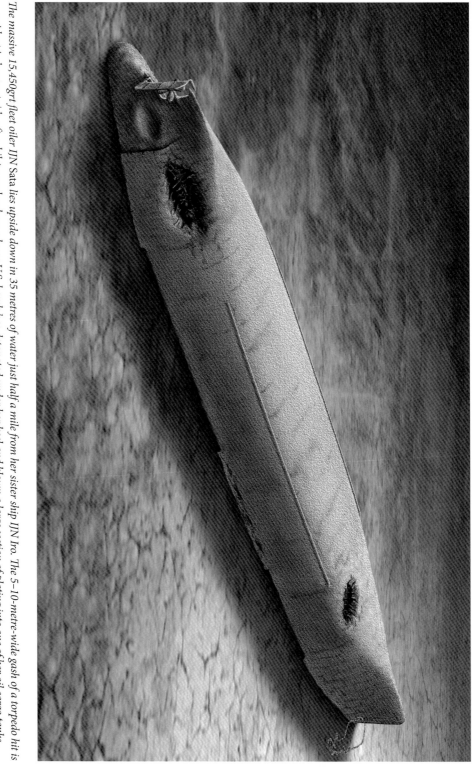

The massive 15,450grt fleet oiler IJN Sata lies upside down in 35 metres of water just half a mile from her sister ship IJN Iro. The 5–10-metre-wide gash of a torpedo hit is evident in her port side aft, whilst near her bow a large U.S. bomb has detonated under her keel and blown a large section of plating into one of her oil cargo tanks.

stern. The resulting explosion blasted a large 10-metre-wide hole directly into her cavernous engine room, which immediately started to flood. She began to smoke and settle by the stern – but remained afloat. Later that day, she took several hits or near-miss 500lb bombs from *Enterprise* Avengers.

Sata, in the middle of the bay, settled deeper into the water until finally her stern hit the seabed and began to take the huge weight of her buoyant forward section that was now bearing down upon it. Her rudder was pushed forward and her keel bar broke, allowing the rudder to be jammed up against the large prop. *Sata*'s structural strength and internal subdivisions however kept her stubbornly afloat. *Iro*, not far away to the south, was also attacked and was soon on fire, with a plume of black smoke coming from her stern.

The following day, at about 0700, *Sata* was bombed at mast level by Grumman Avengers and Douglas Dauntless dive bombers from TG58.3 carrier *Lexington* in Strike 3A-2. She took two or three further hits: one bomb was a near miss between the torpedo damage and her rudder, whilst another bomb – a large 2,000lb bomb with a delayed fuze – was dropped from 150 feet and was a near miss forward of the bridge superstructure along the waterline on the port side. Being aimed into the water intentionally at an oblique angle, the bomb travelled directly under her keel before exploding and blasting a large hole, some 10 metres across, directly up into one of her cavernous oil cargo tanks.

By this time, *Sata*'s foredeck was already awash. The loss of much of her remaining buoyancy in her forward tanks with this strike was too much – she finally gave up, rolled to port, capsized and then disappeared from sight beneath the waves.

The wreck appears not to have been worked by post-war salvors, as the large, valuable propeller – normally the first thing most easily removed from a wreck – is still present. Given that the ship is upside down and the prop not embedded in the seabed, this would have been a relatively easy salvage job. In addition, the valuable engine room fitments are still present on the wreck. There is no mention of the *Sata* in Fujita Salvage's records, so it is likely Fujita was simply unaware of her existence or location during its works in the 1950s.

Today the wreck of IJN *Sata* lies upside down in 35 metres of water just over half a mile north-north-east of her sister *Shiretoko*-class fleet oiler IJN *Iro*, to the west of Urukthapel Island and to the south of Ngeruktabel, the southern claw of Malakal harbour. The two ships were almost identical sister ships of the same class, and for many years despite the obvious damage to *Iro*'s bow from submarine attack, there was much doubt about which wreck was which – until the bell of the *Sata* was found. Other than the localised bomb and torpedo damage that sank her she is in structurally good condition, her welded shell plating still strong and intact.

As a result of *Sata*'s orientation to the local tidal stream, diving her is somewhat tide dependent. If the current is favourable, the vis will be crisp and clear. Dive her at the wrong time and although the vis will be crystal clear in the shallows and on the upturned hull of the wreck, her massive hull, broadside to the tidal flow, will have produced an impenetrable haze of disturbed sand at the bottom, through which her hull appears majestically, like a mountain range protruding through low cloud.

The least depth to her upturned keel at the bow is 24 metres – but despite being upside down, she is a fascinating dive, with lots to see and impressive penetration possible with care into her cavernous engine room and boiler rooms. The aft torpedo hole leads directly to the large inverted triple expansion engine with con rods leading up to the crankshaft above.

Our dive boat swept into the large bay and slowed as we approached the wreck. On three sides, the jungle-clad green hills of islands rose up steeply from the water. The bay was open out to the west.

This wreck isn't visited as frequently as others in Palau and there was no fixed buoy, but using transits we'd soon picked up the wreck and a weighted shotline was dropped over the side.

Kitted up, I rolled backwards into the warm water and began the descent, the upturned hull quickly materialising beneath me and extending for as far as the eye could see in either direction, its metal now covered in a thick layer of coral. The underwater visibility looked to be about 30 metres.

I could see the sides of the hull almost imperceptibly begin to sweep together towards the bow well off to my right, so I kicked my fins and headed that way. It was surprising just how flat the bottom of her hull was, and the sides of her hull also appeared flat, almost vertical, as well. She was beginning to resemble a coral-covered long rectangular box with only her bilge keels breaking her form, thin strips of steel running along the edge of either side of her keel that are designed to give her flat keel a cutting edge for manoeuvring.

After a long swim, I arrived at the plumb stem, which plunged vertically down to the seabed at 35 metres, and began to drop down. Both anchors were run out, with the starboard chain first running around the stem on the seabed, where it became entangled with the port anchor chain before running off into the distance along the seabed. The chain layout suggested that she had rolled to port as she capsized. And that would make sense as the torpedo hole was on the port side aft and would have caused that side to flood more heavily and begin to list. A row of portholes dotted the fo'c'sle near the seabed and where the fo'c'sle ended, the gunwale of the forward well deck rose up 1–2 metres off the seabed.

I moved back on top of the keel and began to move aft from the narrow bow, which quickly broadened out to its full size. When I had swum about 50 metres aft from the bow, a large hole, some 10 metres across, opened up in front of me. This was the damage caused by the 2,000lb delayed-fuze bomb going off directly under her keel – most likely a deliberate tactic by the U.S. dive bomber to destroy the buoyancy of her forward tanks that was keeping the bow afloat. A large area of keel plating was blown downwards (originally upwards) into the wreck between two of her transverse keel frames. It appeared that there was no double bottom to the keel.

I dropped down into the blast hole and was immediately inside one of the large forward oil tanks, which had a fixed steel ladder running up the tank wall and heating coils here and there. The sides of the tank had escaped relatively unscathed – the power of the explosion seemingly spent as soon as it penetrated the empty tank. As she had been undergoing repairs, it is likely that as a preliminary step her valuable and dangerous oil cargo would have been pumped out of her, no doubt desperately needed by other ships. There would have been little point in leaving the oil in her over a prolonged period of repair. This empty tank had probably been acting as a large buoyancy tank, keeping the bow afloat.

I popped up from inside the tank and continued to fin aft outside the wreck again and dropped back down to seabed level on the port side. The forward well deck was slightly off the seabed, but as I followed it aft, it abruptly descended into the seabed. I had arrived at the bridge superstructure situated forward of amidships, which was now largely buried in the sand. A row of portholes lined the hull here, marking out the officers' accommodation cabins.

An open doorway on the port side allowed me to enter the superstructure where I briefly explored cabins, the galley, the officers' mess, lounge – and heads with WCs and baths. Wanting to see the whole wreck, I quickly emerged once again and continued to move aft at seabed level.

Abaft the bridge superstructure, the hull is largely intact with a little gap between the bulwark and the sand. The vessel is resting on its sterncastle, which is well embedded in the sand.

After what had proved to be a long fin down the side of this 470-foot-long vessel I spotted the unmistakable 10-metre wide hole blown in her by a torpedo some 10–20 metres forward of the stern on the port side. It was slightly above me, well off the seabed below her original water line. This gash in her side opens directly into the huge engine room – the torn hull plating is smoothly bent into the hull from an explosion going off on the outer skin.

I finned through the hole into the engine room and immediately the large upside-down vertical triple expansion engine loomed above me, hanging down from its mounts on the engine room floor above me.

Hard up against the port internal side of the hull, an upside-down passageway led forward from the engine room towards the boiler rooms. The internal wall of this outboard passage is flat steel – it is the fire casing that encloses the engine and boiler rooms. The fire casing was still in good condition, its riveted steel wall seemingly intact but blackened by the fires that swept her after the attack. Below me, in the original roof, rectangular openings led into the stern superstructure compartments and spaces originally above the boiler room and now buried in the seabed. Bunker coal for her boilers was scattered all over the place below me.

After moving up this passage way for some 30–40 feet, I moved into a large space that dropped from the very bottom of the ship (now far above me) down to the original roof of this room. Thick structural transverse steel beams of the roof crossed from one side of the ship to the other beneath me and a fixed ladder ran up (originally down) to the lower spaces that were now above me. At its lower end beneath me, the ladder disappeared down through a rectangular hatch in the roof, and shining my torch down into it I could see at least two deck levels further down into the stern superstructure. Here, deep inside the ship, nearly all the steel walls were still thickly blackened from wartime fires.

With everything cocooned in the eternal blackness of the innards of this huge wreck, the underwater visibility in our torch beams was excellent. My torch beam could penetrate completely across her beam of 58 feet from one side of the hull to the other. There was no life in this strange world – just fire-blackened sheer bare steel walls with banks of silt piled up against them here and there.

Moving over to the starboard side of this vast space, a fixed ladder led down the ship's side from above into a large companionway. I dropped down through the opening, my bailout tank clanking against its metal sides as I squeezed through. I moved forward one deck down as one door opening led to another compartment, and then through another door into another compartment.

I then moved back, upwards into the large open space forward of the boiler room. An upside-down passage way, exactly similar to the port one I had entered through, led down the starboard side of the engine casing and boiler room. I moved down it for some way until a thick slope of silt began to rise up from the bottom and eventually blocked any further penetration down it.

The transverse bulkhead of the fire casing seemed to be solid fire-blackened steel and at first allowed no sight of the boilers themselves. But then high up, towards the original floor, I spotted a small rectangular opening from this room into the boiler room proper. This was perhaps an escape hatch or doorway for crew in the boiler room to get quickly out through the engine casing in an emergency. I rose up and shone my torch inside – the sight that met my eyes was astonishing.

There was a gap before the front of the boilers themselves – each seemed to have two fire doors and be covered in pristine pipes and gauges. An upside-down catwalk ran athwartships, across the room, seemingly hanging in space with a staircase angling its way downwards. The hatch between the two rooms was too small to wriggle through fully kitted – but some of our party did find another way into the boiler room and were able to spend some time exploring this massive space in crystal-clear visibility.

I had now spent a long time in this area of the wreck and had already racked up a lot of deco. Deciding that time was now against me, I moved back to the port side of the fire casing where I was able to swim back along the same passageway I had entered by. In the distance, a bright blue-green triangle of light showed me the way out.

As I moved a little way aft from the torpedo impact hole, a vertical rip or tear in the hull appeared – big enough to accommodate a diver at the lower level where it enters into the aft portion of the engine room. The hull shell plating here had been sprung off its frames, just where the hull starts to rapidly widen from the sternpost to accommodate the engine room. On the corresponding starboard side of the hull I found a similar vertical ripple in the shell plating. This mirror-image damage to both sides of the hull would have been caused by compression of the hull when the colossal waterlogged weight of the stern grounded.

I moved further aft to the delicate fantail of the stern, which sits with its upturned poop deck flush on the seabed at about 32 metres, slightly shallower than the bow.

The massive rudder was jammed hard over at 90 degrees to port, pressing up against the propeller blades. On top of the wreck at about 25 metres, the thin keel bar that runs out aft from the wide expanse of the hull and tapers towards the sternpost is noticeably bent and buckled by the weight of the ship bearing down on it as the stern hit the seabed. At one point, the keel bar has been severed and sprung off the keel just forward of the rudder, which has been driven forward by the weight of the ship pushing it onto the seabed, to jam itself against the prop blades.

It was now time to ascend, and as I rose upwards, I unclipped my DSMB and cracked open the small air bottle to send the 6-foot-long red sausage marker buoy up to the surface so the boat topside would know where I was.

Converted auxiliary submarine chaser

Possibly *Showa Maru No 5*: (ex-whaler *Galicia*)

During our 2015 expedition to survey the Palau wrecks for *Dive Palau – the Shipwrecks*, we were privileged to be taken by Sam's Tours north up to West Passage, the major passage through the barrier reef on the west side of the main island of Babelthuap. We were going to dive a new wreck that had only been found in the previous six months in 50 metres of water on the eastern side of the main shipping channel. It had only been dived once before – at the time when it was found.

To get out of Palauan waters through West Passage from the Western Lagoon anchorages, shipping steams north through the open expanses of Kosabang harbour with the island of Koror and the two claws of Malakal harbour passing astern to the east. Moving north, still inside the protection of the barrier reef, shipping begins to funnel towards the narrow shipping channel that runs up the west side of Babelthuap. On the approaches to West Passage, the channel is scarcely a few hundred metres across, and is a deep blue, a colour that contrasts starkly with the light blues, greens, browns and whites of the shallow sandy reef flats that flank either side of it.

The fast dive boat from Sam's Tours was powered by two Yamaha 150hp outboards and effortlessly whisked us up the channel at speed. Soon we were closing on a lateral channel marker on the east side of the channel, not far from the small settlement of Bkulangriil.

We hove to in shallows on the east side of the channel and began to kit up. There was little point in putting a shotline in here as a steady north/south current was the norm here – this dive would be a tidal drift dive. As we got our kit ready, in the distance a small boat cast off the Bkulangriil jetty and a white foam at its bows told us it had powered up and was heading towards us. Within minutes it came alongside, ID badges were shown and a local dive tax of about $10 a skull was requested. The boat was soon on its way with the cash. Our group of six CCR divers completed prepping to dive – and soon we were doing our final checks, booting up our wrist computers and carrying out a pre-breathe.

Hand on mask, we rolled backwards off the dive boat one by one and gathered on the surface before beginning a free descent in 50-metre deep open water, keeping the steeply shelving eastern side of the shipping channel in view. The current started to drift us southwards as we descended.

Although our dive guide had been given the approximate location of the wreck, no one other than the person who had found it had dived it before, so we'd been briefed up front there would be a bit of a bottom search to find it. The wreck lay in 50 metres of water on flat seabed about 50–100 metres off the vertical reef wall. The plan was that we were being dropped some way up current of the probable location. We'd dive to the bottom of the reef wall, move out from it before spreading out in line abreast, keeping each other in sight. We would then just let the current drift us down south, and hopefully the wreck would appear somewhere in front of our 50-metre wide necklace of divers.

We dropped downwards, following the vertical side of the reef – already being drifted south down the channel by the gentle current. At a depth of about 40 metres the reef wall began to bottom out to a flat seabed visible to our right. We moved away from the reef wall and spread out into our agreed line – the sandy seabed was in sight 10 metres beneath us.

In our loose 50-metre-wide line across the east side of the channel, we drifted southwards in beautifully clear underwater visibility of about 50 metres. I was very aware of the minutes ticking by, and very quickly the requirement for lengthy decompression at the end of the dive if we found the wreck was already beginning to escalate. Basically, after about 7 minutes on the bottom on air at 50 metres you are into the realm of required decompression stops during your ascent.

Then suddenly, at about Minute 10, just as I was beginning to wonder if we would in fact find any wreck, the outline of the sturdy bow of a vessel lying on its port side with its bows facing north towards us came into view. At this point I had no idea what sort of vessel we were now to be diving on.

I kicked my fins and angled my drift towards the bow. On the very tip of the prow, on the foc'sle deck, there was a fairlead and roller for handling wires or cables. I floated in mid-water studying the ship's design, and it became clear that it had an icebreaker bow. With its unusual bow fairlead and roller, it looked like a whaler.

I moved around to my right round the bow, towards the now vertical foredeck, checking my depth gauge at its highest point, just over 40 metres, before dropping down to the seabed, where my depth gauge read 50 metres. Lying on its port beam ends, the vessel rose up some 8 metres – she had a beam of around 25 feet.

Immediately abaft the stem I came to an 80mm (3-inch) bow gun set almost right at the bow on top of a four-legged skeletal steel platform that was at most 10 feet back from the prow. This was clearly a wartime wreck of a small Japanese auxiliary subchaser or patrol boat, converted from a requisitioned whaler – the harpoon would have been set where the bow gun now was.

I looked up to the high starboard side of the ship; a blast hole through the starboard gunwale confirmed she had seen action. The wreck was also orientated with its bow to the north, towards West Passage – the direction in which the Japanese convoy PATA-07 had been heading in an attempt to escape from the Palau lagoon before the anticipated American carrier-borne assault. The large convoy had set off from the Western Lagoon well to the south early on the morning of 30 March, but although a number of IJN vessels in the escort screen had made it through West Passage, most of the lumbering large transport ships were still moving up the shipping channel on the approach to West Passage as the U.S. aircraft swept overhead as Desecrate 1 began. Could this IJN auxiliary subchaser wreck be a casualty of that attack? Perhaps moving ahead of the convoy, searching for enemy submarines? During World War II Japan deployed a large number of small grey funnel naval vessels as submarine chasers (subchasers) and also converted many small civilian vessels such as trawlers, fishing boats and whalers for use as armed auxiliary subchasers or patrol boats.

The background to this is that Japan had begun preparing for an offensive Pacific war in the 1920s – but militarily aggressive, she had not contemplated fully, or prepared for, a defensive war such as she would in the end be forced to fight after the disastrous Battles of Midway and the Coral Sea in 1942. Japan paid little attention during the 1920s and 1930s as to how she would protect her sea transport vessels and shipping lines of communication: only a very small percentage of the resources and finance available for warship construction was allocated to vessels that could protect her merchant fleet.

The Imperial Japanese Navy failed to foresee the protracted nature of the coming war they sought – and they failed to recognise that Japan would inevitably require to protect her supply ships over a vast area. The IJN's obsessive fixation on winning the Decisive Battle monopolised the design and construction of its ships, armaments and preparations; naval training focused on tactics for an offensive war – and left Japan blind to the possibility that destruction of the empire's commercial shipping might also be decisive.

Just before the London Treaty of 1930, the IJN did briefly consider building a sizeable force of specialised craft for commercial shipping protection – but for budgetary considerations

The wreck of what the author suggests is possibly the auxiliary sub chaser Showa Maru No 5 lies on her port side in 50 metres in the main shipping channel alongside Babelthuap Island, just to the south of ToachelMlengui – West Passage. The wreck was only located in 2014, and nothing firm has yet been found to positively identify it.

the plan was abandoned. The net result of this failure to consider protecting her commercial shipping properly was the construction of only four *kaibōkan* coastal defence vessels – originally designed for fishery protection and security in Japan's Kurile Islands. These four *Shimushu*-class *kaibōkan* vessels were the closest vessel the IJN had to British and American destroyer escorts. These *kaibōkan* vessels could fulfil the role of general naval escort and were able to perform coastal defence duties such as mine laying, minesweeping and anti-submarine patrols.

It is quite staggering that to protect the vast maritime commerce required for her empire, only four ships of this class were laid down – and even these were reduced in design displacement from 1,200 tons to 860 tons due to some of the funds set aside for their construction, being diverted for construction of the super-battleships *Yamato* and *Musashi*.

Once the four *Shimushu*-class vessels had been built, the IJN was sufficiently impressed with them to order 14 more of an improved design – but they took so long to construct that none had been completed by the time the Pacific War broke out.

In addition to the *kaibōkan*, in the 1920s the IJN ordered construction of other vessels that, although ostensibly constructed for peacetime civilian purposes, could in time of war be converted easily to serve as naval escorts. The IJN also converted several torpedo boats and older destroyers for escort work and, after becoming aware of the build-up of the U.S. submarine fleet, began to develop a new breed of anti-submarine warfare vessel – the submarine chaser.

In 1931, Japan finally moved to protect her fleet with anti-submarine craft – her first 210-foot-long grey funnel submarine chaser was ordered under the 1931 Fleet Supplementary Programme, and further programmes produced modified versions.

Submarine chasers were given the prefix Ch and an identifying number – as in *Ch 1*, *Ch 2* etc. Eventually 64 purpose-built submarine chasers were ordered, most during the pre-war years. The first 300-ton displacement, twin-shaft subchasers were 210 feet long with a beam of 19 feet 5 inches, and were powered by diesel engines which gave them a speed of 21 knots. They were the smallest IJN naval units, but nevertheless were large vessels that looked like proper warships, unlike the auxiliary subchasers.

More than 200 auxiliary submarine chasers would be built by 16 commercial shipyards that specialised in the construction of civilian fishing craft. These vessels were then equipped for war duties by the naval dockyards at Yokosuka, Kure, Maizuru and Sasebo. They were mainly constructed of wood, with 4mm armour on the bridge and engine rooms. They were initially equipped with one 7.7mm machine gun and carried 22 depth charges.

The auxiliary sub chaser Showa Maru *No 5.*

Artist's impression of Showa Maru *No 5.*

At approximately 85 feet in length, these auxiliary submarine chasers were much smaller than the 185-foot-long IJN submarine chasers, the auxiliary subchasers displacing 135 tons compared to the 300-ton displacement of the subchasers. Whilst the subchasers were usually twin shaft, the purpose-built auxiliary subchasers, being much smaller and more basic craft, were powered by a single diesel engine. There is no confusing the subchasers with the auxiliary subchasers: whilst the larger subchasers had the prefix Ch and an identifying number, the auxiliary subchasers had the prefix Cha and an identifying number, as in *Cha 10*.

The auxiliary submarine chasers were much smaller, slower and more poorly armed than the subchasers – and were, in fact, largely ineffective vessels, only good for harbour and coastal patrol work. With a lamentable service speed of just 11 knots, their feeble armament and low freeboard made them ineffective for their intended purpose.

In addition, almost all of Japan's civilian fleet of whale killers that could be spared from essential fishing were converted to auxiliary submarine chasers for war use. Built for heavy-duty work in inhospitable seas, they proved to be extremely valuable ships with great endurance, seaworthiness, speed and towing power – designed to be able to tow several killed whales back to the factory ship for processing. Their towing power was better than most naval vessels of comparable size.

The requisitioned whalers were fitted out for anti-aircraft defence operations, minesweeping and anti-submarine warfare (ASW) escort duty, with deckhouses being enlarged to house 30–40 officers and men. The foremast was moved abaft the bridge and bow gun platforms, AA guns, depth charge racks and mine sweeping gear were added.

A typical example of war alterations would be an 80mm (3-inch) gun on the fo'c'sle, and six 7.7mm or 13mm machine guns. At least eight depth charges would be ready on the stern launching racks with a number of reloads stored below. Minesweeping floats and paravanes would be carried for both high-speed single ship and low-speed twin-ship catenary sweeping, where the sweep wire is slung between the two ships. Some whalers were fitted out with radio direction finder (RDF), hydrophonic gear and degaussing coils. It is known that a number of whalers were operating at Palau as auxiliary subchasers and sunk during Operation Desecrate 1, although their identities are not clear from the sparse wartime records.

With sight of the bow already having me thinking that this was a whaler converted to an auxiliary subchaser, I began to let the gentle current, which was running from bow to stern, sweep me aft. Immediately abaft the gun platform, the deck was flush – there was no raised fo'c'sle. Aft of the gun itself there was a raised aft-facing companionway doorway with small forced-draught ventilators, either side, leading down into the foredeck spaces. Close behind was a sizeable, slightly elevated, rectangular hatch into the foredeck spaces that was big enough to accommodate a diver, and allowed views inside of stacked depth charges with their fuzes nearby, and 3-inch shells for the bow gun.

Immediately abaft the foredeck hatch, down at seabed level on the port side of the deck, was a large powerful steam-driven windlass such as you see in use on whalers for hauling in harpooned whales and towing them to the fleet factory ships. In its wartime role, this powerful windlass would have been used for working anti-submarine nets or booms, for minesweeping and for towing.

Just behind the windlass, the square frontage of a sturdy steel bridge superstructure rose out horizontally from the vertical deck. Portholes faced forward, and there was a small raised structure at its base with two hatches or skylights. The bridge superstructure had survived relatively well, with ventilators and other roof fitments fallen to litter the seabed below. At the back of the bridge superstructure a now horizontal doorway on the starboard wing at main deck level allowed views inside. Its armoured doorway had fallen backwards, to lie flat against the now horizontal side of the boiler room and engine room superstructure.

Abaft the bridge wings, the superstructure returned inwards on both sides to form a slender central deckhouse, its roof dotted with square hatches that opened down into the boiler room, and open circular apertures from which forced-draught ventilators had fallen.

I spotted the circular base opening for the smokestack and, looking down to the seabed, saw the tall slender smokestack of a coal-burning vessel lying at right angles to the wreck. This was a coal-fired vessel – not diesel.

Behind the circular smokestack aperture, the structural ribs and frames of the deckhouse were buckled and twisted, exposing a large boiler and the engine room, which still held its vertical triple expansion steam engine on the centre line. Con rods led from the bottom of the engine to the crankshaft and to a single prop shaft.

As I moved further aft, the damage increased as the stern came in sight – clearly the devastating effect of being hit by U.S. aerial bombs that had almost completely demolished the deckhouse. Sections of hull shell plating and decking lay strewn about amidst torn and bent pipes and fittings. Any of the crew in the vicinity of the boiler room, engine room or aft spaces would have been killed instantly by the force of this explosion.

I popped up to have a look over the gunwale at the aft section of hull and keel here. There was no damage to the hull, so the bomb had exploded on contact as it hit the topsides of the vessel, wrecking the after part of the ship but not blowing through as far as the bottom of the ship. It wasn't a delayed-fuze bomb.

Immediately aft of the engine block, after another 15–20 feet of debris, the rounded fantail of the stern appeared. I moved out over the fantail and once under the keel, found that the aftmost section of keel bar, the single prop shaft and the stern post, on the pintles of which the rudder sat on its gudgeons, had been bent 90 degrees out of position with such force that even though the vessel was lying on its port side, the keel bar descended vertically 90 degrees to the seabed where the three-bladed prop now sat on its boss with all three blades flat on the seabed. The sternpost and rudder itself were actually now under the port side of the fantail.

Although the wreck believed to be Showa Maru *No 5 rests on her port side, her rudder and prop are 90° out of alignment. The stern of the ship hit the bottom so hard as she sank that her prop shaft was broken and a section of her keel was bent. She clearly went down quickly by the stern. (Author's collection)*

It seemed clear that the devastating bomb strike on the after part of this small vessel had sent it to the bottom stern first very quickly; the stern had hit the seabed with such force that the prop shaft and keel bar were bent or broken – and the sternpost and prop skewed 90 degrees out of normal alignment.

I continued further along the keel and found that the keel bar ran forward on a gently rounded bottom that had no bilge keels, and which was not further damaged at all. Further forward along the intact keel – about 25 feet abaft the bow, and straddling the keel bar itself – was a circular Anti-Submarine Warfare (ASW) sonar pod about 3 feet in diameter.

In the good 50-metre underwater visibility here I could now see the entire length of this small vessel. It was definitely more than the 85-foot length of the purpose-built auxiliary subchasers – but it certainly wasn't the 184 feet of an IJN grey funnel subchaser. I felt the length was more like about 120 feet – the approximate length of many of the steam-driven Icelandic deep-sea trawler wrecks we see whilst diving in the North Sea.

In addition, to being much larger than the auxiliary subchasers, the IJN subchasers were all diesel engined and twin shaft – but here we had a single shaft driven by a triple expansion engine on this wreck, so an IJN subchaser was clearly ruled out. The archive reports narrate that in addition to a number of subchasers, Convoy PATA-07 was led by a number of picket boats.

Towards the bow, a circular anti-submarine warfare (ASW) sonar array pod projects downwards for several feet on the keel bar. (Author's collection)

This wreck wasn't a small fishing boat that had been converted for use as a simple picket boat – she was too well constructed, too big, too sturdy, with too much steelwork. This vessel had an icebreaker bow, and her design revealed her as a former steel whaler converted for use as an auxiliary subchaser with an acoustic ASW sonar pod attached to her keel like modern sub-killer vessels.

After about 35 minutes on the bottom it was time to ascend – we had by this time about an hour of decompression stops to tick off. A line had been laid from the bow across the void to the reef wall to the east, which was well out of sight. The shipping channel is still regularly used, and with a noticeable south current running we didn't want to do a free ascent on DSMBs – perhaps drifting into the middle of the channel and being run down by a vessel.

Once back home in Scotland, I started to investigate possible identities for this wreck – going through all my World War II Japanese reference books such as *Warships of the Imperial Japanese Navy, 1869–1945* by Hansgeorg Jentschura, Dieter Jung and Peter Mickel. I also checked Fujita Salvage records and one Palauan casualty name seemed to leap out at me – the auxiliary subchaser *Showa Maru No 5*, which in her previous civilian life had been the whale-killer *Galicia*.

Such is the fog of war that the Japanese records are sparse and vague at this distance in time. But although she is not listed by name in the convoy records, was *Showa Maru*

No 5 escorting convoy PATA-07 north up the west side of Palau to West Passage in its early morning bid to escape before the imminent U.S. attack? Just as she had escorted an earlier convoy PATA-06, one week before, as it had left Palauan coastal waters.

Having an acoustic ASW sonar pod on her keel, it is likely that that was in use and that she was in the vanguard of the convoy and would have been one of the first vessels to approach West Passage. Her wreck is almost level with West Passage – and it is known that the convoy stretched all the way south to Kosabang harbour in the Western Lagoon. She had clearly been bombed, taking a catastrophic hit in the stern.

The clues all fitted – but no clincher of an ID, such as a bell, was found on this 2015 dive. I returned to dive the wreck in 2016 – by this time the bridge compass had been found but as it was heavily covered in coral, no identifying marks could be seen. Something may yet be found to clear this up – but in the meantime, it is my best guess that the auxiliary subchaser found up beside West Passage during 2014 is that of *Showa Maru No 5* (ex-*Galicia*).

The 218grt steel whaler *Galicia* was built in 1924 by Smiths Dock Co. Ltd in Middlesbrough, England, for Hvalfangersisk Antarctic A/S. She had an icebreaker bow, and was 110.4 feet long with a beam of 23.1 feet and a draught of 13.1 feet. She was registered in Tønsberg, Norway – at that time Norway was the pre-eminent whaling country. *Galicia* was powered by a vertical triple expansion steam engine built by Smiths Dock Co. Ltd, – her cylinder diameters recorded in Lloyd's Register were 14 inches, 23 inches and 39 inches. These figures, which I only discovered on my return to Scotland, might prove pivotal in the ID of this wreck – more of that in a wee while.

From 1909 onwards, Toyo Hogei KK (the Oriental Whaling Co.) had been one of Japan's great whaling companies, and in the 1930s it was pivotal in the greatest decade of whale slaughter in history; in 1931 alone, more than 37,000 blue whales were massacred in the Southern Ocean.

During the 1930s, as this slaughter continued and as whale catches diminished in Japan's coastal waters, Japan expanded her whaling to Antarctica, beginning to use large factory ships to convert the whales caught to oil, and also sending refrigerator ships to freeze and transport the meat back to Japan. By capitalising on both the meat and oil products of whales, Japan continued to outperform other whaling nations.

In 1934, Toyo Hogei KK was renamed Nippon Hogei KK, and became the whaling department within Nippon Suisan KK. In 1935 the whaler *Galicia* was taken over by Nippon Hogei KK. She was renamed *Showa Maru No 5* and registered in Tokyo.

At that time, Japan was the greatest fishing country in the world, and almost all of its overseas and domestic fishery was in the hands of four large companies and their various subsidiaries. The new owners of *Showa Maru No 5*, Nippon Suisan KK (the Japan Marine Products Co. Ltd), was the largest of the four, and perhaps the largest fishing company in the world with subsidiary companies operating in Argentina, Formosa, Borneo, the Philippines, Manchuria and Korea. It also operated fishing vessels and floating canning and processing factories in waters near Kamchatka and in the Bering Sea. (All of its Antarctic whaling factory vessels and half of its fishing fleet would be destroyed in the war.)

In 1935, amidst the largely unregulated slaughter of whales, the Geneva Convention for the Regulation of Whaling was ratified. Japan and Germany refused to sign, thereby effectively becoming the first two outlaw whaling nations. The sale of whale oil had helped

Japan finance its imperialistic activities in Manchuria and its invasion of China in 1937. In the years leading up to World War II, Germany purchased whale oil from Japan, and both nations used whale oil in their preparations for war: neither could afford to give up whaling. The slaughter continued – and in 1937 more than 55,000 whales were killed.

With the outbreak of war in the Pacific in 1941, *Showa Maru No 5* was requisitioned from Nippon Suisan KK and assigned to the 3rd Base Force in Palau as part of Subchaser Division 55, along with the 216-ton *Ganjitsu Maru No 1* (1926) and the 222-ton ex-steam whaler *Showa Maru No 3* (ex-*Leslie* 1926). *Ganjitsu Maru No 1* was sunk off Mindanao on 14 January 1943 whilst *Showa Maru No 3* was sunk on 30 May 1944 east of the Kurile islands – so they can be ruled out.

Japanese wartime records list *Showa Maru No 5* as simply 'lost at Palau' during Desecrate 1. She is recorded as escorting convoy PATA-06 as it left Palau on 24 March 1944 – almost a week before Operation Desecrate 1. Once the convoy was safely away, *Showa Maru No 5* was detached from the convoy and returned to her base in Palau on 27 March 1944, just days before the U.S. assault. The trail of information went dead after that, other than 'lost at Palau'.

Fujita Salvage came to Palau in the 1950s and began large-scale commercial salvage of the war wrecks. They list *Showa Maru No 5* as 'sunk at Palau' and narrate that they worked three unidentified 'whalers': one at 07º 18' 01" N, 134° 27' 22" E in 10 metres of water; another at 07° 17' 59" N, 134° 27' 24" E in 13 metres of water; and the third at 07° 17' 55" N, 134° 27' 25" E in 8 metres of water. The identities of these whalers are not given, but all of the locations they give with precise latitude and longitude positions are in or about the Malakal harbour area of Koror – none are way up north at West Passage. Despite extensive further searching I was not able to trace the identities of these three salvaged vessels.

One of the ways to ID a shipwreck if you don't find anything positive like a bell, maker's plate or branded crockery is to take measurements of the ship – its length and beam – if you can, and to measure the sizes of the bore of the cylinders if the ship is fitted with a triple expansion engine. A simple measurement of the beam is often enough to iron out some ships as possible ID contenders – and to rule some in.

Engines are very specific to ships – often built as a one-off for a specific ship. Conveniently, Lloyd's Register of Shipping (where it could) recorded the cylinder diameters for all ships registered with it – and that was most ships of most countries – outwith war periods.

For ships fitted with a triple expansion engine, steam at high pressure is produced by the ship's boilers. This high-pressure steam is first sent into the high-pressure cylinder – the smallest cylinder of the three cylinders. The high-pressure steam expands in this cylinder, forcing the piston head to move. A connecting rod – a con rod – connects down from the piston to the crankshaft, and as the piston head moves the crankshaft is turned. The turning crankshaft is connected to the prop shaft, which is thus turned by the movement of the crankshaft.

Having expanded in the high-pressure cylinder, the steam is now greater in volume but at a lower pressure – and this expanded, lower-pressure steam is now fed into the intermediate cylinder, which has a bigger bore. The steam expands once more in this cylinder, again forcing the piston to move and turn the crankshaft and thus the prop shaft. The engine is set up so that the movement created on the crankshaft by this much bigger cylinder is exactly equal to the movement produced by the much smaller higher-pressure cylinder.

From the intermediate cylinder, the twice-expanded steam is fed into the much larger low-pressure cylinder – where the same process is repeated for a third time, hence the name triple expansion engine – the steam expanding, moving the piston, the con rod moving the crank shaft and thus the prop shaft. The expansion of low-pressure steam in this much larger cylinder produces exactly the same movement of the crankshaft as the movement created by the expansion of steam in the high-pressure and intermediate-pressure cylinders. It is ingenious that the three phases of expansion are set up so that each delivers exactly the same amount of power to the crankshaft, ensuring the engine runs smoothly. Lloyd's records list the three engine cylinder sizes of *Showa Maru No 5* (ex-*Galicia*) as being 14 inches, 23 inches and 39 inches.

It is relatively simple to work out the cylinder bore sizes of a triple expansion engine on a shipwreck – and here's how you do it:

1. Measure the diameter of each of the three cylinder lids.

2. Measure the distance from the outside of the lid to the middle of the nearest lid-retaining bolt. The bolt is situated in the middle of the cylinder jacket.

3. Multiply the distance at No 2 above by 4. This gives the total thickness of both walls of the cylinder jacket.

4. Deduct the calculated combined thickness of the cylinder jacket at No 3 above from the diameter of the cylinder lid at No 1 above.

The resulting three figures, one for each cylinder, will give you the diameters of the three cylinder bores themselves.

When I visited Palau in 2015 to research the wrecks for *Dive Palau – the Shipwrecks*, I hadn't known that we would be diving this particular unidentified wreck – and on that first dive on it, I was focused on surveying and filming it fully so I could write about it in detail when I got back to Scotland. I hadn't thought to measure the cylinders or beam.

Whilst writing the chapter about the auxiliary subchaser wrecks in Palau, I gave a full description of this one up at West Passage, and indicated that my research suggested that a possible identity for the wreck might be *Showa Maru No 5*. I gave her dimensions and the cylinder bore sizes from Lloyd's, suggested someone should go measure the engine cylinders, and ended:

> If the measurements and calculations bring out cylinder sizes of 14 inches, 23 inches and 39 inches, then it would be fairly safe to say we have got a positive ID on this wreck!

I was really flagging this up for posterity – for someone else to go measure them and have the fun of confirming or refuting the suggestion. But by the time I returned to Palau in March 2016, whilst running a Wreck X – Shipwreck Explorers expedition based at Sam's Tours, during which we would launch the book, no one appeared to have done so.

When I explained about the possible ID to our divers and dive guides, everyone became very enthusiastic about having another look at the wreck and possibly confirming the ID. The wreck appeared not to have been dived again since our exploration the preceding year.

As ever, Sam's Tours were very obliging and without hesitation agreed to take our divers up north to West Passage – and I managed to blag a large underwater 50-metre tape reel. I coerced, bribed and cajoled Chris Rowland to devote a dive with me to this task. The night before the dive, we agreed that when we got down onto the wreck we would measure the beam of the ship and then make a bee-line for the engine room to measure the cylinder heads.

The morning of the dive arrived: beautiful blue sky and intense tropical heat. We rose at 0600 and breakfasted, prepped our kit and loaded it onto the two boats we would use for the day. Ropes were off by 0800 and we sped west out through the claws of Malakal harbour before turning the boat's head to the north.

About an hour later, we were speeding up the main shipping channel up the west side of Babelthuap as we closed on West Passage and the wreck of this auxiliary subchaser. Having dived the wreck the previous year, this time there would be no search in 50 metres of water. We should be able to find it almost straight away.

As with the year before, we all dropped into the water close to the eastern reef wall of the channel and well to the north of the wreck. A gentle current drifted us slowly southwards as we began to gently drop down the side of the reef wall.

We soon spotted the line that had been left running from the reef wall to the bow of the wreck – which was well below us and out of sight. I left the wall and swam into 50-metre-deep free water and began to fin downwards beside the line at an angle of about 30 degrees – it just disappeared downwards far into the distance into the blue. The line had a big bight in it as a result of the south current, and I made sure to keep it close beside me – it was my only fixed reference point in the expanse of deep water I was suspended in.

As our group of divers got to about 40 metres deep, we were by now well away from the reef wall. Up ahead I started to see the deep blue take on an eerie shape – we were approaching the keel near the bow. The line was tied off to the uppermost starboard gunwale, and the gentle current was again sweeping from bow to stern down the shipping channel.

Chris and I drifted aft with the current for a tour round this lovely small wreck. Once we had a feel for the wreck, I unclipped the large underwater measuring tape, and after signalling to Chris I finned along to just abaft the small bridge deckhouse, thinking that the ship would be at its widest here. I passed Chris the end of the tape and motioned to him to rise up to the starboard gunwale here whilst I began to unreel and descend to the seabed and the port gunwale. As I reached the seabed at 50 metres, as I was breathing standard air as my CCR diluent, I felt the familiar nostalgic wash of nitrogen narcosis coming over me. I rarely venture to 50 metres on air these days, preferring to use trimix to strip away the dangerous narcosis. But out here, helium was rare and expensive and in the lovely clear water, a 50-metre air dive didn't seem a big deal.

Once Chris was directly above me on the starboard gunwale I wound in the reel as much as I could to get the tape straight and taut. Reading off the measurement, it proved to be 22.4 feet. *Showa Maru No 5* had a recorded beam of 23.1 feet. That is the beam at the widest part of the ship, and it may be that the lower port side was partially embedded in the sand or that there was some tumblehome on the ship at the gunwale – that is, that the width of the ship at the gunwale might be slightly less than at the water line. Perhaps the port gunwale was beginning to sag under the weight of the ship. The small discrepancy of just 9 inches meant we were out by about 4 inches on either beam. This was a totally acceptable measurement error and was still consistent with the ship being the *Showa Maru No 5*.

Measurement duly noted on my underwater pad, I wound in the tape and we moved aft to the engine room. The aft portion of the engine room deckhouse had been blown away by the bomb that struck her here – the aft low-pressure end of the triple expansion engine block of three cylinders projected out of the remains of the deckhouse. Access was a little complicated due to sharp, torn deckhouse steel – but you could still get at all three cylinders.

Chris and I moved forward to the high-pressure cylinder first of all, and measured its lid from outer face to outer face – the measurement came out at 21.6 inches.

I then measured from the outside of the cylinder head to the middle of the nearest lid bolt. The measurement was 2.4 inches. Multiplying that figure by 4 gave a total thickness for the two cylinder walls of 9.6 inches. Deducting that figure of 9.6 inches from the 21.6 inches gave the high-pressure cylinder bore as being 12 inches. Lloyd's records stated 14 inches – so we were off, but not by that far.

Chris and I turned next to intermediate-pressure cylinder; he took one end and I dropped down to the bottom and pulled the tape tight. I read the measurement – it was 24 inches. Lloyds figure for the bore was 23 inches after deducting the cylinder wall thickness. We measured the final low-pressure cylinder lid as being 44 inches. Lloyd's figure for the bore was 39 inches.

So, we had the beam as fitting – pretty closely. But disappointingly, the engine cylinder sizes, particularly cylinders 2 and 3, were a little out. *Showa Maru No 5* was however built in 1924 – and the engine cylinder dimensions at Lloyd's are recorded as at that date. The latest Lloyd's entry for the *Galicia* is in 1935, when she was transferred to her Japanese owners. She thereafter appears in Lloyd's under her new name of *Showa Maru No 5* up until a final entry in 1940, when her three cylinders are still listed as 14 inches, 23 inches and 39 inches.

As tensions heightened between the USA, Britain and Japan in the 1930s, to conceal the true nature of its war shipbuilding programme, Japan banned Lloyd's agents from about 1934–35. Lloyd's agents did not thereafter have access to official sources and were reliant on gleaning what information they could from builders' yards. Britain and Japan went to war in December 1941, and as the veil of war descended there would be no sharing of information. Whatever happened to this vessel after 1940 is lost in the mists of time.

The engine cylinder sizes are a caveat to *Showa Maru No 5* being this ex-whaler auxiliary subchaser up near West Passage. But it is just possible that when she was converted for work as an auxiliary subchaser that she was re-engined. Perhaps her old 1924 engine was removed and a more modern engine fitted to give her more speed for her ASW duties. The discrepancy in cylinder head sizes is a blow to the possible ID of this wreck – but is not fatal. Perhaps *Showa Maru No 5* was in fact one of the three unidentified 'whalers' Fujita Salvage lists it worked down at Malakal harbour. I am disappointed that they are simply listed as unidentified – as they were in reality small steamships, and the engines and boilers would have had maker's plates and there would have been much on the wrecks to identify them at that time in the 1950s. But now, at this distance in time, it's impossible to tell what exactly happened. I personally haven't been able to find any better ID for the wreck.

The jury is thus still out on the identity of this auxiliary subchaser. I'd like to have someone have a go at more accurately measuring the cylinder heads again: I'll do it myself again, next time I am there. The compass recently located on the seabed near the bridge may reveal some identifying mark or maker's name. Likewise, the helm will still be on the wreck and may have a brass boss to it with the name of the ship. At some point, I am quite sure that something conclusive will be found on this virgin wreck to confirm her identity. I look forward to hearing the outcome either way.

You can dive this wreck with me on my YouTube channel here:

Peleliu

One of the most moving 'musts' on a diving visit to Palau is a battlefield tour to the island of Peleliu. This is a small island of just five square miles that lies at the south end of the Palauan chain of islands. Koror and Babelthuap sit to its north whilst Angaur sits to its south.

During World War II, the presence of a strategic Japanese airfield led in 1944 to a full-scale amphibious assault by the U.S. 1st Marine Division. For all that it was a small island, the battle would develop into one of the most vicious and stubbornly contested of the war – General Geiger called it 'the toughest fight of the war'.

The Battle of Peleliu was fought to secure the flank for U.S. forces that were preparing to attack Japanese forces in the Philippines. Codenamed Operation Stalemate II, an amphibious assault saw U.S. Marines and later U.S. Army 81st Infantry Division forces landing on the Palauan islands of Peleliu and Angaur. Peleliu alone had a fortified garrison of some 11,000 well-dug-in Japanese 14th Infantry Division troops.

The Battle of Peleliu took place between September and November 1944. At the outset, the commander of the 1st Marine Division predicted that the island would be secured within four days. With Japanese defenders well dug into pre-prepared and heavily fortified cave defences, offering stiff resistance, the battle lasted over two months.

As a result of heavy losses during the U.S. assaults in the Solomons, Gilberts, Marshalls and Marianas, the IJA had decided to abandon its previous tactic of trying to stop the American

The powerful Japanese airbase on the southern Palauan island of Peleliu. (National Archives)

amphibious assault on the beaches. Instead, a limited beach defence holding action would take place to disrupt the amphibious assault, whilst the majority of the IJA forces would be secure in a prepared defensive position further inland. Heavily fortified bunkers, gun positions and cave systems would form an interlocking honeycomb system through the natural terrain.

The Japanese defence of Peleliu was focused around Peleliu's highest feature, Umurbrogol Mountain. Rather than being a mountain as its name suggests, it was a collection of hills and steep ridges, running north–south along the middle of Peleliu, that overlooked a large portion of the island – including the crucial airfield. An estimated 500 interconnecting caves and tunnels were prepared into an almost unassailable defensive position.

Japanese engineers added sliding armoured steel doors to the caves, and built multiple openings for artillery and machine guns emplacements so that the weapons could be moved around as required. As a defence against the feared flamethrowers and grenades, cave entrances were built slanted, with internal corners and walls angled at 90 degrees to give troops protection from artillery and grenade blasts. This interconnecting honeycomb of caves and tunnels allowed the Japanese to quickly evacuate or reoccupy positions as need be.

The Japanese defenders were well equipped with portable and easily concealed 81mm and 150mm mortars. These rapid fire mortars could be fired out of caves or slit trenches, and the 81mm had a range of 2,800 metres. The 150mm mortar was the largest IJA mortar and had a range of 3,900 metres.

In addition, the Japanese used the natural protection of high cliffs and caves to dig out and install artillery gun emplacements in elevated positions that commanded views over large areas of land below where U.S. forces would require to operate: 20mm AA cannons were installed and a light, mobile anti-infantry tank unit was brought to readiness.

Wherever they could, the Japanese used the natural features of the terrain to their advantage. At the north end of the anticipated U.S. landing beaches on the south-west coast, a coral headland projected outwards and had a field of fire directly down the beach. The Japanese blasted emplacements for 47mm anti-tank guns and 20mm cannons into the coral – and once the guns were installed, the positions were sealed shut, leaving only a slender horizontal firing slit. This defensive feature would come to be known as 'The Point' by the Marines. Similar reinforced concrete gun emplacements were set up all along the treeline overlooking the two-mile stretch of potential landing beaches. These reinforced concrete bunkers were covered in coral and foliage, and were almost impossible to detect.

Thousands of beach obstacles for landing craft and amphibious tanks were set up. Hemispherical anti-invasion beach mines (such as seen in the foredeck holds of *San Francisco Maru* in Truk Lagoon today) were dug into the sand, and in addition heavy artillery shells were buried upright with their fuzes exposed and ready to detonate when run over. A sacrificial IJA infantry battalion was deployed along the beaches in these pre-prepared bunkers and firing positions to harass the first waves of U.S. invaders and delay their advance inland.

Whilst the Japanese had departed from their previous beach defence strategy, the American amphibious assault would take place in the same fashion as previous assaults, despite having recently suffered some 3,000 casualties during two months of Japanese delaying tactics at the Battle of Biak in the New Guinea campaign.

U.S. planners selected the two-mile-long string of beaches to the south-west of Peleliu for their main amphibious assault. These beaches lay only about one mile away from the airfield, and would allow a direct assault. All along the beaches, coral reef flats only a few metres deep extended out for several hundred yards to the coral reef drop-off offshore.

The 1st, 5th and 7th Marine Regiments would make the assault – with the 1st Marines landing at the northern end of White Beach. The 7th Marines would land at the southern end on Orange Beach 3 and the 5th Marines would land in the middle on Orange Beaches 1 and 2.

The 1st and 7th Marines would drive inland, guarding the right and left flanks of the 5th Marines as they assaulted and seized the airfield which was located about a mile inland. The 5th Marines were tasked to push right across the slender island, essentially cutting it in half. The 1st Marines were to push north into the Umurbrogol mountain area whilst the 7th Marines cleared the southern end of the island. The army's 81st Infantry Division was held in reserve at Angaur.

On 4 September 1944, the U.S. Marines LST assault ships departed their Solomon Islands staging post of Pavuvu, just to the north of Guadalcanal. A screen of heavy warships, anti-submarine warfare (ASW) equipped destroyers, minesweepers and aircraft would protect the assault group for the long slow insertion passage of some 2,000 nautical miles at the group speed of 7 knots. Faster transports left later – all due to rendezvous during the early hours of D-Day, by which time the fire support warships would have been softening up the landing zones for three days.

The navy's underwater demolition team (UDT), an elite special-purpose force, went in first – reconnoitring the beaches and waters just offshore in daylight and under direct enemy observation from the shore. They located reefs, rocks and shoals that would interfere with landing craft, and used explosives to demolish Japanese underwater obstacles. Wearing dark blue navy swim trunks, canvas shoes, knee pads and gloves, and carrying only a large knife, to accurately measure depths they turned themselves into human measuring sticks by painting black rings and dashes every 6 inches around their legs and torsos – right up to the full height of their upstretched arms. To accurately record water depth across the reefs and beaches they laid lines across the seabed to form a grid with knots every 25 yards, where the water depth would be sounded.

The development and deployment of the demolition team had followed on from the Battle of Tarawa in November 1943, when aerial reconnaissance had incorrectly led planners to believe that dangerous coral reefs and flats were submerged deep enough to allow assault landing craft to pass right over them safely. In the event, the landing craft foundered on the shallow reefs – and the heavily laden U.S. Marines were forced to abandon their landing craft in chest-deep water some 1,000 yards from shore, terribly exposed to Japanese fire. They suffered heavy casualties.

On 12 September, the pre-invasion naval bombardment of Peleliu began as the battleships *Pennsylvania*, *Maryland*, *Mississippi*, *Tennessee* and *Idaho*, the heavy cruisers *Columbus*, *Indianapolis*, *Louisville*, *Minneapolis* and *Portland*, and light cruisers *Cleveland*, *Denver* and *Honolulu*, led by the command ship *Mount McKinley*, opened up with their big guns on the tiny island. The punishing pre-invasion bombardment lasted three days – only pausing to allow air strikes from the three fleet carriers, five light aircraft carriers, and eleven escort carriers of the attack force to take place.

The Americans were of course unaware of the new Japanese defence tactic, and the initial U.S. assessment of the pre-invasion bombardment was that it had been a success. The navy

Fortified Japanese command building on Peleliu which took a direct hit from a shell from the battleship USS Mississippi. *The shell made short work of the reinforced concrete wall. (Author's collection)*

came to believe they had run out of targets to hit with their big guns – the reality was however very different: the IJA battalion assigned for the beach defence delaying tactic was heavily dug in in deep fortified bunkers and firing posts – they survived the bombardment virtually unscathed.

Whilst obvious military targets above ground, such as fortified buildings, command and communications centres, were taken out, the main bulk of Japanese troops and their equipment, sheltering in the deeper cave complexes inland, were largely unaffected. The Japanese troops maintained strict firing discipline, holding fire to avoid giving away their positions as they patiently waited in their caves and bunkers, ready to attack.

The Japanese had mined the sea passages around Angaur, Peleliu and the Kossol Passage, where U.S. forces were likely to assemble during any amphibious assault. On 13 September, a U.S. minesweeper unit swept Kossol Passage to the north of Palau whilst other units swept around Angaur and Peleliu in the south. The destroyer USS *Wadleigh* struck a mine and was heavily damaged whilst the minesweeper *YMS-19* also stuck a mine and sank. The minesweeper USS *Perry* struck a mine and sunk while sweeping along the south-east coast of Angaur.

On the morning of 15 September, just after 0800, U.S. Marines began their amphibious assault, moving towards the shore from their mother ships in their landing craft – a combination of tracked landing vehicles (LVTs) and amphibious trucks (DUKWs or 'Ducks').

Left: On 15 September 1944, as the three-day-long pre-invasion softening-up Spruance Haircut bombardment hits Peleliu, the first waves of U.S. Marines are inbound in their LVTs and DUKWs. (National Archives)

Below: Waves of U.S. Marines head for the west Peleliu invasion beaches of White Beach and Orange Beach. (National Archives)

As the vulnerable landing craft, packed full of U.S. Marines approached White and Orange beaches, Japanese shore defence troops opened the steel doors guarding their dug-in gun positions on the coral promontories projecting out to the north and south of the beaches on each flank. As the Marines came into range, the Japanese then opened up with their 47mm anti-tank guns and 20mm cannon. The exposed Marines were caught in a vicious artillery crossfire and by 0930, accurate Japanese fire had destroyed 60 LVTs and DUKW amphibious trucks.

The 1st Marines began their landings at 0832 but were quickly bogged down on the beaches by heavy fire.

The 7th Marines, to the south, faced a cluttered Orange Beach 3, with natural and manmade obstacles that forced the LVTs to approach in column.

The 5th Marines, in the centre, made the most progress on the first day, using cover provided by coconut groves. They pushed towards the airfield, which was only a mile or so inland. There, as they reached the outskirts of the airfield, they were met with the first Japanese counter-attack as a company of 13 Japanese light anti-infantry tanks raced across the airfield towards them. The Marines engaged the Japanese tanks and called in support from offshore naval guns and dive bombers. The light Japanese tanks and escorting infantry were quickly decimated.

By the end of the first day, U.S. Marines were ashore in great strength and held their two-mile-long invasion beachhead – but they had only managed to push inland by about a mile in the centre. To the north end of the beach, the 1st Marines were still bogged down by heavy resistance and had made little progress. Already 200 Marines lay dead, with 900 wounded.

As daylight of day two of the operation came, the 5th Marines in the centre assaulted and overran the airfield, taking heavy casualties from IJA infantry and from the artillery that dominated the area from the Umurbrogol Highlands to the north. Once the Marines held the airfield they pushed across to the east side of the island.

With the airfield finally secured, the 5th Marines were sent to capture the tiny island of Ngesebus, just a few hundred metres to the north of Peleliu and connected to Peleliu by a small causeway. Ngesebus harboured many Japanese artillery positions and was the site of an airfield that was still under construction. The 5th Marines commander elected to make a shore-to-shore amphibious landing, believing that the Japanese would have been aware of the obvious route to take the island across the causeway and would have made careful preparations.

A coordinated pre-landing bombardment of the island began on 28 September by army 155mm (6.1-inch) guns, by naval guns from the ships offshore and howitzers from the 11th Marines as well as strafing runs from VMF-114's Corsairs. The assault LVTs opened up with their own 75mm (2.95-inch) weapons as they approached. The naval bombardment successfully degraded the Japanese positions to the extent that the island quickly fell, with relatively light U.S. casualties.

After capturing The Point, the 1st Marines moved north into the Umurbrogol Pocket, soon to be named 'Bloody Nose Ridge'. It proved to be a series of ridges, honeycombed with some 500 interconnecting caves and firing positions. The 1st Marines mounted several assaults, but as they sought to press their attack higher they became trapped in crossfire in the narrow paths between the ridges. They took increasingly heavy casualties to accurate Japanese fire, with Japanese snipers targeting stretcher bearers.

Once night fell, Japanese troops stealthily infiltrated the American lines to attack the Marines in their foxholes as they slept. The Marines soon began to dig out two-man foxholes so that one Marine could sleep as the other stood guard.

When the 1st Battalion of the 1st Marines attacked Hill 100, over six days of fighting the battalion suffered 71 per cent casualties, running out of ammunition and being forced to fight with knives, bayonets and their bare hands.

The stalemate continued – and by the time they were relieved in October 1944 by the 5th Marines under the command of Colonel Harold D. Harris, the 7th Marines had suffered

46 per cent casualties. Pushing from the north, Harris adopted siege tactics, using bulldozers and flamethrower tanks to seal IJA troops in their caves or burn them out of their defensive positions.

Some of the caves had been hewn downwards so that any attackers would be silhouetted as they approached and entered; however, this feature was used by the Americans to their advantage – U.S. bulldozers rolled 55-gallon drums of aviation fuel into the caves and then set the fuel on fire. On 30 October, the U.S. Army 81st Infantry Division took over command of Peleliu operations from the battered Marines. Using the same tactics, they took another six weeks to reduce the Umurbrogol Pocket and secure Bloody Nose Ridge.

After two months of the most bloody defence, on 24 November Colonel Kunio Nakagawa, commander of the Japanese forces on Peleliu, proclaimed, 'Our sword is broken and we have run out of spears.' He solemnly burned his regimental colours and then performed ritual suicide.

On 27 November, the U.S. Army declared the island secure, ending the 73-day-long battle. (Colonel Nakagawa was posthumously promoted to lieutenant general for the valour he had displayed on Peleliu; his remains were discovered in a cave complex in 1993.)

The 1st Marines had been so badly degraded in the battle that they were not deployed in action again until the invasion of Okinawa on 1 April 1945. In one month, the 1st Marines took casualties to more than one third of their strength, some 6,500 men. The 81st Infantry Division suffered 3,300 casualties. IJA losses were estimated at 10,000 killed in action. The new Japanese defensive strategy would be repeated at Iwo Jima and Okinawa.

The battle caused much post-war controversy, as with the airfields, anchorages and shore works of Palau neutralised the Japanese garrison on Peleliu, holed up in their cave complexes, had no means to interfere with U.S. operations in the Philippines. At the end of the day, despite the huge numbers of U.S. troops killed or wounded, the airfield at Peleliu was not used operationally by the Allies, nor were Palau's anchorages used as a U.S. staging point. Instead, the Allies staged at Ulithi Atoll for the invasion of Okinawa.

On the recommendation of Admiral William F. Halsey, Jr., the planned amphibious assault of Yap Island in the Caroline Islands was cancelled. Halsey had previously recommended that the landings on Peleliu and Angaur be cancelled and that the Marines and infantry be deployed to Leyte Island instead – but he had been overruled by Nimitz.

With Palau neutralised, Admiral Nimitz's strategy of island-hopping continued. Rather than attacking the Imperial Japanese Navy in force, his aim was to capture and control strategic islands along a path that would bring U.S. bombers within range of the Japanese home islands and pave the way for a possible invasion of Japan.

By early 1945, leapfrogging U.S. forces led by Task Force 58 (and 38) had advanced as far as Iwo Jima and Okinawa, the carrier aircraft repelling sustained attacks from Japanese kamikaze aircraft as well as providing close air support to the U.S. troops fighting on the ground. U.S. forces were now 340 miles from mainland Japan – but at great cost. On Okinawa alone during 82 days of fighting, some 100,000 Japanese troops and 12,500 U.S. troops were killed with, in addition, 50,000–100,000 Okinawan civilians being killed.

U.S. forces were however, by now, nearing their aim for the next stage of the war – the invasion of the Japanese home islands. American B-24 and B-29 bombers lifted off in February 1945 from captured airfields on Saipan and Tinian for the first of many bombing raids against the city of Tokyo itself. In the first raid alone, 88,000 people are estimated to have died, with 41,000 injured.

On 8 May 1945, Germany finally surrendered. Japan was now left to fight on alone – but steadfastly refused to surrender. On 6 August 1945, the American Boeing B-29 Superfortress bomber *Enola Gay* left Tinian in the Marianas to drop the first nuclear bomb, Little Boy, on Hiroshima; 70,000 to 80,000 people were killed – some 30 per cent of the population – with 19,700 injured and 170,000 rendered homeless.

On 9 August 1945, a second nuclear bomb, Fat Man, was dropped from the B-29 bomber *Bockscar* on the city of Nagasaki, a secondary target, with similar devastating effect. The original target had been the city of Kokura, but on the day of the attack it was obscured by cloud. The third target would probably have been Tokyo itself.

The combined shock of these events caused Emperor Hirohito to intervene and order the Supreme Council to accept the terms the Allies had laid down in the Potsdam Declaration for ending the war. A cease-fire was arranged for 15 August 1945, and the occupation of Japan by the Allies began on 28 August 1945.

The Empire of Japan formally surrendered unconditionally to the Allies on 2 September 1945. The war was over at last.

◆　　◆　　◆

The diving down at Peleliu is spectacular – it has some of the finest reef walls in the Palaus. It is a transfer by fast boat of just shy a couple of hours down to Peleliu from Koror where most of the dive centres are based. It is possible to dive a local wreck early or, on the way south, dive the world famous Blue Holes and Blue Corner coral drop-off, which goes straight down for about 1,000 feet – before heading the rest of the way down to Peleliu for a battlefield tour. The whistle-stop basic tour lasts a few hours, whilst for the enthusiast full-day walking tours lasting up to 8 hours are available. After the short tour, it is possible to then get a second dive done on the way back up north to Koror if you are based there.

During the battlefield tour, you get taken to see knocked-out Japanese command buildings, still with their thick blast doors, Japanese bunkers and a fine museum. At the foot of Bloody Nose Ridge there remain knocked-out American LVTs and Japanese heavy artillery weapons still set in their emplacements, hollowed out from the limestone cliffs. It is possible then to walk up the ridge, passing landmarks made famous by the U.S. Marines. After a pleasant walk up, the final part is up a wooden staircase that rises to a panoramic viewpoint at the highest point from where you can see the whole island, the landing beaches visible in the distance.

To this day there are still some 2,600 IJA troops listed as Missing in Action in Palau; most are still inside the 200 or so caves that have remained sealed since 1944. Archaeologists are now carefully and painstakingly opening up and investigating these cave systems, taking great care as some are still booby-trapped and most hold live ordnance. Every now and then a cave sealed since 1944 is opened to be examined – and inevitably the remains of missing IJA troops are found.

You will be taken into some of the excavated cave complexes – some with the entrances still ringed in black from wartime flamethrowers and fire. The caves are strewn with all sorts

Knocked out U.S. LVT near the foot of Bloody Nose Ridge. (Author's collection)

A walk up to the viewpoint at the top of Bloody Nose Ridge gives panoramic views towards Orange Beach. (Author's collection)

Japanese pillbox near the World War II airfield on Peleliu. (Author's collection)

of bits and pieces, such as bottles and crockery, left over from the war. You get an idea of the harsh conditions the IJA infantry were living and fighting in for a prolonged period.

Unidentified auxiliary subchaser

Bay south of Urukthapel Island

On the way back north to Koror from a day's battlefield tour of Peleliu, our dive boat with Sam's Tours was able to divert into a bay on the south side of Urukthapel Island, where we'd heard that a small wreck had been recently found, parallel to and hard up against the steeply shelving south side of the island. It had only been located and dived very recently for the first time. This was another special dive being laid on by Sam's Tours for us.

We motored into the bay, slowed and began an echo sounder search along the steep jungle-clad slopes of Urukthapel Island, on the north side of the bay. After 30 minutes of searching the familiar shape of a wreck below us appeared on the bottom trace on the sounder. The water was still, an oily calm.

We were at most just 50 metres away from the steeply shelving rock foot of the island, which was thickly covered with dense jungle. Had this ship been moored close into the steep hillside here in an effort to get some protection from U.S. aircraft before Desecrate 1? Some ships had been moored so close to cliffs that they were almost touching them – and then they were covered with nets and camouflaged with branches and leaves to blend into the adjacent jungle terrain. The Japanese almost got away with the ruse – until U.S. analysts, studying reconnaissance photography in advance of the raid, spotted that the jungle had unnaturally straight manmade lines, and guessed the Japanese subterfuge.

A weighted shotline and buoy was dropped, and splashing into the water backwards off the boat, we began the descent down the shotline. It was immediately evident that although there was little current on the surface, the current was strong down on the wreck. It became a very noticeable trait in diving this wreck that due to localised eddies and swirls in the bay the current varied in direction and strength incredibly, almost from minute to minute and at different depths. Underwater visibility was a fine 20–30 metres – not bad for a small tidal bay.

As I neared the wreck, I found a small steel vessel lying in 24 metres of water on its port side with its keel parallel to the shelving side of the island. Both anchors were run out along the seabed: given the strength of the currents we were encountering, her captain had used both to hold her in position close up against the hillside for protection. With two anchors out forward, she probably had a kedge anchor run out from the stern, or even a cable fixed to a mooring point on the rocky shore nearby.

The shot weight itself was lying on the seabed just off the bow, and as I swam over to the wreck I noticed that the top of the stem sported a wide fairlead for ropes or cable handling. I moved aft from the bow and found that the vessel had a beam of about 20 feet, and had a raised fo'c'sle that was still ringed with remnants of her guard rails – there was no gunwale.

Twin squared-off hawse plates for her two anchor chains were set in the deck, but although I'd seen her chains were run out on the seabed, there was no chain in either hawse pipe, and the anchor windlass itself was missing – I was already beginning to think that this wreck had seen attention from salvors who had cut the anchor chains away and removed the windlass.

The wreck of an unidentified steam trawler being used as an auxiliary subchaser lies in 24 metres of water close to the south shore of Urukthapel Island. She has been partially salved post war .

The heavy chains, now free from the windlass, no doubt just ran out from their hawse pipes and fell to the seabed.

I kicked my fins and moved further aft on the foc'sle deck. Immediately aft of the hawse pipes down on the port side there was a high-velocity projectile penetration wound on the deck – and a few feet aft, there was another similar wound. This wreck had been strafed by aircraft and was possibly another casualty of Operation Desecrate 1.

Just in front of the foc'sle bulkhead, a large, sturdy V-shaped horn several feet high was set in the very middle – this would have been used for handling nets, cables or booms.

Fixed steps led up from the well deck to the foc'sle deck either side of an open aft-facing doorway that led into the foc'sle spaces. A complete pristine porthole, with rim and opening light, had been unbolted from the hull and carefully placed upright, ready to lift, on a now flat piece of the port side of the vessel. This looked as though it had been done aeons ago, judging by the coverage of marine growth, which had seemingly welded it onto the steel of the ship. A flat section of steel plating had also fallen over to partially cover it – so whoever had set it there long, long ago to be collected never came back for it. On the starboard side under the cover of the foc'sle deck was a fixed wash hand basin.

I moved aft over the well decayed foredeck, which looked as though it had been wooden, as the decking was now almost completely gone, allowing open views into her innards. I spotted a minesweeping paravane stowed below decks here – she was definitely a war wreck. Fore and aft of the broken-off stump of a foremast were a couple of rectangular raised square hatches – these were the fish hold and ice hold hatches from her civilian days; she had been a pre-war trawler.

Aft of the hatches, the wooden decking appeared to have been burnt away to now expose the structural steel frames around the large fish hold. Moving further aft, I could see a large rectangular opening directly in front of the bridge running from one side of the ship to the other. Exploring around the holds I found a number of 0.5-inch-thick ceramic tiles lying around – perhaps insulating tiles for the ice hold.

Continuing to move aft, I next came to the remnants of her wheelhouse, which was well smashed up and collapsed to port. The lower level of the wheelhouse was made of steel and had a starboard side door into it. The higher wheelhouse deck level would have been largely wood and was completely gone – now just random spars and struts of her skeleton lying about on the seabed.

Aft of the bridge superstructure, the tall narrow funnel of a coal-burning vessel lay flat on the seabed and immediately aft of the smokestack a large single boiler had fallen from its mounts on the centre line of the vessel. Once free, it had rolled out on the seabed and was now exposed and almost in free water. From here I was now able to see right to the end of the vessel, and it was evident that her wheelhouse and engine machinery were situated at the after end of the ship.

Moving aft of the boiler, I came across a gaping hole in the vessel where the engine would have been. Here the shell plating of the uppermost starboard side of the hull had been cleanly cut right down to the keel frames near the bottom of the ship. The area around the engine room was a mass of tangled and bent steel spars and plates, and it was obvious that the area here had been cut away and explosives used by salvors to free up the valuable engine for recovery to the surface.

At the very stern, I moved round the heavily damaged fantail of the vessel and swam underneath the keel to check the rudder and prop. Here I found that the rudder had been neatly cut away and the propeller unbolted and removed, leaving the shaft still *in situ* and perfectly intact.

This wreck appears to be a steam trawler that was being used as an auxiliary patrol boat or auxiliary subchaser. Although a minesweeping paravane was spotted on the wreck, that feature was common to most Japanese vessels, small or large. There was no indication of any bow gun or sonar sub-chasing gear that would nail her as an auxiliary subchaser, although that possibility cannot be ruled out.

The identity of this auxiliary subchaser or patrol boat has not yet been established. It is another of Palau's enduring mysteries that will be revealed in time – and I look forward to hearing of her identity once some vital clue emerges.

IJN *Iro*

15,450-ton *Shiretoko*-class fleet oiler (1922)

The *Iro*, like the *Sata*, is one of the class of ten *Shiretoko*-class fleet oilers ordered by the Imperial Japanese Navy in the 1920s. *Iro* displaced 15,450 tons and had an oil cargo capacity of 8,000 tonnes.

Iro was laid down on 2 September 1921 at Osaka Iron Works in Osaka. She was launched and named on 5 August 1922 and after fitting out afloat was officially completed on 30 October 1922 and registered in the Kure Naval District. Powered by a vertical triple expansion engine, her single shaft gave her a service speed of 9 knots and a maximum speed of 14 knots. She was manned by a crew of 160.

Iro saw service during the Japanese invasion of China in 1937 and then, on 31 October 1941, in the immediate run-up to war in the Pacific, she was assigned to the 4th Fleet. She was fitted with two 140mm (5.5-inch/50-cal) low-angle guns on circular bandstand platforms, one on the fo'c'sle at the bow and one at the stern. She was also fitted with two 80mm (3-inch/40-cal) high-angle (HA) AA guns and four 13.2mm machine guns.

On 15 March 1944, *Iro* departed Balikpapan for Palau in a large convoy of 21 transports and oilers with five escort vessels. On 22 March, west of Palau, the convoy was picked up on radar by the American submarine USS *Tunny*, which began to close on the surface. A Japanese escort destroyer spotted *Tunny* but in poor visibility the submarine was able to evade

The 15,450grt Shiretoko-*class fleet oiler IJN* Iro.

the destroyer and continue to close on the convoy. Once in a firing position, a full bow spread of six torpedoes was fired at two Japanese cargo ships – with hits on both.

Lookouts on the conning tower of *Tunny* spotted the Japanese escort destroyer *Michishio* moving at high speed across the American submarine's stern, and fired a spread of four torpedoes before crash-diving as the first of 87 depth charges were dropped. In the following four-hour-long contact, *Iro* was hit by a torpedo at the very bottom of her bow on the starboard side, well forward of her collision bulkheads. Although damaged, she was still watertight and was able to limp on to Palau for repair.

As *Iro* entered Palau's Western Lagoon at dusk on 23 March 1944 through West Passage, she turned her bows south and moved down to the sheltered Urukthapel anchorage to the south of the southern claw of Malakal harbour, Ngeruktabel. She was still carrying a very volatile and dangerous flammable cargo, and for safety reasons she was being kept well clear of the vessels anchored up within Malakal harbour itself. Her sister *Shiretoko*-class fleet oiler, *Sata*, was already at anchor, undergoing repairs half a nautical mile away to her north-east.

Seven days later, at dawn on 30 March 1944, Operation Desecrate 1 began, as the F6F Hellcats, Douglas SBD Dauntless and SB2C Helldiver dive bombers, and Grumman TBF Avenger torpedo bombers of Task Group 58 swept over the Palau anchorages. Tankers and oilers were priority targets, and the valuable *Iro* and *Sata* were quickly spotted and identified in their sheltered anchorage just to the south of Malakal harbour. Three *Bunker Hill* dive bombers attacked *Iro*, dropping six 1,000lb bombs on the ship at about 0730 (local) and reporting one hit.

The following day, 31 March, as U.S. reconnaissance aircraft overflew Palau, *Iro* was found to be still afloat, and Douglas Dauntless dive bombers were vectored to attack her once again. One 1,000lb bomb hit the ship on the starboard aft quarter just above the waterline, and fitted

U.S. combat photo showing the aft section of IJN Iro *ablaze and billowing clouds of black fuel smoke. (National Archives)*

271

Iro sinks by the stern amidst a slick of fuel oil. Her bow section is so hot from the fires that ragethat steam billows from her metalwork. She strains at her anchor chain and the earlier damage to her bow by the submarine USS Tunny *is clearly visible. 55-gallon fuel drums from her dry cargo spaces bob in the water around her. (National Archives)*

with a delayed fuze, the bomb punched straight through her shell plating, and through a crew accommodation compartment before exploding in her engine room. The large explosion caused a fire to break out, and soon clouds of black fuel smoke were billowing up into the sky from her aft section; 200 of her crew were able to escape the ship – but 50 had perished, including her captain.

Mortally wounded in her cavernous engine room area, she settled by the stern – but such was a tanker's strength, allied to her internal subdivisions and the buoyancy of her forward section, that she did not go under completely. Fuel flooded out of breached compartments causing a large slick, and hundreds of 55-gallon fuel drums floated out from her dry cargo holds.

As her stern sank and grounded on the bottom, her bow rose in the air, straining at her starboard anchor chain. Her bow eventually rose so high that the damage caused to the base of her stem from the earlier submarine attack by USS *Tunny* became visible. The metal of her bow was so hot from fires that boiling white steam billowed up from it. Half a mile away, *Sata* was hit in the stern at the engine room area by a torpedo. She settled by the stern, turned turtle and went under.

Although she had also settled by the stern, *Iro*'s bow and forward tanks retained their buoyancy and kept her bow projecting up out of the water. With her cargo of fuel on fire, she

The wreck of the fleet oiler Iro sits on her keel in just over 40 metres of water and is a stunning world-class wreck dive .

burned for several days after the strike, before finally succumbing and sinking nearly three weeks later, on 17 April 1944. She came to rest perfectly upright on the bottom in just over 40 metres of water.

Today, the massive 470-foot-long wreck of the fleet oiler *Iro* sits upright on her keel in the Western Lagoon. She is a massive, structurally intact vessel that takes several dives to fully understand and appreciate. Sitting upright in an area of generally excellent 100-foot visibility, this large oiler with her guns still in place, towering masts and massive refuelling at sea (RAS) masts still upright, is a stunning world-class wreck and is one of the highlights of diving at Palau.

At the very bow, her slightly raked stem defines the era of her construction. About 5 metres of the base of her stem and part of her keel bar are missing – the stem bar hangs straight down without being connected to her keel. This is the damage inflicted by the torpedo from USS *Tunny* – a large hole, about 8 metres wide. The torpedo that punched this hole appears to have come in from the starboard side just aft of the stem bar, as the entry wound is smaller here than the exit wound on the port side, where torn plating and bent metal, ribs and beams all reveal how the energy of the explosion vented out through the side of the hull. The very base of the stem stands a few metres clear of the seabed at 41 metres, and ripples in the shell plating caused by the explosion extend backwards. The starboard anchor chain runs out of its hawse and drops down vertically before running out along the seabed at right angles to the wreck.

Iro still has a 140mm (5.5-inch) gun with splinter shield set on a large raised circular platform on the fo'c'sle deck. The plating of the bandstand gun platform has corroded away to reveal the structural latticework. This gun was likely an old gun from the secondary battery of a decommissioned Japanese battleship or cruiser; similar guns were used as coastal defence batteries ashore and can be seen at a number of locations. The barrel with its small, curved splinter shield is depressed and is pointed slightly to port off the bow. The anchor windlass sits on deck just forward of the gun platform. Dropping down from the fo'c'sle deck to the forward well deck, you can enter two forward-facing doorways on the aft bulkhead of the fo'c'sle into the fo'c'sle spaces.

On the foredeck immediately aft of the fo'c'sle on the centre line of the vessel is a modest hatch with high coaming that opens into a large open hold with a tween deck where dry cargo would have been stored. The various levels of the hold are now largely empty, barring cargo-handling gear and cargo booms. At the very bottom of the hold, the structural beams of the hull are contorted and bent inwards – again a direct result of the large explosion in the spaces of the bow just forward. Shells for her bow gun can be found stored here. A flying bridge runs about 10 feet above the deck and connects each of the three islands: fo'c'sle to bridge and bridge to sterncastle.

Aft of Hold No 1 stands the foremast, flanked by two tall kingposts which doubled as ventilators. These are connected to the mast by thick horizontal and diagonal bracing, and are reinforced with a cross-bar high up. A topmast rose from the centre foremast and no doubt would have projected out of the water after she sank; it has broken or been cut away to reduce the danger to shipping.

Aft of the foremast and kingposts is a cluster of four small oil cargo tank hatches on the centre line, some with their lids open. A larger open hatch for dry cargo flanks this cluster of four access hatches on the starboard side.

The tubular jumbo derrick boom used for heavy lifts runs aft from the base of the starboard kingpost. It would have no doubt been secured upright when not in use at the top of the starboard kingpost. In the archive combat photo of her sinking by the stern with her bow raised high, the jumbo derrick can be seen passing diagonally aft from the starboard kingpost, to rest on the port side of the well deck just in front of the bridge – exactly where it remains today.

The slender bridge superstructure is set slightly forward of amidships and is three deck levels high. The higher levels have a central steel deckhouse that is flanked by skeletal wings that extend out to either side of her beam. The top deck level has a much smaller steel deckhouse and the same skeletal bridge wings arrangement. The wooden front walls of these higher deck levels have been burnt or rotted away to leave just the steel latticework.

Moving aft from the bridge superstructure, the flying bridge continues just in from the port side of the deck with a cluster of several more cargo tank access hatches on the centre line of the ship, flanked by larger open rectangular hatches in the same fashion as on the foredeck. Lifeboat davits dot the gunwales of the ship in the swung-out position on the port side, indicating the crew here had time to abandon ship. The lifeboat davits on the starboard side are in the swung-in position – those boats were never launched.

Midway between the bridge superstructure and the sterncastle, one of the most striking and characteristic sights of this wreck comes into view – the massive goalpost RAS masts with a latticework of horizontal and diagonal thick bracing steel spars now well encrusted with sealife. A tubular jumbo derrick boom is goosenecked high up on the port kingpost (on the opposite side to the foredeck jumbo derrick) and runs aft until its derrick head rests on the deck beside a cluster of four more oil cargo tank access hatches mirroring the layout forward of the RAS masts.

As the flying bridge approaches the sterncastle, it starts to sag, and then collapses down to the main deck as it meets the deckhouse, as though the intense fires had weakened and almost melted the metal.

The sterncastle begins with a narrow deckhouse set well in from both sides of the deck with guardrails along its roof. On top is a smaller superimposed deckhouse and a long covered rectangular athwartships hatch, which opens down towards the boiler room – a coaling hatch for her bunker coal. This deckhouse runs back towards where the sterncastle extends out to the full width of the ship at either side, and here it is noticeable that the deckhouse roof is sagging – again weakened by fire.

The large refuelling tripod used to support RAS transfer hoses rises up for almost 10 metres on the port side of the vessel here, with a large fixed oil tank athwartships on mounts inboard of it. Oil was most likely pumped by the ship's low-pressure pumps up to this tank, which may have held high-pressure pumps to force the oil high up the transfer hoses via the tripod and over to the ship being refuelled.

The massive smokestack rising from the boiler room has fallen to port and now lies collapsed on top of the superstructure. It projects out over the port gunwale and is still ringed by reinforcing banding.

A rectangular hatch aft of the fallen smokestack allows divers to drop into the large engine room. Here the large vertical triple expansion engine running fore and aft on the centre line dominates, with gratings and catwalks around, all jumbled up and bent out of shape by the catastrophic bomb explosion and subsequent fires. Doorways open aft to deck on either side at its highest level – and internal stairwells allow divers to swim down several deck levels to the bottom of the engine room. The smaller high-pressure cylinder is the furthest forward – nearer to the boiler room where the steam is created – and the larger low-pressure cylinder is the aftmost. Large con rods connect the engine to the crankshaft, and dwarf divers. Spare piston rings can be found clamped onto the engine room bulkhead – failure of piston rings was a very serious problem during voyages and from time to time a piston had to be re-ringed.

I love exploring the engine room on this wreck – it holds so much to see and understand. On one exploration in 2015, I swam over to a large silt-filled room on the starboard side of the engine. Staying well above the silt I carefully frog-kicked my way into the room to avoid stirring it up. A frog kick is a technique that divers use in confined spaces such as caves and wrecks where careless finning can stir up dangerous clouds of silt. With a standard, up/down fin stroke, the fins produce a powerful down-draught which when it hits a silty bottom can produce huge clouds of silt. In a bad silt-out, the vis can be reduced to zero – with no visibility, divers can get lost and many have died, panicking, before running out of air, inside the bowels of a rusting wreck. But the draught from a frog kick moves horizontally, inwards from each fin, the one draught being dissipated against the other and the silt remaining undisturbed.

As I entered the room, there were upturned beds and chests scattered about, some upside down, their legs protruding from the silt of what appeared to be crew accommodation; the officers would have messed in the more pleasant spaces of the bridge superstructure.

On the starboard hull shell plating of this room, there was a circular hole to the outside – the edges of the hole were smoothly bent inwards towards me. This looked like an entry gash for an aerial bomb – perhaps I was looking at where the bomb that mortally wounded her entered the vessel.

Exiting the engine room, I moved towards the very stern. Here a 140mm (5.5-inch) defensive gun, similar to the bow gun, is mounted on a large, now skeletal, circular platform on top of the stern superstructure. Its large barrel, still with its semi-circular splinter shield, points aft, and there are boxes of ready-use shells lying nearby, one directly under the barrel.

The sterncastle extends right up to the fantail, with covered promenade walkways ringing the deck level below the platform and doors opening into internal corridors – portholes lining the walls of what was most likely crew accommodation. All the wooden decking and roofing of the various spaces here has been burnt away to leave only a skeletal framework.

The very stern compartments hold the steering gear below decks, and on deck there is an auxiliary steering position with twin helms for direct turning of the rudder should command from the bridge be lost such as by a bomb hit.

As you drop over the stern and head down to the very bottom, the sternpost emerges from the beautiful counter stern and leads down to the tall, narrow rudder that still hangs on its pintles. The propeller itself, if still present on the wreck, is well buried in deep silt and out of sight. Rising up to begin my return, I noticed familiar degaussing cables lining the hull, designed to give protection against magnetic mines.

The *Iro* is an amazing world-class dive with so much to see – she ranks as one of my favourites. I have dived her many times and each time see something new or find areas I have not seen before.

The wartime chief engineer on *Iro*, Mr Tomimatsu Ishikawa, who lived in Mie prefecture near Osaka in Japan after the war, was just 26 when *Iro* took a massive bomb hit towards the stern of the vessel on the first day of Desecrate 1, 30 March 1944. He was in the engine room at the time and had about 50 junior engineers under his command. The bomb exploded close to him and he was knocked unconscious by the blast for about 30 minutes. When he came to, the engine room was filled with black smoke and the ship was sinking. Knowing the area so intimately, he managed to feel his way out.

He managed to unload a life raft and climbed down a rope ladder into it with five other survivors. They drifted away from the stricken burning ship in the raft for some 6–7 hours as the Operation Desecrate 1 strikes went on all around them. U.S. aircraft reappeared and as they swooped down from the skies, fearing that the raft was going to be strafed, he jumped into the water and duck-dived as the aircraft flew overhead.

Now separated from the raft, he swam for the closest islands – only to find sheer cliffs rising out of the water, with no possible way of getting onto the land. He continued swimming to other equally impossible islands where he was still unable to get out of the water. Then, finally, just as it was getting dark, he reached a small island where he was able to climb out and take shelter in a cave. He was spotted about 2200 the next evening by a Japanese rescue ship and taken aboard.

Iro remained afloat by her bow and on fire for 10 days – she had been carrying a lot of gasoline and fuel oil at the time she was hit. And every day he watched his old ship burning and suffering – knowing that the remains of his crew mates were still inside.

Mr Ishikawa remained in Koror for one and a half years as the war progressed to its nuclear finale. Racked with guilt at having survived when he felt he should have given his life, he repeatedly applied for kamikaze suicide squads, applying to serve on *kaiten* human torpedo submarines. These one-man torpedoes carried a powerful 1,550kg warhead – and once the pilot had entered the submarine and the hatches were closed, he could not unlock them.

Japanese command planned an attack on a large U.S. ship known to be based near Peleliu – and he was selected to be one of the pilots for the mission. On the Japanese torpedo ship, the night before the planned attack, he was given a special beefsteak dinner that was reserved for *kaiten* suicide squad, who were expected to die the following day.

Just as he was starting dinner, the torpedo ship was suddenly attacked by U.S. aircraft and set on fire. The ship began to capsize and he abandoned ship – once again finding himself back in the water, swimming for his life towards an island. When he made landfall, he was able to climb out onto a limestone island, cutting his bare feet on the razor-sharp rock, but feeling little pain at the time. A second torpedo ship that did not get attacked that night went to Peleliu the next morning to carry out the attack as planned. It never came back.

After the war, Mr Ishikawa worked back in Mie prefecture at his father's shipping business until he was 65 years old. When he subsequently saw an NHK TV documentary that featured his old ship, he contacted NHK and was put in touch with an underwater wreck photographer, Mr Koichi Tsubomoto, who had photographed *Iro* for the programme. Mr Ishikawa, believing that he was the last living crewman from the ship, subsequently returned to Palau when he was 77 years old. He performed a small religious memorial ceremony on the surface at that time.

In March 2004, the 60th anniversary of the sinking of the *Iro* was approaching – and sad because no one in Japan seemed to care for his fallen comrades, he determined to dive on *Iro*. Rather than throwing a flower from the boat, despite now being 86 years old, not trained as a diver, and uncomfortable under water, he determined that he would dive on *Iro* and perform an underwater memorial service.

Mr Ishikawa was taken out to the wreck site along with some other divers and TV journalists. At about 1000, exactly the time *Iro* had been attacked 60 years previously, the dive began. Dive staff descended to the wreck and set a ceremony table on the deck in the upper part of his engine room, and set flowers and a bottle of Japanese sake on the table.

Mr Ishikawa was then taken down to the wreck. Not being a trained scuba diver he was carefully led to the ceremony table. He knelt down before it, took his prayer beads out and began to pray. After 2–3 minutes, they left the table to return to the surface.

On the surface, before they left the wreck site, Mr Ishikawa sprinkled part of the sake on the water for his comrades, tears welling up in his eyes as he bade farewell to them for the last time.

BOOK THREE

LATEST DEVELOPMENTS

14

SS *Creemuir* 1940

North Sea

The 3,992grt British steamship Creemuir off Cape Town. She was leading the port column of a convoy of 31 ships that had set out from Methil in Fife, Scotland, for Nova Scotia to collect war supplies. She was torpedoed and sunk in 1940 on Armistice Day, 11 November, as the convoy approached Aberdeen on Scotland's north-east coast. There were only 13 survivors from her crew of 42.

Those of you who have read *The Darkness Below*, the 2011 prequel to this book, will recollect that the book ends with the story of the loss of the 3,997grt British steamship SS *Creemuir*, which was attacked by German aircraft, torpedoed and sunk 14 miles north-east of Stonehaven in 1940 on Armistice Day, 11 November. In the years following publication of that book however, there were a number of significant developments relating to that ship and I will endeavour to set them out and bring the story up to date. But first a little bit of background to set the scene.

The *Creemuir* was built as the SS *Medomsley* in 1924 by Palmers' Co. Ltd of Newcastle for the Muir S.S. Co. Ltd. She was a sizeable vessel of 360.2 feet in length with a beam of 51 feet and a draught of 24.7 feet. Her name was quickly changed to *Langleemere* and then in 1938 was changed again, to *Creemuir*. She was built as a three-island well deck steamer with a raised fo'c'sle at the bow, a composite superstructure amidships and a stern superstructure.

The well deck between fo'c'sle and bridge superstructure had two holds, with the foremast rising from a masthouse set in between the two cargo hatches. The composite superstructure

281

amidships held the navigation bridge forward, which had wooden wings on a steel framework projecting to either side of a central steel section. The boiler room, and the engine room, housing the triple expansion engine, were set low down immediately abaft the bridge. The tall smokestack of a coal-burning vessel rose from the boiler room and was surrounded by a forest of forced-draught ventilators, with more either side of the pitched roof of the engine room. Lifeboats swung in their davits at either side of the boat deck, and the galley was housed at the aft end of the superstructure.

Two large holds were set in the aft well deck, with the mainmast rising from the section of deck in between the hatches. At the stern, a poop deckhouse held the steering gear, auxiliary steering position and crew accommodation. Once war was declared in 1939, she was fitted with a DEMS (defensively equipped merchant ship) gun set on a platform on top of the stern superstructure.

On 11 November 1940, she was the lead vessel of the port column of convoy EN23, which was made up of 31 merchant vessels. The convoy had left Methil in Fife northbound at 0500 and was scheduled to run up the east coast of Scotland, pass through the Pentland Firth (the channel between the north of mainland Scotland and the Orkney Islands) and then pass down the west coast to Oban. Here, in the deep-water convoy gathering point known as the Oban Roads, she would form up again in convoy for an Atlantic crossing in ballast to Yarmouth, Nova Scotia, where she was to load a cargo of pit props. The Oban Roads was a relatively safe convoy gathering point – chosen because of its deep water that made German attempts at minelaying ineffective. The day was overcast and chilly, and a beam wind blew steadily, causing a moderate swell.

The swept channel was a marked channel for Allied shipping that at this point of the war ran all the way up the east coast of Britain from London to Fraserburgh. It was later extended up to Orkney. The swept channel was approximately a half to one mile wide, lay some five to ten miles off the coast, and was marked by buoys every ten miles. On the seaward or eastern side were the minefields of the east coast mine barrage. As the name implies, the channel was regularly swept for mines. There was no such channel marked out in the Pentland Firth itself, as it was believed that no German vessel would dare come so close to the very heart of British naval power in Scapa Flow.

At 1500, some ten hours into the voyage, the convoy was attacked by a German aircraft flying from Norway. Its bombs failed to score a direct hit, but did explode in the water close enough to one ship to stove in some plating and allow water in. That ship was forced to detach from the convoy and head to port for repairs.

Just over two hours later, at 1730, having just passed Stonehaven on her port beam, *Creemuir* was moving north towards Aberdeen when the convoy was attacked again. This time it was a German Heinkel He 115 seaplane, which came in beam on and loosed an aerial torpedo when it was just 150 yards from the *Creemuir*. There was no time for *Creemuir* to manoeuvre out of the way and comb the track of the torpedo, which struck *Creemuir* in the engine room causing catastrophic damage. The ship was 'light' – that is, she was in ballast with her large holds empty and able to quickly fill with immense volumes of water. She sank in just 2–3 minutes. Sadly, there were only 13 survivors out of a crew of 42.

In April 2009, my group of divers located the wreck lying far offshore in 70 metres of water about half a mile to the west of (or inside) the Dog Hole, the underwater canyon that runs north-east to south-west off the north-east coast for about 20 miles. The Dog Hole is around one mile wide and has almost sheer sides that drop down from an average seabed of 70 metres to depths of 125 metres or more.

I set up a dive for my group on what was a completely undived wreck at the time. We had two RIBs, each with four divers and a cox. The dive was interesting but marred by poor pitch-black visibility of about 5 metres down on the wreck.

My publishers at the time, Random House, had been developing their own website and had given each of their authors an individual section. They populated the site with basic book details and blurb, and each author was then able to go into the site and tweak their section and pad it out. A blog for the author was provided, which also allowed members of the public to post online comments.

As the 2009 diving season came to a close for the winter, I began to work on the Random House site and made an initial blog posting about our north-east wreck projects for 2010. In passing I mentioned the *Creemuir* as one wreck we planned to revisit – and thought nothing more of it.

In early March 2010, I checked the site and was staggered to see a comment from one Noel Blacklock, who posted that he had been the radio officer on *Creemuir* when she was sunk and believed that he was the only member of the crew still alive. I managed to get Noel's email address from Random House and fired off an email to him. Noel was soon in touch and sent me his first-hand account written at the time. He kindly allowed me to reproduce it verbatim in *The Darkness Below* and I will repeat it here by way of background to set the scene.

This is Noel's account:

ARMISTICE DAY 1940

This is the account as written by 2nd Radio Officer W.N. BLACKLOCK at the time. He was just nineteen years old.

~~~

RN Radio Officer Noel Blacklock during World War II. © Noel Blacklock

The afternoon of November 11th, 1940 found SS *CREEMUIR* in latitude 57 degrees north about seventy-five miles north of the River Forth and just inside the swept channel which extends almost ten miles out at this point. The day, although fine was overcast; there was a distinct nip in the air, and a beam wind was steadily blowing up causing a moderate swell.

SS *Creemuir* owned by Messrs Muir Young Ltd, of London, a ship of 3992 tons, was leading the port column of convoy EN23, consisting of 31 merchant vessels which left Methyl, north about, at 5 a.m. for Oban, and her final destination would have been Yarmouth, Nova Scotia, for a fresh cargo of pit props, had fate been kind to her.

She was moderately well armed with one four-inch gun, one Holman Projector, one Hotchkiss on the boat deck and two Lewis guns on the wings of the bridge. All the automatic weapons were manned when at three p.m. a large twin engined bomber appeared ahead of the convoy, travelling towards it at a low altitude; to myself it seemed to be an enemy plane (a fact which I mentioned to one of the gunners at the time, but he, and one of the escorting vessels, one sloop and two armed trawlers were of a different opinion, and they held their fire.) Slowly and gracefully the large bomber sailed over the *Creemuir* and passed towards the rear of the convoy, making the typical thrumming noise of a German diesel engined plane. While it was in view my eyes never left it; I was temporarily petrified, and by no means surprised to see a stick of bombs leave it in a row as it passed over the sternmost ships. Terrific splashes appeared in the water but no material damage was done except in the case of one ship where a few plates were loosened and she had to put into port.

Not being on duty until 5 p.m. I had watched this episode from the main deck; only two ships of the convoy had time to fire on the aircraft and their shots did not seem to affect it. An Avro Anson of Coastal Command then dived down to the attack from the north and chased the Bosch into the A.A. fire of our escorting sloop from which it swiftly turned away and made off with the slower Anson in pursuit.

The fun being over for the present, it was decided that the 4th Engineer and myself should have a game of chess which we had previously arranged, but it was not a success, our thoughts being far from the chess board. Just previous to going on watch I left the 4th's cabin and proceeded to tidy up my own, making the bunk etc. which took about half an hour and was invariably left until the afternoon as I slept from 6 a.m. till lunch time. (In the early days when there were only two radio officers per ship it was not possible to keep a continuous watch, as we did later in the war, so I would have been on watch from midnight to six every morning with two more hours in the afternoon).

Promptly at five p.m. I marched into the tiny wireless room on the starboard side of the bridge deck and my mate, Mr. Gawthorne went down to the saloon for tea. By the time Portishead (GKU) had completed his transmission, and his messages been decoded, my mate had reappeared to relieve me for tea. It was half past five.

As I went down the companionways the sun was settling down on the horizon, the wind was increasing and I could see we were in for a dirty night. My tea of egg and bacon pie was more than welcome, as the sea air had made me hungry.

The third officer, Mr. R. Gilchrist, who had been relieving the chief officer was tucking away with great gusto when I walked into the saloon, and as was his wont, immediately started to comment on the lousy food in no uncertain terms. We had not been chatting more than fifteen minutes when a dull resounding thud rent the air; the lights went out, and I was hurled from my seat towards the door. On picking myself up the steward's raucous voice came to my ears as the noise of the explosion passed away;

"Lifebelts, get your lifebelts."

Without stopping to think, I ran along the corridor to the main deck and mounted the steps up to my cabin in record time; grabbed my lifejacket which had given excellent service as a bolster, and unfortunately put it on inside out, rendering it almost useless. For about two seconds I tried to think of something important that I could slip into my pocket, but it was in vain. (£8 in cash was one of the many things only waiting to be picked up).

Out on the bridge once more, Captain Mankin was standing by the companionway, having just given his last order:

"Take to the boats."

To me he seemed to be calmness personified; he made no effort to secure his own safety, and he went down as he would have wished in the execution of his duty.

I made my way aft without undue haste, thinking that the damage was only slight, but on climbing the vertical metal ladder to the boat deck, my mental perambulations were swiftly shattered. A loud hissing noise, which obliterated the hum of human voices, was coming up from the engine room. The after well deck was completely submerged, hatch covers and wooden spars were being tossed about by the waves, and the gun on the poop was steadily sinking into the cold black water. Even at this early stage the ship had taken a heavy list to port.

Although a trifle dazed, I remembered I had been scheduled for the port lifeboat, but on reaching it my heart sank, for it was already floating, at the top of the davits, with none of the ropes severed. A veritable hive of men was standing in it and a few, notably the chief officer, were struggling to loosen the falls, but no knife could be found, and the axe which could have solved the problem, was dropped into the sea.

I remember standing in the after end of the boat with water surging round my legs, and the davits gradually pushing it under, when a huge wave completely swamped the whole outfit, and I passed into oblivion for a short period. My next recollection is of opening my eyes as I came up through the water, and striking my head against a piece of floating debris. Trying desperately to reason with myself as to what was the best thing to do, I grasped a piece of timber and swam away from the ship, fearing that when it took the final plunge there would be a considerable suction.

By now it was almost dark, and in the few glimpses I had of my old ship over the waves, she was silhouetted against the sunset in a truly magnificent manner. As the boilers blew up with a pronounced thud which could be heard over the din of falling wreckage, the funnel and the masts came adrift amid clouds of soot and black smoke, and fell to starboard. The last mental picture I had of her was that of her bows, from the bridge forwards, standing vertically in the water, proudly defying the waves.

Having swum what must have been over a hundred yards through the waves I sighted one of the ships rafts in the gloom rapidly drifting away, and leaving my companionable piece of wood I made for it post haste. Two pairs of willing hands pulled me out of the water and within a few minutes, when I had recovered my wind, I was shouting like a tipster for my comrades to swim to us; for although the craft was fitted with two paddles, these were useless in such a heavy swell.

Pathetic voices could be heard coming from the floating debris requesting assistance, but it would have been madness to leave the raft once we got hold of it for we should never have got back in the state we were in. Apart from that there were eight of us clinging on to it as we passed away from the scene of the action, and being only about five feet square it almost turned turtle several times.

There was the bosun, one gunner, two sailors, one fireman, one galley boy and myself the only officer. For almost two hours we drifted aimlessly, gripping on to each other and the raft, trying to keep warm and to prevent ourselves being carried away by the heavy seas. Other ships of the convoy seemed to approach us periodically only to fade away again into the darkness. To one side of us, another ship clothed in a cloak of flame from stem to stern and surrounded by black smoke was gradually settling down; She was the SS *Trebartha*, and a steady stream of tracer bullets continued to pour into her and into the surrounding water from above.

The intense cold combined with heavy rain proved to be agonising; my limbs and face were completely numbed, and I could only move them with difficulty. Up till then I had never known what it was to be really cold. At this stage, when we were all feeling very much under the weather we happened to drift right across the bows of a ship, and shouting at the top of our voices it was soon obvious that we had been spotted.

A line was thrown to us but it fell short and we continued to drift further and further away from our goal, until she was almost out of sight. But they were coming to our assistance even though it meant endangering their own ship. No lights could be used for the enemy was still close at hand. A lifeboat had been launched, and was even now racing towards us manned by a crew of brave Dutch lads. As it came alongside we stumbled into it and laid down amid pools of water, crouching to avoid the biting wind. The poor little galley boy was by this time in a very bad way and terribly sick; I put my arms round him and rubbed him to restore his circulation, but even I was close to being exhausted.

For what seemed like hours we remained nestled at the bottom of the boat, our shivering bodies entwined round the legs of the Dutch seamen, and on one occasion we heard the voices of our crew as they were taken on board. (Five of them, who had clung to an upturned lifeboat all that time including the first Radio Officer, were in a worse condition than ourselves, as I learned later). Eventually, with a feeling of intense relief, I felt the small craft bump against the ships side; Two rope ladders were lowered; it was the Dutchman SS *Oberon*.

At once it was evident that both my legs were paralysed with cramp and franticly [*sic*] I rubbed them before attempting the lofty ascent to her main deck, for she was light. The wind was now terrific; our small boat was being tossed up and down like a cork and it was a case of gripping the ladder whenever it came within reach. With my last ounce of energy, I clambered up the slippery rungs with my arms alone, and on reaching the top, three hefty lads lifted me over, and carried me to the saloon.

There, amid some of my pals I was deposited on the deck by the radiator; willing hands removed my wet clothing, took it to the engine room to dry, and came back with dry clothes and bedding etc. together with steaming hot coffee. Cigarettes and tobacco were next supplied out of the pockets of the Dutch seamen, who did without these luxuries for our benefit, and which proved to be a Godsend. From our vantage point on the deck we watched the remainder of our fellows being brought in, some much worse than others, and several of them out for the count. All of us were black as the ace of spades from head to foot, and looked more like trimmers than anything else. Naturally I thought I was different, for there seemed no reason for it, but to my disgust I was far and away the worst; my hair was absolutely matted with black grease and grime.

Shortly afterwards the thirty-six survivors of the *Trebartha* joined our miserable company; although only four were missing most of them were severely wounded by machine gun bullets and blast, and most of the newly acquired clothing was given to them, leaving us in our birthday suits.

~~~

The following details concerning the attack on our ship came to light after questioning the Chief Officer, shortly after he came round.

An unknown seaplane, flying about six feet above the water had shown recognition lights, and those on the bridge thought it was going to land; instead, when only about one hundred and fifty yards from the ship, and broadside on a torpedo left it, and a white feather was seen coming towards us. The chief officer on the monkey island immediately shouted an order to the man at the wheel through the voice pipe:

"Hard to starboard – there's a torpedo coming."

But it was of no avail; the wretched missile hit us plum in the engine room, and must have torn the bottom out of the ship, for she went down in approximately two minutes. (Being light hastened the inevitable).

Falling beams and concrete slabs had peppered the mate from all sides, and it was more by luck than judgement that he reached the boat deck comparatively unhurt. It had been his intention to prevent the boats being launched too soon, for even he did not think the damage was really serious.

The *Trebartha* had received a direct hit from an HE bomb, which penetrated the bridge and the saloon and set the bridge space bunkers on fire. The three radio officers were trapped in the wireless room and had no chance of escape, and one of the gunners was killed instantly by the blast.

In our ship, as far as I know, only 13 were saved out of 42; these included the chief officer (who wrote a report which we saw and copied at the Public Records Office at Kew), the Canadian gunner and another fireman who were picked up from the upturned lifeboat, plus three who were on the raft with myself. Mr. Gilchrist, the third officer and a good swimmer, was seen to dive in, but nothing more has been heard of him; the steward and cook are known to have lost their lives. It is just possible that others of the crew were rescued by another ship in the convoy, but unfortunately no vessels were actually detailed for such work.

At about 3 a.m. the Dutchman SS *Oberon*, put into Aberdeen, piloted by the cox of the Aberdeen lifeboat, which was launched on seeing the fire in SS *Trebartha*. Stretcher cases were first removed to hospital by men of the first aid post, then we were taken in a large ambulance to the Seaman's Mission, and given tea and cigarettes before turning in. Right from the start, Aberdeen treated us in a truly magnificent manner, and I have nothing but the highest praise for those kind Scots who did so much for us. The spotlessly white sheets we were given must have been practically ruined by our filthy anatomies, for not one of us was able to get as much as a wash until the following day; the bathing facilities being on the top floor, we should have disturbed the other residents.

Later it was learned with much joy from a radio report that two Junkers 87 Dive Bombers had been shot down in the vicinity of our convoy on that eventful night.

My compatriot, Mr. Gawthorne the first radio officer, was a survivor and was rescued. He managed to cling onto the upturned boat. I know because we came together later on in the war and worked on the same ship together.

On 28 June 1941, SS *Oberon*, (1996 grt), the Dutch ship that had so gallantly come to our rescue was sunk by a U-Boat, U-123, off Freetown Sierra Leone, West Africa.

Six lives were lost. The remainder were picked up by a Corvette and taken to Freetown. They were later repatriated on *Empress of Australia*, a big old three funneller used for trooping.

Noel's account was fascinating and gave me a real insight into how the ship had sunk. It was a privilege to spend time with him – we had a shared affinity for the sea and had both spent time in the same stretch of water and touched the same ship – albeit in very different circumstances in two different centuries: I had been cocooned inside a modern 21st-century drysuit whereas Noel had had nothing but the clothes he had been standing in.

Another comment was posted on my Random House Author's Place website on 26 March 2010 by a Betty Treacy:

> Dear Sir, My late father Pakie (Patrick) Bowe from Waterford, Ireland was also on the SS *Creemuir* during the Second World War, and I would be most interested to hear how the ship was sunk. My father was born in 1902 and died at 60 years of age on 1st January 1963. I was the eldest of his three children and was only just gone 16 years when he died, so would love to hear any news about the torpedoing of the ship. I was always told he was torpedoed and while in the water was fired at by Germans, against all the rules of war. Needless to say, this is only hearsay.

I was able to put Noel and Betty in touch with each other, and Noel was able to fill in all the gaps that Betty had about the sinking. On 22 May 2010, Noel posted the following comment:

> Treacy and I wish to thank you most sincerely for bringing us together after all these years. 70 to be exact. It does not seem possible. We now know that her father and I shared the only raft that survived after the sinking of the SS *Creemuir* off Aberdeen in 1940. To be truthful I cannot remember him, but I know there were four of us on this raft. Her father, who was a stoker, a cabin boy, a sailor and me, 2nd Radio Officer. It really is wonderful to be reunited and we are most grateful. The other Radio Officer, Mr. Gawthorne also survived by clinging to an upturned lifeboat. I sailed with him later in the war on another ship. I think he came from Northampton. Again, many thanks, Rod.

After that Helen King, whose uncle had been lost on *Creemuir*, contacted me. He had been a young deck hand, sadly only on his first trip to sea. And then there was a further posting by an Austin James whose great-grandfather, a master mariner, had been lost on *Creemuir* as well.

It had been quite amazing and very rewarding to see what had transpired from a simple one-line post, made in passing, on my blog about a single wreck we had dived. Noel got in touch with each of the relatives and gave them what information he could and was of great help to me in writing the full account in *The Darkness Below*, his selfless purpose being to help other relatives and to highlight the role of the Merchant Navy during World War II.

I often wondered what it must have been like from Noel's perspective, after 70 years, to meet the daughter of a man he had shared a raft with from a sinking ship. Likewise, imagine what it must be like from her perspective to meet a man who her father had shared a raft with, and to hear first-hand what had taken place that cold November day in 1940.

In 2012, Noel and his wife, Muriel, were in touch; they were flying up to Aberdeen for a holiday in Scotland and would be catching the ferry up to Orkney but had a few hours in Aberdeen – would we like to meet? 'Of course!' I said, and arranged to pick them up from the airport. But at this point I hadn't met them in person and so I asked how I could recognise them. Noel said they would look out for me, but that I couldn't miss them as they'd be the only couple in wheelchairs getting off the flight. I was driving a large Vauxhall Frontera 4×4 at the time that had quite a step up to get into it. I asked if they'd be able to get into my 4×4 and Noel assured me that it wouldn't be a problem – so the die was cast.

On the day of their arrival, I drove through to Aberdeen airport, got parked up in the short stay car park and went into the arrivals hall to wait for their plane to arrive. About 20 minutes or so after its arrival, the doors opened and here came Noel and Muriel, getting pushed along by very kindly Aberdeen airport staff, who also went and collected their bags from the carousel. Given that they were the only people in wheelchairs coming off the flight, I walked over and said, 'Noel, is it?' Noel stood up straight away, as did Muriel, and with a cheeky grin, pointing at the wheelchairs, he said, 'We don't really need these – it just makes travelling so much easier.'

I went and got my 4×4 and they were both able to get up into it. First of all, I drove them down to Aberdeen harbour where I was able to point out the Seamen's Mission where Noel and other survivors had been given refuge when he was landed. After that I drove them south to Cove Bay, where I was able to point out the wreck site of the *Trebartha*, the vessel Noel had seen nearby, ablaze in flames from stem to stern as her crew abandoned ship. She had drifted, unmanned before the easterly wind, the miles in from the swept channel before beaching broadside onto the rocks just to the north of Cove Bay Hotel the following day, 12 November 1940. She eventually broke up, and today her scattered remains are a well-known shore dive.

After filling in that piece of the puzzle for Noel, I drove them down to Stonehaven and took them for a short stroll around the picturesque harbour. Then it was time to drive Noel and Muriel back through to the ferry terminal at Aberdeen harbour for their voyage up to Orkney.

For some reason, we didn't get back to visit *Creemuir* again that year – but the following year, 2013, we decided to have a go at diving her again during a period of settled weather and beautiful underwater visibility. We dived the vessel four times over the coming weeks, and in the glorious visibility were able to make out large sections of the wreck at any one time and get a really good understanding of it. The stern section had actually split from the remainder of the ship – it looked as if the ship had broken its back on the surface where she had been torpedoed. As she went down the two sections had separated; the stern section we found now lies on its port beam ends with the DEMS gun still in place. There is then a gap of about 30 feet between the stern section and the rest of the ship, which sits upright on its keel, with its bows to the north.

The foredeck holds have collapsed, and as this happened, the upright fo'c'sle was pulled backwards and downwards – the bow is now high and the fo'c'sle deck runs downwards aft towards the well deck holds.

Above: Paul Haynes, fully rigged for a technical dive, sits astride the port sponson of our dive boat Stoney Haar *above the site of the Creemuir.* (Author's collection)

Left: The author at the helm of Stoney Haar *far offshore.* (Author's collection)

In the bridge superstructure, we spotted two telegraphs fallen amongst the debris. Moving aft along the bridge superstructure, we located the galley at the aft end on the starboard side, its innards exposed where the ship broke in two, seemingly sheared straight across. Piles of gleaming white crockery dazzled in our torch beams.

On the last of four dives, Jim Burke and I were diving with Paul Haynes on a Saturday afternoon. The descent was dark and moody with underwater visibility of about 20 metres. As our eyes became dark-adjusted, by the time we were at about 50 metres down the wreck came into view just off to one side – the shotline was on the seabed just off the port side of the bow. We clipped our strobes to the downline, set them flashing and swam over to the wreck, which was covered in a rich carpet of white soft corals, known as dead men's fingers, and sponges that seemed to fluoresce in our torch beams.

We moved aft towards the bridge and explored around there, hoping to catch a lucky glimpse of Noel's old radio room and his equipment. If we could get a photograph or video of that for him it would have been amazing. The bridge however was starting to collapse and we couldn't identify where it would have been in the confusion. We pressed aft to the end of the superstructure, where the ship was sheared off. At the limit of our visibility we could see the dark brooding mass of the stern section, which we had explored on one of our earlier dives.

Ever conscious of bottom time ticking away, we turned here and headed back towards the forward part of the ship, passing the bridge and swimming high over the collapsed foredeck holds. The fo'c'sle materialised into view and after a short swim around the bow, with a bottom time of about 30 minutes now elapsed at 70 metres, I signalled to the others that it was time to head up. We turned and began to fin over to the downline, our strobes blinking away brightly in the fine visibility.

As I reached the downline, I swam up it for 5–10 metres and busied myself retrieving my strobe and clipping it onto my harness. When I turned around, Jim was right beside me having done the same – but Paul wasn't there. I looked down, following the downline down to the wreck, which was easily visible below me, and saw that something had very much distracted Paul's attention and stopped him coming up. He was in a confused mess of plating on the starboard side of the wreck, just where the collapsed foredeck holds met the downward sloping fo'c'sle deck. He was animatedly signalling up to us, his arms moving about as he tried to demonstrate something completely unfathomable to us; whatever he was trying to convey was lost in translation. He clearly wasn't in any distress and as I'd committed to the ascent – unless he was in trouble, which he clearly wasn't – I wasn't going back down to the bottom again. He gave up waving and started to ascend towards us.

We finally broke the surface after an hour of decompression and our dive boat came in to pick us up. We busied ourselves getting our stage tanks off inwater and passed up into the boat, getting our rebreathers off and then hauling ourselves up into the boat.

Once were all aboard, Paul said, 'Guys, I've found the bell; it had rolled under a piece of metal plating.' He had spotted it at the very end of our dive, just as he was getting ready to follow Jim and me as we began our ascent. Once he'd seen what it was, he'd been trying to

The author (left) and Paul Haynes (right) back on Stoney Haar *after the dive where Paul had spotted the bell of the* Creemuir. *(Author's collection)*

signal to us above him what he had found – but we hadn't understood. He had quite properly just left it in position so we could have a chat about what to do.

I said, 'Paul, there's only one place that bell is going.'

He replied, 'I know, I totally agree, it's going to Noel.'

Late the following day, Sunday, a few hours before slack water was due, we blasted the 14 miles out to the wreck site, over short seas at about 30 knots in our RIB, *Stoney Haar*. At that speed, we were on site very quickly – just about half an hour in advance of slack water. The weather was due to turn for the worse – but we thought we could just sneak it, get the dive done and get back ashore before it blew up. With a low-pressure system due to arrive and the North Sea off our coast always being temperamental, if we didn't get the bell today it could be weeks before we could get this far out again in diveable conditions.

Once we arrived on site, we quickly picked up the wreck on our echo sounder. We were by now very familiar with the orientation of the ship, and so I was able to manoeuvre the boat over the wreck and then essentially drive north on top of the wreck until the echo sounder trace began to stop. We would then be at the bow.

I moved forward on top of the wreck, crisscrossing from one side of the ship to the other to get a feel for it. When the thick brown silhouette of the wreck on the sounder came to an abrupt drop down to the seabed at 70 metres, I knew we were at the bow. Then, as the bell was on the starboard side, I followed the starboard side of the bow aft a little way before giving a shout that the shotline should be dropped. Hopefully the shot would be pretty close to the bell – I didn't really want to end up in the wrong part of the ship and have to go searching for it and eat up valuable bottom time.

The weighted shotline disappeared over the side of *Stoney Haar* and plunged down to the wreck, the coiled rope paying out at speed from our rope bucket as I held the boat steady into the gentle current and wind. We clipped on a couple of bailout cylinders to the line as it went over the side and plunged into the depths. Buoys were clipped onto the end of the rope as the shot hit the bottom and the rope went still.

I moved the boat away and then came in again, into the wind towards the buoys until they were steady on our port side. Paul clipped on a one-way mountaineering ascender with two fishermen's floats attached to it. He pulled the downline taut and upright – and moved the ascender down the rope, bit by bit, as far as he could. The gentle buoyancy of the two fishermen's floats was enough to suspend the rope vertically in the water column, without dragging the shot away from the wreck. Doing this meant that it would be a straight descent for us down beside the vertical rope, minimising the work we would have to do.

Satisfied with the setting of the shot, Paul and I started to get kitted up as Gary took over the helm. We were quickly ready and, pre-breathe done, we splashed backwards off the boat into the water, which was by now almost perfectly slack. We dumped air from our buoyancy wings and suits, and slowly started to sink beneath the surface, falling down beside the downline to the wreck.

The visibility in the shallows seemed much cloudier than the day before, and it got darker as we pressed on downwards. Finally, in a murky 5-metre visibility, the wreck began to appear out of the gloom beneath us. The shot was lying on the seabed hard up against the starboard side of the wreck in the vicinity of the front of Hold No 1. We were just abaft the fo'c'sle, and the bell could only be about 12 feet away from us. So far so good.

Fixing our strobes to the downline and setting them flashing, Paul and I moved off, swimming over to the starboard gunwale. Paul was leading into the gloom as he knew where the bell was – but he didn't need to lead for long, as in less than a minute we were at the bell – just where Paul had left it.

For some reason, there was an issue with Paul's lifting bag, so I fished mine out, passed it to him and he quickly roped it off securely to the bell. He pulled out an air inflator attached to a small auxiliary lifting bottle he was carrying and stuck it under the bag's open bottom, and started to fill it with air.

The large red lifting bag inflated slowly – then the bell moved, and began to get ready to go up to the surface. He filled the bag a bit more until the bell was slightly positively buoyant and lifted off the seabed. Holding it with one hand, he filled enough air into it so that the bell now began to rise steadily upward into the gloom above us before disappearing.

With the bell now out of sight, we had a cursory swim around the forward part of the wreck, without much enthusiasm. We were here for one purpose, to recover the bell – and we didn't want to leave Gary alone for too long up there in conditions that were due to deteriorate. Plus … we wanted to see the bell! The whole thing had been done and dusted in 15 minutes, and we headed back to the downline, retrieved our strobes and began what was an unusually short ascent for our sort of diving.

As our heads broke the surface, we could see straight away that conditions had noticeably deteriorated. It was already a bouncy Force 4 with a grey leaden sky, and the wave tops were starting to break. Gary gave us the OK signal, which we returned – and he deftly came up beside us in the RIB, into the wind. Bags can bloop at the surface, lose their air and sink to the seabed, or there can be problems getting them back into the boat – but he quickly shouted down to us in the water that the bell was safely in the boat.

Paul and I derigged inwater and Gary hauled all our kit inboard – then we were kicking our fins and pushing up with our arms to flop into the safety of the RIB.

We each had a good look at the bell – it hadn't seen the light of day since 1940. The bell was large and very green with verdigris that had obscured any lettering on it. We secured our rebreathers and stashed all our other tanks and kit safely in anticipation of a bouncy ride home. A thermos of coffee was cracked open and we had a celebratory cuppa.

We jumped into our seats and Gary throttled up the RIB, turning its head towards the distant land and Stonehaven. As we motored home, the seas began to build in a strong westerly headwind. Soon we were bashing into sizeable waves, the splash billowing right over the boat in the wind. It may have been a short scream out in good conditions on the way out, but now, we wouldn't be able to make any decent speed against these seas without each of us losing a few inches in height by having the discs on our spinal cords severely compressed! And it was only going to get worse.

There was no option other than to head back at an oblique angle, crossing the seas rather than bashing into them and aiming for a point several miles north of Stonehaven, where the land would give us a lee as we neared the coastline. We were able to make about 20 knots in this fashion – and as we finally neared the land, so the seas began to settle. Once we had a bit of shelter from the land, Gary stopped the boat and took a photo of Paul and me holding the bell. That safely done, we could turn the boat's head to the south and pick up the speed again. Decompression pints of Guinness all round followed in HQ, the Marine Hotel, once the boat had been put back on our mooring.

Far left: Once the Creemuir *bell had been cleaned up it revealed the ship's original name,* Medomsley. *(Author's collection)*

Left: Rod and Paul set off at 0700 on a fine June morning in 2013 and drove down to Noel's house in Bedford to give him an unexpected surprise – by presenting him with the bell of his old ship. (Author's collection)

Paul took the bell up to his house and spent some time over the coming weeks carefully cleaning it up and removing the verdigris. As he did so, the original name of the ship, *Medomsley*, appeared. A report of the find was duly made to the Receiver of Wreck.

One morning in June 2013, Paul and I set off in my 4×4 at 0700, bound for Bedford where Noel then lived, about an hour north of London. It was a bit of a drive south for us, about eight hours, from the frozen north down to deepest darkest London – but we arrived at the hotel we'd booked into by 1530.

We checked in and then, following the satnav, drove round to Noel's house. I'd been in touch with Noel in advance, keeping quiet about the bell and just saying that we would be in the area and could we come and visit, and take him and Muriel out for dinner.

We found his house, parked up and leaving the bell covered in the 4×4, walked up and rang the doorbell. Noel appeared and warmly welcomed us in. Very soon we had a glass of his home-made wine in our hands and were talking about his wartime experiences on the Atlantic convoys and looking at his World War II medals.

After a pleasant catch-up, I said to Noel and Muriel: 'Noel – we've got something for you.'

Leaving him looking rather bemused, I disappeared out the front door to my 4×4. I took the bell in, covered by a cloth, and then with rather too much pomp and ceremony, I unveiled it and presented it to Noel. I'd swear I could see a tear in Noel's eye in amongst the elation as he took hold of the bell – seeing it for the first time since he'd last seen it on Armistice Day 1940 as the ship sank.

We talked for a long time about his time in the Arctic convoys. One of his most poignant memories was when the then British prime minister, Winston Churchill, was crossing the Atlantic to Newfoundland to meet the American president, Franklin D. Roosevelt, for the Atlantic Charter Conference on Churchill's favourite and newest battleship HMS *Prince of Wales*. The *Prince of Wales* had closed on Noel's convoy to allow Mr Churchill (as Noel politely called him) to inspect the convoy ships. It certainly raised morale for the crews to see such a fine new battleship, and see the interest that Churchill was clearly displaying.

When I mentioned that we were going to visit the famous World War II code-breaking centre of Bletchley Park, just 12 miles away, he mentioned that he had met Alan Turing during the war – and didn't speak very kindly of him! After a pleasant morning at Bletchley Park it was time for another eight-hour drive back up the road to Stonehaven.

But the story still isn't finished there. I was invited to speak at Europe's largest technical diving conference and exhibition, Eurotek, at the Birmingham ICC in September 2014. Being an older sort of chap now, I've met a lot of World War I and World War II veterans in my time, but for younger divers attending, I thought they would love to hear a personal account directly from a World War II shipwreck survivor. I checked with one of the conference organisers, Leigh Bishop, if it would be OK if I gave Noel the last 15 minutes of my second talk. He was very onside and thought it was a great idea.

And so I arranged with Noel that his son Charles Blacklock would drive him to Birmingham on the Sunday morning of Eurotek and that we'd meet in a parking area near the ICC. Noel would need his wheelchair – and would take the bell.

At the appointed time, a couple of hours before my talk, I met Charles and Noel on a pleasant sunny Birmingham morning. I took over pushing Noel through the streets from the car park and into the ICC, whilst Charles carried the heavy bell under a cover. We threaded our way through crowds of diver attendees – who had of course no idea what was going on.

We reached the lecture hall and made our way down to the side of the stage where a MC got us into position off stage, but close to the podium. It was only a few minutes to go before I began my talk, and I asked Noel if he wanted me to come and push him onstage in his wheelchair when it was time for him to talk. With great spirit he said, no – he was standing for this, and was going to walk on.

I began my one-hour talk about diving technical shipwrecks to an unsuspecting audience. After about 30 minutes I began to tell the story of our location of the *Creemuir* and how this had led us to Noel and then to other relatives.

I then said: 'And now, I'd like you to welcome a very special guest to Eurotek – Royal Navy Radio Officer Noel Blacklock.'

At that cue, Noel stood up from his wheelchair and walked onto centre stage as Paul came on stage and placed the bell on a stool in the middle of the stage. I clicked my PowerPoint presentation to the next slide, and a black and white still photo of Noel in his World War II uniform filled the screen behind him. Noel was such an unassuming and lovely old gent – and with great poise and dignity he began to tell his story. He spoke about the convoy – and told the assembled couple of hundreds of delegates what it was like to be torpedoed in World War

When Rod was asked to speak at the Eurotek Advanced Diving Conference in 2014, by agreement with the conference organisers, after recounting the story of the loss of the Creemuir, *he handed the stage over to Noel for the last 15 minutes of his talk. Noel bewitched the crowd as he recounted his side of the story – and delegates got to hear from a man who was there exactly what it was like to be torpedoed in the North Sea during World War II. (Author's collection)*

II. The audience listened in complete silence, spellbound, as this quiet gentleman gave them a glimpse of a war that is now passing into the history books as the veterans pass away. They were hearing directly from one of the last survivors of the Atlantic and Arctic convoys. In the coming months, I met several people who told me they'd been in the audience and that there hadn't been a dry eye in the house. To this day, when I retell the story to divers, it is not uncommon to see a few tears rolling down cheeks – yes, you guys know who you are!

After the talk was over, Charles, Paul, Noel and I went for a coffee – with the bell. A camera man for the diver training agency RAID filmed us speaking to him and looking at the bell. RAID intended to make a short film to put on their website to show what can be achieved by diving.

As we studied the bell and talked around the houses with Noel, we noticed a 7.92mm wide bullet-shaped dink on the outside of the bell. The cameraman turned out to be ex-forces and, knowing about this sort of thing, he looked on the inside and showed us where the metal had been pushed out and deformed as the bullet's energy was spent. We set the bell up in position as it would have been on the fo'c'sle of the *Creemuir* during the attack – and the bullet dink came from exactly the right direction as the torpedo attack – so we now know that the Heinkel He 115 was strafing the *Creemuir* as she completed her torpedo run.

Sadly, Noel passed away in late 2016 – one of the last survivors of the Atlantic and Arctic convoys. I feel privileged to have known such a fine old-school gentleman, to have spent so much time with him, to have learned of his story and been able to preserve it for posterity – and to have reunited him with the bell he last saw as his ship sank 70 years before.

15

MFV *Spes Nova*

Isle of Skye

On 30 November 2007 the fishing boat *Spes Nova* sank in deep water after getting into difficulties at about 1800 GMT near the small island of Holm, six miles north-east of Portree on the Isle of Skye on the west coast of Scotland. The three crew members were taken aboard a nearby vessel, the *Arnborg*, and were then brought ashore by the local RNLI lifeboat.

The vessel's insurers, faced with having to pay out for the loss, wanted to investigate the incident. The wreck lay in water deeper than could easily be commercially dived; the claim didn't justify a full HSE mixed-gas diving operation from a barge. They were a bit stuck.

Paul Haynes and I were by chance to be diving in the Skye area in early 2008 and so through a tangled web of contacts, we were asked that if we happened to be diving in the vicinity, could we have a look at it and give a report on its condition and any obvious signs of why it sank. We were given a GPS position by a marine surveyor and told it lay in about 50 metres of water – certainly no more than 60 metres.

On a late Friday afternoon in February 2008, Paul, Niall Crichton and I drove the five hours over from Aberdeen to Skye for our weekend's diving, towing my 5.5-metre Humber Destroyer dive boat *Stonehaven Diver*. We had decided that we would go and have a look at the *Spes Nova* – it's always interesting to see a wreck no one has seen before. As the wreck lay in quite deep water, we decided to make finding and diving the *Spes Nova* the first dive of the weekend, and we would then move on to dive our other intended targets.

We drove west in darkness on the A96 road from Aberdeen towards Inverness, before driving down the north-west shore of Loch Ness to Drumnadrochit, scene of the most famous of the Loch Ness Monster sightings. At Invermoriston, we turned off onto the picturesque A87 that runs through Glen Shiel to Loch Duich; sadly, the famous three Munro ridge walk of the Five Sisters in Kintail was lost in the darkness.

We drove along Loch Duich, passing the beautiful castle of Eilean Donan on its small island to our left, before we reached Kyle of Lochalsh. From here we drove over the Skye

297

Bridge over Loch Alsh onto Skye itself, where the long and winding road took us up to the small fishing town of Portree, where we had booked a B&B with a driveway so we could get the RIB off the street overnight.

We had assumed that no one would know we were coming over – the marine surveyor we had talked to had told us to keep it to ourselves, which we had religiously done. No one was meant to know we were going to have a look at this local fishing boat – but word does get about in the Highlands in the strangest of ways. As we drove into a quiet Portree in darkness at about 2100 towing *Stonehaven Diver*, I'd swear I could see the curtains twitching and eyes looking out and clocking us: 'Och well, that'll be the divers then, here to look at the *Spes Nova*.'

The next morning, we were up early to find *Stonehaven Diver* covered in about half an inch of frost. It had been exceptionally cold overnight, and in the early morning darkness of a west coast winter's morning it didn't feel much warmer now as I stuck my head out the door for a look. Nevertheless, after a hearty breakfast, and after the weak winter sun had risen, things didn't appear quite so bleak. We hitched up the RIB to our 4×4 at about 0900 and drove down to the harbour to launch at the slip. We'd checked the pilot book in advance, which stated you could launch and retrieve on the slip at all states of the tide, so getting the boat launched and retrieved shouldn't be a problem. Slack water was several hours away – we were allowing plenty of time to launch, get to the site, find and shot the wreck in time to dive at slack water.

We threaded our way through Portree's narrow streets down to the harbour, where Paul started to gingerly and skilfully reverse *Stonehaven Diver* down a very steep and narrow slip. We were slightly bemused when a crowd of about 10–15 folk started to gather around about us. There was no hiding that we were going diving, and persistent questions from them failed to get a straight answer from us about our target. Did they know what we were up to after all?

Once we had the RIB in the water, Paul dragged the trailer out of the water up the slip and parked the 4×4 and trailer nearby. We soon had all our kit loaded into the RIB – but whilst the exercise had warmed us up no end, the RIB was still thickly covered with white frost and the orange sponsons were very slippy underfoot.

We got dressed into our drysuits and then boarded the RIB. I sat at the helm and turned the engine over – despite my misgivings about the oil being so cold, the Yamaha 90hp outboard sprang into life and I let it tick over and warm up for a few minutes. Once satisfied all was well, we cast off our ropes and motored out slowly from the small harbour into Loch Portree. Our routing would take us out of Loch Portree into the Sound of Raasay, which separates the small island of Raasay from much larger Skye. From there we would run up north to the wreck site.

As we motored slowly out of the harbour into Loch Portree, I punched in the GPS position we had been given into my Humminbird Combo plotter, sounder and side-scan sonar unit, which was set on top of the steering console. Automatically, and without thinking, I pressed the GOTO button to give us our route and distance up to the target. Immediately the display corrected to give me a course to run – and the distance to the site came up as more than 120 miles. Something was very wrong – that was up around Orkney!

I rechecked the coordinates we had been given; the figures I had punched in were indeed correct and it wasn't a case of fat fingers pushing the wrong button. Then my brain came off autopilot and began to apply some fading grey matter to the problem – and of course, when I paused to think about it, the answer seemed obvious. The latitude I had been given was 59°N – but checking the plotter, Portree's latitude was 57°N. Each degree of latitude is 60 nautical miles, so if I simply corrected the latitude that might give us the correct position. But if the latitude was about 120 miles off, how far off would the longitude be? The coordinates might be complete and total mince – completely inaccurate.

I edited the latitude of the waypoint on the GPS and punched the GOTO button again. This simple change gave us a distance to run to the target of six miles – and the target now showing on the plotter looked to be in roughly the right place that we had been expecting. Problem possibly solved – or not. If there was nothing there, we would go find something else to dive.

I throttled *Stonehaven Diver* up as we entered the Sound of Raasay, and soon we were up on the plane moving at about 20 knots, skipping over an oily calm sheltered sea, with the hills of Skye to our port side. Although the sea conditions were fine, it was still very cold and I pulled the fur-lined side panels of my trapper hat down and tied them under my chin.

As we got to within half a mile of the target, I brought the RIB down off the plane to let the echo sounder and side-scan sonar kick in fully. By doing this well before the given marks, over the years, I've found a lot of wrecks – many lying well away from the reported sinking positions. Ships can drift after they've been abandoned – being moved by wind or tide – and so by experience, I always run in to a site from about half a mile away with all my instruments blazing, in case of a lucky find. We began to close in on the precise GPS position for the wreck.

Once we were a few hundred metres away, I took the boat down to about 5 knots – and closed even further before driving precisely over the GPS position we had been given, which should be correct to a few metres. But there was just nothing showing itself there on the echo sounder – just a steeply shelving bottom running down from Skye itself on my port side down into the very deep water of the Sound of Raasay. The tiny island of Holm was nearby – close to Skye itself, to port. We had been told that the *Spes Nova* had hit rocks near it, causing flooding and the vessel's ultimate loss.

I wasn't deterred in any way by not finding the wreck on this, our first pass – it's very common in wreck hunting. We could have missed the wreck by just a few feet on the sounder; it could be lying very close to us. It wasn't even 1000 yet, so we had plenty of time for a bit of a search. I've spent days looking for wrecks and not finding them – it comes with the turf.

I did a sector search pattern, the sort we used on the Stonehaven lifeboats when I was crew. I drove north from the GPS position for 200 metres, then turned to starboard on a bearing of 120 degrees for a similar distance before then turning another 120 degrees and heading back to the GPS mark on 240 degrees. We would pass through the GPS position, going to its south-west still on a bearing of 240 degrees, for another 200 metres.

Once at the end of that double length leg, we would come about and repeat the procedure: head north for 200 metres, turning to run on 120 degrees for 200 metres before turning to run on 240 degrees passing through the mark, and continuing for another 200 metres. After repeating this pattern for a third time you find yourself on the last leg running north back up to the GPS mark. The whole sector would then have been quickly and closely searched. If nothing is found, you can adjust the initial north bearing to 030 degrees, and then adjust the other legs to 150 degrees and 270 degrees, and essentially fill in the gaps in between the three sectors searched in the first sweep. If nothing is found then the target isn't in the search area and you may have to expand the search area and do longer legs.

By the time we had finished the first sector search it was about 1030 – and there hadn't been the faintest trace of a wreck at the position either on the echo sounder or side-scan sonar. Whereas an echo sounder essentially looks directly downwards under the dive boat, side-scan sonar shoots out beams to either side of the boat and Humminbird's very clever small boat unit we were using could give us pretty good coverage of the seabed out to 150 metres either side of the RIB. With nothing showing up on either bit of technology, we were pretty clear the wreck wasn't in the immediate search area.

We decided to search further afield, and so dropped a weighted line with a big orange danbuoy attached to it at the exact GPS coordinates we had been given for the wreck, as a visual marker of the location. We then started another type of search, 'mowing the lawn' as it's called, as we carried out a grid-like search of the seabed, and then when that didn't reveal anything, we began an expanding box search radiating out from the buoy.

Things didn't go well. After a further two hours of searching, by about 1300 we were clear there was nothing on the seabed at or near the position we had been given. We motored back forlornly to the buoy, tied off, and cracked open a thermos of tea and scoffed some sandwiches. We were all feeling deflated, cold and miserable – the temperature was barely above freezing and the cold air gnawed at our exposed skin. No one wanted to break off this search and go do a dive elsewhere at this point – it would be dark in a few hours anyway.

We chatted about what we would do. Holm Island itself lay perhaps between half a mile to a mile away from our search zone. The vessel was reputed to have hit rocks near the island, then come off the rocks and sunk. With this scenario in mind, we decided to search between our position and Holm Island itself, along the route the sinking vessel was likely to have taken, to see if anything could be found.

Another hour's searching took us to 1400 and even though we had searched close to Holm Island itself to a depth of just 35 metres, we still hadn't found anything – and we were well away from the original GPS position we had been given. We decided to abandon this area, return to the danbuoy and search deeper – much deeper.

It was about 1430 by the time we arrived back at the danbuoy and our original GPS position. This time we started our search further out into the Sound in deeper water of about 60–80 metres.

For another hour, we searched fruitlessly – and then, the late afternoon winter daylight began to fade. Our surroundings were starting to become darker, the hills of Skye off to our port side now black and brooding.

Then, at the very moment I said to Paul that we should perhaps call it a day, when we were about half a mile away from the original GPS mark, on the side-scan sonar about 90 metres off our starboard side, the unmistakable silhouette of a small vessel lying on the seabed came into view. With the reactions of an Olympic sprinter at the starting gun, I immediately pressed the Mark button on our GPS to save the position, and brought the RIB round to face where the submerged vessel lay, now some 100 metres dead ahead of us.

I motored slowly forward against the current – and as we neared the position we spotted a few droplets of oil in the water.

I kept motoring forward – and more and more droplets of oil started to pepper the water, rising up from below and being carried towards us in the ebb tide. As we continued forward, driving through the stream of oil droplets, the oil got thicker and thicker until we came to a spot where we overran the oil droplets as they rose – and we were in clear water.

The oil had suddenly stopped, unable to reach the surface at this point because of the current. I continued motoring directly forward for another 20 or so metres until a large bump on the bottom trace of our echo sounder revealed the wreck directly below us. I pushed the Mark button once again to save the exact location in our plotter – so we could never lose it again. We had arrived – the *Spes Nova* was directly beneath us. I checked the depth – it was 70 metres down to the wreck, which seemed to lie on a shelving seabed, the plunging shore of Skye itself disappearing down into the depths of Raasay Sound. It was a lot deeper than the 50–60 metres we had been told.

We dropped another weighted shot and danbuoy onto the wreck, and motored around it taking screenshots of the vessel lying on the seabed on our echo sounder and on the side-scan sonar. It looked at first sight as though the trawler was upside down with the keel bar seemingly visible. If that was the case, this would make identifying how the vessel sank and filming the damage very straightforward.

By now it was 1600 and getting pretty dark. I was all up for a quick bounce on the wreck there and then – it didn't matter that it would be dark below; it was going to be dark anyway. But wiser heads than mine prevailed. There was a definite risk in doing a night dive so far offshore in unfamiliar waters, we would have to leave Niall alone in the RIB for at least an hour in pitch darkness. There could be difficulties picking us up in darkness if we became separated from the shotline; what if another vessel came our way when we were ascending an unlit buoy line? On balance, I knew they were right, I was being over eager. We were chilled to the marrow – and the wreck would still be there tomorrow.

With the position marked on our GPS, we could drive right up to it at slack water tomorrow and dive it in daylight when we were rested, warm and better fuelled. With our red, green and white power-driven vessel navigation lights glowing brightly in the darkness, we recovered both shotlines and danbuoys, and turned thankfully to roar back to Portree. Our minds were filled with thoughts of tomorrow's dive – it wasn't particularly deep as tek diving goes, but the vessel had been trawling, so there could be nets and ropes billowing up around it, which could ensnare us.

We were soon back in Portree and recovering the boat onto its trailer in a darkness that was broken only by a few street lamps. There was no one about – it was cold and miserable. Once we'd got the boat safely back to the B&B, the three of us went to the local Indian restaurant and I warmed up with a fine vindaloo and a few Guinnesses – just the job for a deep dive tomorrow.

The next day, Sunday, we had the boat launched by 0900 and were soon roaring once again up north through Raasay Sound to the wreck site. This time we were able to drive right up to the target, and as we prepped our shotline and closed, we started seeing the droplets of oil rising up from the wreck below. When the wreck appeared on the sounder, we dropped our shotline with danbuoy attached and then let the RIB drift away with the wind and tide, as we started to get dressed into our rebreathers and bailout tanks. Niall would again boat-handle for us – Paul and I would dive. As we began to finalise getting ready, Niall motored the RIB slowly over to the shotline.

Once we were prepped to dive, Paul and I sat fully rigged on opposite sponsons of the boat pre-breathing our rebreathers. As Paul was clipping off the underwater video camera he was taking down onto his rebreather harness webbing, I looked down into the water. Although it was dark, I could see the shotline going some distance down into the depths and was hopeful of some decent visibility down on the wreck. After an exchange of OK signals, we rolled backwards off the sponsons, splashing into the water.

Righting ourselves, we swam over to the downline and started the descent. I could see a good 10 metres down the line in fairly decent underwater visibility, so my optimism about getting some good results continued to rise. We pressed on downwards – the *Spes Nova* lay 70 metres – 230 feet in old money – beneath us.

As we reached about 30 metres down, we started to enter a layer of fine silty brown water. The visibility started to close in on us, dropping quickly to just a few metres. By 50 metres down, it was pitch black; all we could see was the downline fluorescing in our torch beams. Nothing untoward in that – it's standard North Sea diving most of the year. As I began to approach 60 metres, the heads-up display on my rebreather started flashing red indicating a spike in my oxygen levels in the breathing mixture. This is again fairly standard, and is caused by the unit reacting to the increase in depth and the higher partial pressure of oxygen in the compressed gas I was breathing. The PO2 can spike and then settle down. The wreck was still 10–20 metres beneath me, invisible in the pitch blackness and poor visibility.

I moved further down, cautiously sweeping my torch all around me, slowly looking for any fishing nets suspended on buoys that could be billowing up from the wreck. 60 metres came and went – and then, a metre or two beneath me at 70 metres I finally saw the silty side of a steep underwater hill. The shot was off the wreck.

As Paul arrived above me, I unclipped my trusty strobe and fixed it to the downline. In such pitch-black water, with poor cloudy visibility, we would never find the shotline to ascend again once we left it if we didn't have it lit. We knew the path down the downline was clear of nets – but we didn't know what else was around us. The thought that there could be unseen nets billowing over me just a few metres away in the darkness clouded my mind.

Once my strobe was clipped on I switched it on – Murphy's Law in action, it gave one flash and then stopped. Fek. No matter how hard I clunked and dunted it with my hand, it had chosen just this precise moment to end its life. I unclipped my cave reel and clipped it to the downline – I could still reel off it, make a search and then rewind my reel and follow it back to the downline. The *Spes Nova* was tantalisingly close in the darkness beside me – perhaps towering over me. With the prospect of nets hanging over me as well, there was no way we could do a free ascent in safety away from the downline.

Paul arrived beside me and I signalled that my strobe had died and that I was going to reel off. He gave an OK signal, clipped his own strobe to the downline and unclipped his video camera and began to get it set up as I moved off into the darkness.

I hadn't gone very far, perhaps just 5–10 metres, grimly frog-kicking my way on my own along the side of a manky, silty underwater slope that plunged away into the depths to one side of me, when I came face to face with the brightly painted incongruous hull of a fishing vessel. My torch revealed red beneath a white plimsoll line and blue topsides above it. I'd seen photos of the *Spes Nova* afloat – this was certainly her, and she was upright, not upside down!

I appeared to be on the seabed on her starboard side; she was well buried into the soft silty hillside. I moved forward along her hull towards the hillside, and the plimsoll line disappeared into the seabed. It became apparent that she had ploughed into the hillside at some speed. As she went down, the natural shape of her hull and the heavy ballast of a trawler had kept her upright and caused her to plane forward. She seemed to have smacked into the hillside bow first, the bottom of the hull in the bow area burying itself deeply into the soft silty hillside. We had been told that she had run onto rocks whilst trawling, so already there was no chance of seeing any damage to the underside of her hull.

The nagging wariness of ropes and nets possibly above me in the darkness was never far away. So at this point, knowing that I couldn't see any keel damage, I swept my torch upwards. The torch beam quickly revealed thick trawl ropes and nets streaming out directly above me. Being under all this trawling gear was a very scary place to be and at this point, as there was no sign of Paul yet, I decided to call the dive. Staying near the seabed underneath the ropes, I started to wind in my reel line. The *Spes Nova* was immediately consumed by the darkness again as my reel took me on a short route across an open expanse of hillside towards the downline.

As I finned towards the shotline, I saw a dim flash of Paul's strobe. Paul was right there at the bottom of the shotline, having a problem with his video camera. I signalled to him that the wreck was not far away but that I was calling the dive and going to ascend.

As we rose up through 50 metres and then 40 metres, our surroundings became lighter and some ambient light started to trickle down. It was as though we came out of a layer of disturbed water, as by 40 metres we were once again back in clear water. I wanted to tell Paul all about what I had seen – but only basic conversation is possible through the rebreather mouthpieces, and it took an hour of decompression before our heads could break the surface. As we dekitted inwater, I briefed Paul about the wreck. Until then, he'd not been sure if I had seen the wreck at all.

By the time we arrived at Portree the tide was out – and contrary to what the pilot book had said about being able to launch and retrieve on the slip at all states of the tide, the slip ended in an abrupt drop of a few feet to the water.

There was no way we could get our RIB onto its trailer for another hour or two – but conveniently, there was a pub right beside the slip. We tied up the RIB, got changed into our dry clothes and went for a decompression pint of Guinness.

The bar went very quiet as we sat down and began to talk in hushed tones about what we had seen. The *Spes Nova* was a local boat and by now everyone in Portree knew we'd been diving it. Although, politely, no one asked us directly about it, everyone wanted to see if they could hear what we were saying. Our tones got even quieter, and as there would be insurance claims and possible litigation flying around in time we kept our own counsel and knowledge for the marine surveyor alone.

16

SCAPA FLOW

I have been going to Scapa Flow to dive just about every year since 1982, and generally on the last day of a dive trip there I like to have a bit of an adventure and do something different. So let me tell you about an adventure I had there with my long-time dive buddy Paul Haynes a few years ago.

Scapa Flow is a great natural deep-water harbour some 12 miles across and almost completely encircled by the Orkney Islands. In its black foreboding depths, it holds the largest easily accessible collection of German World War I naval shipwrecks in the world. It has justly become one of the world's top dive locations, and each year thousands of divers journey to Scapa Flow to explore the three massive 25,388-ton German battleships *Markgraf, König* and *Kronprinz Wilhelm*, and the four *kleiner kreuzers, Brummer, Dresden, Karlsruhe* and *Cöln* – as well as the countless other shipwrecks that lie in the depths of the Flow, such as the German war prize *F2*, the German World War I submarine UB 116 and the many blockships sunk deliberately in the east and west channels into the Flow during World War I and World War II in an attempt to seal them off against enemy incursion.

As a condition of the Armistice that halted the fighting of World War I in November 1918, the finest ships of the German High Seas Fleet were to be disarmed in Germany and sent into internment at Scapa Flow until the Allies and Germany thrashed out a final peace settlement, the Treaty of Versailles.

A few weeks after the Armistice, 74 disarmed warships of the High Seas Fleet rendezvoused with a huge Allied force of warships in the Firth of Forth, and after being searched and checked by the Allies they were led up to Scapa Flow into their internment anchorages in the Flow. In all, 5 battlecruisers, 11 battleships, 6 light cruisers, 2 minelaying cruisers and 50 torpedo boats and torpedo boat destroyers arrived at Scapa Flow, and anchored for internment. The bulk of their crews were soon repatriated to Germany, leaving skeleton caretaker crews aboard. German naval flags were banned on the vessels and all radios had been removed – the ships were cut off and isolated.

High Seas Fleet vessels at anchor, taken from above Houghton Bay

The German caretaker crews aboard the anchored ships had to endure the harsh Orkney winter – and even as spring arrived, the final peace terms had not been yet agreed. By June 1919, after seven months of internment, it appeared to the German commander, Admiral Ludwig von Reuter, that the peace was about to shatter and fighting possibly start again. With his ships disarmed and with only caretaker crews, he would be powerless to stop the seizure of the fleet; he simply could not let that happen.

Thus, on 21 June 1919, as the British warships guarding the interned German fleet went to sea for a torpedo firing exercise, leaving only three destroyers and a handful of patrol boats on guard, he issued the famous pre-arranged coded order to scuttle the fleet: 'Paragraph 11. Bestätigen' which translates as 'Paragraph 11. Confirm.'

One by one the mighty ships began to sink into the dark depths of Scapa Flow. As they did so, in a gesture of defiance the ships ran up the prohibited German battle ensign, as sailors saluted, some dancing hornpipes on deck, before abandoning ship into small boats.

When the British battle squadron at sea on exercise learned of the scuttle, they raced back to Scapa Flow – but although a few German ships were taken in tow and beached, it was too late to stop the majority of the fleet going to the bottom. Only the cruisers *Emden*, *Frankfurt* and *Nürnberg* were successfully beached, whilst only one capital ship, the battleship *Baden*, was saved.

The battlecruiser Hindenburg rolls to starboard as she goes under. (C.W. Burrows)

In the 1920s and 1930s, in an amazing feat of salvage, which itself deserves a whole book, the majority of the sunken German ships were raised to the surface, some from deep water, by divers physically sealing all the openings in the hull and then using compressed air to float the massive ships to the surface. Only seven complete ships were left on the bottom: those that lay in too-deep water and at awkward angles that made them simply economically unviable for salvage.

If you are interested in this fascinating piece of British naval history, there is a full account of the scuttle of the fleet, the subsequent salvage work and the history and disposition of each of the remaining big seven German ships along with all the other wrecks in Scapa Flow, in my book *Dive Scapa Flow*.

SMS *Bayern*

In the late 1980s and 1990s, there was a flurry of diving activity when it was realised that where the massive warships that had been raised had lain, there were depressions in the seabed that were filled with all sorts of bits and pieces of ships that had rotted off, or been cut off by salvors, and which had remained on the seabed as the great ships were lifted to the surface.

The depressions in the seabed were littered with spotting tops, masts, pinnaces and the like – important and substantial parts of some very famous warships. Perhaps the most famous of these depressions is where the battleship *Bayern* had lain upside down. As she was lifted to the surface, her four massive 15-inch gun turrets remained on the seabed in a line in the depression. Before telling the story of the turrets, we need a wee bit of background.

The battleship *Bayern* was the latest in state-of-the-art warship construction when she came into service in the High Seas Fleet in 1916 as the lead ship of the *Bayern* class of battleships. She was laid down in January 1914, launched in February 1915 and entered service in July 1916 – too late by just two weeks to fight at the Battle of Jutland. The original intention was that she would form the nucleus of a fourth battle squadron in the High Seas Fleet, along with three other planned sister battleships, *Baden, Sachsen* and *Württemberg*. Only one of the other planned three ships, *Baden,* was however completed – the other two

The fo'c'sle deck and forward main gun turrets of Hindenburg *rise above the water as she is pumped out.*

Left: The Kaiserin *successfully raised – she still has her eight airlocks attached to her hull and secured by guys.*

Right: The upturned battleship Kaiser *en route for Rosyth. One hut housed the pumps and compressors necessary to keep the hull positively buoyant on its 200-mile journey south from Orkney to Rosyth for scrapping. A salvage team lived in the other hut to man the pumps during the voyage.*

were cancelled later in the war, when materials and production requirements focused on submarine construction.

Bayern was 591 feet long with a beam of 99 feet and a draught of 31 feet. Her design displacement was 29,080 tons, and fully loaded for combat she displaced 31,690 tons. Her main vertical armour belt along either side was 14.5 inches thick. She had a range of 5,000 miles at 12 knots and, driven by her three Parsons turbines, she had a top speed of 22 knots. She carried a crew of 42 officers and 1,129 men.

Bayern is an important vessel as she was the first German ship to be fitted with eight of the new 15-inch guns set in four twin turrets, in place of the 12-inch guns of the earlier classes. A super-firing pair of turrets was set on the centre line of the vessel in front of the conning tower and superstructure. The other two turrets were again set as a super-firing pair towards the stern. The turrets and the ammunition hoists, which ran down to the magazines and shell rooms (below the horizontal armour deck at the bottom of the ship) sat in vast armoured barbettes (hollow armoured cylinders) that were an integral part of the ship's structure. The turrets largely relied on their great weight and gravity to keep them in place, rotating on a ball race of large steel ball bearings at the top of the barbette, with their ammunition hoists rotating in unison beneath them.

Her secondary armament consisted of sixteen 5.9-inch guns (the standard main armament of the light cruisers), six 3.45-inch guns, and five 23.6-inch underwater torpedo tubes set one in the bow and two on each side of the ship.

After the scuttling of the German fleet, with a profusion of scrap metal after the war, prices were at rock bottom and the British Admiralty's initial reaction was that the German warships would be left to rot on the bottom of Scapa Flow where they lay. But almost immediately, local vessels started snagging and going aground on the submerged hulls. By the early 1920s however, the price of scrap metal was picking up.

In 1924, the scrap metal firm of Cox and Danks Ltd (which had only begun ship-breaking in 1921), bought the battlecruisers *Seydlitz* and *Hindenburg* from the Admiralty. They then went on to buy the rest of the fleet – earning the director, Ernest Cox, the title of 'The Man Who Bought a Navy'. When Cox made his decision to lift the fleet, he had never salvaged anything before. He was simply an enterprising scrap metal merchant filled with enthusiasm but with no engineering qualifications. Cox went to Scapa Flow and worked out what had to be done, ignoring the experts who told him it was impossible.

In his first year, Cox raised 18 ships, averaging 750 tons each, and by the summer of 1925 he had recovered half of his initial capital outlay of £45,000. Buoyed with success, Cox then purchased a larger floating dock, with which he intended to lift the larger destroyers that were too heavy for the previous pontoons. With this dock, he raised all of the remaining destroyers, with the last, the 1,116-ton *G 104*, being raised on 1 May 1926. Cox sold his salvage rights in 1933 to another salvage company called Alloa Shipbreaking Co. Ltd which become part of the giant Metal Industries Group.

After the *Bayern* had been languishing on the bottom of Scapa Flow for 14 years, in June 1933, Metal Industries Ltd started to prepare the great ship for lifting to the surface, using compressed air. When divers inspected her, they found that she, like the other battleships, had turned turtle as she sank because of the enormous weight of her turrets, conning tower and superstructure bearing her over to one side as seawater flooded in. She lay with the flat

The 28,080-ton battleship Bayern *goes down by the stern
during the scuttle of the High Seas Fleet. (C.W. Burrows)*

bottom of her hull facing upwards and much of her superstructure embedded in the seabed beneath. Once a number of airlocks made of old boilers welded together had been fixed to the vessel and pressurised, Cox's workers climbed down ladders inside the cylinders to the wreck far below to start clearing her out and preparing her to be lifted.

On one occasion, a compressed air hose inside the hull burst, overfilling the hull with air. Luckily this happened when all the workers who had been working inside the submerged hull had finished for the day and gone home, leaving only a small crew topside to keep the compressors running on board a surface work boat.

The submerged hull started to become buoyant and strove to tear itself from the clinging grasp of the surrounding mud and the weight of the turrets, which had not yet been secured for lifting.

The fastenings for the 15-inch gun turrets were not designed with these huge stresses in mind – and they failed. Suddenly, the hull was missing the massive weight of the four huge turrets and was positively buoyant, rising to the surface in a mass of white foam and bubbles. The four twin 15-inch gun turrets easily broke free from their mounts and were left upside down on the seabed, complete with attached ammunition hoists.

As the hull rose to the surface, some of the airlines going to the airlocks from the workboat ruptured. Air started to escape from the hull, and she soon became negatively buoyant and started to sink again, slowly settling back down into the waters of the Flow. The tide, however, had played on her hull during her temporary freedom on the surface, drifting her round slightly, so that when she eventually sank back down to the seabed, she landed at an oblique angle to her original position. Part of the ship landed on top of one pair of turrets, its great weight easily crushing the unarmoured hoists.

After three further months of painstaking work, *Bayern* was finally ready for a controlled ascent. This time everything went according to plan. *Bayern* lifted off the seabed and rose to the surface amidst frothing eruptions of white water at her sides as expanding air escaped from her.

◆　◆　◆

Fast forward to today – the four twin 15-inch gun turrets of the *Bayern* remain upside down on the seabed in a line, marking where the ship lay after the scuttling, and before its first unexpected journey to the surface. The business part of the turrets – the gunhouse that housed the massive breeches of the 15-inch guns – was protected by 14 inches of armour plating. Each turret had a revolving weight of 1,020 tons.

The upper part of the main turret, the heavily armoured revolving gunhouse, was turned by electricity on top of the fixed armoured barbette, which was some 30–40 feet wide and was integral to the structure of the ship. Shells and propellant passed up from the shell rooms and magazines at the bottom of the ship to the transfer room and thence to the gunhouse inside the shelter of the armoured cylindrical barbette, which did not turn. The ammunition hoists turned as the turret revolved.

The barbette reached down through several deck levels to the horizontal armour deck at its base. The interior of this barbette was divided into several tiers – the transfer room, the switch room, the magazine and the cartridge magazine. In all, including the gunhouse of the

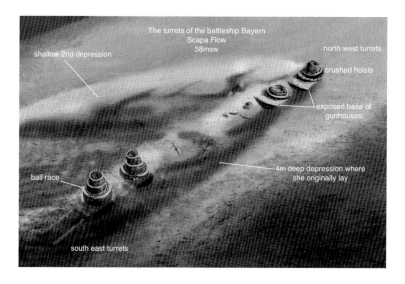

The four great turrets of Bayern *remain on the seabed in a 4-metre-deep depression where the great battleship formerly lay. A smaller depression to top of shot shows where she came to rest after she sank again. The ammunition hoists of the south-east turrets rise up from a depth of 38 metres to about 24 metres. The hoists of the north-east turrets were crushed when the ship sunk back down to the bottom after its accidental voyage to the surface. The spotting top can be seen near the topmost pair of turrets .*

turret, the barbette was some five storeys high and housed 70–80 men – a total of some 350 men in all four turrets.

The four *Bayern* turrets are grouped in two pairs of two, the aft two super-firing turrets to the southeast and the forward super-firing pair to the northwest. The two pairs of turrets are separated by a gap of some 100 metres and lie in a 4-metre-deep depression – the outline of where the ship lay on the seabed before it was lifted. A second, less obvious, depression marks where the ship came to rest on the seabed after it sank again. The second depression shows that the forward part of the ship actually sank onto the forward pair of turrets, which still lay on the seabed.

The gunhouses of all four turrets are now almost completely buried beneath the seabed at a depth of 38 metres. The upturned turrets still have the circular ball race visible – great steel ball bearings, each about 6 inches in diameter, running around the circumference of the gunhouse mount. The ammunition hoists and turning machinery for the southmost aft turrets rises up from the seabed at 38 metres to a least depth of 24 metres – some 45 feet in old money. The hull has crushed the ammunition hoists and turning mechanisms for the northmost forward pair of turrets as it sank after the first accidental lift.

The gunhouses are large rooms that are now buried entirely beneath the level of the seabed – but you can still get glimpses down into them in a number of places through parts of the ammunition hoist machinery and shell ejection hatches. Some openings are large enough to allow divers, with care, to enter the subterranean turrets and inspect the massive 15-inch breeches. It is dangerous however – and there have been several diver fatalities inside them.

In the illustration, the four turrets can be seen in line astern along the depression in the seabed that reveals *Bayern's* first resting place. The second depression lies at an oblique angle towards the top of the illustration. In between the two sets of turrets in the depression lie sections of the mainmast, the foremast and spotting top near the turrets at the top of the illustration.

In 2012, at the end of a week's diving at Scapa Flow, after a refreshing evening in the Flattie Bar in Stromness with local pioneering skipper John Thornton the night before, a slightly groggy author and Paul Haynes decided to have our traditional last day adventure – and decided to have a go at roping the two sets of turrets. Ever since I'd started diving at Scapa, it was the practice to only dive one set of turrets at a time. A few enterprising people had dived both sets of turrets in one dive by following the edge of the 4-metre-deep scour for the length of a battleship to the other set of turrets – but it was a long way between the two sets of turrets and easy to get lost in often limited visibility.

After John Thornton had dropped a shot for us at one of the pairs of turrets, Paul and I jumped into the water from the MV *Karin* with our DPVs (diver propulsion vehicles, aka scooters). Righting ourselves, we began to scooter down into the darkness, staying close to the shotline.

At about 20 metres down, the high tops of the ammunition hoists of the south turrets came into view slightly below but beside us. As we dropped down to the seabed beside the towering hoists, we could see sections of the buried gunhouses peeking through the seabed and these gave us our bearings. We worked our way around to the northmost of the two south turrets.

Moving forward and to the right on my DPV, I found the edge of the scour, a firm compressed bank of seabed, 4 metres high, the sand compacted into place more than 90 years ago by the weight of the *Bayern*.

Paul fished out a cave reel with a long line on it and started to tie it off beside the turret, and then moved forward, slowly unreeling. I moved along the outside of the scour until I spotted a large mangled metal pipe or spar sticking out of the seabed amidships which would make a good tie-off spot for the line. I nipped back into the gloom following the scour back until I found Paul diligently reeling off and led him over to the spar, where we tied off the reel before continuing.

We repeated the procedure, Paul reeling out and me zipping forward on my DPV before tying off again at a suitable point. Rinse and repeat again, and we were at the spotting top which had originally been situated far up the foremast – and which now lies not far from the northmost forward turrets. A final tie-off there and then, a little further forward, the dark brooding mass of the north turrets began to materialise out of the gloom, their ammunition hoists crushed beneath the ship as it sank to the bottom again. Large flat sections of the armoured back of the gunhouses on the bow turrets are visible.

With our caving line now in place, once we'd had a good look around the bow turrets we were able to zip back at speed along the middle of the scour, following our cave line to the aft turrets to ascend.

In the coming months, local divers replaced our thin caving line with more robust rope, and nowadays instead of just diving one set of turrets as in the past, a dive on both sets of roped turrets is a popular and different dive at Scapa Flow.

In 1970, new salvors had arrived in Scapa Flow when Dougall Campbell and David Nicol negotiated a deal to purchase the assets of Nundy (Marine Metals) Ltd which had latterly owned the German wrecks and had been carrying out small-scale salvage works. The newly formed Scapa Flow Salvage company began salvage work on the battleships *Markgraf* and *Kronprinz Wilhelm*, by taking off the valuable and easily accessible vertical armour belt plates, before starting on the four cruisers, *Brummer, Dresden, Cöln* and *Karlsruhe*.

As well as working the main German wrecks, Scapa Flow Salvage also considered lifting the *Bayern* turrets by passing leader wires under the upturned turrets and barrels. Using a Smit 1,000-ton A-frame crane barge, the turrets would be broken out of the mud and raised to the surface. At the end of the 1977 season, however, as the law of diminishing returns made itself felt, a commercial decision was made to stop all salvage at Scapa Flow.

On the one hand, for Scapa Flow diving it is best that the turrets were left where they are on the seabed so divers can see them and understand the complicated chain of historical events that surrounds them. Made of best German armour plate, the gunhouses will still be in pristine condition today, but they are often overlooked as a dive by visitors to Scapa Flow in favour of the much larger complete German warships that hold so much of interest. Only a handful of divers see the turrets each year.

I love diving them – but I sometimes muse that it might be good for tourism in Orkney if they were lifted, conserved and then put on display, say, at the entrance to Stromness, on either side of the road into the town. That certainly would be eye-catching!

Orcas in the Flow

Orcas – sometimes erroneously called killer whales – are found in significant numbers off the northern coasts of Scotland. The adult male of these black and white mammals can reach almost 10 metres long, with a large black dorsal fin that can stand 6 feet high. They live in social groups called pods, and the oldest female is the leader. Pods of several orcas are very common – but super-pods of up to 150 have also been spotted from time to time off Orkney.

Some pods of orcas are resident in one area; one group of nine was well known and dubbed the 'West Coast community'. Others are migratory, following the mackerel and herring shoals.

Usually, the migratory orcas spend the winter months in Norway and Iceland, feeding on mackerel and herring and chasing seals. In May, they return to Scottish waters, and between May to September is the best time to see them, before they depart to winter in Norwegian and Icelandic waters again.

Orcas are large highly mobile mammals. They can reach speeds of 35 mph and travel large distances in quite a short time. They are very intelligent, approaching boats, spy hopping and tail slapping. They are a common sight up the west coast of Scotland, around the Hebrides, and Skye, and also in numbers around the Orkney and Shetland Islands. They are also seen in the Moray Firth on the east coast of Scotland, and from time to time are spotted around North Sea oil platforms. In 2016, a lone orca was spotted in the Firth of Clyde. But some 90 per cent of all orca sightings in the UK are off Orkney and Shetland.

Orcas often shadow a deep-sea fishing trawler; they have come to recognise the sound transmitted through the water of the trawl winch being started to haul in the nets – and many such trawlers have their own accompanying orcas. As the nets are hauled in and the net closes, trapped fish are compressed together towards the cod end. Some of the smaller fish, some dead, some alive, pop out through the net gauge. The orcas know this, and will be there, waiting to pick up an easy free snack.

The footage of orcas surging up a shingle beach in the Arctic to snatch an unwary seal on the shingle at the water's edge is amazing. But this same event has happened in Shetland where orcas have surged up a shoaling beach to try and snatch a quick snack of a dog being walked along the water's edge.

Orcas used to come into Scapa Flow in the 1970s, and salvage divers working the German fleet reported that they could get aggressive. Seeing them as a threat to safety, the salvage divers were withdrawn from the water when they were about. During my time diving in Scapa Flow in the 1980s and 1990s, I never saw any orcas inside Scapa Flow itself, though I was once in the water off Marwick Head, to the north-west of Orkney, when a pod of orcas passed by, followed later by a large male.

Over the last ten years or so, it has become increasingly common to see orcas back inside Scapa Flow once again. I haven't heard of any approaching divers in the water as yet; they don't seem to hunt around the wrecks, preferring the turbulent fish-rich waters around Hoy Sound, Hoxa Sound, Marwick Head.

In about 2012, whilst diving off the *Karin* with John Thornton, our group had just finished the days diving and was heading back to Stromness. We were motoring up Clestrain Sound with Hoy Sound on our port beam as we entered the sheltered Bay of Ireland just outside Stromness. Just off the shallows of Mallow Bank, John called out to us that he had a pod of orcas off his bow. Our divers quickly nipped up the fixed steps that led from the well deck up to the fo'c'sle deck, where we had a close-up bird's eye view of about six or seven orcas fishing for mackerel. They worked as a team, encircling and corralling all the mackerel into one big ball before beginning to feed on them. Mackerel are a very oily fish, and very soon the surface of the water had taken on an oily sheen.

After a while, an inquisitive seal appeared on the scene looking to grab himself a free meal courtesy of the hard work by the orcas. The seal darted into the thronging ball of mackerel and started to pinch some. Bad move – he was spotted and very soon from being the hunter, he himself became the hunted.

The orcas began to play with the seal, chasing him, allowing him try to escape, then cutting him off and keeping him corralled. After about 10 minutes of this, the seal dived down and several of the orcas dived down after him. Suddenly there was an explosion of bright red just underneath the surface. The red colour spread out and then bits of seal came floating up towards us.

We watched from the fo'c'sle, looking down as the orcas began to feed once more on the mackerel bait ball just about 20 feet away from us – Nature at its rawest.

Drifters and a RN pinnace

During 2015 and 2016 three new wrecks of steam drifters were located in Scapa Flow, largely as a result of side-scan sonar surveys of the seabed by local commercial diving and subsea specialists, Sula Diving. The identity of two of them has been deduced from research, but nothing definite has yet been found to positively identify them. However, they are an exciting new addition to Scapa Flow's already long list of shipwrecks.

Drifters were a very common type of Scottish fishing vessel, designed to catch herring in a long drift net. With the outbreak of World War I, the Royal Navy requisitioned many existing civilian steam trawlers and drifters for naval use. The Royal Navy also ordered the construction of 362 new drifters that would be built along existing shipyard designs but were modified for naval use. The idea was that after the war they could be decommissioned and sold to commercial fishing companies for civilian use.

There were two types of Admiralty-built drifters: wooden-hulled and steel-hulled. The wooden drifters displaced about 175 tons and were 86 feet long with a beam of 19 feet. They were usually armed with a 6-pounder gun and could make 7–9 knots. The steel purpose-built naval drifters had the same length, beam and armament, but had a greater displacement of 199 tons.

Naval trawlers and drifters were extensively used in Orkney for patrol duties and for manning and operating the booms. The present-day wreck of HMT *Strathgarry* was a boom defence vessel during World War I. Steam trawlers were also used for convoy escort duties during World War II.

1. The remains of a wooden steam drifter were located south of Scapa Bay in 2015 during bottom scans by Sula Diving. The wreck is orientated east/west and lies on its port side. It is well broken up with the wreckage strewn over an area approximately 30 metres long by 8 metres wide. A large engine stands on the sandy seabed with a pile of ballast stones forward of it, and an Admiralty pattern anchor sitting on top of the pile. A smaller spare or kedge anchor sits aft of the engine – it was common to keep such an anchor stowed near the stern of such vessels.

A small Cochran-style cross-tube boiler sits forward of the engine, and not far forward towards the bow a steam anchor capstan and anchor chain can be found. This wreck was initially believed to be possibly that of the 52grt wooden drifter His Majesty's Drifter (HMD) *Susie Ross*, built in 1900 and lost in 1918 but that possible ID is now in doubt, and the vessel remains unidentified at the time of printing but may well be the herring drifter *Edindoune*.

2. The previously unknown wreck of a drifter was located in Longhope Bay by Sula Diving during side-scan operations with the Scapa Flow dive boat MV *Valkyrie* in 2016. This wreck lies in 11–12 metres of water and its well-dispersed remains consist of a large degraded boiler, copper piping, sections of plating and riveted tanks. This wreck is believed to possibly be that of HMD *Imbat* – but no positive identification has been made as yet.

The 92grt wooden drifter *Imbat* PD105 was built in 1918 by Jones, Buckie for the Admiralty, and she was sold off after World War I ended and she was no longer required for war duties. She had an oil engine and single shaft. In 1940, she was hired for harbour service and began operating at Scapa Flow.

At about 1940 hours on 4 February 1941, the log of HMS *Iron Duke* records that a signal was received aboard that two drifters had been in collision close to the nearby hospital ship HMHS *Amarapoora* off Longhope. A search was carried out using searchlights, and at 2045 *Amarapoora* reported that *Imbat* had sunk, although all her crew had been saved.

3. A third drifter was located north of the island of Flotta in 2016 by Sula Diving. This wreck has now been identified as the 92grt wooden drifter HMD *Chance*, built in 1908 by Donald Alexander of Wick for F. Millar & George P. Simpson of Wick. She was 88 feet long with a beam of 19 feet, and was powered by a compound engine made by Lidgerwood of Coatbridge.

This Wick drifter was requisitioned by the Admiralty for war service during 1915 and was sunk on 26 January 1916 after a collision.

The wreck lies not far from the tanker *Prudentia* and is well degraded. It is still being investigated – but holds much of interest. The wheelhouse still has the remains of its helm, and the steam anchor capstan can be found among the wreckage near the bow whilst at the stern, the prop and rudder are still present.

4. RN pinnace: during the Scapa Flow 2013 Marine Archaeology Project (Christie, Heath and Littlewood), a seabed anomaly was discovered off the old, now ruined, pier at Rinnigill, near Lyness – a major anchorage for Royal Navy vessels during World War II.

The site was dived in 2014, and the remains of a pinnace were found lying on its port side in 14 metres of water. The bell had been recovered some time previously by a scallop diver, but had no distinguishing marks. The boiler plate had also been previously recovered, and an old photograph of it was sourced that revealed the boiler had been fabricated by J. Samuel White's Yard at Cowes, and delivered during 1919/20.

Picket boats or pinnaces were assigned to all large Royal Navy vessels, which were fitted out with heavy-duty booms for launching and retrieving them. By 1914, the Royal Navy had 634 pinnaces in service, and although there were varying types the length was usually 40–50 feet with a beam of about 9 feet. They were used for transferring officers and crew to shore and to other vessels. They were often fitted with a QF 3-pounder gun on the bow and would be used to patrol and guard the parent ship when it was at anchor and vulnerable.

Grumman Wildcat Fm-2 Mk VI

The remains of a Grumman Wildcat aircraft lost from HMS *Trumpeter* on 2 December 1944 were located and identified in 2014 by Sula Diving from Stromness and ARGOS member Kevin Heath.

This single-crew carrier fighter was almost 9 metres long with a wingspan of 11.5 metres, and was armed with four .50 Cal Browning machine guns in its wings. It could make a creditable 330 mph and had a service ceiling of almost 40,000 feet.

On 2 December 1944, this Wildcat was launching from HMS *Trumpeter* in Scapa Flow for RNAS *Hatson* when the retaining ring of the catapult mechanism broke and the aircraft

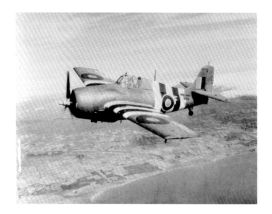

The Grumman Wildcat naval fighter bomber.

went over the port side of the carrier. It appears that the aircraft flipped over before sinking. The pilot was rescued but the aircraft sank to the bottom of the Flow.

Today the Grumman Wildcat lies inverted on the seabed at a depth of about 35 metres. The large radial engine lies exposed and in good condition, with inverted sections of the fuselage and wings, fuel tank wheels and tyres. The propeller appears to have been torn off on the surface and now lies a little away from the main wreckage.

SMS *Dresden*

The *Dresden* is one of the four *kleiner kreuzer* wrecks on the bottom of Scapa Flow today. She was laid down in Kiel in 1916 by Howaldtswerke and launched on 25 April 1917. Fitting out afloat was a lengthy process, as resources were being diverted to the submarine campaign, so it was almost a year after her launch until she was declared completed and commissioned into the Kaiserliche Marine (Imperial Navy) on 28 March 1918.

One of a planned class of ten such vessels, only she and her sister light cruiser *Cöln* (II) were completed – they being the last ships commissioned before Germany's defeat.

Dresden displaced 5,531 long tons (5,620 tonnes) and at full load, laden with ordnance and fuel, she displaced 7,368 long tons (7,486 tonnes). Eight coal boilers and six oil boilers provided steam for two sets of geared turbines that powered her two screws to push her to 28 knots – much faster than the 21-knot fleet speed of the battleships of the day. She was 510 feet long with a beam of 47 feet and a draught of almost 20 feet.

Dresden was protected by tapered 2.4-inch (60mm) vertical main belt armour plating along either side of her waterline and 2.4-inch (60mm) horizontal deck armour. She was fitted with eight powerful SK L/45 5.9-inch (15cm) guns in single pedestal mounts with splinter

The 5,620-tonne light cruiser SMS Dresden. *(IWM)*

shields and a range of 11 miles. Two were set side by side on the fo'c'sle deck in front of the fire control tower and bridge superstructure. Another two were set one either side of the bridge on the upper deck. A further two SK L/45 guns were set one either side of the mainmast towards the stern, and two super-firing guns were set on the centre line at the stern.

With her speed and manoeuvrability, she was ideal as a scout for the main fleet, being heavily enough armed that she could engage British cruisers and overpower British destroyers, armed trawlers and lightly armed merchant shipping. *Dresden* was equipped to carry 200 mines and a crew of 559 officers and men.

Following the Armistice of November 1918, *Dresden*, being one of the most modern and recent additions to the Kaiserliche Marine, was selected as one of the naval units to be taken into internment at Scapa Flow. Turbine failure however delayed her departure – but, leaking badly, she finally arrived at Scapa Flow on 6 December. She was one of the last two ships to enter internment there.

On her arrival in Scapa Flow, she was moored to the north-west of the rocky outcrop in the centre of the western expanse of Scapa Flow known as the Barrel of Butter. The light cruisers *Bremse* and *Cöln* were anchored to her north-east and *Frankfurt* to her north. Not far away to her north-west in deeper water, the battleships *König* and *Markgraf* swung at their moorings.

During the scuttle, of the cruisers, *Brummer* went at 1305, *Cöln* at 1350 and *Bremse* at 1430. Soon the only cruisers remaining afloat were *Karlsruhe* and *Dresden*.

In the authoritative *Jutland to Junkyard*, S.C. George narrates that the small British drifter *Clonsin* was tasked to take the much larger *Dresden* in tow and try to beach her on the nearby shores of the island of Cava to the west. (The *Clonsin* was a 193grt German war prize, formerly known as *Dr. Robitzsch*. She was just 119.8 feet long with a beam of 22 feet and powered by a small triple expansion steam. This German drifter had been detained at Aberdeen on 4 August 1914, the day Britain declared war on Germany following her refusal to pull her troops out of Belgium. *Clonsin* carried a single 6-pounder gun.)

The diminutive *Clonsin* got a tow cable made fast and began the tow – to Cava, if S.C. George is correct. But her progress in attempting to tow the 5,620 tonnes of *Dresden* was made painfully slow by the dead weight of her hull – which was rapidly filling with water. *Dresden* was now so low in the sea that her decks were awash.

S.C. George continues that the tow was 'only a mile from Cava beach' (better described perhaps as 'shallows') when she sank so quickly that there was no time to cast off the towing cable. Other reports suggest that an internal bulkhead perhaps gave way to water pressure, and that she lurched down by the head and sank quickly at 1530. She came to rest on the seabed on her port beam ends.

Interestingly, the wreck today has her port anchor and chain run out straight, almost taut, on the seabed. Although some RN vessels cut German anchor chains with explosives, it appears that *Clonsin* may not have had that ability and took her in tow despite her anchor being set. The large anchor on the seabed today is similar to a modern Danforth-style anchor and is not set in the seabed. It lies upside down with its two large flukes pointing upwards – they should ordinarily be embedded in the seabed whilst the vessel is at anchor. The anchor chain runs from the anchor tight along the seabed in a straight line to the bow.

Skippers today are aware that when anchored with a Danforth, if the wind markedly changes direction with force – and a yacht swings excessively at anchor – that the anchor can

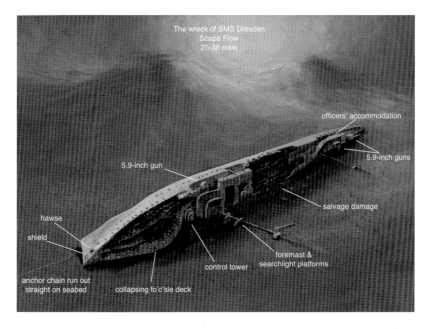

Artist's impression of the wreck of the Dresden, Scapa Flow.

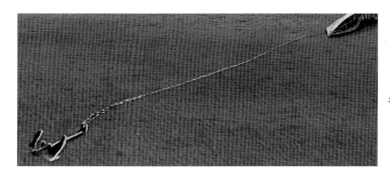

Artist's impression of the upside-down anchor of Dresden with the chain lying straight out on the seabed as it runs back to the wreck. This suggests that she was taken in a stern tow for shallower water.

break out of the seabed and flip over. Danforth anchors don't reset themselves automatically if dragged along the seabed. The yacht will thus no longer be set at anchor, and will just have the dead weight of the chain and upside-down anchor on the seabed to hold it. In this state, yachts can then be blown by the wind, dragging the upside-down anchor and chain along the seabed straight out behind them – exactly the same effect as we see on *Dresden* today.

Although it is not recorded anywhere to this effect, the evidence on the seabed today suggests that the *Clonsin* took *Dresden* in a stern tow. *Dresden* would have been anchored, as most of the German ships were that day, including *Cöln* and *Brummer* nearby, with her bows facing into the north-west wind.

The 193grt *Clonsin* was a small vessel just 119.8 feet long, and her small triple expansion steam engine according to Lloyd's Register developed just 39 rhp (rated or nominal horse power). *Dresden* was 510 feet long and displaced 5,531 tons. If her anchor had been properly set then it is improbable that the *Clonsin* could have successfully begun a tow.

If, however, *Clonsin* took her in a stern tow, and her stern was pulled round for more than 100 degrees for the tow south-west to Cava, this would possibly have flipped her anchor. Perhaps this was fine seamanship by the skipper of the *Clonsin* – deliberately breaking out the anchor in the knowledge that his small 119-foot long drifter would never have been able to tow the massive *Dresden* with her anchor properly set.

If *Dresden's* bows were already going under, then the capstan engine, at the bottom of the ship near the bow, may well have already been flooded and inoperative. It is likely that there was no power to lift the anchor – and in any event, with the crew having abandoned ship, there would have been no one left to operate the capstan even if it was functional, and so lift the anchor.

If, as I suspect, it was a stern tow – and if the anchor flipped – the chain and upside-down anchor would then have been dragged taut and then streamed out along the seabed from the bow as the ship was towed by her stern. If so, no wonder history records that the tow of the *Dresden* was painfully slow – it wasn't just that her hull had taken on a lot of water – she had the deadweight of her anchor and chain dragging on the seabed.

Another thought … the area of south Cava, close to where *Dresden* now lies, has only steep cliffs – there is no beach there, only shallows. *Dresden* lies on the side of a charted underwater hillock – a submerged hillock that is essentially an extension of the Barrel of Butter rocky outcrop to the north-east. This underwater hill rises from depths of around 40 metres to a least depth of about 16 metres at lowest astronomical tide (LAT). The bow of *Dresden* today rests in 25 metres of water whilst her stern is deeper down the hillside at 38 metres.

When I first had the wreck of the *Dresden* illustrated by Rob Ward in 1989, we deliberately put in two underwater hillocks: the submerged one that *Dresden* rests upon and the second in the distance – the small rocky islet of the Barrel of Butter.

Looking at the orientation of the wreck itself, the taut anchor and chain allow us to work out the bearing of the tow – and where the tow was headed. I have the bows of the *Dresden* bearing about 305 degrees and the stern bearing about 125 degrees. If it were a bow tow, then the *Dresden* would be heading up towards where the battleships had just sunk in deep water to the north-east of Cava – not realistic.

But if it was a stern tow, as the gear on the seabed indicates, then the tow was no longer heading for Cava – it was heading towards distant Flotta, which is unlikely.

Is it possible that the skipper of the *Clonsin* realised that *Dresden* was sinking so quickly that they wouldn't make the shallows at Cava before she sank? Rather than let her sink in deep water and become a total loss, did he in fact try to deposit his charge in the shallow water on top of this submerged hillock, where her superstructure and top hamper would have remained proud of the water and she could more easily be salved?

These are simply my idle musings looking at the layout of her gear on the seabed today – and wearing my yachtsman and lifeboatman's cap as I write, having had perhaps too much coffee! Please do not take this as gospel – more as a possibility to get people thinking. But it is personally interesting, that after believing for 35 years that the *Dresden* was taken in a bow tow to beach on Cava, the reality may be that she was taken in a stern tow in an attempt to ground her on a submerged hillock.

17

THE DESECRATION OF NAVAL WAR GRAVES IN THE SOUTH CHINA SEA, JAVA SEA AND JUTLAND

Frankly, it is personally disappointing for me to have to write about this next topic towards the end of a book that I hope has shown diving in a decent light and shown the good that divers can do, the knowledge that can be gained, and the joy that our deeds can bring to survivors and relatives. To me, the last resting places of our fallen servicemen at sea, often called war graves, are sacred, special places. Sadly, for some commercial salvage operators the fact that there are human remains on these sunken warships is of little or no relevance. There is now however a growing concern being expressed around the world, not just in the diving community but amongst military veterans and indeed sections of the general public, about the shocking desecration of naval war graves – all in pursuit of the salvage dollar. By writing about this now, I hope that I will highlight and summarise what is going on, and raise public awareness.

These unscrupulous salvors do not seem to care that those who perished on these vessels have relatives living today – sons, daughters, grandchildren – all of who have special feelings about their lost ones. It is apparently of no relevance to those salvors. There are still many survivors of many of the sinkings alive today – they know that their shipmates and best buddies are still in those vessels – and that is equally of no relevance. The military wrecks are simply seen as holding large amounts of best quality metals that are ripe for salvage. It's all about the money.

To be fair, Britain wasn't quite so sensitive in the past as it is now, about the fact its sunken ships held the remains of service personnel. In the immediate post-war period, the marine salvage company Risdon Beazley Ltd salvaged, with government backing, most of the accessible wartime wrecks – a vast treasure trove of valuable material that had to be brought back into commercial circulation.

Risdon Beazley himself was born in 1904 and formed his salvage company in Southampton in 1926 when he was just 22 years old. By the 1930s, his company was involved in demolition work and the dismantling and removal of shipwrecks.

At the outbreak of World War II, the Admiralty requisitioned a large number of salvage barges, and many of these were placed under Risdon Beazley's control even though they were manned by civilians.

By 1945, the company operated 61 vessels, including 29 that were owned by the Admiralty, and the company operated around the UK and as far east as Sri Lanka. The other salvage barge managers together operated less than 20 vessels between them – so the scale of Risdon Beazley's domination of the salvage market is very apparent.

Risdon Beazley Ltd's salvage barges went to France for D-Day in 1944, making up all but three of the salvage vessels involved. Their ships cleared war torn ports in France, Belgium and the Netherlands. Manned by civilians, the only military personnel aboard were DEMS gunners who would operate the stern defensive gun and AA weaponry. The company also built motor gun boats, motor torpedo boats and harbour service launches.

After the war had ended, Risdon Beazley Ltd specialised in cargo recovery from sunken merchant ships, and over four years in the 1950s they contributed £187,000 to the UK Treasury and were able to take two new recovery vessels, *Twyford* and *Droxford*, into their fleet.

Risdon Beazley Ltd in all recovered some 56,000 tons of non-ferrous metals in the post-war years, down to depths of 300 metres, working around the world. In the 1960s, the company was involved in saving Isambard Kingdom Brunel's ship SS *Great Britain*. Launched in 1843, this famous ship was the longest passenger ship in her time and the first iron steamer to cross the Atlantic. She was retired to the Falkland Islands in 1884 and used as a warehouse, quarantine ship and coal hulk until she was scuttled there in 1937. Risdon Beazley Ltd was brought in by the SS *Great Britain* Project and successfully refloated her, mounted her on a pontoon and towed her via Montevideo to Bristol, where the great ship has been restored as a museum ship and is now open to the public.

Risdon Beazley sold his interests between 1969 and 1971, and the new company, Risdon Beazley Marine Ltd., expanded – but ultimately, perhaps with the law of diminishing returns at work, the company became run down and closed in 1981. Risdon Beazley himself died in 1979.

I have dived many wrecks that were salvaged by Risdon Beazley Ltd – a lot of them show signs of a standard *modus operandi*. The prop of a large ship was most often made of non-ferrous bronze alloys such as manganese bronze or phosphor bronze. The prop shaft could be cut by explosives, and the freed prop could then be stropped and lifted to the surface – money in the bank.

The engine rooms held a lot of non-ferrous fitments, such as condensers, condensate de-aerators, seawater filters, freshwater evaporator distillers (to produce fresh drinking water from sea water), Weir pumps and the valuable engines themselves made of best steel and non-ferrous metals.

Condensers were particularly valuable. Once steam had passed through a turbine or the three cylinders of a triple expansion engine, the steam was passed through the condenser, a large piece of engine room equipment that held a mass of copper tubes inside its chamber. Cold sea water was circulated through these tubes inside the condensing chamber, and as the expanded steam passed through the chamber the steam condensed on the surface of the cold tubes. The resulting hot condensed water was not contaminated by the salts in sea water and could then be pumped back to the boiler as pure, or nearly pure, water. With no dissolved solids in the boiler water, there was no need to blow it overboard, and higher temperatures and pressures were achievable without risk of encrustation.

Weir pumps were also very valuable. They were an essential element of the closed feed system on condensing expansion engines, with different pumps carrying out different jobs and ranging in size from 2 to 9 feet tall. The pumping cylinder was made of cast iron for condensate, or brass for condenser cooling by sea water.

To get at this multitude of valuable metals, Risdon Beazley Ltd would set explosive charges on the hull around the engine room. Once they were blown, a mechanical grab would lift the now free hull and superstructure around and above the engine room off the wreck, and dump it at the side, on the seabed. The engine room was thus wide open and accessible, allowing the non-ferrous metal fitments to be grabbed out or stropped by divers and lifted out. Engines were usually held in place on their mounts by gravity and a number of thick steel pins. Blow these pins with a small explosive charge and the engine could be lifted out in one piece.

There are a number of wrecks around north-east Scotland, where I do most of my diving, that have been salvaged in this fashion. The SS *Anvers* lies on the seabed about 5 miles north of Rattray Head, south of Fraserburgh on the north-east tip of Scotland. She is a large 4,398grt steam ship built in 1908 that was sunk on 13 November 1940 (just a few days after the *Creemuir* was sunk, not far south) by German torpedo bombers flying from Norway while she was en route from Philadelphia to London with a large cargo of 6,000 tons of mixed steel.

This 383-foot-long steamship sits on its keel in about 55 metres of water and is almost, but not quite, perfectly intact. The impressive bow and two foredeck holds containing the remnants of the cargo of steel are intact – and the lovely stern and two aft deck holds are perfectly intact. In between however, the composite superstructure of the bridge and engine room is completely gone. The ship has been cut down with explosives almost to the seabed – and then the freed-up superstructure above it has been grabbed out. It's as though a giant undersea monster has taken a huge bite out of it – and every single piece of brass and copper in the area has been carefully removed. The large boilers sit in the midst of the debris – unworthy of salvage – but you can see how copper pipes leading to them have been carefully hacksawed off by divers.

Risdon Beazley Ltd worked a large number of the reachable, and commercially viable, wrecks around the UK in this fashion – there was little thought given to the fact that the remains of fallen merchant sailors would be still in the wrecks. The value of the metal that could be recovered and put back into commercial use outweighed the sentiment of preserving the remains of the fallen. It was a different time, following on just after the horrors of a world war – a time that is hard for those who were not involved to understand at this distance in time.

Likewise, the Admiralty sold Metal Industries the salvage rights for the British battleship *Vanguard*, which blew up at anchor in Scapa Flow on 9 July 1917 with the loss of 843 men. In the 1950s, they used commercial blasting techniques to remove and lift the battleship's vertical side armour belts, the gunhouse armour of the turrets and anything else of value, despite the remains of the 843 service men being present – something that would be unthinkable and totally unacceptable nowadays. Salvage rights were again sold as recently as the 1970s.

Among other historic vessels sold or licensed by the Admiralty for salvage for their scrap value were the armoured cruisers *Cressy*, *Hogue* and *Aboukir*, sunk in one action by the

German submarine U 9 on 22 September 1914 with the loss of 1,459 lives. These war graves were sold for scrap in 1954.

The Hospital Ship HMHS *Anglia*, which was sunk by a mine laid by UC 5 off Folkestone on 17 November 1915 with the loss of 134 wounded soldiers, crew and nursing staff, was sold to the Folkestone Salvage Company in 1965. The German submarine UB 81 lay in the English Channel with 29 crew still inside her; she was sold for scrap as recently as 1975.

Among other vessels lost with major loss of life, where salvage was allowed, are the British armoured cruiser *Natal* which, in similar fashion to *Vanguard*, blew up at anchor in the harbour area of the Cromarty Firth from an internal magazine explosion on 30 December 1915, with the loss of some 400 crew. After commercial salvage had been carried out, her remains were further dispersed by explosives in the 1970s to remove the hazard to navigation for the developing oil industry vessels that now sought to use the firth.

In 1981, the wreck of the cruiser HMS *Edinburgh* in the Arctic Ocean off Russia (sister ship of HMS *Belfast*, currently moored as a tourist attraction in the River Thames) was worked for the consignment of 4.5 tons of gold bullion she was carrying. She was scuttled following a combination of U-boat attack, German bombers and destroyer attacks on 2 May 1942 with the loss of 58 crew. The gold was a partial payment by Russia for war supplies from the Allies, and the British government was anxious to recover its gold. (After the war, in 1954, the British government had offered the contract to Risdon Beazley Ltd – but salvage attempts were not made due to the blossoming Cold War, souring relations between Britain and Russia.)

By 1981 however, when the *Edinburgh* job was being contemplated, a growing sensitivity about naval war graves was beginning to manifest itself. The British government awarded the salvage contract to civilian saturation divers who were to undertake a clinical forensic salvage job, carefully cutting into the wreck with minimal disturbance.

I must admit that this subject causes me some amount of personal discomfort. During World War II, an uncle that I never knew, my mother's brother, Sergeant Alan Whyte (Service No 1571167) of the Royal Air Force Volunteer Reserve, was lost on 9 January 1945 at the age of 22, whilst flying out of Alexandria in Egypt. His aircraft and his remains have never been found – he is still missing in action, his name being recorded on the Alamein Memorial. It pains me greatly to think of my uncle's remains still trapped in his aircraft at the bottom of the Mediterranean. The thought that his remains could be thrown aside like trash for commercial interests if the wreck of the aircraft was found is deeply disturbing and leaves me cold.

So, with that perspective, it is with deep revulsion and horror that I have watched the recent salvage works being carried out – illegally – on a number of British, Australian, American, Dutch and Japanese naval war graves around the world.

There is a lot of misinformation and ignorance around about shipwrecks and salvage, so I'll don my old lawyer's hat for a second, to explain.

Each shipwreck, each cargo, each artefact lying on the bottom of the sea today still has a legal owner. Rights of ownership are not simply lost by abandonment.

The wrecks of merchant ships may each have a number of owners involved. There could be multiple owners of the vessel itself, and it was common for the hull and the cargo to be separately insured. When a ship is lost, the relevant insurance company may have paid out for the loss to the owner and been given ownership of the sunken ship and its cargo. Through ordinary commerce, an insurance company that paid out in say World War I, may have been bought out or amalgamated in subsequent years – so although the original World War I insurer may no longer exist, ownership may well vest in a present-day insurer.

Where a civilian ship was requisitioned or chartered by the British government for war use, if it was sunk on war duty, the British government would pay compensation to the owners for the war loss – and acquire ownership of the sunken ship. Those rights are today held by the UK Department of Transport.

It is perfectly legitimate to 'buy' the hull or its cargo from those insurers or the Department of Transport. You then own the wreck, are responsible for it and can do as you like with your property as long as you obey any relevant statutes or rules that may be in force. Thus, the wreck of a merchant vessel can be legitimately salvaged.

In the UK, whether or not you own the wreck, if any items are recovered (and this applies right down to a diver who finds and lifts a shiny trinket on a wreck), such wreck material must be reported to the government body called the Receiver of Wreck. The Receiver is allowed a period of one year to trace the legal owner of the wreck material recovered. If traced, the wreck material then gets offered to the owner, say the insurance company. If it wants the material, then it must pay the salvor a salvage fee, usually a percentage of its assessed value. If it does not want the material, then the item can be adjudged by the Receiver to belong to the salvor. That's how a diver can perfectly properly get legal ownership of, for example, the porthole they have found on a wreck.

The legal position for naval or military wrecks is, however, very different. The wrecks of military vessels are state-owned vessels. Under Article 14 of the Brussels Convention on Salvage 1910 (as amended) and Article 4 of the International Salvage Convention 1989, this means that they are still the legal property of the sovereign state and are immune from salvage unless the sovereign state consents to their salvage. A sovereign state must grant a licence before salvage work can legitimately be carried out on its naval wrecks.

Sadly, this rule has been, and is being, brutally ignored by commercial interests who are plundering naval war graves around the world, most notoriously, the World War I wrecks from the Battle of Jutland in the North Sea and those in the South China Sea and Java Sea. No salvage rights are being applied for – and no concern or compassion has been shown for the remains of often hundreds of sailors still present in these wrecks.

I will summarise what is going on here to try and highlight the scurrilous practice.

Jutland

Jutland is the large peninsula rising up northwards from the north of Germany, which holds the main land regions of Denmark. This Danish peninsula separates the North Sea to the west from the Baltic Sea to the east. To its north-east and east, across the Kattegat sea channel, lies Sweden. The Kattegat leads westwards from the Baltic Sea into a wider channel, the Skagerrak, between Denmark's Jutland peninsula and Norway, and the Skagerrak in turn leads westwards out into the North Sea.

The Battle of Jutland (called the *Skagerrakschlacht*, the Battle of the Skagerrak, in Germany) was fought in the North Sea to the west of the Jutland peninsula between the British Royal Navy and the Imperial German Navy on 30 May and 1 June 1916. It was the largest clash of steel warships there had ever been, and was the first major fleet encounter between the

British Grand Fleet and the German High Seas Fleet. Although in terms of numbers of ships sunk and men killed the Royal Navy came off worse, the Imperial German Navy had a higher number of ships badly damaged and tactically was outplayed when the main element of the British Grand Fleet joined the battle after arriving from Scapa Flow.

The bloody opening skirmishes of the Battle of Jutland took place between the five battlecruisers of Vice Admiral Franz Hipper's I Scouting Group and the six battlecruisers of the British 1st and 2nd Battlecruiser Squadrons under the command of Vice Admiral David Beatty, which had put to sea from Rosyth. The British battlecruisers were supported by the four fast *Queen Elizabeth*-class battleships, *Barham*, *Valiant*, *Warspite* and *Malaya* of the 5th Battle Squadron and by a screen of 14 light cruisers and 27 destroyers.

The German force had sortied as part of a general strategy intended to draw out and isolate a portion of the British Grand Fleet and destroy it – before the might of the British Grand Fleet from Scapa Flow could retaliate. The German High Seas Fleet was numerically inferior in numbers of capital ships to the Royal Navy, and Germany hoped that by isolating and destroying small sections of the British Fleet, along with attrition from mine laying and submarine attack, British sea power could be gradually diminished and the British naval blockade of the North Sea broken. This would allow German merchant supply shipping to operate – and allow her warships to break out of the North Sea to threaten British supply shipping. The German plan was that once an equality of strength had been achieved, the High Seas Fleet would seek out battle with the Grand Fleet in favourable circumstances.

As the opening skirmish of the Battle of Jutland took place between the two battlecruiser squadrons on the afternoon of 31 May, two of the six British battlecruisers, *Indefatigable* and *Queen Mary*, blew up in catastrophic secondary magazine explosions. A third battlecruiser, *Invincible*, would also be destroyed later in the battle.

Battlecruisers were a relatively recent innovation and whilst they had the same powerful guns as battleships, they had sacrificed armour to gain greater speed. They were less protected against plunging fire than were battleships – but at this point the battlecruiser concept had not been truly tested in battle and their vulnerabilities were not fully appreciated. These would be tragically exposed during the battle, when the frailty of the British version of the battlecruiser concept would be starkly revealed to the world.

On *Indefatigable*, 1,015 men died instantly as she blew up; only two of her crew, who had been some 180 feet high in the foretop, survived.

Just over 20 minutes after *Indefatigable* blew up, *Queen Mary* took a hit that detonated a forward magazine of either A or B turret. The ship was mortally wounded and began to sink as crew frantically tried to escape from deep inside the ship and get into the water. She heeled over to port at an angle of more than 45 degrees as repeated explosions from inside her tore her apart, the last explosions being so violent that the shock killed many men in the water. As she sank, the suction of her passing pulled others below. Of her 1,286 crew, there were only 20 survivors.

At 1814, as the dreadnoughts of the Grand Fleet, racing down south from Scapa Flow, finally reached the battle and began to deploy, British armoured cruisers acting as a dispersed screen found themselves in a dangerous position. The four lead *König*-class battleships of the German High Seas Fleet vanguard, coming up from the south, along with the battlecruiser *Derfflinger*, fired heavily on the British cruisers. In the ensuing melée, the British armoured cruiser *Defence* was struck by several heavy calibre shells. One salvo penetrated the ship's aft ammunition magazines, and at 1820 she erupted in a huge explosion and broke in two, leaving nothing but a gigantic smoke cloud. There were no survivors from the crew of 903.

Lützow and *Derfflinger* sighted the British battlecruiser *Invincible* silhouetted on the northern horizon 10,000 yards away and commenced firing at her. At 1834, *Invincible* was struck by a shell that penetrated Q turret amidships – the flash raced down through the working chamber, down the barbette and ammunition hoists into the magazines below and set off a catastrophic secondary magazine explosion. An enormous sheet of flame shot hundreds of feet up in the air, dissolving into a cloud of black smoke. When it cleared, *Invincible* had practically disappeared; she had broken in two and was left with the tips of her bow and her stern proud of the water. Of her crew of 1,032, only 6 survived.

In all, the battle lasted for 11 hours, during which time the German High Seas Fleet lost one pre-dreadnought battleship, one battlecruiser, four light cruisers and five torpedo boats, with 2,551 German sailors killed and 507 wounded. The British Grand Fleet came off numerically worse, with the loss of three battlecruisers, three cruisers, one light cruiser and seven destroyers. A total of 6,097 British servicemen were killed in action, 674 were wounded and 177 taken prisoner.

Between both sides a total of some 25 major warships were lost, and these wrecks are the graves of a combined 8,648 sailors who perished in this famous battle. They should be allowed to rest in peace – yet unscrupulous salvage companies have viewed these wrecks not for their historic importance but simply for the scrap value their metal represents. The scale of the salvage works that have been carried out on them, most notably by a Dutch salvage company in recent years, is staggering.

An investigation by a group of maritime archaeologists took place some years ago into allegations that a Dutch-based salvage company had been involved in the illicit, systematic looting for profit of the wreck of the battlecruiser *Queen Mary*. The wrecks were being located by side-scan sonar, and then explosives or a free-fall chisel weighing several tons used to break open the wrecks to free up the valuable metal, particularly condensers and props, which could then be lifted by mechanical grabs guided by closed-circuit television cameras, or by divers stropping specific items. It has been found that *Queen Mary* has been almost totally destroyed.

Indefatigable is known to have been repeatedly worked since the 1950s.

The entire 839 crew of German pre-dreadnought battleship SMS *Pommern* were killed when she was torpedoed and split in half by the British destroyer *Onslaught*. A war grave, *Pommern* was the only battleship sunk in the battle, and has been heavily salved. Many other battle losses have been worked, such as the light cruiser SMS *Rostock* (14 crew lost), as recently as 2009.

It is believed that 15 of the British and German Jutland wrecks, some 60 per cent of the total lost, have been commercially worked.

South China Sea, Java Sea, Sunda Strait and the Philippines

Simultaneously with the Japanese attack on Pearl Harbor on 7 December 1941, Japanese troops began to seize large amounts of territory in the Pacific as it sought to create an empire to rival the existing great colonial powers. With an Allied oil and economic embargo now beginning to cripple Japan, Japan believed that it had to secure by force of arms the natural resources that it so badly needed to hold onto its dominions in China and Asia.

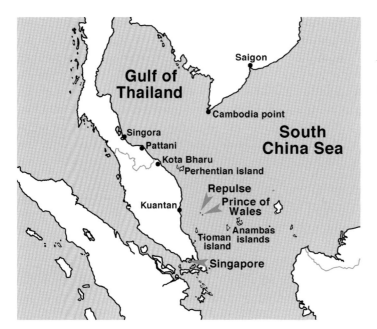

Chart of present day Malaysia and the Gulf of Thailand showing the final resting places of Prince of Wales *and* Repulse.

Japanese troops landed in Siam (modern Thailand) and northern Malaya, and began to fight down the Malayan peninsula towards their ultimate goal, the great British fortress of Singapore. At the same time, American airfields in the Philippines were seized and Japanese troops began to land there in numbers.

The strategically important American island holdings of Wake, Guam and the Gilbert Islands were seized, whilst Japanese forces also attacked the small British garrison at Hong Kong.

This area of the Pacific became heavily fought over as America entered the war, and eventually turned the Pacific War with the Battles of Midway and the Coral Sea. There are literally thousands of World War II wrecks in these waters, many the last resting places of service personnel who gave their lives so that we can enjoy the freedoms we do today.

In the run-up to the Japanese invasion operations in 1941, the Royal Navy was stretched to the limit in Europe by the war against Germany. But despite that, as Allied intelligence became aware of Japanese forces advancing into Indo-China, and threatening Malaya and Singapore, Churchill demanded that a small powerful naval force be sent to Singapore as a symbol of the might of the British Empire, to deter Japanese aggression. Force Z had been conceived.

Churchill's much beloved and newest battleship, *Prince of Wales* would be sent along with the reconstructed World War I era fast battlecruiser *Repulse*. *Prince of Wales* had been launched in 1939, and in May 1941 had recently seen action in the Battle of the Denmark Strait as *Bismarck* and *Prinz Eugen* broke out into the North Atlantic, intent on terrorising Allied shipping. *Prince of Wales* was at the time one of Britain's newest and most formidable fast battleships, with ten powerful 14-inch guns. An aircraft carrier was tasked to provide air cover for the two British capital ships, but it ran aground en route in the West Indies, and had to go for repair to an American naval shipyard. It would not reach Singapore in time.

Left: The 36,727-ton King George V-class battleship HMS Prince of Wales. *(IWM)*

Right: The 26,854-ton battlecruiser HMS Repulse. *Built on the Clyde during 1915–16,
after several post-war refits she was fully modernised and reconstructed in 1933. (IWM)*

Now missing its own fleet air cover, as Force Z reached and entered Singapore on 2 December 1941, amid great fanfare, the two capital ships were already exposed and almost indefensible, reliant on Fortress Singapore's own defences and older land-based RAF aircraft based in Malaya and Singapore.

Just five days later, on 7 December 1941, the Japanese carrier fleet crept up on the American base at Pearl Harbor, Hawaii and delivered their savage early morning attack. This devastatingly successful surprise attack crippled the American Pacific Fleet at anchor and triggered America's entry into the war. The same day, Japanese aircraft bombed Singapore.

Reports subsequently arrived at British intelligence that the Japanese had begun a land invasion 200 miles further north up the Malayan peninsula, at Kota Bharu. Thus, at 1700 on 8 December 1941, Force Z, comprising *Prince of Wales* and *Repulse*, with four escort destroyers, set out to locate the invasion forces, if any, and attack them. It was a bold and daring plan that was reliant on monsoon rain and clouds to allow Force Z to arrive undetected with the element of surprise. Force Z headed out into the South China Sea, hoping to surprise the Japanese forces at dawn on 10 December. The series of events which would lead to the beginning of the end of the battleship era now started to unfold.

En route to the possible invasion site, a signal was received advising that shore-based air cover, on which Force Z, in the absence of its own carrier aircraft, was now reliant, could not be provided due to heavy RAF losses to Japanese bombers attacking RAF airbases in the north of mainland Malaya. *Prince of Wales* and *Repulse* had become very vulnerable.

A Japanese submarine spotted Force Z as it steamed north towards Kota Bharu. Worse still, the poor visibility, which had masked the British warships as they sped to investigate, cleared just an hour or so before the cloak of darkness fell on 9 December – and Japanese reconnaissance aircraft spotted Force Z. Without air cover and now lacking the element of surprise, the two British capital ships and their escort destroyers under cover of darkness belatedly turned and headed back for Singapore, making a night detour to Kuantan to investigate further reports of troop landings.

Just before dawn the following morning, Japanese reconnaissance aircraft were despatched from Saigon to sweep south in a large fan to locate the British naval squadron. Once they were well on their way south, 85 Japanese torpedo- and high-altitude bombers took off from Saigon – following slowly and waiting for reports from the reconnaissance aircraft of Force Z's exact location so that they could be vectored in to attack.

At the end of one of its sweeps, a lone Japanese reconnaissance aircraft spotted Force Z, and the armada of 85 bombers was directed to the location. The bombers attacked the two exposed British capital ships in wave after wave of torpedo and bombing runs. As British AA fire opened up, the commanders of the two British warships vigorously tried to comb the tracks of the torpedoes, turning their ships to face into the torpedoes streaking towards them so that they would pass harmlessly down the side of the ship.

A single torpedo struck *Prince of Wales* right at her most exposed point, her unarmoured Achilles heel around the port propeller shaft. The strike blew a hole in the hull right beside where the outboard port side propeller came out of the hull – and at the same time, weakened the supporting struts that held the free section of the shaft in position.

She had four screws, two on either side.

The outboard port propeller was driven by the forward engine – and the shaft ran more than 200 feet along inside the ship. With the supporting struts weakened, the propeller shaft vibrated until the supporting struts broke. The unsupported section of propeller shaft that projected outside the hull now corkscrewed around until the 17.5-inch thick shaft itself broke and a section of the shaft, along with the huge propeller itself, fell away – damaging the port inner propeller as it went and forcing it also out of action. Suddenly, from one critical torpedo strike, the great ship was reduced to her two starboard propellers for propulsion.

The thrashing of the shaft inside the ship caused massive damage internally to bulkheads and seals. Tons of water flooded into the hull through the gaping hole, searching through the damaged bulkheads of the shaft alley to the engine rooms. As she flooded with water into her port compartments she settled by the stern and took over a heel to port. Electrical power to the stern part of the ship was cut off and both steering motors failed. Her rudder could not be turned – the ship could not be steered.

The list to port caused the starboard side of *Prince of Wales* to rise up in the water, raising the vulnerable unarmoured hull that lay beneath her armour belt and was normally safely buried deep in the water.

Another wave of torpedo bombers now swarmed at *Prince of Wales* on her raised starboard side, with some aircraft breaking off to simultaneously attack *Repulse*. With her rudder jammed, *Prince of Wales* could not manoeuvre to take avoiding action. She had lost power at her stern and some after AA guns could not function. The AA guns on her raised starboard side could not depress sufficiently to counter the low-flying torpedo bombers streaking towards her only 100 feet above the water.

Repulse faced her own battle for survival bravely – but against overwhelming odds. At one point, there were 16 torpedoes in the water – and her commander valiantly tried to manoeuvre his ship to comb the tracks. Finally, however, her fate was sealed when a mass of Japanese torpedo bombers attacked in a pincer-like star formation – torpedoes streaked towards her from every direction. *Repulse* could not comb all of these differing tracks – and she was hit by five torpedoes in rapid succession. Only 11 minutes after being struck by the first torpedo, she rolled over and sank quickly, with the loss of 508 officers and men.

A photograph taken from the destroyer HMS Express, *on the starboard side of* Prince of Wales *as she settles by the stern and lists to port. Crew crowd the decks and scramble across ropes from the sinking battleship – gun crews remain at their stations. (IWM)*

Three torpedoes struck the now raised and vulnerable starboard side of *Prince of Wales* in quick succession. One hit her bow about 20 feet back from the stem – the blast blew right through her hull and out the port side. The second torpedo hit slightly forward of amidships under the protective armour belt, blasting open the unarmoured soft underbelly of the ship. The third torpedo hit the aft section of hull behind the armour belt, causing substantial damage. She now had four holes in her hull – each some 7–10 metres in diameter – and a large section of her hull had now been opened up to the sea. The end was inevitable. She slowly turned turtle and sank; 327 officers and men were killed. Force Z had been destroyed.

The wrecks of these two famous British warships became deeply respected by divers, and when I first dived them on a military joint services expedition in 2001, both strongly built ships were in extremely good condition, as though they would float today. They were almost pristine, their size dominating divers, and a fitting testament and memorial to those who perished and whose remains still rested inside them. Our military group flew Royal Navy ensigns suspended on buoys on both wrecks, and the buoys on these ensigns were periodically renewed by civilian divers in the coming years to keep the ensigns flying.

But sadly, in about 2010, salvage barges from up north in Malaysia and China started coming south and pillaging these two famous British war graves for their metal. These vessels still remained the legal property of the British government and no salvage licence had been applied for or granted. Barges loaded with rusted salved metal were photographed in Terengganu, a port on the north-east coast of Malaysia, to the north of where the wrecks lay. The salvage work was an open secret.

In about 2015, divers from Aberdeen coming back from a trip to dive the Force Z capital ships, reported that when they got down on the wrecks they found explosives set in place over large sections of them, all linked by det cord and ready to be blown. After they had finished their dive and moved away from the site, they heard a loud boom. The salvage vessel had perhaps seen the approach of their dive vessel on radar and moved away. Once the salvors had seen the dive vessel itself move away on radar, they returned to the site to continue their activities.

The battleship Prince of Wales now lies upturned in 70 metres of water, 50 miles offshore east of Malaysia, in the South China Sea. Although this wreck is the war grave of 327 officers andmen and is a protected place under U.K. legislation, the wreck has recently been heavily blasted and salvaged by illegal salvors .

The battlecruiser HMS Repulse lies wellheeled over on her port side in 55 metres of water, 50 miles off the east coast of Malaysia and just 8 miles away from the wreck of the battleship Prince of Wales. She too has recently been heavily blasted and illegally salvaged despite being the war grave of 508 of her officers and men and protected under UK legislation.

All four valuable propellers from *Repulse* have been removed, and the hull has seen heavy blasting to free up steel and allow access into the wreck. The entire aft section of the keel is now gone, probably as a result of salvage blasting around the boiler and engine rooms to get at the valuable condensers and other non-ferrous fitments. The three massive propellers that remained on *Prince of Wales* have also been removed from the wreck, and salvage blasting has been carried out on her hull. Oil is now leaking from both vessels, causing marine pollution.

Many other wrecks have suffered a similar fate in this area. In December 1941, the Dutch submarine HNLMS *K XVII* hit a Japanese mine and sunk whilst leaving the Gulf of Siam (now Gulf of Thailand). The wreck of this submarine, holding the remains of her crew of 36, has now been completely removed.

In Usukan Bay, off Sabah, Borneo, the three Japanese World War II wrecks *Kokusei Maru* (79 dead), *Higane Maru* (15 dead) and *Hiyori Maru* (34 dead) have been dismantled and removed. The Japanese destroyer IJN *Sagiri* was torpedoed and sunk by the Dutch submarine *K XVI* off Kuching, Sarawak, with the loss of 121 of her crew – and has now too suffered at the hands of salvors. The list goes on and on.

As well as naval wrecks, a number of other non-military wrecks in and around the South China Sea have seen the attentions of salvors. Whilst there is no apparent legal impediment to this being carried out if the correct reporting procedures are followed, it is still a great blow to those in the diving industry who rely on taking liveaboard dive trips out to these vessels.

In 2004, I dived the massive wreck of the Swedish 56,630-ton supertanker *Seven Skies* that sank, in mysterious circumstances in some 15 minutes, off the east coast of Malaysia in 1969, whilst en route from Japan to Indonesia, taking four of her crew to the bottom. This large modern tanker was 261 metres long (some 857 feet) and rested upright in 63 metres. When I dived her, she was so large that the whole dive was focused on the towering stern superstructure. The wreck was a massive, almost perfectly intact, artificial reef that thronged with sea life and still had the bridge telegraph *in situ*. Since that time, her top half has been completely removed – and her remains now being so deep, with little of interest left, there is little point in diving what is left of her.

The large 72,741grt modern cargo ship SS *Igara* was built in 1972, and foundered off the east coast of Malaysia on 12 March 1973, as a result of hitting a rock the day before as she passed through the Sunda Strait. The bow sank to the seabed whilst the stern remained projecting above the water. Salvors used explosives to cut the ship in two at No 1 Hold, and the stern section was then towed away to Japan, where a new bow section was added. The old bow section has now been worked by commercial salvors.

The 1,596grt cargo ship MV *Seng Hing* was lost in 1992 – a popular dive, she has now been half-salved. The unidentified tanker 40 nautical miles south of Tioman Island in 64 metres of water close to Pulau Aur, Johor, Malaysia, and nicknamed the Aur Tanker, has also suffered at the hands of salvors.

As a result of the adverse publicity being generated, there have been growing attempts to stop this illegal trade. On 20 April, the Indonesian Navy detained the 8,352-ton grab hopper dredger *Chuan Hong 68* (flagged to a home port of Fuzhou on China's east coast), in waters off Natuna in the Riau Islands of the South China Sea – on suspicion she was involved in illegal salvage. She escaped from detention in mysterious circumstances on 22 April and fled to Malaysia, where she was subsequently detained by the Malaysian Maritime Enforcement

Above: The 560-foot-long Dutch light cruiser Hr.Ms. DeRuyterwas sunk during the Battle of the Java Sea on 27 February 1942 with the loss of 345 crew. The wreck has illegally been completely dismantled by salvors.

Left: Following the Battle of the Java Sea, the 6,380-ton Australian light cruiser HMAS Perth (seen here) and the 9,050-ton American heavy cruiser USS Houston were confronted by a major Japanese naval force and sunk on the night of 28 February–1 March 1942 with the combined loss of more than 1,000 officers and crew. More than half of HMAS Perth has been illegally removed and USS Houston has also been worked.

Agency in the Pengerang waters, east of Johor. Other salvage barges have been seized by Indonesian authorities – but it seems an unstoppable tide. There are so many wrecks in the South China Sea, belonging to so many nations, that they cannot all be policed.

Java Sea

The Java Sea lies between the Indonesian islands of Borneo to the north, Java to the south, Sumatra to the west and Sulawesi to the east. On 27 February 1942, the decisive Battle of the Java Sea was fought between Allied and Imperial Japanese naval forces, and resulted in a heavy defeat for the Allies with eight major warships being sunk: the Dutch vessels Hr.Ms. *Java*, Hr.Ms. *Kortenaer*, and Hr.Ms. *DeRuyter*; the British vessels *Electra*, *Jupiter*, *Exeter* and *Encounter*, and the American vessel USS *Pope*. This battle was followed by a number of smaller actions around Java that included the scuttling without loss of life of the American submarine USS *Perch*.

Of the war graves, two of the Dutch naval vessels off the remote island of Bawean, the 8,000-ton 509-foot-long cruiser Hr.Ms. *Java*, (on which 512 crew were killed) and the 560-foot-long light cruiser Hr.Ms. *De Ruyter* (345 crew lost), have now been completely dismantled. They have simply disappeared from the seabed, leaving only scours in the sand where they once lay. A large section of a third Dutch vessel, the 322-foot-long destroyer, Hr.Ms *Kortenaer* (40 crew lost), has also been removed.

Of the British losses, the 10,490-ton heavy cruiser *Exeter* and the 1,940-ton destroyer *Encounter* have been completely dismantled and removed, whilst the destroyer *Electra* has been gutted. The 300-foot-long scuttled American submarine USS *Perch* has also been completely removed.

Sunda Strait

The Sunda Strait lies between the islands of Java and Sumatra. Following on from the Battle of the Java Sea, on the night of 28 February–1 March 1942, the 6,380-ton Australian light cruiser HMAS *Perth* and the 9,050-ton American heavy cruiser USS *Houston* were confronted by a major Japanese naval force. Both ships were sunk, with the combined loss of more than 1,000 officers and men. More than one half of the wreck of HMAS *Perth* is reported as having been salved; most of her superstructure is gone, as are some of her main battery guns. The *Houston* is still present, but has seen unauthorised salvage works on her.

◆   ◆   ◆

The ships I've mentioned above are given only as examples to highlight the scale of these unauthorised salvage operations – the list of salvaged World War II ships in this area is very long. It has been reported that one salvage company website spoke of 1,000 wrecks having been worked by it alone.

Whilst there can be no legitimate objection to the wrecks of merchant ships and their often valuable cargoes being returned to commerce under the normal laws of salvage, naval war graves, often holding the remains of hundreds of sailors, should be left to lie in peace, the wrecks themselves still belonging to the sovereign states that owned the vessel at the time of its loss.

POSTCRIPT

The state of the art today

For the first 15 years of my diving career, all sport diving was carried out using compressed air down to a maximum recommended depth of 50 metres. Like some other divers, I ventured deeper than that when I had to for a particular reason, but you knew that beyond 50 metres you were playing Russian roulette with all sorts of diving disabilities such as nitrogen narcosis, CO2 blackout, oxygen toxicity and of course the dreaded bends. Back then, the nitrogen in air was such a limiting factor for us – and apart from the physical dangers it presented, it also meant that vast swathes of the sea were simply beyond our reach in any safe way. Pushing the envelope, trying to dive a new wreck in a current, in silty pitch-black, 5-foot visibility at a depth of 58 metres, triggered a serious, potentially fatal incident for me. You can read about what happened in the chapter entitled 'Bail out on the Cushendall' in *Into the Abyss – Diving to Adventure in the Liquid World*. I learned my lesson and never went beyond 50 metres on air again – the recommended limit of 50 metres was there for a reason.

Trapped in a narrow swathe of sea that extended from our coasts out to a depth of 50 metres, most of the wrecks in that tranche of water were already well dived by the time I developed an interest in shipwrecks in the early 1980s. They were also almost completely robbed of any non-ferrous artefacts such as portholes, telegraphs and the like by the generations of divers who went before us. It was as if only the rusted steel shell was left – I thought that's just the way shipwrecks were.

Then, in 1995, we got access in the UK to helium for sport diving – it was an overnight game changer. Almost immediately, as we started to explore deeper into the darkness, I started to see portholes still in position on hulls and deckhouses, telegraphs, helms and compass binnacles in bridges and ship names in brass letters on fo'c'sles. Galleys were still filled with crockery that gleamed white in our dive torches; engine rooms were lined with gauges. We even started to see ships' bells – it was a revelation.

Helium, traditionally the reserve of the commercial diver, replaced much of the dangerous nitrogen in our breathing gas, and this, allied to new accelerated decompression techniques using the new oxygen-rich breathing gases generically called nitrox, stripped away the old 50-metre depth limit. We could dive much deeper, dispense with nitrogen narcosis and enjoy much shorter, more effective, decompression times on ascent.

Almost overnight, in a developing sport in which we early technical divers were essentially human guinea pigs or crash test dummies, we were able to range down to 100 metres or beyond. It was all new – and in the early years of the technical diving revolution, stuck in the past with a mental 50-metre depth ceiling ingrained into our psyches, a dive to 60–70 metres was seen as a significant dive.

To begin with during this experimental time, there were sadly a number of fatalities. But as our sport evolved and we got better at it, depth boundaries began to advance – and it got safer. Soon dives in the 80–90-metre range were becoming increasingly common off our north-east coast of Scotland, and many pioneers were pushing it much deeper. Soon, those at the vanguard of our sport were diving beyond 100 metres – and well beyond. A whole new frontier had been opened up to us, and instantly huge areas of the sea previously out of bounds beyond the old 50-metre depth contour were in play. It meant lots of new, undived virgin wrecks to find and explore. But, as we were warned during our technical diving training, if you walk the frontier you will meet Indians.

We didn't have a name at first for this radical quantum leap forward in the development of our sport until the American diving journalist and technologist Mike Menduno coined the term 'technical diving'. Our branch of the sport now had a name – and Mike went on to serve as editor-in-chief for *AquaCorps: the Journal for Technical Diving* and its sister publication *TechnicalDiver*, both of which helped usher tech diving into the mainstream of sports diving.

Our understanding of the new techniques, of decompression theory and bubble mechanics, advanced – and the kit we carried got better and better. After a few years of diving open-circuit trimix, closed-circuit rebreathers began to enter the market towards the late 1990s. It was yet another quantum leap forward – we were now freed from the cost and wastage of open-circuit deep diving, when expensive helium is lost in large quantities to the atmosphere as you exhale.

When they arrived, rebreathers brought lots of benefits to technical diving. The rebreathed gas was warm, for a start, in comparison to OC trimix, which was bitterly cold. As you continuously rebreathed the same breathing gas, the amount of gas you had to carry was drastically reduced, a saving in weight and money; helium is uber expensive. Rebreathers allowed you to use very high helium-content gases on deep dives at a fraction of the cost of doing the same dive open circuit.

Rebreathers also allowed the levels of oxygen (the PO2) to be strictly controlled, both on the bottom and on the ascent. Rebreathers seamlessly gave you the desired amount of oxygen in your breathing gas at whatever depth you were at. This was a startling change from open-circuit trimix diving, when you had to carry cylinders of travel gas for the descent and the deep part of the ascent. You also had to carry a twin set of bottom gas for the deep part of the dive – and then a separate cylinder or two of deco mix for decompression. Carrying a total of four cylinders was the norm, and some divers carried many more. By giving you the optimum amount of oxygen during decompression, rebreather diving was just much healthier for your body. We began to experiment using inert argon for suit inflation, carried in a separate small cylinder.

But with rebreathers, as with the initial introduction of OC trimix diving, we were once again walking the frontier, and many Indians were indeed met – there were an inordinate number of rebreather fatalities in the early years. It became apparent, that whilst you may be a vastly experienced OC trimix diver, once you moved to CCR diving you were right back at the beginning as a novice – the techniques were so different.

In those early days lessons were learned the hard way from the fatalities, and our sport began to settle down, to become formalised and much safer. Divers began to venture even deeper, much deeper – and for much longer on the bottom. We found that we could do constructive work on the bottom at 100 metres with a clarity of mind that you could never have had on air at half that depth. Technical diving began to bring in astonishing results.

In the North Channel off Malin Head, County Donegal, Ireland, divers are now regularly diving on shipwrecks down to depths of around 160 metres. This just isn't bounce diving, when you go down, touch the wreck and then get out of Dodge; they are spending significant time on the bottom, albeit that they have decompression hangs of 4–5 hours as a result.

Sports divers have visited and filmed the ocean liner SS *Empress of Britain*, torpedoed and sunk on 28 October 1940 on a passage from South Africa for Liverpool. She now lies upside down in 163 metres of water, 68 miles west of Rosguill, Donegal, with her bow section lying on its port side. The haunting video imagery they brought back showed how the great depth had preserved the ship in remarkable condition, slowing rusting and preserving pristine wooden decking. Even sections of the original white paint of this hospital ship still gleamed in divers' torches on hull plates.

Whilst our new technology has allowed us to dive much deeper, we are still the poor relation of diving compared to offshore commercial divers, who live and work in saturation for periods of up to a month. They can dive to incredible depths, unattainable by sports divers doing bounce dives, when we return to the surface after the dive. As at the date of printing, the depth record for commercial diving is 534 metres (1,750 feet).

The deepest open-circuit trimix dive at the time of printing is 332 metres (1,090 feet), the diver taking 14 hours to ascend and fully decompress. In 2014, Will Goodman reached a depth of 290 metres using a JJ-CCR closed-circuit rebreather.

For deep dives in confined waters, such as in cave systems, some divers are now using habitats to alleviate the rigours of decompression in the shallows. Habitats are chambers that can be pressurised to keep the water out and are large enough to accommodate divers. They are pre-positioned, secured and suspended at the desired depth for decompression. In a cave, the habitat can be floated up against the roof at the desired depth and then secured.

Divers who have gone very deep with lengthy decompressions to follow, sometimes of 12 hours or more, can rise up from the depths and then as they arrive at the habitat they take their rebreathers or OC rigs off, clip them outside and enter the habitat, in much the same way as a commercial diver enters a diving bell and subsequently transfers to a living chamber. Some habitats have a shelf or floor that allows divers to get completely out of the water.

Divers in a habitat and out of the water have a greatly reduced risk of hypothermia, and the risk of potentially fatal inwater oxygen toxicity convulsions is lessened. They can breathe the desired decompression gas in relative comfort, either from banks of deco cylinders or surface-supplied – and they can exceed the normal inwater PO2 limits to accelerate decompression further. They can also eat, have hot and cold drinks, and even sleep. But a habitat is complicated, with many ways to run into trouble, so the decompressing divers need surface support and a safety diver to closely watch them. Nevertheless, some remarkable results are being achieved in cave systems at depths of more than 200 metres.

Divers have already brought so much information, seemingly lost to the sea for eternity, back to the present day, from the location of ancient shipwrecks in the Mediterranean, to the exquisitely preserved wooden sailing ships dating to before the birth of Christ that are now being found in the cold depths of the Baltic, and those more modern sailing ships from the 19th century being found in the Great Lakes. Divers have been instrumental in finding and recording legions of more modern shipwrecks previously lost to time through collision or war.

Perhaps the most stunning example of what divers can do has been the important discovery by Richard Lundgren and the not for profit organisation Ocean Discovery, of the exquisitely preserved *Mars the Magnificent*, a warship of King Erik XIV of Sweden, that was sunk in action in 1564 in the south-east Baltic. This has triggered one of the largest archaeological projects in the world.

The recent arrival of relatively inexpensive 3D photogrammetry software now means that sport divers can achieve stunning results, recording shipwrecks in intricate detail, and preserving information about them for future generations: the shipwrecks from both world wars are now rapidly falling apart, literally turning to dust and disappearing before our eyes.

Underwater video cameras are now relatively inexpensive, and produce fine results which are completely acceptable for use with 3D photogrammetry software. Any diver willing to make a modest investment can now start preserving imagery of shipwrecks by both video and photogrammetry.

Merchant vessels are not as robustly built as military vessels, and most wartime wrecks are now showing signs of age, collapsing and decaying, some now a pale shadow now of what they were. I regret that this sort of technology wasn't available during the 1980s and 1990s when the Scapa Flow wrecks were so intact, and when I was beginning to find and explore the shipwrecks off my own stretch of coast. The wrecks are so very different now from what they were – and I have only my memories of them as they were.

The 3D photogrammetry, the hundreds of hours of video and countless numbers of still photographs of HMS *Hampshire* captured during the Explorers Club expedition in 2016 and on the subsequent expedition in 2017 to survey HMS *Vanguard* at Scapa Flow will be available for marine archaeologists to study and learn from forever.

And really, that is how this book should end, with a realisation of the vital role that sport divers can now fulfil by discovering and recording shipwrecks in ways impossible in the past. In this way, divers can help the archaeological narrative by recording and preserving information about our maritime past – before it is lost to the sea.

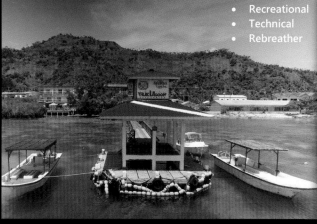

MORE FANTASTIC BOOKS BY ROD MACDONALD

£30.00   978-184995-290-3

£30.00   978-184995-131-9

£30.00   978-184995-170-8

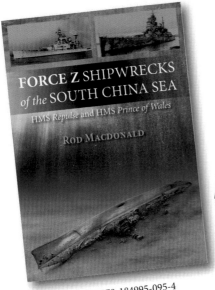

£18.99   978-184995-095-4

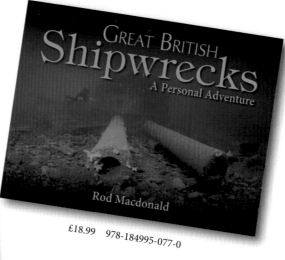

£18.99   978-184995-077-0

www.whittlespublishing.com

PRAISE FOR ROD'S BOOKS

... Macdonald's knowledge comes across in his enthusiastic writing. The prose is clear, definitive and loaded with facts, figures and safety information. ...the ideal book to read... **Deeper Blue**

...Rod's description of the dive scene once you get to Scapa Flow is compelling and every diver's dream scene. It's a beautiful, informative book and a must have for any diver's bookshelf. **SubSea**

...the most enjoyable dive book I have read in a long time. ... If you love diving, wrecks or just like a well-written, true life adventure written with passion and attention to detail, this is the book for you! **Scottish Diver**

...a collection of bite-size ripping yarns. ...The Darkness Below deserves to become a classic. ... It's action packed from the get-go and doesn't let up all the way through. **Conger Alley**

Rod Macdonald's tome is arguably the definitive guide. Dive Truk Lagoon is ... a rich and hugely detailed work ... it's pretty much a must-read. **British Diver**

...a first class book. ... His explanations of the Japanese military build up and campaigns in the Malay Peninsula are both succinct and informative ... a thoroughly enjoyable book... **Warship World**